The Experience of Authority in Early Modern England

The Experience of Authority in Early Modern England

Edited by

PAUL GRIFFITHS, ADAM FOX and STEVE HINDLE

St. Martin's Press
New York

THE EXPERIENCE OF AUTHORITY IN EARLY MODERN ENGLAND
Editorial matter and Introduction © 1996 by Paul Griffiths, Adam Fox
and Steve Hindle
Chapter 1 © 1996 by Keith Wrightson, Chapter 2 © 1996 by Martin
Ingram, Chapter 3 © 1996 by Adam Fox, Chapter 4 © 1996 by Bernard
Capp, Chapter 5 © 1996 by Paul Griffiths, Chapter 6 © 1996 by J. A.
Sharpe, Chapter 7 © 1996 by Steve Hindle, Chapter 8 © 1996 by Andy
Wood, Chapter 9 © 1996 by John Rule

St. Martin's Press, Scholarly and Reference Division,
175 Fifth Avenue, New York, N.Y. 10010

First published in the United States of America in 1996

Printed in Malaysia

ISBN 0–312–16043–7

Library of Congress Cataloging-in-Publication Data applied for

Contents

List of Figures

Introduction

These essays are about social relationships in early modern England. They are concerned with the articulation, mediation and reception of authority; with the preoccupations and aspirations of both governors and governed in English society between the sixteenth and eighteenth centuries. From various perspectives, contributions explore the ongoing set of negotiations between dominant ideologies, groups or individuals, and those subordinate to them, which constitute the exercise of power.

The particular focus of these essays is the light in which structures of authority were seen and interpreted by those subordinates upon whom they variously acted. Such popular perceptions cannot be understood apart from the political processes which determined them, but they were also fashioned by imperatives of their own. Where the initiatives of the authorities collided with the expectations of people, the experience of authority was synthesised.

In this sense, the study of politics, broadly defined, and the study of society cannot easily be separated. The most satisfactory accounts of political actions will seek to explore their social ramifications,[1] while the more rigorous analyses of social relations are bound to acknowledge their conditioning by political power.[2] It is in the light of this much more comprehensive understanding of politics that this collection should be read and its key terms – authority and experience – interpreted. Authority is here taken to be the power or right to define and regulate the legitimate behaviour of others: its experience is the direct contact with that authority and the way in which it was felt and ultimately interpreted. The ubiquity of authority in early modern society is well known. Its exercise was a political expression because its principal purpose was to perpetuate existing ideologies and structures of power by which rule was preserved. To maintain power, governors had to retain control of these structures and make public their ideas of accept-

1

able behaviour. Order was never inevitable; authority had to be disseminated.

Whatever the theoretical dictates and physical embodiments of authority, however, they only ever amounted to claims to, and representations of legitimate power. For the arts of governance and control usually depended upon far more than the ability of rulers and elites merely to enforce their wills by coercion. Authority is most often socially arbitrated and politically contested, involving some level of participation by subjects and inferiors. A reciprocal element lies at the heart of almost all power relations.[3] By examining this reciprocity, and the mutuality which mediates between domination and subjection, we can best appreciate what it was to experience authority.

Early modern English society was organised around a series of overlapping power structures which sought to regulate and order the lives of people at every level. In the governing principles of rank, gender and age, the values of hierarchy and place were ordained and elaborated. The positions of rich and poor, men and women, and young and old were articulated and disseminated in an effort to make them seem natural and inevitable. Through the institutions of Crown and Church, by way of the agencies of the State and the law, and in the fabric of communities, workplaces, and households, the messages of authority were inculcated and enforced.

Underpinning the workings of any political culture are some notions of authority, explicitly enunciated or implicitly understood. In early modern England these notions were expressed in a web of ideological and institutional instruments which have become familiar areas of study. Authority was institutionalised on a national level in Church and State, and the system of courts. It was given distinctive colouring in the forms of local government, including the parish vestry, the manorial court and the urban corporation, as it was in the household and workplace. Authority was also personalised. The monarch was a figurehead, but his right to rule was delegated and exhibited in the person of the judge, alderman, minister, constable or householder. There was a multivalence about many institutions of power and most figures of influence which implies that their workings can only be understood in specific context. The status of some of these authority figures was fluid and even contradictory; they frequently moved from positions of power to situations of subordination. All were subjects: the minister rubbed shoulders with gentlemen, the constable made presentations to the judge, the male adult was expected to oversee his wife, children and servants, but outside his household he was usually a worker and often poor. One characteristic of a social structure which had such a well-developed series of middling ranks was large numbers of people with an amphibious relationship to authority, at once its conduits and receptacles. Some of these transitions of status were familiar and easy to manage but others were more difficult. This was one reason why early modern people were so regularly reminded to keep in their 'place' and observe its limitations.

Officers and institutions were expected to disseminate the letter of the law in print and speech and a complex of performances. Texts such as sermons, catechisms, judgements, writs or proclamations communicated their ideological messages in terms which were at certain times blatantly coercive and, at others, subliminally hegemonic. Such messages were represented more graphically and communicated more accessibly through prosecutions, visual displays or public demonstrations. So, for example, the pomp of a royal or civic progress, or the solemnity of an ecclesiastical visitation sometimes carried a rhetorical force greater than words ever spoken or written. At the theatre of the assizes and in the drama of the scaffold other scripts were enacted, voluble and clear. In the carefully ranked demarcations of church seating, in the finely graded hierarchy of the urban processional, in codes of dress, forms of address, and a host of other insistent proprieties, the order of things was always and everywhere rehearsed and reinforced.

Contemporary governors, therefore, had a formidable repertoire of methods and strategies at their disposal. They could pursue coercion, persuasion, negotiation, reformation, compromise or inculcation, although the mediation of authority was in fact complicated by the many parts from which the political nation was constructed. Authority circulated in these overlapping tiers of government, in which jurisdiction and the formulation of policy were sometimes matters of dispute. The sheer scale of government raised the possibility of authority being misinterpreted, reinterpreted, corrupted or neglected. Structures of authority were extremely 'diffused and extensive' at this time.[4] They could themselves become the issue and location of competition between rival interests, which sometimes exploded into serious factional squabbles. The circuits of authority were not free from tension. Complaints about lax and incompetent officers litter the records of the courts. The poor quality of domestic governors was a persistent grievance and prompted gloomy forecasts about social order.

Moreover, different groups and people invested authority and significance in different things, or offered competing interpretations of a particular source of authority. The written word could be such a territory of multiple meaning; the institutions and forms of the law could be another. Hierarchical relations were expressed in the rhetoric and forms of legal procedure, but the law was not simply a conduit of hegemony and control. For the common people participated in its workings when they asserted their own interpretation of customary rights, or their distaste for the abuse of power by a master or employer. If the value of these vehicles of authority was widely accepted, their meanings were frequently contested.

If authority was contingent upon context, it was also a function of process. During these centuries of far-reaching and sometimes rapid political and socio-economic change, the conditions into which messages of control were refracted altered over time. The environments in which early modern people lived were irrevocably restructured by such forces as the reformations of religion, changes in administrative structures under the Tudors, and the centralising tendencies of the Stuarts. The structural developments which are known to have transformed the economy such as demographic growth, waves of considerable price inflation, and major reorganisations in production and marketing were always revising the background against which power was exercised. New battles over resources ensued, evident in the commercialisation of the land market or the reification of customary use-rights into private properties. New problems of order were raised, consequent upon the increases in poverty, the steady expansion of urban society and the substantial rise in indicated crime. All of these long-term shifts, together with periodic phenomena such as epidemic disease, food shortage, unemployment or campaigns to reform manners, challenged those in authority to re-examine the ideas, reinvent the rhetoric, and reinforce the efforts upon which their government was based.

The articulation of authority in place and time was changeable, adaptable, uneven and fragmentary. The resulting impression is of a society struggling to comprehend sharper differentiation and inequality at a time when agencies of law enforcement had to be flexible and even innovative. The exercise of authority was multi-faceted, and its expression and enforcement was only one aspect of its experience. The dictates of governors were not simply disseminated, they also had to be received and interpreted by the governed.

The realities of power ensured that the dominant and influential in early modern English society were rarely able to enforce their rule without some reference to the sensibilities of those subject to it. Authority was always, to a certain extent, bound by the limits of the possible and mitigated by the need for consent. In such circumstances, the majority of the people were not merely the passive recipients of social and political control but possessed some degree of agency in constructing the terms of their inferiority. Thus, whatever the ideals and intentions of governors, their strictures were liable to be appropriated and reinterpreted in the acts of reception. The resulting (but constantly shifting) pattern of social and political relationships was invariably the outcome of an ongoing set of negotiations. The governors' script called for a series of choreographed and staged responses, including deference, respect, applause, consent and conformity. But the reality of daily relationships was invariably more complicated.

There were, of course, a multiplicity of ways in which men and women responded to the forces which attempted to guide and influence, or sometimes even to intimidate and suppress. Although it is discordance and conflict which often produces the records in which glimpses of the past are bequeathed, it is likely that such sources exaggerate the extent and nature of contemporary antagonisms. The routine of daily life usually passed unremarked by contemporaries and unnoticed by subsequent generations. For the most part, perhaps, early modern people never conceived of challenging authority nor could they imagine alternative constitutions of it. Some clearly accepted the inevitability of circumstance and even became reconciled to the implications of their appointed 'place'. Others positively conspired in confirming prevailing value systems and rejoiced in strengthening conventional structures of authority. The intermingling of Protestantism, patriotism and nationalism was a potent brew, stirring pride and focusing loyalties. From loyalty to Church and State sprang a Protestant popular culture which shaped the commitments of many people. It is also true that at least some parts of the moral code of governors commanded public assent, and that their formulations sometimes took account of the felt needs of the people. In the platitudes of convention many people sought stability and in the familiarities of tradition they found security.

The extent to which ideological and institutional authority was either uncritically absorbed or enthusiastically embraced should not be underestimated, therefore. But there were other responses to power in which contemporaries were neither passive in obedience nor active in endorsement. For on occasion the messages of domination passed unheeded, the mechanisms of control were ignored, and the attempts to govern met with resistance. Indifference and even hostility in the face of authority was variously expressed. To a large extent subversive reactions remained essentially hidden, passing unnoticed by those in authority. Behind the mask of outward deference always lay the face of inner feeling. On occasion, the thin veneer of obeisance was ripped away to reveal an underside of resentment and distrust.[5] By clinging to ancient custom, by preserving collective memory, or by pursuing legal action, early modern people defended their rights and liberties. Through riots and protests, through petitions and threatening letters, through female independence and workers' combination, they questioned the terms of their subordination.

In such situations it was clear that there was nothing inevitable about prevailing power structures and hierarchies, nothing immutable about the world as it was so often presented. In many contexts, the dictates of theory were contradicted by the realities of practice. The experience of subordination was rarely if at all complete and exhaustive. There was nothing ineluctable about subjection, nothing natural about patriarchy, and nothing sacrosanct about orthodox forms of worship.

There is, therefore, never a single or tidy explanation of patterns of behaviour in the lower rungs of early modern society. Instead, it is possible to locate a broad spectrum of interpretative positions, which would include conformity, resignation, passivity, creativity, mockery and opposition. It is very unlikely that individual responses could ever be represented fully by any one of these positions, however. The ideas and actions of a single individual or group might alter greatly according to situation, and the multiple identities of which most people were capable of assuming defies their easy categorisation.

This complexity is rarely revealed either in contemporary sources or in those historical accounts which reduce relations between governors and governed merely to bi-polar models of paternalism and deference, discipline and obedience, inculcation and assimilation, or example and imitation. These dualistic representations of social relations also fail to take account of the existence of those 'middling' groups which occupied such an ambiguous position in the social order. Early modern people were often able to create their own spaces, identities and experiences within existing ideas and structures of authority. The accommodation of social and political power was as variegated as its exercise.

Experience, therefore, is itself adaptable and contingent. But it is also dynamic and compelling, altering in response to change, and shaping social perceptions and affiliations. The store of experience helps to structure 'the popular mentalities of subordination' by mediating between 'social consciousness', or the sense of individual or communal identity, and 'social being', or material environment. A history of the common people in former centuries should always be written 'in terms of their own experience'.[6] Even the most commonplace events have meaning for people in their time. It has been said that 'experience' is neither a robust analytical category nor an organising narrative principle;[7] that it tempts historians into 'exalting the commonplace and demeaning the exceptional';[8] and that the significance of conventional politics is relegated to a minor role.[9] The following chapters seek to locate experience within the context of 'public' life and power structures, interpreting and explaining rather than merely 'celebrating' or 'valorising' it.[10]

It must be emphasised, however, that the experience of authority varied according to geographical and social context and also over time. Like the implementation of authority, its reception was both dependent upon difference in circumstance and subject to change over time. Responses might be conditioned by environment and the particular fabric of communities. The distinctions between national and local jurisdictions, open and closed parishes, agricultural and industrial economies, urban and rural societies, pastoral

and arable ecologies, and learned or popular cultures are among
the many contingencies which are familiar to historians seeking to
explain the politics of local society. Each community had its own
politics, social relations and culture.

Reactions to authority were determined by the broad texture of
chronological development. Both abrupt discontinuities and evolutionary increments as well as enduring structures were among
those factors which coloured the nature of perception. Indeed, the
pace of socio-economic change was never regular and even.
Amongst those transitional developments which touched the experiences of early modern people were the incremental growth of
the State, alterations in social structure, the greater commercialisation of agriculture, technological innovation, and changes in practices of work and leisure. Taken together they resulted in
fundamental economic, cultural and social differentiation. This
prolonged and uneven transition was reflected in different ways in
communities at different stages of development. Early modern
England was in many respects a society of contrary experiences in
which traditional and novel elements co-existed in often uneasy
tension. Only, therefore, by repairing to context can the experience of authority at this time be understood fully.

Some of the contexts in which authority was experienced are explored here. This collection ranges broadly both in time and space.
Each chapter employs different methods and focuses on different
areas of inquiry, though all of them share a concern with the points
of contact between governors and governed. No single chapter
deals exclusively with either the articulation or reception of authority, but it is the point of intersection, the place of resolution,
compromise, rejection or resistance, which is of most concern. It
was at this junction where rulers crossed paths with subordinates
that critical allegiances and identities were constructed. Some essays study developments of national significance through the prism
of local circumstance, including the fabrication of marginality, the
customary consciousness of free miners, and the keeping of the
public peace. Other contributions survey the contours of long-term
change by mapping the details of specific episodes: campaigns to
reform manners, the regulation of the household, and the proletarianisation of labour. Certain authors attempt to analyse shifting
patterns in universal relationships by examining particular bodies

of source material: attention is given thus to the interactions between the social ranks, men and women, young and old, and oral and literate media. Each chapter has its own particular preoccupations, but with significant regularity the contributors return to shared concerns: the ubiquity, diversity, and ambiguity, of authority in early modern society.

NOTES AND REFERENCES

1. P. Collinson, *De Republica Anglorum: Or, History with the Politics Put Back* (Cambridge, 1990).
2. See esp. K. Wrightson, 'The Enclosure of English Social History', *Social History*, 1 (1990), pp. 73–81; revised and reprinted in A. Wilson (ed.), *Rethinking Social History: English Society 1570–1920 and its Interpretation* (Manchester, 1993), pp. 59–77; and Chapter 1 below.
3. Georg Simmel writes that all 'power relations involve an active reciprocity of orientation', extracts from his writings reprinted in L. A. Coser and B. Rosenberg (eds), *Sociological Theory: A Book of Readings*, 2nd edn (New York, 1964), p. 123.
4. M. Mann, *The Sources of Social Power, Volume I: A History of Power from the Beginning to AD 1760* (Cambridge, 1986), pp. 7–8.
5. See esp. J. C. Scott, *Domination and the Arts of Resistance: Hidden Transcripts* (New Haven, 1990); E. P. Thompson, *Customs in Common* (London, 1991).
6. E. P. Thompson, *The Making of the English Working Class* (Harmondsworth, 1968), p. 12; and *The Poverty of Theory and Other Essays* (London, 1978), chs 1, 3.
7. H. Sewell, 'How Classes Are Made: Critical Reflections on E. P. Thompson's Theory of Working-class Formation', in H. J. Kaye and K. McClelland (eds), *E. P. Thompson: Critical Perspectives* (Cambridge, 1990), pp. 50–78, esp. pp. 59–66; D. Cannadine, 'The Way We Lived Then', *Times Literary Supplement*, 7–13 September (1990), pp. 935–6.
8. G. Strauss, 'The Dilemma of Popular History', *Past and Present*, vol. 132 (1991), pp. 130–49, esp. pp. 133–4. Cf. W. Beik, 'Debate: The Dilemma of Popular History', *Past and Present*, vol. 141 (1993), pp. 207–19.
9. Cannadine, 'The Way We Lived Then'.
10. Strauss, 'Dilemma of Popular History', pp. 133–4.

1. The Politics of the Parish in Early Modern England*

KEITH WRIGHTSON

In his Cambridge inaugural lecture in November 1989, Professor Patrick Collinson attempted to re-establish the common ground linking two increasingly separated areas of historical debate when he used his platform to call for 'a new political history' of early modern England, 'an account of political processes which is also social'.[1] In reflecting on what I will call 'the politics of the parish', this chapter also seeks to explore the opportunities for a 'social history with the politics put back in'; but in a rather different sense.

Professor Collinson's concern was with the need 'to explore the social depth of politics, to find signs of political life at levels where it was not previously thought to have existed'. In particular, he drew attention to the opportunities for 'a new and extended political history' at a lower level of political society, along 'the bottom line of early modern government', among the village notables and parish officers who governed the most local of England's many overlapping communities, and whose activities as 'brokers' – 'as much political as administrative in nature' – provide the best hope of grasping 'how nine thousand parishes composed, at a higher level, a single political society'.[2] This is an aspiration with which I for one am wholly in sympathy. My principal concern here, however, is to reflect on the extent to which we already have a social history of early modern England 'with the politics put back in' – if we did but realise it.

To grasp the extent to which this is so we need only to redefine modestly what we mean by the 'political'. If by that term we mean the conduct and management of affairs of state, then it might well appear that politics is somewhat peripheral to the concerns of social history. If, however, we broaden our definition somewhat to include the social distribution and use of power, all those processes which are 'political in the sense that different actors and different meanings are contending with one another for control', and in particular the manner in which relationships of power and authority, dominance and subordination are established and maintained, refused and modified, then it is fair to say that a great deal of the social history of early modern England written in the last twenty years has been quite centrally preoccupied with politics – not simply in the sense of 'micro politics' or 'local level politics', but in its broader concern with the history of social relationships and of the culture which informs them, its concern with the political dimensions of everyday life.[3]

This fact is most clearly revealed in the conceptual and interpretative vocabulary now commonly employed in English social history. Whereas we used to hear most about 'structures', 'systems', 'typologies', 'patterns' and 'regimes', we now have a historiography liberally seasoned with more dynamic and interactive terms. 'Agency', 'negotiation', 'transaction', 'accommodation', 'participation', 'discretion', 'process', 'discourse', 'appropriation', 'brokerage' and 'mediation' are among the current buzz words of the subject: and they are sensitively employed as well as ritually bleated.

All these terms carry charges of 'political electricity'.[4] The second generation of the so-called new social history is pervasively preoccupied with the political. And one of the best ways to appreciate this is to survey parts of the field from a parochial perspective: to consider the rich variety of political processes which can be observed in the local community. For the world of the parish was nothing if not a political forum – not simply as a unit of secular or ecclesiastical administration, nor even as a complex of institutions focusing social interaction intensely within a specific geographical area, but as a tangled, messy, skein of overlapping and intersecting social networks, most of which extended beyond its boundaries outwards and upwards into the larger society, and many of which were networks of power.[5] The parish was in many respects an 'authentic unit of everyday life' – albeit varying in its significance as such socially, geographically and for different purposes – but this was an everyday life replete with 'power laden situations'.[6] It was in many ways a community, an association of neighbours, a unit of identity and belonging, a primary group – but one perennially defined and redefined by processes of inclusion and exclusion. In short, it was 'a system of social relations in motion', part of a larger such system.[7] It is that motion that I want to discuss in reflecting on the politics of the parish.

One way of doing this would be to survey the substantial repertoire of political action available to members of local society in the period: a repertoire now revealed in a clutch of specialist literatures. This included most obviously involvement in local government, and participation not only in the implementation but also in the shaping and contesting of policy: as petitioners, as voters, as subscribers of declarations, sometimes even as rebels. Here already is politics enough. To consider only such matters, however, is to focus, in James C. Scott's phrase, on the 'coastline of politics and miss the continent that lies beyond'.[8] The political topography of that continent included direct action: riot, strikes, and violent intimidation. It encompassed many juridified forms of dispute and resolution: public presentment; private litigation; mediation and formal arbitration. It extended also to more fugitive forms of political action: gossip; verbal abuse; anonymous threats; libellous attacks on the credit of opponents; the use of gestures and symbols; the cacophonous processional mockery of 'rough music'; insubordinate grumbling; footdragging; 'playing dumb'. All these means were available for the pursuit or resolution of conflict, severally or (most often) in various combinations, and it would be possible to examine all of them and the political attitudes which they reveal, tracing the lineaments of a popular political culture.

For present purposes, however, I want to focus on the principal spheres of parochial politics within which these means could be deployed. A useful clue to their identification can be found in recent analyses of the proverbial wisdom of the period – the common adages which were themselves guides to the conduct of daily life. Prominent among the subjects on which they offered traditional wisdom, it appears, were women, marriage and family life; relations with neighbours and kinsfolk; customs of husbandry and work; God (and the devil); law and order; poverty and riches.[9] Taking this cue, I will look briefly in turn at what I will call the politics of patriarchy; of neighbourhood; of custom; of reformation and of 'state formation', before turning finally to the politics of subordination and of meaning.

THE POLITICS OF PATRIARCHY

There can be little doubt that early modern England was a patriarchal society in the sense that authority was conventionally vested in adult males generally and male household heads specifically. At its core lay the family; an institution best defined not in terms of the anachronistic categorisation of nuclear, extended or multiple family types, which we impose for our own analytical purposes, but in contemporary terms as a cluster of related and unrelated dependents living under the authority of a household head who was usually, though not always, an adult male.[10] Parish society can be seen as an association of such households. They formed the most immediate context of life for most people, the spheres within which the roles and associated statuses of men and women, children and servants were defined. This being so, it is easy to assume that the household provided above all a primary socialization into habits of deference, that it fostered the acquisition of habituated responses which sustained established patterns of authority.[11]

In fact, both the conventional definitions of familial relations and the actualities of life in households were shot through with ambiguities and inconsistencies, if not outright contradictions. Familial relationships were hierarchical but also reciprocal. Authority was besieged with obligations of love and care. Obedience and deference lived in juxtaposition with expectations of protection and support.[12] Moreover, the family was a sphere not only of authority but also of interdependence, to an extent not always readily remembered in a more cushioned age. In consequence 'individual lives . . . were more integrated with familial goals' and 'many decisions today considered "individual", such as starting work, leaving home, and getting married, were part of collective family timing strategies'.[13] The family, then, was a structure of authority, a sphere of duty, an experience of interdependence, and a decision-making agency, constituted of individuals of differing gender and age and unequal status and power. (A situation complicated by constraining emotional bonds of the most intimate kind.) This sounds like a political arena: and so it was, at every stage of the family cycle and the life course so far illuminated.

Work on domestic divisions of labour, for example, is still at an early stage, but what we know suggests the existence of 'household work strategies' which involved every member of the household, made no rigorous distinctions between work for production, consumption, and reproduction, and required adaptability in the face of contingent circumstances. (Richard Wall has written of 'the adaptive family economy' and its 'key characteristic – flexibility'.)[14]

Within such economies, most attention has been paid to the elasticity of women's work, and it has been suggested that the demands made upon women were a direct reflection of their subordinate place in an asymmetrical distribution of power: 'What men did was definite, well-defined, limited . . . What the women did was everything else'.[15] Doubtless it could be so, especially perhaps in the case of those urban crafts and trades in which the male role was indeed clearly defined, and 'female economic activity was restricted by the combined forces of patriarchalism and fraternalism'.[16] But it was not *always* so. There were also occupations in which sexual divisions of labour were less rigidly structured, even blurred or unformed, in which male and female roles involved 'overlapping skills' and 'shared competence', and in which the variability of work strategies created space for female initiative and collective decision-making.[17] Husbands' encomiums to the economic contribution of 'careful industrious wives' may seem tainted with patriarchal condescension, but they none the less reflect a working partnership of man and wife in the fundamental imperative of sustaining the family economy. 'I could never have done it without a most careful, thriving, wife', noted Sir John Oglander in his accounts; and much the same awareness can be found in other men throughout the social scale: 'what estate he had, he together with his wife Jane had got it by their industry and therefore he gave and bequeathed all . . . to his loving wife to be at her disposall, and that if it were more his said wife deserved it well'; 'my wife . . . who hath taken very great paines for my profit and benefitt and saved me from many a sore dayes worke'; 'if he had a great deal more his wife was worthy of it and she should have it'.[18]

Effective partnership, of course, does not necessarily imply an equality of decision-making power. Yet it stretches credibility to suggest that within the household economy wives were merely passive enactors of their husbands' directions. When William Gouge preached that wives should not dispose of the common goods of a marriage without their husbands' consent, 'much exception was taken' to this view by his London congregation.[19] Among the poor of Elizabethan Norwich many households depended primarily upon the earnings of the wife and children. In Augustan London most women worked and contributed to the household budget independently of their husbands. The abundant testimony of the wills of the more prosperous householders of early modern England proves beyond question that wives were deemed to be both capable of acting as executors and administrators of their husbands' estates and the most appropriate bearers of such duties. The very confidence with which they were routinely given such authority demonstrates an assumption of their independent decision-making capacity, and the surviving evidence of probate accounts constitutes 'the single most valuable document illustrating ordinary women's economic responsibilities and financial management'.[20]

Such realities make perfect sense in a culture in which women's social subordination as a sex did not preclude expectations of individual competence and self-reliance, and in which their success in managing the myriad responsibilities of 'huswifery' rested on constant activity and careful thrift. Nor is it to be assumed that women raised to meet such expectations would necessarily revert to a submissive role in the face of their husbands' proposals in other dimensions of household affairs. Law and ideology might leave little room for doubt about where ultimate supremacy lay in the family, but that is not to say that a husband's authority was invariably, or even usually, unilaterally imposed. Indeed, it is clear that it was often far from so. The domestic conduct books which dwelt so fulsomely on patriarchal authority also recognised, at the least implicitly, that the prescriptive norm could be challenged – the imperious Gouge conceded that of all subordinate groups wives were 'most backward in yielding'. The Church of England's official homily on marriage was explicit in its recognition of the normality of marital discord, anticipating 'chidings, brawlings, tauntings, repentings, bitter cursings and fightings'. And there is evidence enough that if 'most early modern women were not concerned about equality with men . . . redress for the specific wrongs they perceived had been done to them was of considerable importance to many' both within and beyond the domestic sphere.[21]

We have few such explicit accounts of conjugal negotiation as that given in Adam Eyre's journal entry for 1 January 1648:

This morning I used some words of persuasion to my wife to forbear to tell me of what is past & promised her to become a *good husband* to her for the time to come & she promised likewise she would do what I wished her in anything *save in setting her hand to papers*, and I promised never to wish her thereunto.

But we have more than a few glimpses in other contemporary diaries of the daily domestic chafings of reproach and concession which constituted the negotiative element in marital relations. The many accounts of death-bed settlements of family affairs, to be found in the deposition books of the ecclesiastical courts, also yield examples enough of wives willing to intervene forcibly to argue for or against a husband's testamentary proposals.[22] It is surely of significance that the most commonly employed vernacular term for satisfactory conjugal relations was that of 'quietness'. John and Sarah Welham of Norfolk could not 'agree quietly together as man and wife should do'. William Wright 'lived very disquietly with his wife' and beat her. Bartholomew Musgrave of Brancepeth, Co. Durham had 'no quietness with [his] wife' and 'durst not' offend her.[23] The fingers of blame wagged in both directions. 'Quietness', when it was achieved, might imply merely uncontested patriarchal domination. It seems more probable, however, that it was a condition of dynamic equilibrium between the powerful influence of gender roles as conventionally defined – the only definition available – and the day to day efforts of women to cope, to adapt, to resist, to defend their own space, get their due, and cultivate their own sense of personal esteem within the matrix of the existing system of constraints.

There was much in the contexts of women's lives in early modern England to encourage conformity to the prescriptive pattern of gender roles and to counsel self-restraint in coping with the limitations which it placed upon their personal autonomy. The realities of law and ideology, of demography, economics and material culture, and of exposure to judgemental neighbourhood opinion in small-scale local communities might all foster such conformity. Yet as has been said of these matters in another context, 'power is a relationship, and a relationship which, while shaped by economic and social structures and cultures, is experienced through individuals', and subject to the 'difference arising from personality'.[24] The realities of marital relations in early modern England may not have posed an explicit challenge to the structure of the patriarchal household, but they expressed none the less what has been called 'the ingenuity of many ordinary women in working within a mass-ively restrictive system'. The anonymous author of *The Lawes Resolutions of Women's Rights* could offer 'no remedy' for female subordination, but acknowledged also that 'some women can shift it well enough'.[25] So they could: making something of their own lives; making something, when required, of their menfolk too, making over 'bewildered, sidelong-looking men' into 'husbands, heads of households'.[26]

Recent work on childhood, youth, service and apprenticeship also tends to stress how the socialisation process in the household involved not only the reproduction of authority structures and the inculcation of skills but also a gradually developing participation in decision-making – for example over choices of occupation – which constituted a process of maturation leading to adult autonomy.[27] Fostering such a developmental, participatory process was a charac-teristic of good parenthood, good mastership, and prudent youth. At the same time such relationships – and in particular that of master and servant or apprentice – could be highly unstable. There were abusive, negligent masters and mistresses; cocky, idle and disorderly apprentices or servants – who were not necessarily much younger than their masters and could be as much like assertive younger brothers as dutiful sons. Undoubtedly there was a politics of service, conducted in 'unfitting words' and 'slanderous speeches', in blows, and in malicious gossip – the servant's peren-nial ultimate sanction, employed, for example, by one malcon-tented youth who put it about that his master 'was not able to pay his debts, and if every man were paid he was not worth a groate'.[28]

Youthful initiative and participation in decision-making is per-haps most fully illustrated in the best researched sphere of familial decision-making, and that about which least need be said here: matchmaking. Where the operative social ideals were parity in a match and what Martin Ingram has dubbed 'multilateral consent' in decision-making, there was scope for politics aplenty, as has been abundantly demonstrated – among the eligible young, between parents and children, among the 'friends' who constituted the effective kin: advising, mediating, negotiating, facilitating, block-ing, conceding.[29] And so one could go on. Kinship ties in the dispersed family, for instance, were bonds of varying strength. They were frequently negotiable if not effectively optional. They could be drawn upon for a host of purposes, or they could be ignored –

another dimension of familial politics (or perhaps of diplomacy).[30] In the currently emerging history of death and of death-bed decision-making we can also find together every element of the situation I have tried to describe: recognised household heads; anxiously participating wives; children and kinsfolk; hopefully observing servants – all orbiting the death-bed in the gravitational fields of the politics of patriarchy.[31] Very commonly some of the neighbours were there also, a presence linking the politics of the household to those of the neighbourhood.

THE POLITICS OF NEIGHBOURHOOD

'Neighbourliness' was one of the key words of early modern social relations – a critically important social ideal. I have described it elsewhere as a relationship based on residential propinquity and involving both mutual recognition of reciprocal obligations of a practical nature between effective if not actual equals, and a degree of normative consensus as to the nature of proper behaviour amongst neighbours.[32] Contemporaries believed that neighbours should avoid contention. As the parish clerk of St Botolph's, Billingsgate put it in a neglected contribution to the poetry of the English Renaissance:

> Even as stickes may easselly be broken
> So when neighbours agre not then there is a confucion
> But a great many of stickes bound in one boundell will hardly
> be broken
> So neighbours being ioyned in love together can never be
> severed.[33]

Neighbours should live 'quietly' and 'in charity' – unlike Richard Bowerhouse of Mottram, Cheshire, 'an unquiet and turbulent person amongst his neighbours', or Jane Milner 'a common skowle . . . and disquieter of her neighbours'.[34] Neighbours should be 'of good conversation' and not 'of evyll example'. They should strive to be of 'good credit' and 'honest repute' – both credit and honesty being assessments of individual worth carrying far greater resonance in early modern discourse than in their restricted modern usage.[35] They should pursue agreement and consensus – as they affected to do in the many vestry books and parish accounts through which, it has been said, the words 'consent' and 'agreement' 'beat like leitmotifs'.³⁶ When they fell from grace, as they inevitably did, they should accept reproof and prove willing to be reconciled, 'for quietness sake' – like the Cheshire villager engaged in a bitter quarrel who, being moved by his neighbours and the minister to 'christian reconciliation', publicly declared himself 'willing that all such matters be laid away so as they might live in love and charity as becomes good christians to do'.³⁷ Neighbourliness, then, was a powerful ideal, and an operative ideal, as the local records of the period make abundantly clear. Already we can discern here a politics of neighbourhood; a reconciliatory political culture, of an exceedingly attractive sort.

Perhaps too attractive, for we must be careful not to paint too rosy a picture of neighbourly relations. Somewhat less often dwelt upon are the questions of who was included in these 'tangled webs' of interpersonal obligation',³⁸ and how they were constructed. In a society which witnessed a considerable degree of physical mobility – especially among the young and the propertyless – there was clearly a core and a periphery in every neighbourhood; a continuum of 'belonging'. There was a hierarchy of belonging too. All neighbourhood was overlaid and qualified by rank. People – even gentlefolk – might speak, apparently inclusively, of 'the neighbours'. Yet rank and hierarchy were there for all to see, even at holy communion – a celebration of Christian community among neighbours, who by definition had to be 'in charity', at which it was not unknown for two qualities of wine to be served: malmsey or muscadine for the 'better sort', cheap claret for the rest.³⁹ Neighbourhood was qualified by age too – a factor which bore down with particular force upon the youthful servants who were temporary and fleeting residents – and it was qualified by gender (an issue to which we will return).

All these factors could influence participation in the institutions and occasions from which neighbourhood was constructed. It is overwhelmingly clear that participation in parish office was commonly very circumscribed. Humbler roles might be open to lesser folk, but 'If the lower slopes were pitched shallow so as to encourage participation, the higher ones were correspondingly steep so as to preserve status'. Tenure of the most significant positions was confined for the most part to 'chief inhabitants' of the 'better sort', as in Cheshire, where it was ordered in 1610 that overseers of the poor should be selected from only the 'most substantial' parishioners, and include 'none of the meanest sort who are not fit to be trusted with the stocke of the poore'.[40] We should also avoid assumptions about who participated in the occasions of commensality, the activities of parish guilds, the perambulations, wakes and funeral processions for which we have no attendance lists. Clearly, social relations in parishes criss-crossed the social scale, but many of those of vertical orientation – the provision of alms, work, or protection; standing as a godparent for a dependent; writing or signing a petition for a supplicant – smack less of neighbourhood than of patronage.[41] A different set of meanings might inform such transactions, or a multiplicity of meanings. Again, the realities of mediation, arbitration and reconciliation are rightly stressed in many recent accounts of dispute and litigation. Yet these concepts need to be disaggregated. Reconciliation, for example, might mean a true settling of differences through mutual give and take by equals. But it might also mean in practice acquiescence by a superior willing or constrained to concede a diminution of authority, or by a wronged subordinate powerless to sustain resistance. Were there some neighbours to whom one *needed* to be reconciled – in the interests of securing the future benefits of those 'mutual comforts of neighbourhood' defined by a Norfolk man in 1582 as 'good will for good will and one good toorne for another' – but others to whom the extent of obligation was more unilaterally determined?[42] Were there yet others who were marginal to the 'moral community' or lay outside it altogether?

The case of gender relations is particularly intriguing, the more so in that we face the perennial difficulty of separating the overlapping influences of gender and of rank when attempting to assess the role of women within the community. Clearly women were not passive subjects in the neighbourhood. Individually, some were powerful actors. Collectively, they had their own spheres within which their individual standing could be established and defined. It has been suggested that they were central to the moral community through gossip networks – and work on defamation, witchcraft and infanticide stresses their role in the identification and accusation of deviance.[43] They too had power to include or exclude. Was this, however, a power which could be safely exercised only against other women, against social equals or against inferiors? The complex circumstances of witchcraft accusations provide a pertinent example. They demonstrate both the expectations and the limits of neighbourly obligation, the power which some women were deemed to possess and the risks taken by those of them held to be threatening, especially to their betters.[44] Nor are they the only instances. The humiliating rituals of 'rough music' and the cucking stool also marked the boundaries of female assertiveness, as well as revealing the 'elements of ambiguity and insecurity' which pervaded gender relations in both household and neighbourhood.[45] When Margaret Knowsley of Nantwich spread word amongst her friends and workmates in 1627 that her employer, the minister of the parish, had attempted her chastity, she was probably speaking no more than the truth – it was established that he had been similarly accused in Newcastle some years before. Yet she went 'against the rule of modesty and womanlike behaviour to publish such like matters as also against christianlike discretion', as she was brought to confess, and the defence network he was able to activate led *her* to be sentenced to three public whippings.[46] Women like Margaret Knowsley had to be discreet; a political quality.

So did the poor in general, to judge by the ease with which their 'credit' could be challenged on those occasions when they were called as witnesses. Recent work on the Poor Laws speaks volumes about their ambivalent position and about the larger structures of neighbourhood within which it was negotiated. Stress has been laid on the social significance of the parochial relief system; its vital role in defining rights and obligations; its importance as a framework of interaction involving every level of parish society. Relief embodied a recognition of obligation – it 'presupposed membership of a community'. Yet the system was no simple reflection of paternalism and neighbourhood. Its very establishment in the early seventeenth century was itself a political achievement, sometimes hard fought at the local level. It was run by the 'most substantial' parishioners and increasingly bureaucratised private charity also, subsuming it within a system directed by 'the best sort of the parish'. The system identified and isolated the poor as a group: stressing their otherness; markedly reinforcing the moral differentiation of the deserving and the underserving; defining the boundaries of the community by the recognition of settlement and entitlement.[47]

The whole relief system was predicated on a recognition of eligibility which was discretionary, discriminatory and conditional. It could be remarkably generous; it could harshly exclude; it could be employed to discipline. There was a complex local politics in the administration of the Poor Laws which has not yet been fully explored. It can be discerned not only in the policy resolutions of vestrymen and overseers, but also in the daily assessment of the needs and deserts of individual paupers, the appeals and interventions which such decisions might occasion, the postures of deservingness which needed to be adopted, the exercise of power: 'The overseers shall give old father Cleeves tenn shillinges to releeve him in his necessity, upon condicion he shall remove his son Dennis out of the towne and not receive him any more into his house.'[48] In the politics of poverty, as in so much else, neighbourliness could be an ideal to be appealed to, a tactical claim. The neighbourhood itself, however, was a shifting and unstable entity, constituted by processes of inclusion and exclusion which were not infrequently occasions of contest.

THE POLITICS OF CUSTOM

The neighbourly community, then, could be an episodic and unstable entity. Nevertheless, it had its moments of disclosure as well as of denial. Prominent among these were those occasions when the inhabitants of a locality (or large sections of them) found common ground in the assertion or defence of Custom.

Custom, as E. P. Thompson has powerfully reminded us, was a 'good' word in the popular political discourse of early modern England: an 'operative' word, vital to the 'rhetoric of legitimation'.[49] It is also a familiar word. All students of the medieval and early modern periods know about the importance of custom, and its significance has been particularly eloquently restated in recent years. Custom 'presupposed a group or community within which it was practised', consensus, and collective responsibility. It was vital to the claims of such groups to autonomy and independence. Within them, custom was an 'accumulation of rules about what was right or wrong and about the right procedures for enforcing [them]'.[50] It was a 'lived-in environment of practices, inherited assumptions and rules'; a 'workaday routine of livelihood'; an 'ambience', a 'mentality', 'a whole vocabulary . . . of legitimation and expectation'. It was 'the interface between law and common practice', describing a spectrum from unwritten norms to rights with

legal force.[51] Custom claimed authority from antiquity, continuance 'time out of mind of man', certainty and reason, but was in
fact highly flexible. Some customs were maintained, others cancelled or gradually discarded. New customs evolved; meanings
changed. Operative custom at any one time was the outcome of
processes of 'structural amnesia' – as was demonstrated in Audley,
Staffordshire, in 1618, when the tenants' sturdy assertion that 'the
customes of the said manor doe lye and rest in the breaste of the
coppiehoulders' was outflanked by a smart lawyer's use of court
rolls extending back to the thirteenth century to demonstrate the
historical variability, and therefore invalidity, of the rights which
they claimed.[52]

It is also well known that custom was, and long had been, not only
a field of change but also one of contest, 'an area in which opposing
interests made conflicting claims'.[53] The historiography of early
modern England can boast a substantial literature detailing the
resistance of agrarian communities to efforts by landlords and
agricultural 'improvers' to assert 'unreasonable' claims, challenge
alleged customs, shake off the restraints of tenant rights, extinguish
common rights and so on.[54] Such resistance could take the form of
evasion, as with the tenants of manors in Yorkshire and Northum-
berland in 1628–9 who 'in a subtle combination, mixt with feare'
refused to cooperate with the surveyor sent by their new landlord.[55]
It could result in litigation, as at Wigston Magna, Leicestershire, in
1588, when thirty-one copyholders fought their Lord at law (eventually causing him, after twenty years of stubborn resistance, to cut
his losses and sell them their holdings).[56] It could involve threat, as
when the tenants of Osmington, Dorset, conspired to erect a mock
gallows outside their enclosing landlord's house in 1618 – using his
own firewood for the purpose – and some months later hanged him
in effigy.[57] If all else failed it could explode into the direct action of
riot: usually in response to immediate threats to local customs and
usages; often involving coalitions of interested parties; commonly a
tactic to advance a legal action or provoke authoritative arbitration;
generally purposefully directed and carefully restrained, with a
preference for ritualistic and symbolic violence; invariably infused
with a powerful sense of justification, explicitly articulated in scores
of surviving depositions which truculently assert the authority of
custom, and smoulder with resentment of the allegedly arbitrary or
unreasonable dealings of landlords.[58] Nor were such disputes con-

fined solely to agrarian relations, as witness the century-long defence of their rights and customs by the 'free miners' of Derbyshire against the encroachments upon them of gentlemen mineowners in the Peak.[59]

The defence of custom was 'quintessentially local politics'.[60] As the now numerous accounts of such local struggles should make clear, localised customary consciousness was just as much a form of political consciousness as the knowledge of national affairs fostered by a developing print culture. It involved parochial conflicts, but it was no less an authentic political consciousness for that. It could mobilise whole communities, or sections of them, with a conviction of their rectitude in disputing power, and to those involved their causes might seem every bit 'as dramatic and important as the struggle against arbitrary . . . power within the national body politic'.[61] (Indeed on a few occasions the two became united.) Here if nowhere else, subordinate groups could claim equality of a kind in the assertion of what they took to be their rights.

For all that, it is arguable that the politics of custom are only begining to be explored. Accounts of these matters are too often somewhat elegiac. Like community, custom seems commonly to be in retreat, tactically withdrawing at best, nibbled at episodically, eroded by the long-term 'hardening and concreting [of] the notion of property in land'.[62] This is, of course, a valid theme and one worth extending by a shift of historiographical emphasis from the thick description of particular episodes to more extended explorations of the ways in which customary values and consensus might gradually break down in a community, losing their once compelling force. However, recent work also suggests not only that a world of custom was still very much alive and kicking in the eighteenth century, but also that it was being extended in the early modern period into new spheres. Worlds of custom, and communities defined by them, were being created and established – above all in the growing industrial areas. To take one example, the struggle of the copyholders of Whickham, Co. Durham, in 1619–21 against the coal owners of Newcastle, was presented in the first instance as a defence of their customary manorial rights against unrestrained mining. In fact it was *also* about the maintenance and extension of certain 'new grown customs' regarding their claims to a profitable monopoly of the transportation of coal won in their lands.[63] Similarly, in the woollen districts of Yorkshire and Wiltshire in the eighteenth century, the work structures of rural industry 'developed social systems which had a stronger vested interest in preserving them than in changing them', a 'vigorous and confident culture' of industrial customs which could be appealed to as 'bastions against the threat of detrimental change'. Much the same process of evolution was certainly taking place in the northern coalfield in the late seventeenth and early eighteenth centuries. Such developing industrial cultures were 'premised upon a capitalist economic system', yet assumed and expected a certain stability of relations within it. They were products of market forces, yet demanded that these should be permitted to work 'only within the strict parameters of custom'.[64]

Attitudes and values of this kind and the 'customary' wages, conditions of work, and master–employee relations which they were intended to preserve were often 'invented traditions', as bogus in that sense as George IV's kilt. They were also politically created, enshrining terms and conditions which had been won, or conceded, under favourable circumstances. Once established, however, they acquired compelling force to those whose interests they enshrined, and they too were truculently – and often successfully – defended in negotiation, litigation, riot and strike. This 'moral economy of production', was firmly in being and taken for granted by the mid-eighteenth century.[65] Its emergence presents an agenda to historians of preceding centuries which might reinvigorate the historiography of Tudor and Stuart industrial life, as well as linking it more firmly to the more familiar world of agrarian social relations through the common nexus of an ongoing politics of custom.

THE POLITICS OF REFORMATION AND STATE FORMATION

Custom, of course, was not confined to the economic sphere. Tension between customary practice and innovation can also be found elsewhere, and not least in responses to religious change and to what have been called 'the growing pretensions' of the English State.[66] Both the politics of what we have always called the Reformation and what we are learning to call 'state formation' have large, independent historiographies. They can conveniently be taken together, however, since from the perspective of the parish, with its overlapping civil and ecclesiastical functions, they had a good deal in common in their impact.

Whether or not the English Reformation was initially welcomed – and we can agree at least that this varied – the impact of the 'long Reformation' on parish society was undoubtedly profound. Some places may have witnessed a relatively painless process of adaptation to successive changes – undergoing what has been nicely termed 'a series of conforming experiences'.[67] Many did not. Both the extent to which England became a Protestant nation and the developing nature of English Protestantism in the long term were matters which were determined locally as well as centrally. For a full account we would need to review the local contests occasioned by every stage of change in religious belief and practice from pre-Reformation heresy to the evangelical revival of the eighteenth century, and that is clearly impossible here. Nevertheless, one can confidently assert that every stage of that long process could have its impact on local social relations and that all were fought out somewhere or other at the level of the parish.

No one doubts that religious change could galvanise the politics of the parish. The impact of 'state formation' in the early modern period has been rather more contested. It has been argued forcefully that early modernists stressing the social consequences in the localities of the 'incorporative drive' of early modern government neglect the medieval antecedents of such processes. Medieval villages were not closed corporate communities. Their inhabitants were not isolated from the institutions of the state. Political society already possessed considerable social depth and its development was well advanced through the involvement, at the least, of parish notables in administrative and judicial institutions which were arenas of participation. All this seems fair comment. The essential characteristics of a centralised, unified, integrated polity in which the coordinating roles in local society corresponded to the local social hierarchy, and which permitted – within a framework of law – a participatory, discretionary, accommodative relationship with higher authority, can be readily accepted as established features of the English State.[68]

At the same time, however, none of this precludes the argument that in early modern England what has been called the 'infrastructural reach' of the State became more powerful; that involvement with its institutions intensified; that policy could be more effectively

implemented on the ground.[69] We must not forget the 'increase of
governance'; the 'stacks of statutes' defining and redefining acceptable forms of social activity; the quickening tempo of local government; the substantial increase in criminal and regulative
prosecution and the simply massive increase in civil litigation which
characterised the period.[70] Such developments were occasioned in
part by the direct demands of the state but still more by the
willingness of individuals and groups in local society to employ the
resources of state power for their own particular purposes. None of
this required structural transformation or even institutional innovation – though there was important institutional innovation too,
most notably from the point of view of the parish in the Poor Laws,
the petty sessions, the militia and taxation. It might be said to be
essentially a matter of degree: but degree does matter. Quantitative
change can become qualitative change, not least in the relative
salience of what have been called 'extensive' as against 'particular-
ist' interests in local society.[71] All this could have complex repercus-
sions on local social relationships.

Taken together, both religious change and an intensifying interaction between local people and the institutions of the State could
present a range of potential political problems to be handled and
settled. And despite the large literatures which we have on religion,
law and local government, it remains fair to say that the resultant
political processes have been little studied in depth, or for their own
sake. Rather we have a highly episodic historiography of these
matters: an accumulation of vignettes, a range of encounters –
particular events being sometimes 'unpacked' with great skill, but
often for only a brief period or with respect to particular issues
taken in isolation. The cumulative impact of such episodes, the
longer-term course of accommodating, reopening, consolidating,
or reversing their outcomes, is comparatively rarely explored.
Nevertheless, what we have at least presents a range of possibilities
in the relationships of local people with the institutions of Church
and State, and one which can be characterised.

In the first place, both religious change and the demands of the
State impinged on local societies in ways which could cause real
problems of cooperation and enforcement. Did churchwardens
cooperate with repeated demands for uniformity handed down
from above, or did they mix 'truth with ambiguity and ingenuity in
their efforts to satisfy the authorities, their neighbours and their

consciences' – like those of Tostock, Suffolk, who ingeniously reported to the Archdeacon 'that the mynester do not iuselle [*usually*] wear the surples, nor do he not Refeues [*refuse*] to weare yt'?[72] Did ministers encounter biddable flocks or find themselves embroiled in conflict with some or all of their people? Many ministers found themselves prosecuted by their own flocks – or parts of them – sometimes for negligence, sometimes for excessive zeal. A few faced even more shocking demonstrations of local hostility, like the Wiltshire vicar, locked in combat with both profane elements among his parishioners and a core of truculent dissenters, who in 1686 found his church porch 'shamefully polluted with human excrements . . . to near the quantity of a barrowfull, which they laid against the door and also filled the keyhole'.[73] Again, did constables and jurymen respond punctiliously, even enthusiastically, to the periodic requirements of magistracy, or did they negotiate the demands of authority by selective response, taking advantage of that discretionary 'untidyness of government which was partly involuntary and partly deliberate'? Did their neighbours assist them, support them, or revile them?[74]

Secondly, both the Reformation and the increase of governance could provide opportunities for participation, initiative and activism which went beyond dutiful (or undutiful) response. John Leache, the godly Romford schoolmaster, welcomed local people to his private catechising and expository meetings, and was repeatedly in trouble with the local ecclesiastical authorities for this initiative in the 1580s – though he ended his days as a revered parish lecturer and vestryman.[75] In another context, there were the twenty-four of the 'auntientest and better sort of inhabitants' of Braintree, who achieved constitution as a select vestry in 1611, and thereafter governed their township rigorously and efficiently for a century. Or again, there were the members of the Swallowfield Town Meeting who devised their own set of procedures for local government in 1596 'to the end we may the better and more quyetly lyve together in good love and amytie'.[76]

Thirdly, such participatory initiatives could also involve exclusions. One of the intentions of the townsmen of Swallowfield was to correct the poor if they should 'malapertly compare with their betters and sette them at nought'. The exclusiveness of the Braintree vestry found its eventual nemesis in the revolt of the lesser ratepayers at an acrimonious meeting in 1713, when the latter group 'in a very confused and disorderly manner cryed out with loud voices, noe four and twenty, noe four and twenty'![77] Similarly, the stimulation of religious enthusiasm could breed a distanced attitude towards those neighbours who were 'backward' or 'skorners' in religion. John Rogers, that vigorous exponent of spiritual warfare, advised his followers to be 'friendly in all points of neighbourhood' with such people, but to avoid keeping company with them, intermarrying with them or taking unconverted youths as servants. Such 'shunning' could be the basis of a perilously restricted pastorate and a corroded sense of community.[78] It may also have had a part to play not only in alienating some parishioners from the radical Reformation, but also in creating a constituency for heterodox sects which offered alternative definitions of spiritual integrity and modes of religious participation.

Involvement in the pursuit of order and reformation could also lead to the introduction, or expansion of public debate over policy – a kind of parochial 'public sphere' in which local responses to national policies was critically discussed. From Yorkshire in 1615 we have a glimpse of a group of local notables standing in the churchyard discussing 'some vices which reigned' in their parish 'whereof . . . Mr Clough [the vicar] desired Reformation'. In Cheshire in the 1620s Sir Richard Grosvenor, in his addresses to jurymen and freeholders, forged 'ideological links between the arena of national politics and local society', attempting to 'mould the demands of a collective politico-religious consciousness that can be described only as a sort of embryonic public opinion'. All over Essex in the 1630s and early 1640s, parishioners hostile to Laudian ceremony anticipated the Quakers by keeping on their hats in church as a gesture of protest. 'Are you at Mass again?', hissed a (hatted) tailor to the curate of Radwinter, while at Chelmsford some in the congregation 'did very stubbornly clap on their hats', while others 'with violent glee [did] pluck them off again'.[79]

All this could produce a superimposition of types and levels of conflict within particular communities. Hostile reactions to the religious predilections of the Puritan Harlackenden family at Earls Colne, Essex, in the 1590s, for example, intersected with resentment of their vigorous policies as newly established manorial lords. Personal rivalries over local office took on a religious complexion at Thetford ten years before.[80] Elsewhere responses to the imperatives of order, subordination, godly reformation, or all three tangled together, could exacerbate conflict within households, between old and young, rich and poor, or simply personal rivals.

Finally, what is clear throughout is that both processes were refracted into local communities through their varied social structures in the fullest sense: through their structures of power and authority; their networks of interpersonal connection both within and beyond the local sphere; their localised patterns of expectation and canons of evaluation. Such structures could influence how the requirements of Church and State were locally perceived. Did they make sense? Did they offer solutions to local ills? They could influence the manner in which universalistic ideals of order and salvation were appropriated and mutated in particular contexts. They could determine whether or not there existed interstices in the networks of power through which initiatives could emerge, or whether alternatives were dampened, defused or excluded altogether. In all these ways they could have a powerful influence on the specific local outcomes of processes active in the nation at large.

This consideration provides the essential kernel of truth in the various hypotheses which have been advanced concerning patterns of response to these developments: in particular those associating religious change and the conflicts to which it gave rise, or success in the imposition of tight patterns of local government, with particular economic and social structures and the initiatives of particular social groups.[81] Such hypotheses are important in directing attention to structural influences on social change which are too often evaded. Yet they run the risk of acquiring a predictive rigidity, of assuming that particular patterns of social relations were coincident with given economic structures or positions within them. If more refined models can be developed, they must be ones which leave more room for the contingent element in social processes, for the peculiar configurations of structure, circumstance and individual agency which could prove vitally important in the experience of particular places.[82] Moreover, they must make due allowance for the dynamism and mutability of social formations. For the politics of reformation and state formation could change situations through their cumulative impact on local social networks, power structures and attitudes; all of which were parts of a system of social relations in motion.

What we have is less a finite group of relatively predictable alternatives than a whole range of possibilities for cooperation and conflict which were variously pursued in different contexts. This does indeed provide an exciting field of opportunity for an expanded political history – and one directly linked to some established central themes of national politics. Yet those opportunities are unlikely to be realised if the politics of reformation and state formation at the level of the parish remain bogged down in sterile debates over the 'typicality' of particular case studies or the validity of premature efforts to impose systematic order on the larger picture. What is needed, rather, is appreciation of the larger range of variability in contexts and options which shaped the manner in which the inhabitants of England's 9000 parishes participated in their own ways, and for their own reasons, in the pulsating development of a single political society.

THE POLITICS OF SUBORDINATION AND OF MEANING

We have, then, a prospectus of local society as a system of social relations in motion; one which derived its dynamics from the politics of everyday life. Taken together, as we have seen, all this posed problems not only of cooperation but also of authority and subordination. From the perspective of people in established positions of authority, existing dispensations of power had to be sustained, adjusted, elaborated. From the perspective of those lacking any formal 'voice or authoritie in the commonwealth', advantageous (or at least acceptable) patterns of subordination had to be negotiated and defended; disadvantageous ones resisted or evaded. This was the politics of subordination, informing every aspect of the situation which I have sketched so far.

It might be objected, perhaps, that there is a degree of wishful thinking in the situation as described, a danger of overestimating the interactive and negotiative elements of social relations and of underplaying the role of coercive power. Certainly power could simply be asserted and there are many ways of illustrating how subordination could be enforced by the coercive and manipulative use of superior power, be it physical, institutional, economic or political. Several of these have been touched upon. Nevertheless, there were also limits to the direct assertion of power. There were

legal constraints. There were also sufficient areas of relative independence within the structure of society to remind the dominant in
household, manor or parish of the contingent nature of social
hierarchy. And there were cultural restraints, for it is evident that
coercion was not the preferred means of resolving conflicts of
interest. It was employed selectively to mark the boundaries of
insubordination rather than routinely to repress every challenge to
authority.

The politics of subordination involved rather an ongoing process
of rearticulation in local social relations.[83] From the perspective of
authority, the demands of such a process required efforts to maintain a united front among the dominant figures in a community –
for in the politics of the parish, as in those of the State, it was when
chief men lacked effective unity that they risked losing control of
the situation. They underlined the importance for magistrates,
ministers, landlords or parish officers of winning the support of
those strategically significant social groups whose cooperation as
willing subalterns was essential to maintaining desired patterns of
authority. Above all, they reinforced the need to invest social relationships with meanings supportive of the legitimacy of structures
of hierarchy and subordination – to supplement economic and
political with cultural authority. One example can be found in the
conventions of patronage and deference which gave simultaneous
emphasis to both the powerful realities of social differentiation and
the bonds of personal identification between patron and client,
thereby lending credibility to 'a description of social relations as
they may be seen from above'.[84] Another lies in the habit of describing capitalist labour relations in terms of 'master' and 'servant',
terms connoting personal ties of patriarchal authority.[85] Yet another was the manner in which churchwardens placed parishioners
hierarchically in the seating plans of parish churches – a ranking
often contested in detail, it is true, but at least as significant for the
way in which it routinely inscribed and reinscribed patterns of
subordination within the ritual community of the parish.[86]

Central to the politics of subordination was the elaboration and
reinforcement of such meanings and the social identities to
which they gave rise, in the face of corrosive processes of social
change. This is a large subject in itself, but for present purposes
four aspects can be illustrated, all of which are most easily approached from a top-down perspective, and all of which involve

processes of redescription, significant adaptations of descriptive and evaluative language which together could constitute shifts of meaning.[87]

First, certain key values could be appropriated and reinterpreted in the interests of hierarchy, authority and social distance. Perhaps the best known example is the migration of meaning in the concept of charity, from describing a *condition* of Christian harmony to describing an *act* of benevolence from the wealthy to the poor and needy – those people who by 1700 were routinely described in many parish books as 'objects of charity'.[88] But there are other examples too. Dr Heal has examined how 'hospitality', a public obligation of the wealthy 'routinely offered as part of a holistic view of community', became a private virtue, practised towards chosen others – a shift accompanied by a real decline in public sociability and commensality.[89] Dr Archer has described a 'changing conception of brotherhood' in the companies of London, which meant that while they retained an integrating role among their members 'the communal bond was a more hierarchically articulated one'.[90] The petitions and presentments thrown up by contests of authority in particular parishes also provide innumerable examples of the appropriation of the cultural force of the concepts of law, order, neighbourhood, honesty and true religion by individuals or groups pursuing sectional interests, and collectively reveal comparable processes of restrictive redefinition.[91] One might even speculate as to whether the ideal of family relations described in the conduct books of pre-Reformation humanists and Protestant moralists alike was not appropriated by dominant social groups and employed in both their critique of the domestic relations of the poor, and the closure of their own households to previously routine forms of neighbourhood regulation.

Secondly, other values, or the practices which expressed them, could be eroded or rejected. Custom became an increasingly ambiguous term which by 1700 could be employed pejoratively to denigrate the beliefs and practices of the 'vulgar', as well as positively as a legal term of art. The moral rhetorics of the Reformation era and of the eighteenth-century age of politeness and commercialism alike are riddled with examples of the hostile redefinition of behaviour previously tolerated or even applauded. Whole areas of working practices – and still more of leisure and communal sociability – were redefined. Whole areas of belief and practice became characterised as vulgar errors tainted with social inferiority – as did whole manners of speech.[92]

Thirdly, new self-identities could be established among dominant groups in local society. To take only one example, the self-description of local ruling groups as 'the most sufficient', 'the principal' or 'chief' inhabitants, or above all 'the better sort' of the parish, had late medieval precedents, in towns at least. But it was an expression of a specific and exclusive social identity which was powerfully reinforced in this age of social polarisation and parochial oligarchy.[93]

Fourthly, revised social identities could be imposed on others by their classification in approved or disapproved categories. We might consider the developing implications of such terms as 'the poor', 'the deserving poor' or 'objects of charity' (all of which obscured more than they revealed about the people concerned). Then there was the whole battery of terms associated with the language of 'sorts of people' so much employed in the politics of the parish, contrasting the 'better sort' with the 'poorer', 'ruder', 'vulgar', 'baser', 'inferior' or 'meaner' sorts. These terms derived their specific meanings from particular local contexts, but all were part of a broader vocabulary of differentiation, dissociation and devaluation.[94] Again, there was the characterisation of whole communities as threatening or insubordinate, like the Derbyshire miners, supposedly a 'rude, boorish kind of people' and 'given to unthriftness . . . lavysh and idle', or the Wiltshire weavers, said to be full of 'insolence, disobedience, disregard and contempt . . . towards their masters and superiors.'[95] In all these ways language could be 'used and abused in the service of hierarchy'. In the obscurest of parishes such meanings could come in like cultural 'spores on the prevailing wind looking for any likely place to land, any welcome'. And what could not be achieved by the formal machinery of parish government might be 'sought through the tyranny of vocabulary'.[96]

Sought, but not necessarily achieved. For these instances are drawn from the rhetoric of the dominant, the evaluative vocabulary of an attempted hegemony. Such meanings could be contested too. Among dominant social groups themselves, there were those who, for whatever good reasons of their own, declined to rearrange their mental furniture and participate in the consumption of a new world of cultural goods. Among those occupying subordinate roles, the whole thrust of this discussion of the politics of the parish serves to illustrate the many ways in which hegemonic enterprises of all kinds could be 'rejected, reinterpreted, or simply ignored'.[97]

Such resistance might be openly displayed in those communities in which the networks of power were sufficiently loose to permit expressions of truculent independence. These were commonly the same places denounced by beleaguered ministers and chief inhabitants as sinks of disorder and irreligion; the bastions of E. P. Thompson's insubordinate plebeian culture.[98] In more tightly controlled, dependent and closely overlooked social environments also, the doffed hat and lowered eyes could conceal the 'hidden transcript' of the subordinate: the 'critique of power spoken behind the backs of the dominant', elaborated in sequestered places, expressed fugitively in 'an unobtrusive realm of political struggle', seeping perennially through the unstopped cracks in the wainscoting of power.[99]

Alternative cultural forms could persist or be elaborated. Popular religion, however negatively defined from above and outside, continued in its unrepentantly syncretic and appropriative way to incorporate selectively those elements of reforming, dissenting and evangelical religion which had appeal, while ignoring the rest. The very language of abuse and debasement so often visited on the labouring poor could also be a 'reactive element' in the formation and consolidation of alternative identities.[100] The development of the powerful popular attachment to 'independence', so evidently a central concept in the self-identity of many labouring people by the later eighteenth century, deserves to be explored with the same care devoted to such elite social ideals as 'civility' or 'politeness'. The insubordinate plebeian culture so celebrated by historians of the eighteenth century did not spring into life fully formed in that century, as they sometimes seem to imply. Nor, for that matter, was it the *whole* story. It was one manifestation of the *many* meanings which can be found in dialogue and in contest, within particular social structures, within individual minds, in the cultural dimension of the politics of the parish.

To conclude: throughout this discussion of the politics of the parish I have been at some pains to describe localised systems of social relations in motion without implying that they were subject to any single, linear, pattern of social transformation. This caution does not derive from any reluctance on my part to confront the problem of social change – aspects of change have been repeatedly emphasised in the course of my argument, and the entire discussion has been conducted in a manner which assumes the larger context of demographic, economic, social structural, governmental and cultural developments familiar to every student of early modern England. It reflects rather a concern with the complexities of social change, a preoccupation with the manner in which larger processes were experienced in particular local societies, how they impinged upon individual lives, and how the varied responses which they occasioned helped to shape their outcomes.

Such a perspective does not lend itself to the making of confident generalisations about the dominant pattern of change in English local society over more than two centuries, and for that I make no apologies. Many of the pioneering master narratives of English social history – adapted, as often as not, from the evolutionary assumptions of classical social theory – have gradually lost their interpretative credibility. Their power to convince has been eroded by a growing awareness of the diverse, uneven, incomplete, contradictory, and often highly contingent and unstable nature of social change in early modern England, and also by what has now been revealed about both preceding and succeeding social realities.

Bereft of the old secure assumptions about the stages and direction of social development, we have to think again. This does not, however, mean starting from scratch. We know a great deal about the processes of social change in early modern England which can stand secure without the old scaffolding. We know that they were experienced differently in different social contexts; contexts which presented varying ranges of options to the people of the time. We also know that those contexts themselves were subject to change, and that shifts in the contexts of life – demographic, economic, ideological, legal, sociological, cultural and political – were the product not merely of impersonal forces, but of individual human agency. They were episodic as well as conjunctural. To understand how all this served to expand, or to contract, people's freedom of movement in the conduct of their lives individually, and how it contributed to the making, maintaining, dissolving and recreating of communities and identities over time, is one of our best hopes for a subtler, more nuanced, fairer and more convincing account of cumulative social development in England's mosaic of parochial diversity. Central to that enterprise is consideration of the politics of everyday life, the parochial struggles through which mostly obscure people tried to make their own history. Those efforts seem no less significant in the absence of teleologically predetermined outcomes. Indeed, they may seem all the more impressive because they *lacked* them.

NOTES AND REFERENCES

* This chapter is based upon a James Ford Special Lecture delivered at the Univesity of Oxford in May 1993. I wish to thank Adam Fox, Malcolm Gaskill, Paul Griffiths, Steve Hindle, Naomi Tadmor, Andrew Wood and David Levine, all of whom read and commented upon the original text, for their advice and criticism, and the members of seminars and lecture audiences in Oxford, Cambridge, Durham, Liverpool and Lund who have discussed particular issues with me. I am especially grateful to all those who have generously allowed me to refer to, or quote from, their unpublished doctoral theses.

   1. P. Collinson, *De Republica Anglorum: Or, History with the Politics Put Back* (Cambridge, 1990), p. 14.

   2. Ibid., pp. 15, 30–5.

   3. Quoting J. W. Scott, *Gender and the Politics of History* (New York, 1988), p. 49; and A. Macfarlane *et al.*, *Reconstructing Historical Communities* (Cambridge, 1977), p. 187.

   4. The phrase quoted is from J. C. Scott, *Domination and the Arts of Resistance: Hidden Transcripts* (New Haven, 1990), p. xiii.

   5. For recent attempts to reconceptualise the local community, see C. Phythian-Adams, *Re-thinking English Local History*, Department of English Local History Occasional Papers, 4th series (Leicester, 1987); and Phythian-Adams, 'Introduction: An Agenda for English Local History', in C. Phythian-Adams (ed.), *Societies, Cultures and Kinship, 1580–1850: Cultural Provinces and English Local History* (Leicester, 1993), pp. 1–23. On social networks and power, see M. Mann, *The Sources of Social Power, Vol. I: A History of Power from the Beginning to A.D. 1760* (Cambridge, 1986), pp. 1, 13.

   6. Quoting D. MacCulloch, *Suffolk and the Tudors: Politics and Religion in an English County, 1500–1600* (Oxford, 1986), p. 28; and Scott, *Domination*, p. 3.

   7. W. G. Runciman, *A Treatise on Social Theory, Vol. II: Substantive Social Theory* (Cambridge, 1989), p. 123.

   8. Scott, *Domination*, p. 199.

   9. D. Rollison, *The Local Origins of Modern Society: Gloucestershire, 1500–1800* (London, 1992), ch. 3; and A. P. Fox, 'Aspects of Oral Culture and its Development in Early Modern England' (unpublished University of Cambridge Ph.D. thesis, 1992), ch. 3.

   10. N. Tadmor, 'Concepts of the Family in Five Eighteenth-Century

38   *The Experience of Authority in Early Modern England*

Texts' (unpublished University of Cambridge Ph.D. thesis, 1992), esp. pp. 62–85, 132–7.

11. As is powerfully argued in G. Schochet, 'Patriarchalism, Politics and Mass Attitudes in Stuart England', *Historical Journal*, vol. 12 (1969), pp. 413–41.

12. S. Amussen, *An Ordered Society: Gender and Class in Early Modern England* (Oxford, 1988), pp. 38–9.

13. T. K. Harevan, 'The History of the Family and the Complexity of Social Change', *American Historical Review*, vol. 96 (1991), pp. 107, 115.

14. R. E. Pahl, *Divisions of Labour* (Oxford, 1984), p. 20, and chs 1–2 passim; R. Wall, 'Work, Welfare and the Family: An Illustration of the Adaptive Family Economy', in L. Bonfield *et al.* (eds), *The World We Have Gained: Histories of Population and Social Structure* (Oxford, 1986), p. 265.

15. M. Prior, 'Women and the Urban Economy: Oxford, 1500–1800', in M. Prior (ed.), *Women in English Society, 1500–1800* (London, 1985), p. 95.

16. V. Brodsky, 'Widows in Late Elizabethan London: Remarriage, Economic Opportunity and Family Orientations', in Bonfield *et al.* (eds), *World We Have Gained*, p. 141. This reality is illustrated by the difficulties experienced by urban widows in carrying on their late husbands' trades without remarriage.

17. P. Thompson, 'Women in the Fishing: The Roots of Power Between the Sexes', *Comparative Studies in Society and History*, vol. 27 (1985), p. 15.

18. R. Houlbrooke (ed.), *English Family Life, 1576–1716: An Anthology from Diaries* (Oxford, 1988), p. 65; D. Levine and K. Wrightson, *The Making of an Industrial Society: Whickham, 1560–1765* (Oxford, 1991), pp. 319–20; Brodsky, 'Widows in Late Elizabethan London', p. 147. Cf. S. Wright, '"Churmaids, Huswyfes and Hucksters": The Employment of Women in Tudor and Stuart Salisbury', in L. Charles and L. Duffin (eds), *Women and Work in Pre-Industrial England* (London, 1985), p. 105. It is worth noting that such evidence is most commonly to be found in accounts of the making of nuncupative wills, which not infrequently contain expressions of feeling which were omitted from more formal testamentary documents.

19. Quoted in A. L. Erickson, *Women and Property in Early Modern England* (London, 1993), p. 9. Records of litigation can provide examples of husbands anxious not to make decisions without their wives' consent. One litigant declared that 'hee cannot perfectly answere . . . before hee have had conference' with his wife; another, after 'his wife came to him and did stand with him . . . changed his former speaking, and saide hee woulde pay no money': see T. Stretton, 'Women and Litigation in the Elizabethan Court of Requests' (unpublished University of Cambridge Ph.D. thesis, 1993), pp. 155–6.

20. R. H. Tawney and E. Power (eds), *Tudor Economic Documents, Vol. II: Commerce, Finance and the Poor Law* (London, 1924), pp. 313–16; P. Earle, 'The Female Labour Market in London in the Late Seventeenth and Early Eighteenth Centuries, *Economic History Review*, 2nd series, vol. 42 (1989), p. 337; Erickson, *Women and Property*, p. 36 and chs 9–10.

21. Erickson, *Women and Property*, pp. 9, 14; R. Houlbrooke, *The English Family, 1450–1700* (London, 1984), p. 114. For representations of marital

discord in popular humour, see E. Foyster, 'A Laughing Matter? Marital Discord and Gender Control in Seventeenth-Century England', *Rural History*, vol. 4 (1993), pp. 3–21. Women's activity as litigants is illuminatingly discussed in Stretton, 'Women and Litigation', ch. 2 and passim.

22. Houlbrooke (ed.), *English Family Life*, p. 65 and ch. 2 passim. Cf. K. Wrightson, *English Society, 1580–1680* (London, 1982), pp. 95ff. For death-bed interventions, see e.g. Levine and Wrightson, *Industrial Society*, p. 290; Brodsky, 'Widows in Late Elizabethan London', p. 146.

23. S. Amussen, 'Governors and Governed: Class and Gender Relations in English Villages, 1590–1725' (unpublished Brown University Ph.D. thesis, 1982), pp. 193–4, 206–7; C. Issa, 'Obligation and Choice: Aspects of Family and Kinship in Seventeenth-Century County Durham' (unpublished University of St Andrews Ph.D. thesis, 1987), p. 259.

24. Thompson, 'Women in the Fishing', pp. 21, 26.

25. Erickson, *Women and Property*, pp. 20, 99.

26. Alluding to A. Munro, *Friend of My Youth* (Penguin edn, Toronto, 1991), p. 60: 'One thing she has noticed about married women, and that is how many of them have to go about creating their husbands. They have to start ascribing preferences, opinions, dictatorial ways . . . This way, bewildered, sidelong-looking men are made over into husbands, heads of households.' The same process can work in reverse, of course.

27. I. Krausman Ben-Amos, 'Service and Coming of Age in Seventeenth-Century England', *Continuity and Change*, vol. 3 (1988), pp. 41–64. See also Ben-Amos, *Adolescence and Youth in Early Modern England* (New Haven, 1994).

28. For an illuminating discussion of these issues, see P. Griffiths, 'Some Aspects of the Social History of Youth in Early Modern England, with Particular Reference to the Period, *c.*1590–*c.*1640' (unpublished University of Cambridge Ph.D. thesis, 1992), ch. 7, quoting p. 451.

29. M. Ingram, *Church Courts, Sex and Marriage in England, 1570–1640* (Cambridge, 1987), chs 4, 6. See also, among the many studies of this issue, Wrightson, *English Society*, ch. 3; Houlbrooke, *The English Family*, ch. 4; M. MacDonald, *Mystical Bedlam: Madness, Anxiety and Healing in Seventeenth-Century England* (Cambridge, 1981), pp. 88–98; R. M. Smith, 'Marriage Processes in the English Past: Some Continuities', in Bonfield *et al.* (eds), *World We Have Gained*, esp. pp. 67–9, 76ff, 96; P. Rushton, 'Property, Power and Family Networks: The Problem of Disputed Marriage in Early Modern England' *Journal of Family History*, vol. 11 (1986), pp. 205–19.

30. Wrightson, *English Society*, pp. 44–51; D. Cressy, 'Kinship and Kin Interaction in Early Modern England' *Past and Present*, vol. 13 (1986), pp. 38–69; Issa, 'Obligation and Choice', passim; A. Mitson, 'The Significance of Kinship Networks in the Seventeenth Century: South-West Nottinghamshire', in Phythian-Adams (ed.), *Societies, Cultures and Kinship*, pp. 24–76; K. Wrightson and D. Levine, *Poverty and Piety in an English Village: Terling, 1525–1700*, 2nd edn (Oxford, 1995), pp. 82–103 and postscript.

31. See e.g. K. Wrightson and D. Levine, 'Death in Whickham', in J. Walter and R. S. Schofield (eds), *Famine, Disease and the Social Order in Early*

Modern Society (Cambridge, 1989), pp. 156ff; D. Beaver, ' "Sown in Dishonour, Raised in Glory": Death, Ritual and Social Organisation in Northern Gloucestershire, 1590–1690', *Social History*, vol. 17 (1992), pp. 389–419.

32. Wrightson, *English Society*, p. 51.

33. Quoted in I. Archer, *The Pursuit of Stability: Social Relations in Elizabethan London* (Cambridge, 1991), p. 84.

34. Quoted in S. Hindle, 'Aspects of the Relationship of the State and Local Society in Early Modern England: With Special Reference to Cheshire, c.1590–1630' (unpublished University of Cambridge Ph.D. thesis, 1992), pp. 256–7.

35. Amussen, *Ordered Society*, pp. 104, 152ff. Ingram, *Church Courts*, p. 165, describes 'credit' and 'honesty' as 'the lower class equivalents of gentry notions of honour'. See also the important discussion in C. Muldrew, 'Interpreting the Market: The Ethics of Credit and Community Relations in Early Modern England, *Social History*, vol. 18 (1993), pp. 163–83.

36. N. Alldridge, 'Loyalty and Identity in Chester Parishes, 1540–1640', in S. J. Wright (ed.), *Parish, Church and People: Local Studies in Lay Religion* (London, 1988), pp. 110–11.

37. Hindle, 'State and Local Society', p. 237. There is now an extensive literature on the subject of mediation and reconciliation in medieval and early modern England. See, e.g., M. Ingram, 'Communities and Courts: Law and Disorder in Early Seventeenth-Century Wiltshire', in J. S. Cockburn (ed.), *Crime in England, 1550–1800* (London, 1977), pp. 125–9; M. Clanchy, 'Law and Love in the Middle Ages', and J. A. Sharpe, ' "Such Disagreement betwyx Neighbours": Litigation and Human relations in Early Modern England', both in J. Bossy (ed.), *Disputes and Settlements: Law and Human Relations in the West* (Cambridge, 1983), pp. 47–67, 167–7; E. Powell, 'Settlement of Disputes by Arbitration in Fifteenth-Century England', *Law and History Review*, vol. 2 (1984), 21–43.

38. The phrase is quoted from Muldrew, 'Interpreting the Market', p. 174.

39. J. S. Craig, 'Co-operation and Initiatives: Elizabethan Churchwardens and the Parish Accounts of Mildenhall', *Social History*, vol. 18 (1993), p. 376. For some sceptical remarks on the extent to which neighbourhood transcended social distance, see Archer, *Pursuit of Stability*, p. 80.

40. Alldridge, 'Loyalty and Identity', pp. 106–7; Hindle, 'State and Local Society', pp. 412–13. Cf. the analyses of East Anglian parish officers in Craig, 'Co-operation and Initiatives', pp. 363–4; and H. R. French, 'Chief Inhabitants and their Areas of Influence: Local Ruling Groups in Essex and Suffolk Parishes, 1630–1720' (unpublished University of Cambridge Ph.D. thesis, 1993), ch. 3.

41. A point well made in R. A. Davies, 'Community, Parish and Poverty: Old Swinford, 1660–1730' (unpublished University of Leicester Ph.D. thesis, 1987), pp. 297 ff, where analysis of social networks suggests that rich and poor 'inhabited rather different social worlds' save for those occasions when patron–client ties were activated for specific purposes.

42. Quoted in A. Hassell Smith, *County and Court: Government and Politics in Norfolk, 1558–1603* (Oxford, 1974), p. 193. For the probable influence of status differences on the outcome of mediation, see Amussen, *Ordered Society*, pp. 174–5.

43. See, e.g., J. A. Sharpe, *Defamation and Sexual Slander in Early Modern England: The Church Courts at York* (Borthwick Papers No. 58, York, 1980); Ingram, *Church Courts*, ch. 10; Amussen, *Ordered Society*, pp. 101–4; L. Gowing, 'Gender and the Language of Insult in Early Modern London', *History Workshop Journal*, vol. 35 (1993), pp. 1–21; J. A. Sharpe, 'Witchcraft and Women in Seventeenth- Century England: Some Northern Evidence', *Continuity and Change*, vol. 6 (1991), pp. 179–99; C. Holmes, 'Women: Witnesses and Witches', *Past and Present* 140 (1993), pp. 45–78; M. J. Gaskill, 'Attitudes to Crime in Early Modern England, with Special Reference to Witchcraft, Coining and Murder' (unpublished University of Cambridge Ph.D. thesis, 1994), chs 2, 7.

44. The classical accounts of English witchcraft accusations are A. Macfarlane, *Witchcraft in Tudor and Stuart England: A Regional and Comparative Study* (London, 1970); and K. V. Thomas, *Religion and the Decline of Magic: Studies in Popular Beliefs in Sixteenth and Seventeenth Century England* (London, 1971), chs 16–17. Both explore tensions in neighbourly relations but pay less attention to the question of gender relations. For more recent studies exploring more fully the question of witchcraft and gender, see C. Larner, *Witchcraft and Religion: the Politics of Popular belief* (Oxford, 1984), pp. 61–3, 84–8, 149–52, and the works of Sharpe, Holmes and Gaskill cited in n. 43 above.

45. M. Ingram, 'Ridings, Rough Music and the "Reform of Popular Culture" in Early Modern England', *Past and Present*, vol. 105 (1984), quoting p. 97; D. Underdown, 'The Taming of the Scold: The Enforcement of Patriarchal Authority in Early Modern England', in A. Fletcher and J. Stevenson (eds), *Order and Disorder in Early Modern England* (Cambridge, 1985), pp. 116–36.

46. S. Hindle, 'The Shaming of Margaret Knowsley: Gossip, Gender and the Experience of Authority in Early Modern England', *Continuity and Change*, vol. 9 (1994), pp. 391–419.

47. See, e.g., P. Slack, *Poverty and Policy in Tudor and Stuart England* (London, 1988); A. Fletcher, *Reform in the Provinces: The Government of Stuart England* (New Haven, 1986), ch. 7; T. Wales, 'Poverty, Poor Relief and the Life-Cycle: Some Evidence from Seventeenth-Century Norfolk', and W. Newman Brown, 'The Receipt of Poor Relief and Family Situation: Aldenham, Hertfordshire 1630–90', both in R. M. Smith (ed.), *Land, Kinship and Life-Cycle* (Cambridge, 1984), pp. 351–404, 405–22; J. Walter, 'The Social Economy of Dearth in Early Modern England', in Walter and Schofield (eds), *Famine, Disease and the Social Order*, quoting p. 125; P. Rushton, 'The Poor Law, the Parish and the Community in North-East England, 1600–1800', *Northern History*, vol. 25 (1989), pp. 135–52; A. L. Beier, 'Poverty and Progress in Early Modern England', in A. L. Beier *et al.* (eds), *The First Modern Society* (Cambridge, 1989), pp. 201–40; Archer, *Pursuit of Stability*, p. 86 and ch. 5; Levine and Wrightson, *Industrial Society*, pp. 344–55, 377–81.

48. F. G. Emmison (ed.), *Early Essex Town Meetings* (Chichester, 1970), p. 101.

49. E. P. Thompson, *Customs in Common* (London, 1991), pp. 2, 6.

50. S. Reynolds, *Kingdoms and Communities in Western Europe, 900–1300* (Oxford, 1984), pp. 21, 23, 34, 43.

51. Thompson, *Customs in Common*, pp. 2, 97, 98, 101–2.

52. For the concept of 'structural amnesia', see J. Goody and I. Watt, 'The Consequences of Literacy', in J. Goody (ed.), *Literacy in Traditional Societies* (Cambridge, 1968), p. 33; R. B. Manning, *Village Revolts: Social Protest and Popular Disturbances in England, 1509–1640* (Oxford, 1988), pp. 139–40.

53. Thompson, *Customs in Common*, p. 6.

54. See, e.g., B. Sharp, *In Contempt of All Authority: Rural Artisans and Riot in the West of England, 1586–1660* (Berkeley, 1980); K. Lindley, *Fenland Riots and the English Revolution* (London, 1982); P. Slack (ed.), *Rebellion, Popular Protest and the Social Order in Early Modern England* (Cambridge, 1984); Manning, *Village Revolts*. For protests intended to secure the right ordering of the market in times of dearth and the customary 'moral economy', see also Thompson, *Customs in Common*, chs 4–5; J. Walter, 'Grain Riots and Popular Attitudes to the Law: Maldon and the Crisis of 1629', in J. Brewer and J. Styles (eds), *An Ungovernable People: The English and Their Law in the Seventeenth and Eighteenth Centuries* (London, 1980), pp. 47–84; J. Walter, 'A "Rising of the People"? The Oxfordshire Rising of 1596', *Past and Present*, vol. 107 (1985), pp. 90–143.

55. Wrightson, *English Society*, p. 131.

56. W. G. Hoskins, *The Midland Peasant: The Economic and Social History of a Leicestershire Village* (London, 1957), pp. 104–9.

57. Fox, 'Aspects of Oral Culture', pp. 223–4.

58. See the works cited in n. 54 above. The historiographical emphasis upon the restraint commonly exercised in riot should not obscure the very real anger felt by protesters, or the fact that by engaging in public protest, they were involved in a very dangerous kind of brinkmanship.

59. A. Wood, 'Social Conflict and Change in the Mining Communities of North-West Derbyshire, *c.*1600–1700', *International Review of Social History*, vol. 38 (1993), pp. 31–58; and Wood, 'Industrial Development, Social Change and Popular Politics in the Mining Area of North-West Derbyshire, *c.*1600–1700' (unpublished University of Cambridge Ph.D. thesis, 1994), chs 4–6.

60. J. Bohstedt, *Riots and Community Politics in England and Wales, 1790–1810* (Cambridge, Mass., 1983), p. 3. Bohstedt is here characterising riot in general.

61. Wood, 'Industrial Development', p. 155.

62. Thompson, *Customs in Common*, p. 135.

63. Levine and Wrightson, *Industrial Society*, pp. 106–34.

64. A. J. Randall, *Before the Luddites: Custom, Community and Machinery in the English Woollen Industry, 1776–1809* (Cambridge, 1991), pp. 26, 35, 89; Levine and Wrightson, *Industrial Society*, pp. 359–69, 389–427. Cf. J. Rule, *The Experience of Labour in Eighteenth-Century Industry* (London, 1981), ch. 8.

65. Randall, *Before the Luddites*, pp. 254–5. For a recent survey of eighteenth-century industrial protest, see J. Rule, *Albion's People: English Society, 1714–1815* (London, 1992), pp. 201 ff.

66. Fletcher, *Reform in the Provinces*, p. 372.

67. M. S. Byford, 'The Price of Protestantism: Assessing the Impact of Religious Change on Elizabethan Essex: The Cases of Heydon and Colchester, 1558–1594' (unpublished University of Oxford D.Phil. thesis, 1988), p. 426. Dr Byford uses this phrase to characterise the developing religious position of William Sheppard of Heydon.

68. R. M. Smith, ' "Modernisation" and the Corporate Medieval Village Community in England: Some Sceptical Reflections', in A. H. R. Baker and D. Gregory (eds), *Explorations in Historical Geography* (Cambridge, 1984), pp. 140–79. Other relevant discussions of characteristics of the state and political society include D. A. Carpenter, 'English Politics in Politics, 1258–1267', *Past and Present*, vol. 36 (1992), pp. 3–42; G. Harris, 'Political Society and the Growth of Government in Late Medieval England', *Past and Present*, vol. 138 (1993), pp. 28–57; P. Corrigan and D. Sayer, *The Great Arch: English State Formation as Cultural Revolution* (Oxford, 1985), ch. 1; M. Braddick, 'State Formation and Social Change in Early Modern England: A Problem Stated and Approaches Suggested', *Social History*, vol. 16 (1991), pp. 1–17.

69. Braddick, 'State Formation', pp. 2, 6. Cf. Mann, *Sources of Social Power, Vol. I*, p. 477.

70. See, e.g., Wrightson, *English Society*, ch. 6; Fletcher, *Reform in the Provinces*, passim; J. A. Sharpe, *Crime in Early Modern England, 1550–1750* (London, 1984), esp. chs 3 and 8; C. Brooks, *Pettyfoggers and Vipers of the Commonwealth: The 'Lower Branch' of the legal Profession in Early Modern England* (Cambridge, 1986), chs 4–5. For a superb synthesis of the historiography of state formation in early modern England, see Hindle, 'State and Local Society', ch. 1.

71. Braddick, 'State Formation', p. 5.

72. Craig, 'Co-operation and Initiative', p. 368. My emphasis.

73. J. Maltby, 'Approaches to the Study of Religious Conformity in Late Elizabethan and Early Stuart England: With Special Reference to Cheshire and the Diocese of Lincoln' (unpublished University of Cambridge Ph.D. thesis, 1992), pp. 36 ff; D. A. Spaeth, 'Common Prayer? Popular Observance of the Anglican Liturgy in Restoration Wiltshire', in Wright (ed.), *Parish, Church and People*, p. 127; and Spaeth, 'Parsons and Parishioners: Lay–Clerical Conflict and Popular Piety in Wiltshire Villages, 1660–1740' (unpublished Brown University Ph.D. thesis, 1985), pp. 15–16, 31.

74. See. e.g., K. Wrightson, 'Two Concepts of Order: Justices, Constables and Jurymen in Seventeenth-Century England', in Brewer and Styles (eds), *An Ungovernable People*, pp. 21–46; J. R. Kent, *The English Village Constable, 1580–1642: A Social and Administrative Study* (Oxford, 1986), esp. chs 5–8. The phrase quoted is from MacCulloch, *Suffolk*, p. 342.

75. M. K. McIntosh, *A Community Transformed: The Manor and Liberty of Havering, 1500–1620* (Cambridge, 1991), pp. 206–11. Cf. MacCulloch, *Suffolk*, p. 317.

76. French, 'Chief Inhabitants', pp. 151 ff; Collinson, *De Republica Anglorum*, pp. 30 ff.

77. Collinson, *De Republica Anglorum*, p. 31; French, 'Chief Inhabitants', p. 160.

78. A. R. Pennie. 'The Evolution of Puritan Mentality in an Essex Cloth Town: Dedham and the Stour Valley, 1560–1640' (unpublished University of Sheffield Ph.D. thesis, 1990), pp. 86–7; P. Collinson, *The Birthpangs of Protestant England: Religious and Cultural Change in the Sixteenth and Seventeenth Centuries* (London, 1988), pp. 145–6; C. Haigh, *English Reformations: Religion, Politics and Society Under the Tudors* (Oxford, 1993), pp. 279–84 and conclusion.

79. J. A. Sharpe, 'Enforcing the Law in the Seventeenth-Century English Village', in V. A. C. Gatrell *et al.* (eds), *Crime and the Law: The Social History of Crime in Western Europe Since 1500* (London, 1980), p. 114; R. Cust and P. G. Lake, 'Sir Richard Grosvenor and the Rhetoric of Magistracy', *Bulletin of the Institute of Historical Research*, vol. 54 (1981), 51; T. A. Davies, 'The Quakers in Essex, 1655–1725' (unpublished University of Oxford D.Phil. thesis, 1986), p. 19.

80. Macfarlane *et al.*, *Reconstructing Historical Communities*, pp. 144–8; R. von Friedeberg, 'Reformation of Manners and the Social Composition of Offenders in an East Anglian Cloth Village: Earls Colne, Essex, 1531–1642', *Journal of British Studies*, vol. 29 (1990), pp. 354, 376–7; J. S. Craig, 'Reformation Politics and Polemics in Sixteenth-Century East Anglian Market Towns' (unpublished University of Cambridge Ph.D. thesis, 1992), ch. 4. For further examples of such superimposition, see D. Underdown, *Fire From Heaven: The Life of an English Town in the Seventeenth Century* (London, 1992), pp. 7, 23, 27–32, 34, 39, 42, 151–2; McIntosh, *Community Transformed*, pp. 181–205 and chs. 3, 6.

81. I have in mind both the longstanding debate over the sociology of Puritanism and the more recent controversies occasioned by the arguments of K. Wrightson and D. Levine, *Poverty and Piety in an English Village: Terling, 1525–1700* (New York, 1979) and D. Underdown, *Revel, Riot and Rebellion: Popular Politics and Culture in England, 1603–60* (Oxford, 1985).

82. This issue is fully discussed in my Postscript to the 2nd edn of Wrightson and Levine, *Poverty and Piety*.

83. See the valuable discussion of the changing articulation of social relations in London in Archer, *Pursuit of Stability*, pp. 92 ff. Archer's interpretation has relevance far beyond its immediate context.

84. H. Newby, 'The Deferential Dialectic', *Comparative Studies in Society and History*, vol. 17 (1975), pp. 139–64; Wrightson, *English Society*, pp. 57–61; Thompson, *Customs in Common*, pp. 21–24, quoting pp. 21–2.

85. Rule, *Experience of Labour*, pp. 209–11.

86. Alldridge, 'Loyalty and Identity', pp. 93–5; P. Collinson, *The Religion of Protestants: The Church in English Society, 1559–1625* (Oxford, 1982), pp. 182 n. 71, 195; Amussen, *Ordered Society*, pp. 138 ff.

87. This point and the following discussion are influenced by Q. Skinner, 'Some Problems in the Analysis of Political Thought and Action', in

J. Tully (ed.), *Meaning and Context: Quentin Skinner and His Critics* (Cambridge, 1986), pp. 111, 114.

88. J. Bossy, *Christianity in the West, 1400–1700* (Oxford, 1985), pp. 168–9; F. Heal, *Hospitality in Early Modern England* (Oxford, 1990), pp. 15–16, 124.

89. Heal, *Hospitality*, passim, quoting p. 388.

90. Archer, *Pursuit of Stability*, pp. 120, 124.

91. See, e.g., the petitions quoted in K. Wrightson, 'Alehouses, Order and Reformation in Rural England', in E. and S. Yeo (eds), *Popular Culture and Class Conflict, 1590–1914* (Brighton, 1981), pp. 19–20.

92. Cultural distancing is a central theme of Thomas, *Religion and the Decline of Magic*, and of Thomas, *Man and the Natural World: Changing Attitudes in England, 1500–1800* (London, 1983). Other relevant works include, e.g., Collinson, *Birthpangs*, esp. ch. 5; Underdown, *Revel, Riot and Rebellion*, esp. ch. 3; Rule, *Experience of Labour*, ch. 5; Randall, *Before the Luddites*, pp. 33–4; R. Malcolmson, *Popular Recreations in English Society, 1700–1850* (Cambridge, 1973), chs 6–8; P. Borsay, *The English Urban Renaissance: Culture and Society in the Provincial Town, 1660–1770* (Oxford, 1989), ch. 11; Thompson, *Customs in Common*, pp. 174 ff; Rollison, *Local Origins*, esp. chs 3, 10; Fox, 'Aspects of Oral Culture', esp. chs 2–3.

93. K. Wrightson, ' "Sorts of People" in Tudor and Stuart England', in J. Barry and C. Brooks (eds), *The Middling Sort of People: Culture, Society and Politics in England, 1550–1800* (London, 1994), pp. 28–51. Cf. the later emegence of 'polite society', as discussed in, e.g., Borsay, *Urban Renaissance*, chs 9–10; and P. Langford, *A Polite and Commercial People: England, 1727–1783* (Oxford, 1989), ch. 3.

94. K. Wrightson, 'Estates, Degrees and Sorts: Changing Perceptions of Society in Tudor and Stuart England', in P. Corfield (ed.), *Language, History and Class* (Oxford, 1991), pp. 45 ff. For a fuller discussion, see Wrightson, ' "Sorts of People" '.

95. Wood, 'Industrial Development', pp. 110–11; G. C. Smith, ' "The Knowing Multitude": Popular Culture and the Evangelical Revival in Wiltshire, 1739–1850' (unpublished University of Toronto Ph.D. thesis, 1992), p. 149. Cf. R. Malcolmson, ' "A Set of Ungovernable People": The Kingswood Colliers in the Eighteenth Century', in Brewer and Styles (eds), *An Ungovernable People*, pp. 85–9; Levine and Wrightson, *Industrial Society*, pp. 274–8; Rollison, *Local Origins*, ch. 10; J. M. Neeson, *Commoners: Common Right, Enclosure and Social Change, 1700–1820* (Cambridge, 1993), ch. 1.

96. Quoting, in turn, Fox, 'Aspects of Oral Culture', pp. 122–3; Munro, *Friend of My Youth*, p. 23; Archer, *Pursuit of Stability*, p. 259.

97. R. W. Scribner, 'Is a History of Popular Culture Possible?', *History of European Ideas*, vol. 10 (1989), p. 182.

98. Thompson, *Customs in Common*, pp. 443–4; Smith ' "The Knowing Multitude" ', pp. 198 ff; Randall, *Before the Luddites*, pp. 87–9.

99. Scott, *Domination*, passim, quoting pp. xii, 183.

100. K. Snell, 'Deferential Bitterness: The Social Outlook of the Rural Proletariat in Eighteenth- and Nineteenth-Century England and Wales', in

M. L. Bush (ed.), *Social Orders and Social Classes in Europe Since 1500: Studies in Social Stratification* (London, 1992), p. 162. As has been observed in another context, 'the history of discourse is not a simple linear sequence in which new patterns overcome the old, but a complex dialogue in which these patterns persist in transforming each other': J. G. A. Pocock, *Politics, Language, and Time: Essays on Political Thought and History* (Chicago, 1989), pp. ix–x.

2 Reformation of Manners in Early Modern England*

MARTIN INGRAM

I

On 10 March 1612 the Westminster Court of Burgesses assembled in the 'town court house' for its regular weekly session. The judges were the Dean of Westminster, the Deputy Chief Steward, the twelve Burgesses (representing the twelve Westminster wards) and their twelve Assistants. The jury, convened as necessary, comprised twelve 'honest householders' of the city. Their duty was to hear cases concerning nuisances, illegal inmates, scolding, slander and sexual immorality in all its forms, and as it happened the leading case that day was one of bastard-bearing. Susan Perry, who had borne an illegitimate child, had little option but to confess. Robert Watson, waterman, her alleged partner, denied the charge, but it availed him nothing. After trial by jury he was pronounced guilty, and thereupon it was

> ordered by ye court that the s[ai]d Rob[er]t Watson and Susan Perry should be committed to the prison of the Gatehouse and both of them to be stripp'd naked from the wast upwards and so tyed to the carts tayle and to be whipp'd from the Gatehouse in Westm[inste]r unto Temple Barr and then and there to be pr[e]sently banished from the Citty and Libertyes and if either of them returne again and be taken within the Citty & Libertyes to be likewise whipped.[1]

The penalty that this couple received was exceptionally severe, and the court that inflicted it upon them was, as will be seen, in some respects unusual; but in a sense their experience was quite typical of practice in early modern England. Sexual immorality, and many other forms of personal behaviour that nowadays are not

47

considered criminal or subject to legal sanction, were in this period regulated by courts of law. In other words, they were not regarded merely as matters for the private conscience, but as social and political ills that were subject to the sanction of public authority.

'Authority' may be understood as the exercise of power that claims, and at least in some measure is recognised, to be legitimate. The construction of such authority in the sphere of moral regulation was a complex matter that involved a dense web of beliefs and assumptions. Partly it depended on reciprocal notions of responsible behaviour among neighbours, of the duty of personal restraint for the common good; but these ideas were underpinned by deeper, more far-reaching concepts. Of fundamental importance was the prevailing orthodoxy that social and political order as divinely instituted: that the powers that be were ordained of God. Equally well entrenched was the principle of monarchy: it is significant that the republican governments that were instituted after the execution of Charles I in 1649 rapidly drifted back towards a quasi-royal settlement. Along with monarchy went hierarchy: political and social relations were conceived in terms of inequality that as a principle required no justification, however much the precise gradations of such hierarchy were contested. These inequalities were drawn, moreover, along patriarchal lines. The authority of the prince over his subjects was conventionally thought to be analogous to that of the father over his wife, children and servants; both were mutually validating. Thus women were subject to fathers and husbands, while the young were firmly subordinate to those of riper years. A corollary was that sexuality had to be subject to regulation, confined within the legitimate channels of Christian wedlock. The household – or in contemporary terms the 'family' – itself was thought to be the linchpin of the commonwealth; adolescents of either sex, and others that lacked the means to support a 'family', were supposed to be brought within the framework of order through bonds of service that subjected them firmly to a master or mistress.[2]

On one level all these relationships were seen as 'natural', earthly reflections of the heavenly order and hence immune from serious question. At another, it was recognised that in practice they were likely to be contentious and had to be interpreted and regulated. Youngsters and other 'inferiors' were apt to evade, contravene, or even to rebel against the strictures of lawful authority, while quarrels and disputes were only too likely to arise between neighbours and equals. To an extent the resolution of such problems and tensions could be achieved informally, but when necessary contemporaries looked to the law to mediate social and political relations. Indeed law – in the various forms of common, statute and ecclesiastical law – was regarded as the cornerstone of order and authority, and legal institutions were the favoured means of maintaining them. An elaborate system of overlapping jurisdictions existed to meet this need, including the great common law and equity courts at Westminster; assizes and quarter sessions; city, borough and manor courts; and a hierarchy of ecclesiastical courts operating at the levels of archdeaconry, diocese and province.[3] The Westminster Court of Burgesses was merely a peculiar variant on this theme, set up by statute in 1585 'for the better ordering and government of the people inhabiting . . . within [Westminster] . . . , for repressinge and rootinge owte of vice . . . and for due reformac[i]on of . . . inconvenyences and disordres'.[4]

Yet in itself the law could not resolve all issues. For one thing, it was recognised that the operation of law depended on broader issues of personal and public morality, which in turn related to matters of religious faith and observance: '*Quid leges sine moribus vanae proficiunt?*', asked the Kentish antiquary and justice William Lambarde in 1582, quoting an oft-cited passage from Horace; 'What shall we do with laws without manners?'.[5] Thus the law had to be wielded fearlessly and with vigour (albeit temperately) if it was to achieve good, and could only be effective if its sanctions were reinforced by good example, careful education, and sound religion. On the other hand, the law was not necessarily as powerful and coherent as theory demanded, nor was its use a straightforward matter; thus the apparently confident rhetoric of legislators and judges was in practice belied by numerous underlying uncertainties, ambiguities, and disagreements over the precise scope of legitimate authority and the means by which it was exercised. Further, both the laws and the institutions that administered them were subject to periodic modification, to take account of changing perceptions and altered circumstances. The present chapter relates to some of these more complex issues in the relationship between law and morality, focusing on the concept of 'reformation of manners'. As will be seen, this phrase – and its component elements – was a commonplace, yet had diverse meanings for contemporaries. The term has also been much used by historians in the last twenty years, in their gradual exploration of the society of Tudor and Stuart England; and it is to the historiography that we must now turn.

The phrase 'reformation of manners' is in current historical usage to refer to any major campaign to alter moral standards and behaviour by attacking what the proponents of such activism saw as godlessness, immorality and vice. In practice, however, it has usually been employed with reference to particular periods and episodes. It is self-evidently applicable to the work of the Societies for Reformation of Manners which were active from the 1690s to the 1730s, together with the renewed bursts of reforming zeal along somewhat similar lines that began in the 1750s and in the troubled years of the 1780s. The term also suits the campaigns associated with the Puritan regimes of the 1650s, during which Oliver Cromwell explicitly called for a 'reformation of manners'.[6] Rather more loosely the label has been attached to various attempts to alter religious and moral standards in the century before the civil wars. Here usage has varied considerably. Some authors attach the label to very specific episodes, such as Archbishop Laud's attempt to reduce the University of Oxford to order, discipline and sobriety in the 1630s. Others, such as Anthony Fletcher and Derek Hirst, seem to envisage something more comprehensive, if not a unitary movement then a cluster of interrelated campaigns in the early seventeenth century. Keith Wrightson, and others following him, have used the term even more generally to embrace the coercive aspects of some very broad social and cultural changes that occurred in Elizabethan and Stuart England – the enforcement of Protestant religious practice, governmental efforts to regulate the drink trade, the exercise of social discipline over sex and marriage, and so on. Following Wrightson's early work, the idea of 'reformation of manners' in the century before 1660 has most commonly been associated with Puritans, and equally it has often been argued or assumed that the main targets of reformation were the 'manners' of the poor.[7]

The fact that the term 'reformation of manners' has been applied to a range of historical circumstances over a long period suggests that it captures an historical phenomenon of central and recurrent significance. On the other hand, the diversity of modern usages and the assumptions that underlie them indicate the problematic nature of the concept. In an attempt to elucidate matters, this chapter will first comment briefly on the semantics of the term 'reformation of manners'. Building on recent work, it will go on to emphasise how many of the features associated with 'reformation of manners', far from being an innovation of the century after 1560, stretched well back into the fifteenth century if not before; and (a related point) that thinking in terms of 'campaigns' can be misleading if we do not at the same time recognise how firmly based these were in a *routine* system of regulating behaviour. The final section will review (albeit briefly and schematically, since space is limited) the range of motives that underlay action, and in so doing will examine *variations* in the agenda of moral regulation – both variations over time and, more particularly, variations in the way the scope and limits of reform activity were conceived by different groups and individuals. Implicitly this discussion will go some way towards explaining how more activist campaigns periodically developed out of the context of routine regulation, though the intricacy of that issue precludes a full analysis on this occasion.

Other limitations of the chapter must likewise be noted at the outset. The period before 1550 is given privileged treatment precisely because it has hitherto been relatively neglected; the following two centuries, on which there already exists a substantial literature, are more lightly dealt with. One consequence of this approach should be particularly noted. Ideally the chapter should go on to consider the factors that were by the end of the seventeenth century leading to the decline of the system of social discipline that had operated for so long, and that were eventually, if not to vitiate further attempts at 'reformation of manners', then at least to change their form. Some peculiar features of the campaigns of the years around 1700, notably the organisation of reform societies, the extensive use of informers, and the limited impact of the movement outside London and a few other urban centres, may be seen as symptoms of this incipient shift. However, these are complex matters that cannot be dealt with adequately here but must be set aside to await separate treatment.[8]

II

It is a curious fact that the term 'reformation of manners' and its component elements, though plainly problematic, have not in themselves attracted much attention. The word 'reformation' in this period did not necessarily, or even usually, bear the associations with religious upheaval that it does today, though the notion that the changes inaugurated by Luther in Germany and by Henry VIII in England did constitute a great 'reformation' of religion was firmly established by the end of the sixteenth century.[9] The word did, however, carry connotations of decisive action, and it could be used to mean 'improvement', 'reform', 'reconstruction', or 'restoration' in the sense of a major overhaul or radical change. Something of this sense of urgency was often present in contemporary usages of the phrase 'reformation of manners', as it was also, on occasion, in the use of the term 'reformation' in parliamentary bills and statutes. But equally 'reformation' could be used to denote a relatively minor, routine correction, amendment, or repair in either a physical or a moral sense, or the kinds of remedy available through legal action. These meanings of the word were a commonplace of parliamentary bills and debates, of proclamations, of petitions to the courts of equity, and of the work of county and borough magistrates. Likewise they were part of the stock-in-trade of constables and presentment juries in quarter sessions and in manorial courts, and of churchwardens and other local officers when they were called upon to make their regular reports – variously called 'presentments' or 'detections' – about the state of the parish church or the behaviour of the clergy and the local inhabitants. Thus the churchwardens of Hankerton, Wiltshire, reported in 1590 that 'o[u]r chancel is downe flat: heretofore p[rese]nted but no reformac[i]on'. As will be seen, it is of significance that the word 'reformation' embraced the routine and the radical.[10]

'Manners' is a more complex and in many respects more interesting word, the meanings of which all branched from 'manner' in the sense of 'way of doing things'. In *Leviathan* (1651) Hobbes wrote: 'By manners, I mean not here, decency of behaviour, as how one man should salute another, or how a man should wash his mouth, or pick his teeth before company'. This disclaimer reflects the fact that in the seventeenth century, and indeed long before, the word 'manners' could carry its modern sense of polite behaviour and deportment. However, its alternative meaning approximated more closely to what we would call 'morals' or, more generally, 'moral climate', albeit with the emphasis not on the inward state of mind but on the externals of behaviour, and shading off into usages more nearly equivalent to what we mean by 'habits' or 'customs'. The word 'manners' was in fact the equivalent of, and regularly used to translate, the Latin *mores*. Thus John Northbrooke wrote in 1579 of 'our dailie conversation, our maners, and all that ever we do'. Discourse often centred on 'ill', 'evil' or 'corrupt' manners, but this was balanced by a strong ideal sense of 'good' or 'sound' manners. Concern about either good or bad manners was in turn associated with the concept of the well-ordered common-wealth or public weal, and was often found in juxtaposition with a discourse of 'civility'. Thus the Elizabethan Puritan writer Thomas Beard condemned certain behaviour as 'contrarie to good man-ners, and to the laudable customes of all civill and well governed people'.[11] In the sixteenth century all these usages were mainly the preserve of moralists, preachers, judges and justices, but as time wore on they gradually found their way into the presentments and petitions of local officers. Thus in 1614 the jury of the court leet of Nettleton, Wiltshire, presented two unruly women who, having been 'heartofore pr[e]sented for the like faulte and admonished to reforme the same . . . have not amended their mann[er]s'.[12]

The link with the term 'civility', which in this period was gradually shifting its signification from conduct within a commonwealth to matters of etiquette and deportment,[13] brings us back to the ambi-guity of the word 'manners'. In a pedagogic or, more broadly, educational context, the two senses of 'manners' were hardly distin-guishable, given that contemporaries so closely associated personal development, and moral and religious instruction, with other forms of 'good learning' – whether academic knowledge, the 'mysteries' of crafts or trades imparted through apprenticeship, or the practi-cal skills of husbandry and housewifery taught to children and servants. Hence 'manners' featured prominently in educational discourse. As the Boy Bishop explained in his Childermas sermon at Gloucester in 1558, 'Mary! That is the very thyng that is meanyd in all good educacion, to discorage youth utterly as touching vice and vicious maners, and to bolden and corage them in all probitye and vertue, and vertuose maners'. The means by which this was to be done were not merely sound instruction and worthy example, but also wholesome correction administered by 'parentes, fathers, mothers and scolemasters', on the familiar grounds that to spare the rod was to spoil the child. As will be seen, writers on the subject of 'reformation of manners' sometimes had young people espe-cially in mind. But it was not only the behaviour of children and adolescents that needed to be regulated. In the wider world and among adults, the task of correction lay with the public authorities. It was their duty not only to pass and enforce good laws to inculcate sound manners, but also to repress corrupt manners, the manifestations of which were commonly discussed in two main ways. Sometimes they were conceived in terms of the medical and organic imagery of corruption, and hence seen as 'diseases', 'infirmities', 'imposthumes', 'ulcers', which required 'salves', 'remedies', or (sometimes sharp) 'medicine', lest they spread their deadly contagion. Alternatively – sometimes in conjunction with the medicinal metaphor – they were thought of more legalistically and expressed in a series of overlapping concepts: 'faults', 'sins', 'vices', 'crimes', 'enormities', the repression and punishment of which lay with the public authorities or, in default of effective action by them, with God.[14]

The public regulation of personal behaviour through legal institutions, which could administer condign punishment, was thus crucial to the concept of 'reformation of manners'. This context was, moreover, well established by Tudor and Stuart times. For centuries the church had exercised jurisdiction over 'religion and manners'. Sin was ultimately a matter between the individual and God, and before the Reformation, and to some extent afterwards, hidden sins were dealt with in the secrecy of the confessional. But outward or public sin, especially when it became an open scandal, a 'common' or 'public fame' and hence an affront to the Christian community, was punishable in the external forum of the spiritual courts. These episcopal and archidiaconal courts operated *pro salute animae* and *pro correctione* (or *reformatione*) *morum* – for the health of the soul and for the reformation of manners. This role was indeed a commonplace of late medieval and early modern life. Thus around 1527 Archbishop Warham commended Bishop Longland of Lincoln for his 'fervent zeal', evinced in his sermons, for 'reformation to be made as well of heretycell doctrynes as of mysbehaviours in maners'; while in 1612 the minister, churchwardens and sidesmen of Loddington, Northamptonshire, reported the misdoings of one of the parishioners to the officials of 'Mr Archdeacons court unto whom it app[er]taynes to reforme manners and punishe synnes'.[15]

However, the secular courts were also concerned with 'reformation of manners'. For the lawyer and publisher John Rastell, writing around 1513, 'the comon wel restith nother in i[n]cresyng of riches, power, nor honoure, but in the incresyng of good maners and condicions of men . . . for the which thing to be atteyned, yt ys to men most expedie[n]t to have ordinancis & lawes: for likwyse as the brydel and the spurr directyth & co[n]straineth the hors swyftly & well to p[er]forme hys journey, so doth gode & resonable ordina[n]cis and laws lede & direct me[n] to use gode maners & co[n]dicio[n]s'. For William Lambarde, the Elizabethan author of one of the best known handbooks for justices of the peace, 'corruption of manners' and 'amendment of manners' were key themes, to which he returned time and again in his charges to the juries at quarter sessions. The precise scope of secular court action in matters of personal morality was not entirely certain, and was to some extent subject to flux and also to dispute; it was, moreover, in general subsidiary to the spiritual power in this area. Yet despite this imbalance the secular and ecclesiastical authorities formed an effective, if sometimes uneasy, alliance to regulate behaviour for the good of the commonweal and the Christian community as a whole. This alliance, well established by the fifteenth century, was the long-standing basis for any attempts to further the 'reformation of manners'; the decay of the alliance was ultimately to undercut this legalistic system of moral regulation.[16]

III

Research into the legal regulation of personal morality has revealed that it was a recurrent, indeed almost continually persistent, feature of English social life over several centuries, albeit subject to shifts and fluctuations in scope and intensity. However, the way the results of such research have entered the historical consciousness has had a somewhat distorting effect on our conception of the phenomenon, giving undue emphasis to the century after 1560 at the expense of earlier and later periods. To arrive at a rather different view it is necessary to peel back the historiographical layers. The Societies for Reformation of Manners in the reigns of William and Mary, Queen Anne, and the first two Georges attracted historical attention quite early, but for long they were regarded as something of a curiosity. They may still be seen as distinctive, in that the voluntary associations that were formed to combat vice were in themselves a new departure, even though many of the targets for prosecution were of old stock. The Adultery and Blasphemy Acts and the sabbatarian legislation of the 1650s, together with the activities of the Major-Generals and of zealot Puritan justices, were for a long time likewise viewed by historians as little more than a bizarre aberration.[17] However, in the 1970s and 1980s, some of the context and antecedents of the Puritan 'reformation of manners' came rapidly to light as it emerged that, in the eighty years or so before the civil war, church courts, assizes, quarter sessions and manor courts mounted thousands of prosecutions to combat sexual immorality, alehouse disorders, unlawful games, and lax religious observances. This work – which is now being complemented by research into the activities of borough and city courts under Elizabeth and the early Stuarts[18] – was the shared endeavour of a number of researchers, but Keith Wrightson was particularly important in drawing together diverse materials into a coherent whole. He was able to argue that – setting aside the special case of the Societies for Reformation of Manners – the century 1560–1660 was a highly distinctive, perhaps even unparalleled, period of moral activisim, explicable in terms of a powerful amalgam of four elements: Protestant if not Puritan zeal; the growing pretensions of the State, and the administrative and governmental developments that this entailed; economic and social pressures springing from the population pressure and price inflation of the 'long sixteenth century'; and cultural changes (notably the spread of literacy in the middling and upper ranks of society and a vast expansion of printed materials) that made possible an alliance between activist magistrates and clergy and responsive elements in the upper half of local society in town and country.[19]

Further work has, however, modified this model. The effect of a spate of recent work on the Societies for Reformation of Manners in the reigns of William and Mary and their successors has been to re-emphasise the scope and longevity of this episode – or rather, series of episodes – of moral activism; and, in contrast to the view that saw the Societies as aberrant, to show how closely they were linked with other important social and political developments such as innovations in poor relief, new expressions of religious revival and missionary zeal, and the articulation of a distinctive 'country' ideology in politics. Joanna Innes's demonstration that there was more of the same in the middle and later eighteenth century, particularly in the 1780s and 1790s, adds extra weight to the argument. On the other hand, John Spurr has emphasised the antecedents of the Williamite reformation of manners in the efforts of Anglicans in Charles II's reign; while one of the most notable achievements of Anthony Fletcher's study of local government in Stuart England (confined though it effectively is to county government, with little attention to cities and boroughs) has been to show that Restoration justices were often far from supine in such matters as alehouse regulation and the pursuit of bastard-bearers; on the contrary, they could on occasion be as active as their Jacobean and Caroline forebears. Derek Hirst has recently proposed that the moral regulation of the seventeenth century should be seen in terms of 'three peaks of activity at the beginning, middle and end'. This formula is itself problematic, because it leaves unclear just what is meant by the early peak and what levels of activity obtained in the supposed troughs; moreover, it privileges the seventeenth century at the expense of periods before and after. None the less, it does reflect a search for a new paradigm.[20]

Claims for the intensity of moral regulation before about 1560 have been more tentative. It is now clear that the work of the 1970s and early 1980s exaggerated the novelty of some features of the moral reform activities of Elizabethan and early Stuart times, seriously underestimated the vigour in this sphere of the pre-Reformation church courts and of some secular tribunals, and drew probably misguided conclusions about the related issue of popular attitudes to Christian morality in the late Middle Ages. The reasons for these false perspectives lay partly in misleading continental parallels, found in the works of writers such as Delumeau and Muchembled.[21] But it is also the case that the necessary comparative data on moral regulation in England in the high and late Middle Ages has been slow to accumulate. The most spirited use of the information then available was Margaret Spufford's comparison of moral regulation in, on the one hand, the late thirteenth and early fourteenth and, on the other, the late sixteenth and early seventeenth centuries. This reveals interesting parallels between the two periods. However, it has nothing to say on the centuries in between, whilst in so far as the analysis implies that bursts of moral regulation were contingent on rising population and growing poverty, it may itself be misleading. Most other discussions of moral regulation in the pre-Reformation period, whether penned by early modern historians or by medievalists, have stressed the limited or transient nature of reform offensives. Ian Archer, for example, whilst recognising and indeed stressing the ambiguity of the evidence, suggests that in pre-Reformation London action against prostitutes and other moral offenders was 'exceptional and rarely sustained'; Gervase Rosser, commenting on the expulsion from Westminster in 1508 of thirty-one people said to be 'ill-governed of their bodies' is at pains to point out that this was 'strong action of a sternness unprecedented' in the franchise; and Jeremy Goldberg, while surveying a series of measures against prostitution and other forms of sexual immorality in fifteenth-century towns, implies that many authorities condoned or even profited from offences and that repressive action was fitful.[22]

A more positive line has been taken by Marjorie McIntosh, principally on the basis of her study of leet records for Havering-atte-Bower, Essex, and other manors in south-east England. She finds that in the period 1460–1500 certain larger villages and small towns mounted what were in effect campaigns against sexual immorality, illicit games and pastimes, railing and scolding, woodstealing, hedgebreaking and other disorders. However, she suggests that these prosecutions fell away in the early sixteenth century, only to resume from the mid-Tudor years or the reign of Elizabeth. There is room for debate about the reasons that McIntosh offers for these developments, and it is open to question how far the chronological pattern she describes is generally applicable. Despite her stress on the early sixteenth century as a lull between two periods of activism, she does cite some manors, such as Walden, Essex, which had an active programme of prosecuting misdemeanours in the reign of Henry VIII. Other communities that fit this pattern are not hard to find, which suggests that we should take pause before accepting the idea of a marked contrast between the late fifteenth and the early sixteenth centuries. It is probably only when a great deal more research has been done (including McIntosh's current investigations) that a definitive pattern, taking proper account of regional and local variations, will be established.[23]

But McIntosh's main point, arguing the existence in the late Middle Ages of legal activity directed against immorality and petty misdemeanour similar to that associated with 'reformation of manners' in the reigns of Elizabeth and her Stuart successors, can be not only accepted but actually reinforced. McIntosh concentrates on manorial jurisdictions, but of course many other tribunals were active in England at this time. Regrettably little survives to illustrate the workings of county quarter sessions and of the assizes at the close of the Middle Ages, but the church courts are better represented. It is true that their fifteenth-and early sixteenth-century records are for the most part fragmentary and hard to interpret, but what does survive suggests impressive levels of prosecution. This appears to be the case, for example, in the diocese of Canterbury (covering much of Kent) and the archdeaconry of Buckingham (more or less co-terminous with the county).[24] But the most striking evidence is Richard Wunderli's study of the London Commissary Court in the period from about 1470 to 1520. He himself lays emphasis on a decline in the level of prosecutions after about 1500, hence suggesting that Londoners lost faith in ecclesiastical sanctions and preferred to take action against prostitutes by means of the city courts. This interpretation, the evidence for which is almost entirely inferential, is in fact questionable; and the decline of business may actually be part of a broader series of adjustments between the spiritual and secular courts. But in any event, from the perspective of the later sixteenth century the most striking feature of Wunderli's data is not the post-1500 decline in prosecutions – which still left the court handling hundreds of cases a year – but the dramatic peak of cases under the Yorkists and Henry VII. To judge from the surviving records the high point of activity was in 1490 when as many as 1515 prosecutions were processed by the commissary; another peak was in 1472 when there were 1305 cases. In each year a high proportion involved sexual offences, together with considerable numbers of defamation suits – which in this period were often sexual immorality cases under another guise. The figures gain added significance when it is recognised that the Commissary Court was only one of a group of church courts operating in London. The business of the Archdeaconry Court and the Bishop of London's Consistory Court at this time cannot be properly assessed because their records have not survived; they were certainly very active later, and it is most unlikely that their work in this earlier period was negligible.[25]

If the records of the city courts had not for the most part perished we could get a truer sense of the intensity of moral regulation in late medieval London in a regime in which the secular and and spiritual courts combined to punish sin. What does survive may at least serve to *illustrate* their activities. Wunderli himself draws attention to a civic drive against some forms of illicit sexuality – and other offences too – in the 1520s. In June 1529, for example, five women were convicted for being 'p[er]sones not dredyng godd ne the shame of thys worlde but contynually usyng thabhomynable custume of the fowle & detestable synne of lechery & bawdry to the gret dysplesure of Almyghty Godd and to the gret noysaunce of their neighburs', whereupon the mayor and aldermen gave judgement that

> according to the olde & auncyent lawes & customes of this citie in that behalf used & tyme oute of mynde contynued that the foreseid p[er]sones shall suffre suche penance as heraft[er] folowyth, that ys to say the seid p[er]sones shalbe conveyd from the Counto[u]r [prison] to Newgate w[i]t[h] mynstralsye that ys to say w[i]t[h] pannes & basones ryngynge before theym and they to were ray hod[es] & to have in their hand[es] whyte roddes in tokyn of comyn bawd[es], strumpett[es] & harlott[es]; and so from thens to be conveyed to the Standerd in Chepe and there this p[ro]clamac[i]on to be made, and so to be conveyd through Chepe into Cornehill and there to stonde under the pyllarye duryng this p[ro]clamac[i]on, and from thens to be conveyd to Algate and there to be banyshed the citie for ev[er].

In the same month Robert Dobynson was convicted 'for a co[mm]en barrato[u]r among[es] his neighbors and a grete resorter of suspicious p[er]sones to his house both by nyght & by day, & a grete occupier of tabull[es] & card[es] in his house contrarye to the kyng[es] comaundeme[n]t', while a batch of seven women (probably scolds) were recorded as being 'brought in by John Margetson, depute to thalderman of the Warde of Portsoken & . . . adiuged to be had to the cukkyng stole'. There were similar proceedings against a variety of offenders earlier in the decade, most notably in 1523.[26]

Some of this judicial activity seems to have been triggered by the summoning of the parliaments of 1523 and 1529. But, *pace* Wunderli, there was really nothing new in this kind of moral regulation. As the judgement quoted above clearly indicates, the punishment of bawds, prostitutes and other offenders in London rested firmly in long-established custom. Similar proceedings, employing exactly the same rhetoric, are recorded, albeit sporadically, throughout the later fifteenth and early sixteenth centuries, while periodically the moral temperature was raised by 'drives' occasioned by special circumstances or initiated by zealous individuals. In 1483, the Lord Mayor and Aldermen had issued a proclamation against 'the stynkyng and horrible synne of lechery'; while the so-called Great Chronicle of London records that in 1474 – in fact an error for 1473 – the mayor, William Hampton, 'dyd dyligent & sharp correccion upon Venus['s] servauntys, and cawsid theym to be garnysshid & attyrid wyth raye hodys, and to be shewid abowth the Citye wyth theyr mynstralsy beffore theym . . . and sparid noon for mede nor for favour'. Surviving records, probably incomplete, show that over sixty people, predominantly women but including a sizeable minority of men, were indeed the victims of this civic clean-up, many of them suffering not merely the shame of penance and pillory but also banishment from the city. Fragmentary survivals of wardmote presentments indicate, moreover, that such initiatives were based in more routine legal regulation; extant returns from Portsoken Ward in the reign of Edward IV include numerous charges against barrators, scolds, bawds, 'common strumpets' and 'strumpetmongers', the 'maintainers' of the womenfolk among these offenders, 'receivers of suspicious and misruled people', and other transgressors. These proceedings, it is evident, were in turn but the tip of an iceberg of informal disciplinary and admonitory action by the Aldermen and their deputies and by ordinary householders. A stray survival from the neighbouring jurisdiction of Westminster in 1519, now accessible (as far as is known) only in a typescript abstract, records even more intense activity. In a single sessions held on 20 August, the bailiff, headboroughs, constables, and their 'fellows' – the various local officers of Westminster and St Clement Danes – made presentment, on a street by street basis, of dozens of 'suspicious persons that were then warned'. These included people accused of scolding and other quarrelsome behaviour, lodging suspicious persons, allowing unlawful games, bawdry, 'lechery' and prostitution. It is not known how long such a court had been established or how characteristic this lengthy tally of offenders was; but there are no signs that it was an innovation.[27]

It is sometimes suggested that such efforts at moral discipline were belied and vitiated by the existence of licensed prostitution in the capital. But in fact prostitution was officially proscribed within the City. The regulated brothels or 'stews' at Southwark were in the liberty of the Bishop of Winchester and represented an administrative anomaly beyond the control of the City fathers. Even so an attempt was made to close the stews in 1506, and when they reopened it was on a smaller scale; they were eventually to be closed down for good by royal proclamation in 1546, after the spate of jurisdictional and religious reforms of the previous decade had made such action irresistible. (This did not eliminate prostitution in London, of course, but it ended any implication of overt official tolerance.)[28]

In any case, the existence of licensed brothels was a phenomenon largely confined to the metropolis; with a few limited exceptions such as Sandwich and Southampton, such institutions appear not to have been countenanced in provincial towns and cities. Given the patchy survival and often cryptic nature of the evidence relating to rural areas, it is in fact some of these towns that best illustrate the intensity of late medieval moral regulation in provincial England. In the case of many towns the position is the same as for London: there are indications of at least occasional drives against illicit sexuality and other moral offences but, owing to the vagaries of survival in town archives, detailed evidence of prosecutions and year-by-year records of policing activity are lacking. In Leicester in 1467, for example, there was an elaborate ordinance against unlawful games, scolds and quarrellers, and brothels and bawdry; while in 1484 there was a supplementary ordinance that established a ward system so that these and other offences could be more readily repressed. In Coventry, ordinances and other measures against 'bawdry' and related disorders were issued in 1445, 1474, 1490 and 1492. The last of these forbade any citizen to 'kepe, hold, resceyve nor favo[u]r eny tapster, or woman of evell name, fame or con-dic[i]on to whom eny resorte is of synfull disposic[i]on, hauntyng the synne of lechery'; further ordered 'that no tapster nor oth[er] p[er]sone fro[m] hensforth resceyve nor favo[u]r eny mannes p[re]ntes or s[er]va[u]nt of this citie in his house, ther to spend eny money or to company with eny woman of evell name, or other p[er]son of unsadde disposici[o]n, or other p[er]son diffamed, ayenst the will of his maist[er]'; and finally laid down, in a remarkable attempt (later modified) to control the activities of women, 'that no senglewoman, beying in good hele & myghty in body to labo[u]r, w[i]t[h]in the age of 1 yer[es], take nor kepe fro[m] hensfurth housez nor chambers be the[m]-self; nor that [they] take

eny chambr[e] w[i]t[h]in eny oth[er] p[er]sone, but th[a]t they go
to s[er]vice till they be maried'.[29]

More revealing, because more detailed, is the information available for Nottingham. This was a moderately sized borough in the
late Middle Ages: in terms of taxable wealth it ranked twenty-third
among provincial towns in 1334, with a population approaching
3000 that may have declined to around 2000 by 1525. Regrettably
the pre-Reformation records of the church courts in this area have
perished, though from incidental references we do know that they
were active. What have survived in unusual quantity for the period,
albeit not completely, are presentments of constables and jurymen
(for the west and east parts of the town) made at the quarter
sessions. Henry VI's charter elevated the borough to the status of a
county and gave the mayor, aldermen and sheriffs extensive jurisdiction over felonies and misdemeanours. The original orders and
proclamations of the court in the first century of its existence are
lacking, but from later abstracts of records now lost we know that in
1463 the mayor and burgesses – much like those of Leicester and
Coventry – made ordinances 'agaynst light women', 'agaynst keep-
inge of bawdy houses', and 'for alehowses receyvinge suspicious
p[er]sons or kepinge theyr howses open after 9 of the clock'. These
offenders and offences formed a staple of prosecutions in session
after session over the next century. They were supplemented by
numerous presentments for keeping disorder or misrule; receiving
or harbouring servants to waste their masters' goods; playing or
maintaining unlawful games, especially for money; scolding and
quarrelling, particularly on the part of women; nightwalking and
nocturnal disturbances; and 'petty bribery' or theft – the urban
equivalent of wood stealing and the snapping up of unconsidered
trifles. In practice many of these offences were related, and particular individuals were often accused of several of them in successive
courts. The details of repeated presentments evoke a world of
ill-regulated alehouses and lodgings, in crowded tenements sometimes in peripheral parts of the town, where servants and others,
including certain of the borough's supposedly celibate clergy,
drank, whored, gambled, stole, embezzled, quarrelled, ran riot and
sometimes ended up dead. *Mutatis mutandis*, the picture is one that
is very familiar to students of disorder in Elizabethan and early
Stuart England.[30]

The numbers and pattern of prosecutions fluctuated from year to year, in part depending on chance factors such as the make-up of particular jury panels and the assiduity of individual constables. Because the records are incomplete, while part of what does survive is damaged and sometimes illegible, a reliable time-series of presentments cannot be constructed. However, certain years or individual rolls are complete enough to give a vivid impression of the scale of operations. In a single sessions in October 1484, for example, there were over sixty presentments for bawdry (i.e. allowing illicit sexual activities) and maintaining disorder, together with a variety of other presentments for receiving servants, petty bribery and other offences. A more characteristic pattern was in the year Michaelmas 1505 to Michaelmas 1506. Again the records are incomplete, but those that survive comprise 19 presentments (including 13 women, 1 husband and wife and 2 couples) for keeping 'bordel houses' or brothels, 'keeping bawdry', 'occupying bawdry', or being a bawd, pimp or prostitute; 5 (including one female) for harbouring thieves or receiving beggars or servants; 3 (of whom one was a woman) for keeping misrule at night; 6 (all men) for playing bowls; and 10 (including 5 women) for scolding and quarrelling; together with a variety of trade offences and nuisances. There were overall perhaps 50 presentments with moral connotations, including an accusation against 'ye scheref Johnson' for 'okkepying' Alice, the wife of Richard Copeland, and 'ye [s]cheref['s] s[er]wand Wyllyam Danson for okepying Copland['s] wyfe['s] s[er]wande'.[31]

The evidence from London, Westminster, Nottingham, and other places, together with church court and manorial material for rural areas, gives some grounds for asking whether the late fifteenth and early sixteenth centuries experienced moral regulation on a scale comparable to later, better researched periods. However, it is doubtful whether such a straightforward comparison can really be made. The fragmentary nature of the late medieval evidence, and the regional and local patchiness of the materials for later periods, in themselves give pause. Other problems to contend with are drastic changes in the size and distribution of the population, major alterations in the functions of different courts, shifts of business from jurisdiction to jurisdiction, and the decline of some courts including many local leets. The picture is further obscured by changes in prosecution methods, the recording of cases, and the kinds of court record which were either produced or preserved. For these and other reasons, some of which will emerge later in the discussion, any attempt to compare in simple numerical terms the intensity of regulation under the Yorkists and early Tudors with later periods is bound to fail. What can be said with certainty on the basis of the available evidence is that in the late fifteenth and early sixteenth century the public regulation of morality through legal action was commonplace; in this light, later developments should be seen as at most an intensification, in some respects merely a continuation, of an earlier pattern.

It might, none the less, be suggested that a key feature of the century after 1560, marking it out from preceding regimes of moral regulation, was an insistence on harsher punishments for moral transgressions. There are some indications to this effect, for example the increasing use of the cucking stool against scolding women, the provision made in numerous Tudor and Stuart statutes for the use of the stocks against petty offenders, and probably also the greater use of whipping as a sanction. However, on closer examination the outlines of the development become blurred. Physical penalties of various sorts were in use in some borough courts, leets and other jurisdictions in the fifteenth and early sixteenth centuries. On the other hand, even by the early seventeenth century many offenders seem to have received little or no punishment. A high proportion of the presentments made at quarter sessions either led nowhere or were quashed on the grounds of insufficiency. Many others were settled by fines, many of them very small. In the post-Reformation church courts, a substantial segment of the accused, especially those who failed to appear to answer charges, were excommunicated; generally, this meant that they were excluded from the church premises but received no more tangible penalty. Most other offenders before the ecclesiastical courts were simply admonished, or received a mild form of penance, such as a simple acknowledgement of the offence before selected members of the congregation; only serious sexual offenders (fornicators and adulterers, for example), plus a sprinkling of other people accused of grave crimes, were subjected to the full rigour of public penance, involving the wearing of the white penitential sheet and open confession in church or market-place. The late fifteenth-and early sixteenth-century church courts had, in general, hardly been more severe; but some of them had on occasion prescribed the rod in addition to ordinary penance for sexual sin, and in this respect the trend after 1560 was towards greater laxity.[32]

The issue of increased severity is particularly pertinent to sexual offences dealt with by the secular courts, but again the picture is far from clear. In theory the apogee of severity was reached in 1650, when the Commonwealth's act 'for suppressing the detestable sins of incest, adultery and fornication' made the first two of these offences felonies, punishable by death without benefit of clergy; prescribed three months' imprisonment for fornication, to be followed by a year's security for good behaviour; and laid down that brothel-keepers were for a first offence to be whipped, pilloried, branded and gaoled for three years, and for a second offence to suffer death. However, the most extreme of these penalties proved virtually a dead letter, while even the three months' imprisonment for fornication was sparingly used in most areas; and the whole measure was repealed at the Restoration. It is true that behind the Adultery Act lay more than a century of efforts by various interests to secure statutory approval for severe physical penalties against sexual offences. But the crucial point is that, until the unique circumstances of the Commonwealth, these initiatives had always been resisted by more moderate members of Parliament, and the most that the zealots had been able to achieve were measures (enacted in the context of poor relief and vagrancy legislation in 1576 and 1610) to ensure the maintenance of poor bastard children and the punishment of the guilty parents. As a result, some of the latter were whipped or (especially in the case of the mothers) sent to the House of Correction for a year. But regionally and locally the impact of these measures was very patchy, and even in areas of relatively intense enforcement they applied only to a small proportion of the bearers and begetters of illegitimate children. The regular use of whipping against sexual offenders in the Westminster Court of Burgesses, illustrated at the beginning of this paper, was exceptionally rigorous; even here, two burgesses moderated the regime by successfully maintaining in a case in 1612 that 'when a young man and a maid did commit incontinency together they ought but to be carted & not whipp'd'.[33]

Other physical penalties against sexual offenders were under Elizabeth and the early Stuarts largely confined to cities and boroughs, whose right to inflict them rested on claims of special custom. The most characteristic of these punishments was the 'carting' mentioned by the Westminster burgesses – that is, the parading of culprits through the streets in a waggon, often wearing 'papers' on which the offence was written in large letters and with basins ringing or music playing before them. Frequently the effect was aggravated by the mud or ordure thrown by the crowd, which no doubt seemed particularly appropriate for what were regarded as the 'filthy' offences of 'whoredom' and bawdry. Sometimes the offenders were banished from the city or borough after this experience, and forbidden to return on pain of branding or flogging; occasionally a whipping was administered anyway as part of the original punishment. But while London, Westminster, Norwich and some other cities and boroughs retained these penalties into the seventeenth century, some communities were hampered in the infliction of them by challenges to their jurisdiction, or simply let them fall into disuse. Indeed it was precisely these developments that fuelled some of the early seventeenth-century agitation for stricter statutory measures. On the other hand, it is clear that in many communities the use of carting and similar penalties long predated the reign of Elizabeth. Hence it may well be – though the subject does require more research – that in cities and boroughs the peak period for the use of physical sanctions against sexual offenders was before the end of the sixteenth century.[34] But even when such penalties were not used, or employed only sporadically, by Yorkist and early Tudor authorities, it does not necessarily imply lack of firm action against moral offences. Revealing in this respect is the court record from Westminster in 1519, which shows a graduated system of penalties in operation. Many offenders were simply 'warned', others were made to give bond for their good behaviour; but these measures were given credibility by the fact that notorious or repeated offenders were ordered to 'avoid the town' or, in the case of scolds, threatened with the cucking stool.[35]

A more interesting qualification of the idea of continuity of moral regulation from the late Middle Ages into the early modern period relates to the cultural context. The complexity of later fifteenth-century culture, and the rate of circulation of ideas, should not be underestimated. None the less, the explosion of relatively cheap printed literature from the sixteenth century onwards undoubtedly created a different, and in some ways more sophisticated, milieu. The reformation of manners campaign at the end of the seventeenth century manifested itself and achieved momentum through the medium of scores of pamphlets and printed sermons, which portrayed it as a 'national' movement; to an extent the same was true of 'reformation' initiatives of the period 1560–1660. Save for preaching from the pulpit and the circulation of statutes, proclamations and town ordinances – there are some intriguing indications of the influence of London on provincial towns in the sphere of moral regulation – there was no late fifteenth-century equivalent. It must be recalled in addition that the broadest treatments of the concept of 'reformation of manners' by modern historians (notably Keith Wrightson) include shifts in education and lay culture, and above all the massive religious changes associated with the Reformation, that plainly had no analogue in the earlier period. By concentrating on the core activity of moral regulation through courts of law, it is possible to conclude that 'reformation of manners' was a constant or at least recurrent feature of social life. However, the meaning of such activity, how it was understood and experienced by contemporaries, was bound to alter with changes in the wider context. For example, the ending of compulsory clerical celibacy, which in the late Middle Ages had helped to sustain prostitution, inevitably affected attitudes to sexual offences. So also did other changes in attitudes to the married state associated with the Reformation, though just how profound these alterations were is open to question.[36] A particularly telling index is changing attitudes to drama. In the fifteenth and early sixteenth centuries the didactic function of plays seemed secure, and a production such as *Mankind* (*c.*1460s) was clearly a medium of moral reformation. More than a century later, in a preface to the first edition of his *Anatomy of Abuses* (1583), Philip Stubbes still thought it expedient to admit that 'some kind of playes, tragedies and enterluds . . . may be used, in tyme and place convenient, as conducible to example of life and reformation of maners'. Indeed this was to remain a stock defence of the drama. But for a variety of reasons, including the development of the London theatres as well as profound changes in religious attitudes, from Elizabeth's reign onwards plays were more often seen as the enemy than as the ally of reformation.[37]

It will be evident that, in these conditions of cultural shift over a long period, simple notions of 'continuity' and 'change' are hardly adequate for understanding the history of reformation of manners; more appropriate, perhaps, are musical metaphors invoking ideas of theme, variation, transposition and transformation. But whatever metaphor or analogy is employed, it is not merely changes over time that need to be considered. At any point between the fifteenth and the eighteenth centuries, 'reformation of manners' was understood differently by diverse groups and interests. It is to such different meanings that the discussion now turns.

IV

The phrase 'reformation of manners' has a deceptive simplicity. By implication it evoked a former period of 'good manners', perhaps a Golden Age, and suggested consensus among right-thinking people about sound morals and decent behaviour. At the same time, it assumed that the 'manners' of at least some groups in society had lapsed into corruption and vice, and made a bid for the moral high ground to secure 'reformation'. Hence it was apt to be a contested concept, liable to appropriation by different interests for particular ends. What these ends were conditioned precisely what forms of behaviour were thought to require reformation; at the same time, the agenda of reform was influenced by legal constraints and by changing notions of what was amenable to public regulation. These complexities have not always been appreciated by historians, who have often tended to see 'reformation of manners' in unitary terms. The following brief discussion of certain of the issues will go over some well-known ground but, it is hoped, shed new light by seeing it in longer-term perspective and by introducing some less familiar material.

Stubbes's *Anatomy of Abuses* is rightly seen to embody many of the concerns of the Elizabethan Puritan 'reformation of manners', and has often been quoted with reference to bastardy, drunkenness, dancing, Maygames, and so forth. It has been less often emphasised how much attention Stubbes gave to usury, excesses in apparel, and covetousness. Yet these were prominent targets of 'reformation' in the fifteenth and sixteenth centuries. They were denounced not only by Puritans such as Stubbes but also by bishops such as Edwin Sandys and, in Tudor and Stuart times as in earlier periods, condemned in innumerable sermons.[38] The reasons why they have tended to escape the attention of historians of 'reformation of manners' in the seventeenth century are twofold. The first is that prosecutions relating to these matters do not feature prominently in the quarter sessions and ecclesiastical court records that such historians have mostly relied on. The second is that, for complex reasons, they had by the end of Elizabeth's reign largely disappeared from the agenda of legal regulation while still remaining to some extent moral issues. Apparel was regulated from the fourteenth century by means of sumptuary laws: there were important Acts of Parliament in 1337, 1363, 1463, 1483, 1510, 1515, 1533 and 1554, complemented by a stream of proclamations including some significant ones in 1562, 1566, 1574, 1580, 1588 and 1597. This legislation owed very little to what we would think of as the 'economic' motives of regulating trade or promoting manufactures. It was much more concerned with the maintenance of social order and due distinction of rank, but was also shot through with moral implications which related 'inordinate' or 'outrageous' excess in apparel to other sins. Thus the Act of 1533, animadverting on 'the p[er]verse and frowarde maners and usage of people', referred to the 'utter impov[er]isshement and undoyng of many inexpert and light p[er]sones inclyned to pride, moder of all vices'; while Acts of 1463 and 1483, scandalised by changes in male fashion, forbade most men to wear a jacket 'unless it be of such length that the same may cover his privy members and buttocks'. There were, however, two main problems with sumptuary legislation: the principles of social distinction enshrined in such Acts were highly controversial, and could only become more so as the social structure grew more complex, social mobility increased, and the range of textiles, ornaments, and fashions available to the populace widened inexorably; and, more basically, the legislation was almost impossible to enforce. It was because these problems proved irresolvable that Parliament failed to renew the sumptuary laws in 1604, though bills on the subject were repeatedly introduced in the early seventeenth century.[39]

The story of prohibitions on usury is rather similar. Traditionally this had been a matter for regulation by canon law administered by the church courts, but concern about the evasion of the prohibitions on usury through a variety of financial devices was among the factors that led to parliamentary legislation in 1487, 1495, 1545 and 1552 (the last being a highly rigorist measure, reflecting reformed Protestant thinking on the subject). However, in an increasingly sophisticated financial context the moral status of money-lending and the charging of interest came to be perceived as a difficult matter, in which considerations of motive, circumstance and economic practicality had to be taken into account. There were in any case massive problems of enforcement. As a result the prohibitions were in effect restricted by the ambiguous act of 1571 and neutralised by the statute of 1624.[40] Similar considerations apply in the case of covetousness, which sixteenth-century moralists and government officials saw manifested in emparkment, enclosure, conversion of tillage to pastoral land, rack-renting, and similar activities by landlords. There was, of course, a great deal of Tudor legislation to deal with these issues, but its efficacy was always limited and after 1600, in the face of inexorable economic pressures which eventually encouraged a change of attitude, the laws gradually fell into decay.[41] Thus by the early seventeenth century apparel, money-lending and certain other economic activities had become matters for exhortation and the private conscience but had essentially escaped from legal regulation – not necessarily because there was widespread opposition to such regulation, but because no one could any longer agree on how it should be done. This shift foreshadowed what was to happen to many other issues of personal morality in the eighteenth century.[42]

As is well known, legislation on apparel, usury and tillage was usually sponsored, if not always initiated, by the royal government. It is less often recognised that the crown also had particular interests in other aspects of 'reformation of manners', which in the centuries under discussion led to repeated royal initiatives in this field. The dynastic struggles of the fifteenth century involved a propaganda war, pursued through sermons, proclamations and royal letters, in which the contestants strove for support and legitimacy; each claimed to be zealous in the defence of traditional morality and the correction of sin, while opponents were implicitly or explicitly denounced as irresponsible and immoral. The Yorkists came close to appropriating the rhetoric of 'reformation' in church, government and commonweal – hence rendering nugatory the claims to sanctity of the Lancastrian Henry VI. But Edward IV's allegedly invalid marriage to Elizabeth Woodville laid him open after his death to the accusation that, far from being the champion of Christian morality, he had 'lived . . . sinfully and damnably in adultery'. This background helps to explain why Henry VIII's divorce from Catherine of Aragon and later matrimonial changes were linked with an aggressive attack on sexual immorality, whether of the religious orders or of the denizens of the Southwark stews. The Protestant counsellors of Henry's successor, casting him in the role of a new Josiah, built on this tradition of royal reformation: a proclamation of 1551 commanded all subjects of whatever degree 'to dread and fear God and his plagues, to convert and amend their manners and to live according to the profession of Christian men'.[43] The association of the monarch with 'reformation of manners' was further reinforced in the early to mid-sixteenth century through the influence of humanist social thinkers in government circles. Indeed they played an important role in revitalising and extending the tradition; though to see humanists as the originators of such reformation, as some historians have done, is as misleading as to see Puritans in the same light.[44]

A more specific crown concern with 'reformation of manners' related to war and defence. The tillage acts were designed, amongst other things, to secure 'the defence of this land ageyn oure enne-myes outwarde' and to preserve 'the husbandman . . . a strong and hardy man, the good footman . . . a chief observation of good war-riors'.[45] Likewise the determination of fifteenth- and sixteenth-century governments to foster archery and prevent the decay of manly pursuits was among its reasons for legislating against un-lawful games such as bowls, tennis, football, quoits, cards and dice. These matters were dealt with in Acts of 1388, 1409, 1477, 1495, 1503, 1511 and 1515, culminating in the definitive statute of 1541, and were repeatedly noticed in proclamations. Among other facets of these military concerns, it should be noticed, was an emphasis on the training of youth. While the focus of the Acts was apparently on the activities of the common people, there were also fears that the availability of brothels, taverns, bowling alleys, gaming houses, and similar places of resort in the burgeoning metropolis would destroy 'the marow & stre[n]gth of this happy realme, I mean the abilitie of the gentlemen'; and here military concerns were but part of the wider, humanist-inspired debate on the role of noblemen and gentry in the state. This was the background of Whetstone's *Mirour for Magestrates* (1584), which reiterated some of the themes adum-brated by Thomas Starkey and others earlier in the century.[46]

However, government concerns over unlawful games were re-lated not merely to military matters or state service but also to issues of 'idleness' and public order; in these contexts young people again featured prominently, but this time (along with labourers) as servants and apprentices who frittered away their time or wasted their masters' goods. In the conditions of price inflation, the growth of poverty and vagrancy, trade fluctuations, repeated dislocations of the labour market by plague and other epidemics, and the inexorable growth of London that characterised the sixteenth century, government preoccupation with these more 'economic' issues became increasingly marked. A memorandum drawn up some ten years after the passage of the Statute of Artificers (1563) made a characteristic link between the short-term hiring of craftsmen and artisans and 'hauntinge of ale howses, usinge of unlawfull games, . . . cosinages, deludinge of mens wifes, daughters, and maidens, procuringe theim to whoredome and to pilfer for their maintenaunce' and other more heinous crimes; and concluded that proper enforcement of the statute would, among other benefits, 'refourme the unadvised rashnes and licentious manners of youthe'.[47]

By the early seventeenth century, crown initiatives in the sphere of reformation of manners were somewhat less in evidence. Elizabeth and her Stuart successors were inclined to leave matters of morality as far as possible to the church courts; the concern with archery had disappeared; and – in the matter of alehouse regulation, for example – the royal government sometimes seemed more interested in revenue than reformation. Yet the traditional concerns were by no means dead. Charles I's Book of Orders has been called 'an official blueprint for a reformation of manners', while the Declaration of Sports (issued by James I in 1618 and by his son in 1633) may be seen in part as an effort to revive royal sponsorship of manly pursuits. Protector Oliver's promotion of moral reformation, which drew on his experience of military discipline and looked to the Major-Generals for effective enforcement, was a more explicit reassertion of the link with military prowess and national security. It was no accident that he was concerned above all with 'the nobility of this nation especially, and the gentry', and the education of youth. In this light his concerns have a very traditional cast, and reflect the quasi-monarchical position he was gradually assuming. At the end of the century, the link between kingship and moral rearmament was again strongly reaffirmed by William III: anxious both to vindicate his legitimacy as monarch and to involve England in a major continental conflict, he and Queen Mary were initially foremost in sponsoring the campaign for Reformation of Manners in the 1690s.[48]

In so far as successive royal governments were concerned with economic and public order implications of 'evil manners', they were likely to strike a chord with local interests, and in particular with middling or wealthier householders. It was they who, throughout the whole of the period under review, characteristically served as jurors, constables, tithingmen and churchwardens; they thus bore much of the responsibility for the local enforcement of penal statutes and canon law, the burden of day-to-day policing, and the relief and management of the poor. It would be wrong to see their motives wholly in prudential terms; but matters that affected such people's purses, their personal safety, and the subsistence needs of themselves and their families inevitably gave a hard, practical edge to their understanding of morality. The degree to which this was so did vary to some extent with the economic context. The late sixteenth- and early seventeenth-century combination of increasing population, rising prices, recurrent epidemics, and burgeoning numbers of the poor was especially likely to stimulate concern about personal morality, especially in populous and rapidly expanding communities. The connections were only too obvious: bastardy had implications for poor relief, bridal pregnancy and simple fornication raised questions about the marriage of poor people, alehouses and unlawful games raised spectres of idleness and the wasting of goods. Thus Paul Slack has emphasised how closely poor relief measures in Elizabethan and early Stuart towns were connected with 'reformation' – in Gloucester in 1635, for example, the new orders for the city hospitals appointed an 'overseer of the manners of the poor' – while a variety of studies illustrate increasing resort to local courts in this period to combat what one historian has labelled 'immiserating vice'. None the less, it would be a mistake to overemphasise the century after 1560. McIntosh has argued plausibly that activism could likewise be generated in the very different demographic regime of the later fifteenth century. Some larger manors in Essex and elsewhere, especially clothworking communities and market centres on major routeways, were strongly affected by the stimulus of the London market and experienced considerable immigration. Thus *locally* such communities experienced problems not unlike those of many villages in Elizabethan and early Stuart England, even though the general context was one of low population levels. On the other hand, Jeremy Goldberg has linked concern over sexual immorality in later fifteenth-century cities and boroughs to the effects of economic *recession*; on this view, it was declining employment opportunities for women that drove them into prostitution and, more generally, into unregulated activities that made them seem a threat to order. More generally, problems of poverty, disease and migration were rarely far away in late medieval and early modern England, providing a context in which bursts of legal action could be triggered with ease. This was especially so in the case of towns and cities; and this circumstance – combined with others, such as the superior administrative and governmental resources of most towns – meant that urban initiatives towards the reformation of manners were particularly prominent, just as they were in the related sphere of poor relief. The predominantly urban, and especially metropolitan, focus of the Societies for Reformation of Manners in the decades around 1700 exemplified this pattern with particular clarity.[49]

However, the link with economic problems should not be taken to imply that the targets for reform were invariably, or even predominantly, the poor; and when they were, that their poverty was their only relevant characteristic. Recent studies indicate that at least as prominent an object of reform were the young, especially mobile youngsters including servants. Here again, crown concerns expressed in legislation and proclamations united with grass-roots interests. Their responsiveness no doubt varied according to the precise local context, which was shaped by such factors as age structure, gender ratios and economic opportunities. But it is clear that young people's drunkenness, sexual immorality, tendency to waste their masters' or parents' goods in drinking and gambling, and simple rowdiness were matters of recurrent concern, whether in early Tudor Nottingham, Jacobean Earls Colne, Caroline Dorchester or late Stuart London.[50]

While prudential concerns guaranteed some popular support for 'reformation of manners', they also restricted the agenda of local activism and limited its impact. In the context of the work of the Societies for Reformation of Manners in London in the years around 1700, Robert Shoemaker has argued that informers for the most part concentrated their activities on matters that immediately threatened order in their local communities, especially prostitution and 'lewd and disorderly practices' that included pickpocketing and theft. More generally, it is clear that throughout the fifteenth, sixteenth and seventeenth centuries, the offences that were most consistently pursued in towns and villages were precisely those that had financial or other practical implications as well as moral or religious significance. The outstanding example is bastard-bearing, which was condemned without question in many parts of the country. Others were prostitution, in localities where it was likely to occur; and a cluster of offences centring on gambling and drink.[51] Of course, consensus was not total, even in the case of illegitimacy. As I have emphasised before in another context, 'private' attitudes to bastardy – in one's own family, for example, or if one were well paid to harbour an unmarried woman – could be considerably more lax than attitudes to other people's bastards or to the 'bastardy problem' in general.[52] As for alehouses and similar establishments, licensing and other kinds of regulation were bound to be to some extent contentious, since so many livelihoods depended on these institutions and they served such a variety of functions and played such a complex role in local economies – to the extent that Wrightson can plausibly argue that in the century after 1580 'the struggle over the alehouses was one of the most significant social dramas of the age'. Gradually, a system of regulation and licensing came to be accepted, a process that began in the fifteenth century if not before. But *extreme* attempts to bridle drink-selling (such as those associated in some areas with the Puritan regimes of the 1640s and 1650s) aroused opposition, while perennially there was resistance in Parliament and in the localities to sanctions against *personal drunkenness* as opposed to the institutions of ale-selling. The obvious danger was that such a vaguely defined offence could provide a snare for ordinary people engaged in normal kinds of recreation or sociability. 'We cannot define a . . . drunkard, and therefore crave advice (how to present such) untill the next courte', the churchwardens at King's Sutton, Northamptonshire, declared cannily in 1619.[53]

The reasons why some groups and individuals were prepared to embark on a more thoroughgoing assault on the evils of drink, and also to confront other issues outside the 'prudential' or 'commonsense' range, requires consideration of another factor – religious zeal. Here again we enter some well-trodden ground, but also areas where more research is needed; and again a long-term perspective proves helpful, revealing a complex landscape of contest and consensus, continuity and change. The religious Reformation inaugurated a battle over 'reformation of manners', as Protestants and their conservative opponents each tried to seize the moral high ground. The reformers' share of this activity has been documented in, for example, Bishop Hooper's stern rule in the consistory court of Gloucester diocese in the reign of Edward VI, and the anti-prostitution campaign – in which a distinctively Protestant rhetoric was strongly evident – that Ian Archer has uncovered in Elizabethan London. The Catholic case was hampered by the fact that the Church had tolerated the Southwark stews before their abolition by Henry VIII, and that licensed brothels still existed in Rome, Venice and other Catholic states. None the less, the argument did not go all one way. There are indications of sharp and exemplary action against sin, in London and other towns, during the brief reign of Mary. In Chester, in 1557, the mayor not only banned the selling of drink at unlawful times, 'espetially on the Sunday in the tyme of devine service doinge in the churches', but also tried to curtail Christmas festivities: the practice of going 'abrode muminge . . . their faces beinge covered or disgised' was sternly forbidden, as also were Christmas day breakfasts given by the 'worshipful' of the city, 'by reason wherof many discrett p[er]sons have used them selves all the day after idley in vise & wantonesse'. More generally Catholics claimed that the pretended 'reformation' of religion had let loose a torrent of vice, and indeed blamed on that event the whole gamut of sixteenth-century social evils that historians associate with population pressure and price inflation. Such accusations stung the Elizabethan government to search for means 'whereby the reformation of religion may be brought in credit, with the amendment of manners, the want whereof hath been imputed as a thing grown by the liberty of the Gospel'.[54]

In longer-term perspective, it can be seen that the Reformation led to a permanent tilt in the pattern of regulation, and contributed significantly to an apparent upsurge of prosecutions in the later sixteenth and seventeenth centuries. As George Hakewill commented, certain activities 'in former times were scarce known to be sinnes; but being now by the light of the Gospell discovered to be such, and that in an high degree, as they are straitly forbidden by *God's* law, so is the edge of our lawes turned against them'. In particular, the enforcement of church attendance and regular communion became an important part of the work of the church courts and, to an extent, of secular tribunals too. Sabbatarianism likewise emerged as a strong force. Working, trading and other forms of profanation of Sundays and holy days were fiercely denounced by late medieval moralists, and prosecutions and orders against them in the pre-Reformation spiritual and secular courts were by no means unknown; but such action was stepped up in Elizabeth's reign and was pursued with even greater vigour by the seventeenth century. As Kenneth Parker has emphasised, it was by no means confined to Puritans but was also a major concern of the church hierarchy. In London in the 1630s, for example, the authorities mounted huge drives against shopkeepers and victuallers who opened on Sundays and holy days; in the archdeaconry court between November 1639 and November 1640, nearly 1300 people were prosecuted for offences of this kind. Such activities emerge as commensurate in scale, and netting the same kind of offenders, as the campaigns against sabbath-breakers sponsored by the Societies for Reformation of Manners around 1700 – though these bodies ignored holy days other than Sunday, and depended on the parliamentary legislation that had been enacted at intervals during the seventeenth century to supplement ecclesiastical law on sabbath observance.[55]

Throughout the period under review, the most intense bursts of moral activism, and the widest range of targets outside the prudential range, were associated with groups and individuals who were fired by a peculiarly intense religiosity. The sources of such zeal were complex and are sometimes hard to decipher. Craig Rose has emphasised the connection between the movement for moral reform in the 1690s and aspirations towards Protestant unity. More generally, Tim Hitchcock suggests that the Societies for Reformation of Manners should be seen in the context of the millenarian expectations circulating in the closing years of the seventeenth century and the early years of the eighteenth. Such beliefs, held in more or less extreme versions by different groups and individuals, and taking a bewildering variety of forms, created 'a powerful sense of impending change which suggested the need to reform society, control the wicked, convert the heathen and witness God's miracles'. On this view the Societies for Reformation take their place alongside activities ranging from utopian experiments to the SPCK. The 'godly rule' of the mid-seventeenth century certainly had a millenarian dimension, while it was a commonplace of zealous Protestants in the reign of Elizabeth, James and Charles I that these were the 'last days' prophesied by Scripture, in which 'corruption of manners should abound'. The eschatological tradition had been reinforced during the sixteenth century – and given a 'national' dimension through emphasis on England's particular role in God plan – by the writings of Bale and Foxe. But such ideas were in themselves not entirely new. Closely related notions, emphasising decline and decay, are found in the *ubi sunt?* tradition which underpinned much moral diatribe at the close of the Middle Ages.[56]

A similar thread of continuity at the core of changing theological emphases is seen in the linked theme of God's providence. Recent work has underscored the importance of such doctrines to the Societies for Reformation of Manners at the end of the seventeenth century: they reflected both a sense of the providential deliverance through the agency of William of Orange from the threat of Roman Catholic tyranny, and a heightened awareness of the threat of divine judgement on the nation for its profligacy and sin. Similarly powerful ideas were at work in the century before 1660, animating many clergy and some laymen of various social ranks and extending in their influence even to the grass-roots in some places. But these beliefs also had deep roots in the past, springing from a tradition that was shared by both Protestants and Catholics. 'What man canne denie these manifest plages, manifestly to come of God, for the manifest corectio[n] of this his daughter Englande?' asked James Brooks, preaching at the beginning of Mary's reign. The link between providence and 'reformation of manners' was certainly no innovation. Fifteenth- and early sixteenth-century statutes bearing on moral issues customarily invoked the 'great displeasure of God' as a spur to urgent action; while the absorption of such ideas at the local level is suggested by the ordinance of the lawday of Gloucester which around 1504 denounced 'the vicyous lyvyng' of some of the inhabitants, including the 'to excidyng nowmbre of commyn strompettes and bawdes', 'which, yf hit be not shortly remedyed and punysshed, hit is to be feryd leste Alle Myghty God wole caste his greate vengeaunce uppon the said towne in shorte tyme'.[57]

These religious ideas, of course, operated in conjunction with prudential concerns and other motives, and their precise impact at the local level is often hard to trace. In the Book of Sports controversy in the reign of Charles I, the religious view became highly visible when it clashed directly with Charles's own vision of 'reformation of manners' (though the agitation drew some of its strength from ministers, magistrates and other laymen who, irrespective of the religious issues, feared that the royal Declaration of Sports offered a licence for popular disorder). At other times the imprint of godly zeal can be discerned in the peculiar scope or intensity of local activism. It emerges to some extent in certain country parishes, such as Earls Colne and Terling in Essex, but is generally clearer in urban contexts.[58] Thus at Bury St Edmunds, in Suffolk, in 1579, a group of godly justices produced a code of exceptionally disagreeable penalties for sin: for example, fornicators, adulterers and incestuous persons were to be tied to the whipping-post for twenty-four hours, to have their hair cut off (if they happened to be female), and to receive 'thirtie strypes well layed on till the blood come'. Here an extra twist of zealous cruelty marks these provisions out from the common urban tradition of severity towards sexual offenders. In Puritan Dorchester in the 1630s, the magistrates went beyond the, by then, normal insistence on church attendance to the regular punishment of people who came late to church. Equally they were not satisfied with alehouse regulation and the *occasional* prosecution of personal drunkenness, but undertook the routine punishment of drunkards and 'tipplers'. They also regularly fined swearers and blasphemers. The Societies for Reformation were, at least for a brief period in the 1700s and 1710s, to chalk up considerable numbers of prosecutions for profane swearing; but Dorchester appears to have been one of the few places where much was done about this form of sinful behaviour in the early seventeenth century.[59]

In fine, a 'Puritan reformation of manners' did exist but it was a subset of a genre, one variant on a multifarious phenomenon. Other variants are visible in some royal initiatives, which drew on traditional ideals of kingship and often had a military flavour; and the stolidly prudential framework which shaped much local action. Depending on motive and purpose, the rhetoric and agenda of reform were apt to vary; diverse combinations of ideology, economic context, group concern, and individual initiative translated themselves into differing levels of zeal for reform, the intensity of which therefore varied over time and space. In broader terms the understanding and implementation of 'reformation of manners' were inevitably affected by the cultural shifts which England experienced between the Wars of the Roses and the Hanoverian Succession. Yet there were some important continuities. If concern about the disorders of the poor was a recurrent theme, so also was worry about the behaviour of the young, especially since ideas about 'manners' were often found in an educational context. Underlying all these activities was a tradition, taken for granted until the eighteenth century, of the regulation of personal morality through the secular and ecclesiastical courts, supported and justified by princes and magistrates, schoolmasters and preachers, masters, mistresses and 'honest' householders. This was the tradition of *reformatio morum* or 'reformation of manners'. Far from being an innovation of post-Reformation England, it had strong and deep roots in the medieval past. If the Puritan version is of special interest, this is as much for negative as for positive reasons. For extreme emphasis on sins that outraged only the zealot was bound to arouse opposition. In Dorchester and other Puritan strongholds before the civil wars, the magistrates and constables were denounced by some townsmen as 'hollow-hearted men', 'dissemblers'; the agents of reformation during the Commonwealth and Protectorate were dismissed as 'fanatics'; the informers who worked for the Societies for Reformation of Manners were condemned as 'hypocrites' and 'pharisees'.[60] Such criticism was one factor – among many – that ultimately undermined this long-established system of moral regulation and ensured that, though efforts to alter the manners of the people did not cease, they were by the late eighteenth and nineteenth centuries to take a rather different form. But that is another story.

NOTES AND REFERENCES

* Early versions of this paper were presented at seminars in Oxford, Cambridge and Birmingham. I am grateful to the participants for their helpful comments.

1. Westminster City Archives, WCB 1, pp. 150–1.

2. For general discussions of these ideas, see P. Laslett, *The World We Have Lost Further Explored* (London, 1983), chs 1–3; S. Amussen, *An Ordered Society: Gender and Class in Early Modern England* (Oxford, 1988).

3. J. A. Sharpe, 'The People and the Law', in B. Reay (ed.), *Popular Culture in Seventeenth-Century England* (London, 1985), pp. 244–70.

4. 27 Elizabeth I c. 31; on this court see also W. H. Manchée, *The Westminster City Fathers (the Burgess Court of Westminster) 1585–1901* (London, 1924); J. F. Merritt, 'Religion, Government and Society in Early Modern Westminster, c.1525–1625' (unpublished University of London Ph.D. thesis, 1992), ch. 3.

5. C. Read (ed.), *William Lambarde and Local Government: His 'Ephemeris' and Twenty-Nine Charges to Juries and Commissions* (Ithaca, 1962), pp. 68–9.

6. G. V. Portus, *Caritas Anglicana, Or an Historical Inquiry Into Those Religious and Philanthropical Societies That Flourished in England Between the Years 1678 and 1740* (London, 1912); J. Innes, 'Politics and Morals: The Reformation of Manners Movement in Later Eighteenth-Century England', in E. Hellmuth (ed.), *The Transformation of Political Culture: England and Germany in the Late Eighteenth Century* (Oxford, 1990), pp. 57–118; W. C. Abbott (ed.), *The Writings and Speeches of Oliver Cromwell*, 4 vols (Cambridge, Mass., 1937–47), IV, pp. 273–4, 493–4, 499.

7. B. Sharp, Review of D. Underdown, *Revel, Riot & Rebellion, American Historical Review*, vol. 92 (1987), pp. 1204–5, referring to K. E. Sharpe, 'Archbishop William Laud and the University of Oxford', in H. Lloyd Jones *et al.* (eds), *History and Imagination: Essays in Honour of H. R. Trevor-Roper* (London, 1981), pp. 146–64; A. Fletcher, *Reform in the Provinces: The Government of Stuart England* (New Haven, 1986), ch. 8; D. M. Hirst, 'The Failure of Godly Rule in the English Republic', *Past and Present*, vol. 132 (1991), pp. 32–66; K. Wrightson, 'The Puritan Reformation of Manners, with Special Reference to the Counties of Lancashire and Essex, 1640–1660' (unpublished University of Cambridge Ph.D. thesis, 1973); K. Wrightson, *English Society, 1580–1680* (London, 1982), chs 6–7. On the specific issue of popular festivities, see R. Hutton, *The Rise and Fall of Merry England: The Ritual Year, 1400–1700* (Oxford, 1994). For the association of 'reformation of manners' with Puritanism and poverty see, e.g., W. Hunt, *The Puritan Moment: The Coming of Revolution in an English County* (Cambridge, Mass., 1983), pp. 79–84 and passim; but cf. P. Collinson, *The Religion of Protestants: The Church in English Society, 1559–1625* (Oxford, 1982), p. 222 and ch. 5 passim; and K. Fincham, 'Introduction', in Fincham (ed.), *The Early Stuart Church, 1603–1642* (London, 1993), pp. 19–20.

8. I intend to deal with these issues on another occasion.

9. For example, J. Strype, *The Life and Acts of John Whitgift*, 3 vols (Oxford, 1822 edn), I, p. 494.

10. [W]iltshire [R]ecord [O]ffice D3/7/1, fol. 48v; for similar examples, see D5/28/10, nos 27, 40.

11. T. Hobbes, *Leviathan, Or the Matter, Forme and Power of a Commonwealth Ecclesiasticall and Civil*, ed. C. B. Macpherson (Harmondsworth, 1968), p. 160, cf. pp. 166, 717, 727; J. Northbrooke, *A Treatise Wherein Dauncing, Vaine Plaies or Enterludes with Other Idle Pastimes &c. Commonly Used on the Sabboth Day, Are Reprooved* (London, 1579), sig.A3v; T. Beard, *The Theatre of Gods Iudgements* (London, 1597), p. 321. The relationship between 'manners' (in all its senses) and 'civility' is an important and complex issue that requires separate treatment; some of the issues are explored in A. C. Bryson, 'Concepts of Civility in England, c.1560–1685' (unpublished University of Oxford D.Phil. thesis, 1984) and F. A. Childs, 'Prescriptions for Manners in English Courtesy Literature, 1690–1760, and their Social Implications' (unpublished University of Oxford D.Phil. thesis, 1984).

12. [B]ritish [L]ibrary Add. MS 23151, fol. 52v; London Guildhall

Library MS 9057/1. fol. 175v. For an earlier example, see WRO D5/28/5, no.3 (1582).

13. Bryson, 'Concepts of Civility', pp. 38–55.

14. J. G. Nichols (ed.), 'Two Sermons Preached by the Boy Bishop at St Paul's, Temp. Henry VIII and at Gloucester, Temp. Mary', in *The Camden Miscellany VII* (Camden Society, new series 14, London, 1875) [items separately paginated], pp. 23. 26–7; G. Whetstone, *A Mirour for Magestrates of Cyties* (London, 1584), fols. 23, 25; Read (ed.), *William Lambarde & Local Government*, pp. 68–71 and passim.

15. E. Cardwell, *Synodalia: A Collection of Articles of Religion, Canons and Proceedings of Convocations in the Province of Canterbury from the Year 1547 to the Year 1717*, 2 vols [consecutively paginated] (Oxford, 1842), I, pp. 229, 230, 311, 312, II, pp. 468, 695; F. Clarke, *Praxis . . . tam jus dicentibus quam aliis omnibus qui in foro ecclesiastico versantur apprimè utilis* (Dublin, 1666), pp. 405–6; cf. H. Consett, *The Practice of the Spiritual or Ecclesiastical Courts* (London, 1685), pp. 379–80; M. Bowker, *The Henrician Reformation: The Diocese of Lincoln Under John Longland, 1521–1547* (Cambridge, 1981), p. 11 (quoting Warham); Northamptonshire Record Office, Peterborough Diocesan Records, X615/42, p. 124, cf. ML 637, fols. 43, 63 (for the Latin forms *correctio sive reformatio morum*, etc).

16. J. Rastell, *The Booke of Assizes* (London, ?1513), 'Prologus'; Read (ed.), *William Lambarde & Local Government*, pp. 68–9, 76, 78, 95 and passim. On the relationship between the spiritual and the temporal power, see M. Ingram, *Church Courts, Sex and Marriage in England, 1570–1640* (Cambridge, 1987), pp. 150–3.

17. Portus, *Caritas Anglicana*; D. W. R. Bahlman, *The Moral Revolution of 1688* (New York, 1957) (for later work on the Societies for the Reformation of Manners, see n.20); S. R. Gardiner, *History of the Commonwealth and Protectorate, 1649–1660*, 3 vols and supplement (London, 1894–1903), III, ch. 42; cf. K. V. Thomas, 'The Puritans and Adultery: The Act of 1650 Reconsidered', in D. Pennington and K. V. Thomas (eds), *Puritans and Revolutionaries: Essays in Seventeenth-Century History Presented to Christopher Hill* (Oxford, 1978), pp. 257–8.

18. For example, M. S. Byford, 'The Price of Protestantism: Assessing the Impact of Religious Change on Elizabethan Essex: The Cases of Heydon and Colchester, 1558–1594' (unpublished University of Oxford D.Phil. thesis, 1988).

19. Wrightson, *English Society*, chs 6–7, and the references there cited.

20. T. C. Curtis and W. A. Speck, 'The Societies for the Reformation of Manners: A Case Study in the Theory and Practice of Moral Reform', *Literature and History*, vol. 3 (1976), pp. 45–64; T. B. Isaacs, 'Moral Crime, Moral Reform and the State in Early Eighteenth Century England: A Study of Piety and Politics' (unpublished University of Rochester Ph.D. thesis, 1979); Isaacs, 'The Anglican Hierarchy and the Reformation of Manners, 1688–1738', *Journal of Ecclesiastical History*, vol. 33 (1982), pp. 391–411; A. G. Craig, 'The Movement for the Reformation of Manners, 1688–1715' (unpublished University of Edinburgh Ph.D. thesis, 1980); D. Hayton, 'Moral Reform and Country Politics in the Late Seventeenth-Century

House of Commons', *Past and Present*, vol. 128 (1990), pp. 48–91; R. B. Shoemaker, 'Reforming the City: The Reformation of Manners Campaign in London, 1690–1738', in L. Davison *et al.* (eds), *Stilling the Grumbling Hive: The Response to Social and Economic Problems in England, 1689–1750* (Stroud, 1992), pp. 99–120; J. Spurr, ' "Virtue, Religion and Government": The Anglican Uses of Providence', in T. Harris *et al.* (eds), *The Politics of Religion in Restoration England* (Oxford, 1990), pp. 29–57; Fletcher, *Reform in the Provinces*, pp. 240, 242–3, 260–1; Innes, 'Politics and Morals'; Hirst, 'Failure of Godly Rule', 65 n.

21. M. Ingram, 'The Reform of Popular Culture? Sex and Marriage in Early Modern England', in Reay (ed.), *Popular Culture*, pp. 129–65, and the references there cited.

22. M. Spufford, 'Puritanism and Social Control?', in A. Fletcher and J. Stevenson (eds), *Order and Disorder in Early Modern England* (Cambridge, 1985), pp. 41–57; I. Archer, *The Pursuit of Stability: Social Relations in Elizabethan London* (Cambridge, 1991), pp. 249–50; G. Rosser, *Medieval Westminster, 1200–1540* (Oxford, 1989), p. 244; P. J. P. Goldberg, 'Women in Fifteenth-Century Town Life', in J. A. F. Thomson (ed.), *Towns and Townspeople in the Fifteenth Century* (Gloucester, 1988), pp. 118–21.

23. M. K. McIntosh, 'Social Change and Tudor Manorial Leets', in J. A. Guy and H. G. Beale (eds), *Law and Social Change in British History* (London, 1984), pp. 73–85; McIntosh, 'Local Change and Community Control in England, 1465–1500', *Huntington Library Quarterly*, vol. 49 (1986), pp. 219–42; McIntosh, *Autonomy and Community: The Royal Manor of Havering, 1200–1500* (Cambridge, 1986), esp. ch. 6; and cf. McIntosh, *A Community Transformed: The Manor and Liberty of Havering, 1500–1620* (Cambridge, 1991). For preliminary findings from McIntosh's more recent work, see McIntosh, 'Finding Language for Misconduct: Jurors in Fifteenth-Century Local Courts', in D. Wallace and B. Hanawalt (eds), *Representing Fifteenth-Century England* (forthcoming, Minneapolis, 1995). I am very grateful to Professor McIntosh for the opportunity to read this paper in advance of publication.

24. On Canterbury diocese and other late medieval jurisdictions, see B. L. Woodcock, *Medieval Ecclesiastical Courts in the Diocese of Canterbury* (London, 1952), esp. pp. 79–82; D. J. Guth, 'Enforcing Late Medieval Law: Patterns of Litigation During Henry VII's Reign', in J. H. Baker (ed.), *Legal Records and the Historian* (London, 1978), pp. 89–91. For some proceedings, see E. M. Elvey (ed.), *The Courts of the Archdeaconry of Buckingham, 1483–1523*, Buckingham Record Society 19 (Aylesbury, 1975); K. L. Wood-Legh (ed.), *Kentish Visitations of Archbishop William Warham and His Deputies, 1511–12*, Kent Archaeological Society 24 (Maidstone, 1984).

25. R. M. Wunderli, *London Church Courts and Society on the Eve of the Reformation* (Cambridge, Mass., 1981), esp. pp. 20, 22, 142–7 and chs 3–4 passim. Commissary court books for the period 1518–29, which Wunderli believed to have disappeared, survive in Guildhall Lib. MS 9065J/1–2 (cf. Wunderli, *London Church Courts*, pp. 11–12, 161). I hope to discuss the issues arising from Wunderli's interpretation at greater length on another occasion.

26. [C]orporation of [L]ondon [R]ecord [O]ffice Journal 13, fols. 141v, 143; Repertory 8, fol. 43v; Journal 12, fols. 10, 40, 169, 237, 238, 239, 277; see also Wunderli, *London Church Courts*, pp. 94–6, and the references there cited. I am grateful to Ian Archer for kindly communicating references to proceedings against bawds and scolds in London in the period 1509–58.

27. R. R. Sharpe (ed.), *Calendar of Letter-Books . . . of the City of London: Letter Book L, Temp. Edward IV-Henry VII* (London, 1912), p. 206; A. H. Thomas and I. D. Thornley (eds), *The Great Chronicle of London* (London, 1938), p. 222, cf. R. Fabyan, *The New Chronicles of England and France*, ed. H. Ellis (London, 1811), pp. 613, 663; cf. Archer, *Pursuit of Stability*, pp. 249–50, and the references there cited; Guth, 'Enforcing Late-Medieval Law', pp. 92–3; CLRO Journal 8, fols. 46v–50v and Journals 6–13 passim; Portsoken Ward Presentments, 242A; [G]reater [L]ondon [R]ecord [O]ffice Acc. 518/80 (I am grateful to Faramerz Dabhoiwala for this reference); for other proceedings against moral offenders in Westminster, see Westminster Abbey Muniments 50778 and 50782 (I am grateful to Gervase Rosser for advice about Westminster).

28. R. M. Karras, 'The Regulation of Brothels in Later Medieval England', *Signs: Journal of Women in Culture and Society*, vol. 14 (1988–9), pp. 405–6, 408–11; Archer, *Pursuit of Stability*, ch. 6, passim.

29. Karras, 'Regulation of Brothels', 407, 411; M. Bateson *et al.* (eds), *Leicester Borough Records*, 7 vols (London, Cambridge and Leicester, 1899–1974), II, pp. 290–1; M. D. Harris (ed.), *The Coventry Leet Book: or Mayor's Register Containing the Records of the City Court Leet or View of Frankpledge AD 1420–1555*, 4 parts, Early English Text Society, original series nos 134, 135, 138, 146 (London, 1907–13), part I, pp. 219–20, part II, pp. 399, 538–9, 544–5, 552, 568.

30. A. Dyer, *Decline and Growth in English Towns, 1400–1640* (London, 1991), pp. 70, 74; [N]ottingham [A]rchives [O]ffice CA 1a–47c (Borough Quarter Sessions Rolls, 1453–1556); selections printed in W. H. Stevenson *et al.* (eds), *Records of the Borough of Nottingham*, 9 vols (London and Nottingham, 1882–1956), II–III, passim. For the abstract of the 1463 orders, see ibid., II, p. 425.

31. NAO CA 4, 13a–d (for the quotation see CA 13c, no.10).

32. M. Ingram, ' "Scolding Women Cucked or Washed": A Crisis in Gender Relations in Early Modern England?' in J. Kermode and G. Walker (eds), *Women, Crime and the Courts in Early Modern England* (London, 1994), pp. 48–80; McIntosh, *Autonomy and Community*, p. 250; J. A. Sharpe, *Judicial Punishment in England* (London, 1990), p. 20; Woodcock, *Medieval Ecclesiastical Courts*, pp. 97–8; R. Houlbrooke, *Church Courts and the People During the English Reformation, 1520–1570* (Oxford, 1979), pp. 46–7; Ingram, *Church Courts*, pp. 52–4.

33. Thomas, 'Puritans and Adultery', pp. 257–82 passim; Ingram, *Church Courts*, pp. 151–3, 338–40, but cf. S. K. Roberts, *Recovery and Restoration in an English County: Devon Local Administration, 1646–1670* (Exeter, 1985), pp. 198–208. Fletcher, *Reform in the Provinces*, pp. 252–62 surveys evidence from a wide range of counties. For the Westminster case, see Manchée, *Westminster City Fathers*, p. 113.

34. I intend to discuss these issues more fully on another occasion; meanwhile, for some suggestive indications, see Thomas, 'Puritans and Adultery', pp. 265–7, and the references there cited.

35. GLRO Acc. 518/80.

36. These issues are complex and cannot be discussed in detail here. For a selection of recent viewpoints, see K. Davies, 'Continuity and Change in Literary Advice on Marriage', in R. B. Outhwaite (ed.), *Marriage and Society: Studies in the Social History of Marriage* (London, 1981), pp. 58–80; M. Todd, *Christian Humanism and the Puritan Social Order* (Cambridge, 1987), ch. 4; L. Roper, *The Holy Household: Women and Morals in Reformation Augsburg* (Oxford, 1989); M. E. Wiesner, *Women and Gender in Early Modern Europe* (Cambridge, 1993), pp. 21–5; P. Crawford, *Women and Religion in England, 1500–1720* (London, 1993), ch. 2.

37. D. Gray (ed.), *The Oxford Book of Late Medieval Verse and Prose* (Oxford, 1985), pp. 236–64; F. J. Furnivall (ed.), *Phillip Stubbes's Anatomy of the Abuses in England in Shakspere's Youth, AD 1583*, 2 parts in 3, New Shakspere Society, series 6, nos 4, 6, 12 (London, 1877–82), pt. I, p. x; G. Walker, *Plays of Persuasion: Drama and Politics at the Court of Henry VIII* (Cambridge, 1991), pp. 8–15; R. L. Greaves, *Society and Religion in Elizabethan England* (Minneapolis, 1981), pp. 445–54; P. Collinson, *The Birthpangs of Protestant England: Religious and Cultural Change in the Sixteenth and Seventeenth Centuries* (London, 1988), pp. 112–15.

38. *Stubbes's Anatomy of Abuses*, I, pp. 27–88, 114–29; J. Eyre (ed.), *The Sermons of Edwin Sandys*, Parker Society (Cambridge, 1841), pp. 49–50; G. R. Owst, *Literature and the Pulpit in Medieval England: A Neglected Chapter in the History of English Letters and of the English People* (Cambridge, 1933), pp. 404–11; Greaves, *Society and Religion*, pp. 502–20, 596–611 and chs 13–14 passim.

39. 11 Edward III c. 4; 37 Edward III cc. 8–14; 3 Edward IV c. 5, 22 Edward IV c. 1, 1 Henry VIII c. 14, 6 Henry VIII c.1, 7 Henry VIII c.6, 24 Henry VIII c. 13, 1 and 2 Philip and Mary c. 2 (for quotations, see *Statutes of the Realm*, 11 vols. (London, 1810–24), II, pp. 401, 470, III, p. 430; cf. *Stubbes's Anatomy of Abuses*, I, pp. 27–8); P. F. Hughes and J. F. Larkin (eds), *Tudor Royal Proclamations*, 3 vols (London, 1964–9), II, pp. 187–95, 202–3, 278–83, 381–6, 454–62, III, pp. 3–8, 174–9. More generally, see N. B. Harte, 'State Control of Dress and Social Change in Pre-Industrial England', in D. C. Coleman and A. H. John (eds), *Trade, Government and Economy in Pre-Industrial England: Essays Presented to F. J. Fisher* (London, 1976), pp. 132–65.

40. N. Jones, *God and the Moneylenders: Usury and Law in Early Modern England* (Oxford, 1989).

41. The literature on enclosure and related legislation is extensive: the best introduction is J. Thirsk, 'Enclosing and Engrossing', in J. Thirsk (ed.), *The Agrarian History of England and Wales, Volume IV: 1500–1640* (Cambridge, 1967), pp. 200–55.

42. Cf. Jones, *God and the Moneylenders*, p. 5.

43. A. Allan, 'Royal Propaganda and the Proclamations of Edward IV', *Bulletin of the Institute of Historical Research*, vol. 59 (1986), pp. 146–54; M. Levine, *Tudor Dynastic Problems, 1460–1571* (London, 1973), pp. 135–7; Hughes and Larkin (eds), *Tudor Royal Proclamations*, I, p. 516.

44. Cf. Todd, *Christian Humanism*, pp. 3, 7, 16, 18, 33, 178, 193, 203–4; L. Hutson, *Thomas Nashe in Context* (Oxford, 1989), pp. 23–5.

45. *SR*, II, p. 542 (4 Henry VII c. 19); A. E. Bland *et al.* (eds), *English Economic History: Select Documents* (London, 1914), p. 274.

46. *SR*, II, pp. 57, 163, 462–3 (12 Richard II c. 6; 11 Henry IV c. 4; 17 Edward IV c. 3), III, pp. 25–6, 123–4, 837–41 (3 Henry VIII c. 3; 6 Henry VIII c. 2; 33 Henry VIII c. 9); Hughes and Larkin (eds), *Tudor Royal Proclamations*, I, pp. 88–92, 113, 152–3, 174, 177–80, 206, 239–40, 266–8, 515, II, pp. 359–62, 517; Whetstone, *A Mirour for Magestrates*, sig. A4 and passim; cf. J. W. Cunliffe (ed.), *The Complete Works of George Gascoigne*, 2 vols (Cambridge, 1907–10), I, p. 4; T. F. Mayer (ed.), *Thomas Starkey: A Dialogue Between Pole and Lupset*, Camden Society, 4th series 37 (London, 1989), pp. 106–7.

47. R. H. Tawney and E. Power (eds), *Tudor Economic Documents, Vol. I: Agriculture and Industry* (London, 1924), pp. 360, 363. See also the contribution of Paul Griffiths to this volume, Chapter 5 below.

48. J. F. Larkin and P. L. Hughes (eds), *Stuart Royal Proclamations, Volume I: Royal Proclamations of King James I, 1603–25* (Oxford, 1973), pp. 360–2, 409–13; J. P. Kenyon (ed.), *The Stuart Constitution, 1603–1688: Documents and Commentary*, 2nd edn (Cambridge, 1986), pp. 451–5; cf. Sharp, Review of Underdown, *Revel, Riot and Rebellion*, p. 1205; S. R. Gardiner, *The Constitutional Documents of the Puritan Revolution, 1625–1660*, 3rd edn (Oxford, 1906), pp. 99–103; Abbott (ed.), *Writings and Speeches of Oliver Cromwell*, vol. IV, pp. 493–4; Bahlman, *Moral Revolution*, pp. 15–17.

49. Wrightson, *English Society*, pp. 222–4; M. Ingram, 'Religion, Communities and Moral Discipline in Late Sixteenth- and Early Seventeenth-Century England: Case Studies', in K. von Greyerz (ed.), *Religion and Society in Early Modern Europe, 1500–1800* (London, 1984), pp. 177–93; P. Slack, *Poverty and Policy in Tudor and Stuart England* (London, 1988), pp. 149–52, quoting (on Gloucester) P. Clark, ' "The Ramoth-Gilead of the Good": Urban Change and Political Radicalism at Gloucester, 1540–1640', in P. Clark *et al.* (eds), *The English Commonwealth, 1547–1640: Essays in Politics and Society* (New York, 1979), p. 176; McIntosh, *Autonomy and Community*, pp. 261–2 and ch. 6 passim; Goldberg, 'Women in Fifteenth-Century Town Life', p.121; Shoemaker, 'Reforming the City', pp. 99–101 and passim.

50. R. von Friedeberg, 'Reformation of Manners and the Social Composition of Offenders in an East Anglian Cloth Village: Earls Colne, Essex, 1531–1642', *Journal of British Studies*, 29 (1990), pp. 372–3; Craig, 'Movement for the Reformation of Manners', p. 21; D. Underdown, *Fire From Heaven: The Life of an English Town in the Seventeenth Century* (London, 1992), pp. 79–84.

51. Shoemaker, 'Reforming the City', passim; Ingram, 'Religion, Communities and Moral Discipline', pp. 184–91.

52. Ingram, 'The Reform of Popular Culture?', pp. 152–3.

53. Wrightson, *English Society*, p. 167, and see also K. Wrightson, 'Alehouses, Order and Reformation in Rural England', in E. and S. Yeo (eds), *Popular Culture and Class Conflict, 1590–1914* (Brighton, 1981), pp. 1–27; and, more generally, P. Clark, *The English Alehouse: A Social*

History, 1200–1830 (London, 1983), chs 1–9; S. A. Peyton (ed.), *The Church-wardens' Presentments in the Oxfordshire Peculiars of Dorchester, Thame and Banbury*, Oxfordshire Record Society 10 (Oxford, 1928), p. 294.

54.   F. D. Price, 'Gloucester Diocese Under Bishop Hooper, 1551–53', *Transactions of the Bristol and Gloucestershire Archaeological Society*, vol. 60 (1938), pp. 51–151; Archer, *Pursuit of Stability*, ch. 6, esp. pp. 248–54; BL Harley MS 2150, fol. 128v (I am grateful to Paul Slack for this reference); A. G. Dickens, *Tudor Treatises*, Yorkshire Archaeological Society Record Series 125 (Wakefield, 1959), pp. 90, 133–4; [R. Broughton], *An Apologicall Epistle: Directed to the Right Honourable Lords, and Others of Her Majesties Privie Counsell* (Antwerp, 1601), pp. 5, 8–9; Tawney and Power (eds), *Tudor Economic Documents, Vol. I*, p. 325.

55.   G. Hakewill, *An Apologie of the Power and Providence of God in the Government of the World* (Oxford, 1627), p. 433; K. Parker, *The English Sabbath: A Study of Doctrine and Discipline From the Reformation to the Civil War* (Cambridge, 1988) (though his stress on consensus and continuity, especially in the doctrinal sphere, is exaggerated); W. H. Hale (ed.), *A Series of Precedents and Proceedings in Criminal Causes From 1475 to 1640* (London, 1847), pp. lii–liii; Isaacs, 'Moral Crime', pp. 47–50, 252, 259.

56.   C. Rose, 'Providence, Protestant Union and Godly Reformation in the 1690s', *Transactions of the Royal Historical Society*, 6th series 3 (1993), pp. 151–69; T. Hitchcock, ' "In True Imitation of Christ"; The Tradition of Mystical Communitarianism in Early Eighteenth-Century England', in M. Gidley with K. Bowles (eds), *Locating the Shakers: Cultural Origins and Legacies of an American Religious Movement* (Exeter, 1990), pp. 13–22; Wrightson, 'Puritan Reformation of Manners', pp. 10–11; Collinson, *Birth-pangs*, ch. 1; J. W. Blench, *Preaching in England in the Late Fifteenth and Sixteenth Centuries* (Oxford, 1964), pp.228–32.

57.   Craig, 'Movement for the Reformation of Manners', pp. 4, 293–307; Rose, 'Providence, Protestant Union and Godly Reformation', pp. 152–9; Wrightson, 'Puritan Reformation of Manners', pp. 11–14; J. Brooks, *A Sermon Very Notable, Fruictefull and Godlie, Made at Paules Crosse the .xii. Daie of Novembre, in the First Yere of . . . Quene Marie* (London, 1553), sig.Iv; *Historical Manuscripts Commission: Beaufort MSS*, p. 435.

58.   Von Friedeberg, 'Reformation of Manners', esp. pp. 373–8; Wrightson and Levine, *Poverty and Piety*, ch. 5.

59.   On Bury, see BL Lansdowne MS 27/70, fols. 154–5; E. Rose, *Cases of Conscience: Alternatives Open to Recusants and Puritans Under Elizabeth I and James I* (Cambridge, 1975), pp. 158–68; Collinson, *Religion of Protestants*, pp. 157–9. For Dorchester, see Dorset Record Office DC/DOB 8/1 (Dorchester Borough Records, Offenders Book, 1629–37), passim; Under-down, *Fire From Heaven*. On prosecutions for swearing by the Societies for the Reformation of Manners, see Shoemaker, 'Reforming the City', pp. 104–5.

60.   Underdown, *Fire From Heaven*, chs 4–5; Bahlman, *Moral Revolution*, ch. 3.

3 Custom, Memory and the Authority of Writing*

ADAM FOX

I

Writing is a source of power: it is both a symbol and an agent of authority. As a technology of communication, it has the ability to revolutionise the transmission of information; as a means to objectify ideas, it has the capacity to transform mental process; and as an act of record, it has the potential to assume iconic significance.

The evidence from many societies in different times and places demonstrates the impact which the introduction and dissemination of the written word can have as an agent of change. In religious life and economic affairs, cultural expression and social structure, the role of government and the rule of law, writing has been both cause and effect of major historical development. Moreover, for those people in the past who have had access to it, it has often acted as a reservoir of authority, a means through which to control and coerce or to protect and preserve.[1]

In England, writing in the vernacular was already widely dispersed by the Anglo-Saxon period. It was the enormous expansion in the use of written documents in the centuries after the Norman Conquest, however, which may have witnessed the decisive shift 'from memory to written record'. In administrative, legal and commercial contexts, writing came increasingly to be relied upon as a medium of communication, a method of preservation, and a means of legitimation. Even the humblest of people found that it was scarcely possible to live their lives without running up against written records, prescribing, defining and codifying the world. They, too, learned to harness this resource for their own purposes: some 8 million charters may have been written, in the thirteenth century alone, simply for smallholders and serfs.[2]

By the early modern period, therefore, the written word had long been familiar in a wide variety of guises and at all social levels. England was a society permeated by documentary standards of reference and proof, a culture deeply imbued with literate habits of mind. At the same time, however, in an environment in which literacy levels were limited and oral traditions continued to enjoy considerable respect, the paradoxes and ambiguities inherent in writing remained keenly felt. On the one hand, it derived prestige as the vehicle for transmitting government and law: an 'authority' was not merely a person of privileged knowledge or power, it was also a canonical or official text. On the other hand, the notion long endured that writing, as the mere symbol of speech, was a poor substitute for personal contact and verbal exchange. In some senses, writing was prized as a standard of proof, its fixity, durability and longevity giving it value over oral testimony. In other respects, the idea that the spoken word of an honourable person was sufficient guarantee in matters of trust was slow to perish. The long-standing suspicion of writing as a vehicle for deception and chicanery, and the difficulty in distinguishing between the many forged documents and their originals, did little to dispel this attitude.

Concerns about the corruptibility of documents were evident, for example, in the statute of 1563 'agaynst the forgyng of evydences and wrytinges', prompted by the perception that the falsification of written titles 'hathe of late tyme been verye muche more practised, used and put in use in all partes of this realme then in tymes passed'. It was directed partly at the property market and against anyone found fabricating a 'false dede, charter or writing sealed, court roll, or the will of any person or persons in writing' with the intent of defrauding another of hereditaments. It was also concerned with commercial transactions in general and the forgery of 'any obligacon or bill obligatorye, or any acquitance release or other discharge of anny debt accounte, action sute, demande or other [thing] personall'. By the time the statute 'for prevention of frauds' was enacted in 1677, it was the case that titles to property and leases which were created only 'by parole and not putt in writeing and signed by the parties soe makeing and creating the same . . . shall not either in law or equity be deemed or taken to have any other or greater force or effect'. Equally, no goods could be granted or surrendered in any legally binding manner 'unlesse

it be by deed or note in writeing'; no contract of marriage, agreement to convey lands, or bargain to sell goods worth over £10 could
be enforceable at law unless recorded in 'some note or memorandum in writeing'.[3]

In a variety of contexts, therefore, the courts came increasingly to
give priority to written evidence over verbal witness wherever it was
available. It had long been the case that a hierarchy of value and
authority existed between a 'record' or sealed document, a mere
'writing' on parchment or paper, and an averment, or oral statement. Without 'records' or 'evidences' as proofs in legal disputes,
judges and juries were left simply with one person's word against
another.[4] As the Elizabethan Justice, William Lambarde, put it,
'One may affyrme a thing, and another may deny it, but if a record
once saye the worde, no man shall be received to averre (or speake)
against it.' The twin pillars of a manorial surveyor's work were
'information and record', as John Norden noted, 'although record
be alwaies preferred before verbal intelligence'. The crux of the
matter, identified by John Evelyn in the 1650s, was that

> verbal reports we experimentally find so very inconsistant and apt
> to err, and misrepresent things, done even in our own time and
> very neighbourhood . . . Nay, why (if this be otherwise) do men
> take such wonderous care about their deeds and legal evidences,
> which concern their temporal estates only, if writing be not more
> certain and less apt to err than words?[5]

These developments in legal and economic spheres did much to
create a general cultural climate in which written testimony was
privileged over oral report in a number of different circumstances.
The huge expansion in the production of documents and manuscripts of all kinds in this period, together with the ever greater
outpouring of printed books and pamphlets, helped, in the long
run, to promote a mentality which valued the fixity of writing over
the casualness of speech. People of varying ideological persuasions
and with different aguments to win could agree on this point. 'As
for orall traditions, what certaintie can there be in them?' asked
Bishop Joseph Hall in 1628 when accusing centuries of Catholic
teaching of corrupting the original word of God. Similar considerations provoked John Tillotson's denunciation of 'the authority of
oral tradition' in the 1660s. Over many years, he observed, 'oral
tradition might receive insensible alterations, so at last to become

quite another thing from what it was at first, by passing through many hands', which 'mistakes and corruptions' occur 'either through ignorance, or forgetfulness, or out of interest and design'. The same point was made by another commentator on human testimony at the end of the seventeenth century. In oral transmission everyone is liable to tell a different story, he argued, 'but in written tradition the chances against the truth or conversation of a single writing are far less; and several copies may also be easily suppos'd to concur; and those since the invention of printing exactly the same'. It was for these reasons that antiquaries and topographers were coming to take an ever more sceptical view of verbal evidence when collecting research for their county histories and local surveys. In the 1720s, Daniel Defoe reflected what was, by that time, a commonplace incredulity in dismissing the otherwise unsubstantiated tales told to him by the people at Tintagel Castle in Cornwall: 'as for the story of King Arthur being both born and killed [here], 'tis a piece of tradition, only an oral history, and not any authority to be produced for it'.[6]

Despite these developments, however, the ascendance of the written word was never complete nor absolute. There always remained circumstances in which oral testimony was required or had to be relied upon, and others in which it remained the only available form of evidence. A central place in the English legal system has continued to be allocated to verbal presentments and the spoken depositions of witnesses. In other contexts a preference for the immediacy and the personal contact implied by vocal delivery remained strong. Many preachers were reluctant to set down their sermons in writing, many scholars were loath to give up the verbal and visible inducements of the lecture. Script, and especially print, replaced the persuasions of viva voce with the dead letter of text. In general, the feeling that writing was somehow removed and divorced from the authorial voice, was slow to fade even from the thinking of those accustomed to using texts.[7] Among the majority, meanwhile, there remained 'more trust in an honest score chaulkt on a trencher, then in a cunning written scrowle, how well so ever painted on the best parchment', as Gervase Markham believed in 1635. For them, documents were less to be trusted than the word of an honest person, 'for the one may be falsified and corrupted, the other if it be found will hardly be shaken'.[8]

II

One way in which these ambivalent attitudes towards writing and some of the changing perceptions of its authority may be explored further is by an examination of the evolving relationship between local custom and national law in the sixteenth and seventeenth centuries. In thousands of manors, parishes and boroughs throughout the country at this time, the legal, economic and social relationships between landlords and tenants, clergymen and their flocks, or a corporation and its citizens were governed by sets of customary rules and regulations which determined the rights and obligations of all parties. These customs might dictate the terms of tenancy and ownership, the value of rents and tithes, or the amount and usage of common land. They might act differently upon rich and poor, men and women, young and old. In both rural and urban areas, agricultural regions and industrialised communities they comprised a set of rules and a body of lore which structured the practices and rhythms of daily life.[9]

Customs enjoyed full force at law so long as they could be shown to be 'reasonable', consonant with common right, binding upon those to whom they applied, certain and consistent over time, and anciently used.[10] Contemporaries defined the particular customs of local jurisdictions, as they did the general customs of the realm which made up the common law, to be laws 'unwritten', by which they meant non-statutory or not matters of record. In the standard formulation, a custom was said to be 'a law, or right, not written, which being established by long use and the consent of our ancestors, hath been and is daily practised'.[11] Samuel Carter's late seventeenth-century discussion of parochial customs copied directly from Sir John Davies' definition of the common law in 1612:

> A custom which hath obtained the force of a law, is always said to be *jus non scriptum*, for it cannot be made or created, either by charter or by Parliament, which are acts reduced to writing, and are always matter of record: but being only matter of fact, and consisting in use and practice, it can be recorded and registered no where but in the memory of the people.[12]

In some cases, local customs had no basis in writing at all, being born out of practice and preserved in verbal transmission and continual usage. Indeed, the multiplicity of these different uses, varying not only between manors, parishes and boroughs, but applying variously to different groups and individuals within them, made for a bewildering complexity which reflected the variegation typical of oral traditions. In London, for example, there were once said to be so many 'liberties, priviledges, and customes' that 'no man can remember them all to set them downe in writing being only recorded by mouth'.[13]

More often, customs had some written foundation, having been recorded in one form or another at an early date. Since at least the thirteenth century, court rolls, surveys and custumals had set down the customary regulations governing many manors and boroughs. They noted the fines payable to the lord on the descent or alienation of land and property, the amount and due dates of rents and tributes, the rules governing the rights of widows and the provisions for minors, and other rights and obligations of customary tenants. In a number of instances, privileges had been specifically bestowed by a lord upon his tenants, in the form of deed or grant, which over time had become customary. The extent to which such documentation could be relied upon, however, was often limited. For in the case of certain customs, such as the exercise of common rights, the taciturn and unspecific references in many manorial documents recorded only the lineaments of practice, the bare outline of what was in reality a much more complex fabric of densely woven rights and usages. These were fashioned and elaborated in the exercise of everyday social relations, in the reciprocities between landlord and tenant which were constantly adapted and renegotiated over the centuries. Indeed, one of the virtues of custom being only partially written was that it allowed for such flexibility, for subtle changes over time to be accommodated without fear of contradiction from the records of past practice.[14]

The unreliability of documentation in such cases was enhanced, in an age still unscrupulous and unsystematic in the keeping and storing of records, by its sheer lack of survival. Typically, the surveyor, Sir Robert Johnson, could complain to Robert Cecil in April 1602 that on the royal estates 'of every tenne mannors their is not one perfect surveigh, that not one court roll of a hundred that ought to be are to be seen or come by, and I think fewe or none (onelesse it be for Duchie lands in which I think some good course is holden) are to be found in anie of those storehowses in which they might and owght to have bene kept and preserved'. The reason, he believed, was largely the failure of manorial stewards in 'not troubling their heads with anie curious preservation of ancient customes, nor their pennes with ingrossing anie records at all, but kepe their momentarie remembrances . . . in rough paper bookes which are commonlie loste or embeseled with the death or change of the steward and almost suppressed altogether at the change of the quenes tenant'.[15]

This lack of adequate records meant that when contention over custom arose between landlords and their tenants, or between the tenants themselves, there was often insufficient evidence to settle the matter easily in the manorial court or at common law. 'To what height the controversies that have growen (through want of sucessyve preservation of records) have brought our comon lawiers, nedeth no argument', as Johnson observed. The solution, therefore, was to be found in resort to the courts of equity, most often in the form of the court of Exchequer where Crown lands were conerned. In disputes where '(for want of ancient records) little or nothing can be said or averred, yt were mete that pecemeale the points might be drawn into question before the Barons of her Majesties Exchequer to be by theme allowed or reiected as to equitie appteieneth'. The Exchequer was one of a number of tribunals at Westminster with equity jurisdiction, including the courts of Chancery, Requests and the Duchy of Lancaster, which heard cases referred from manorial courts baron and other local jurisdictions.[16]

The following discussion is based largely on the records of the equity side of the court of Exchequer in the period of its greatest activity, from the reign of Elizabeth I to the end of the seventeenth century. In the first instance, the court heard only suits in which the Crown had some interest, but as it became increasingly popular it was able to assume a general jurisdiction in 1649 by means of the legal fiction that the plaintiff was a debtor to the Crown. There were an average of 84 bills filed every year in the period 1558 to 1587, rising to an annual mean of 334 between 1587 and 1603, growing again to 456 during the Interregnum and finally reaching a peak of 739 at the time of William and Mary. Among these cases were a large proportion of disputes involving the rents, fines and heriots due on customary lands, together with contention over tithing customs, the boundaries between manors, and over common rights such as grazing, gleaning and mining. Westminster litigation was not, perhaps, representative of the bulk of manorial disputes settled in the localities, and the pattern of Exchequer cases may not be consistent with those of other central courts, but the records of its business do offer one body of evidence through which to examine the relationship between oral and documentary forms of evidence as revealed in that between custom and law.[17]

III

Given that the Exchequer and other equity courts were called upon to arbitrate in cases in which documentary evidence was often partial, their judges were compelled to place considerable store in the oral testimony of witnesses, taken either centrally or by commission in the localities. If written records could be forged and corrupted, however, their propensity to deceive was small when compared to that of verbal information. For added to the problems of faulty memory and deliberately selective amnesia was the fact that many protagonists interviewed by surveyors, commissioners and judges clearly engaged in invention and special pleading in order to make their cases. They often presented under oath, perhaps on the advise of legal counsel, plausible fictions in the guise of ancient traditions. Certainly 'overordennrie experience' had taught Sir Robert Johnson

> that moste parte of tenannts in these daies, when inquisitions of surveigh or inquests of office are taken, do not so much studie to answere what is true as (by all possible meanes) devise to sett forth and aver such customes and usages as are eyther directly preiuditiall to the inheritance or at the least onelie good and profitable for theme selves, and I have scarcely found anie other course holden; speciallie when they knowe not of court rolls or ancient surveighes to impugne theme.[18]

Nevertheless, oral testimony could be valuable in determining the validity of manorial custom since its defining conditions included current, consistent and uninterrupted usage to which those directly involved could best attest. There was also a sense in which such witness was more likely to yield the truth of the matter than the ancient documents, so often produced and counter-produced by opposing parties to substantiate their claims, which were found to be flatly contradictory. In one such case, heard before Chancery at the beginning of the seventeenth century, Lord Keeper Egerton instructed a jury to decide the disputed manorial customs by what 'had gone by usual reputation sixty years last, and not to have it paired, and defalked by such ancient deeds'. Sometimes the best way to establish practice exercised within living memory, and often to gauge tradition beyond it, therefore, was through the interrogation of the eldest inhabitants of a community whose long memories made them in this, as in other contexts, the repositories of local knowledge and the custodians of ancient wisdom. In 1607, the civil lawyer John Cowell commented that if a custom was to be decided at common law 'by witness', it was sufficient 'if two or more can depose, that they heard their fathers say, that it was a custome all their time, and that their fathers heard their fathers also say, that it was likewise a custome in their time'.[19]

Thus, in the depositions given by old men and women before manorial, common law and equity courts, whether accurate in detail or not, it is possible to gain some insight into the workings of memory and oral tradition in early modern English society. Many ordinary tenants seem to have displayed the long and accurate recall of those who had lived the customs they described for many decades. In a typical Exchequer dispute of 1630, ten witnesses were produced to testify that the tenants of the manor of Okesey in Wiltshire had always enjoyed rights of common pasture in the Forest of Braydon: their average age was 78 years, the most senior being husbandman Thomas Wigmore, a centenarian who claimed to have known these rights for ninety years. In order to establish immemorial usage, however, it was necessary to reach back beyond direct experience into the realms of inherited tradition. In 1628, William Messenger, a yeoman of Chelworth in Wiltshire, testified that tenants from the manor of Leigh also enjoyed rights in Braydon Forest, something he knew to have existed not only from personal experience 'dureinge all the time of his remembrance', which was fifty years, but also by report from 'before his tyme and tyme out of minde, as he has credibly heard by the relacion of [his] father who well new the same beinge aged one hundred yeares or thereabouts att the tyme of his death'.[20]

In this way, 'the memory of man' might extend back with some reliability for at least a century and could involve several generations, as many deponents were quick to establish. In 1565 Richard Hobbes, a 70-year-old husbandman, claimed to know the customs of the manor of Southam in Gloucestershire as one born and bred there, 'and also for that he hathe heard bothe his grandfather and his own father, sometyme beying tenants of Southam, so say and declare'. Richard Mogiar, a husbandman aged 56 in 1574, had been told the bounds of the manor of Gillingham in Dorset 'by ould aunccient men, as by his grandfather and father'.[21]

As a result of such oral transmission there were many in Elizabethan and early Stuart England who had strong memories, at first or second hand, of the days before the dissolution of the monasteries, especially if they lived on lands formerly owned by religious houses. In 1603, for example, a 96-year-old butcher from Horsington in Lincolnshire could recapture the customs of the locality as he had 'hearde his father and other auncyent men of Horsington' speak of practice in the days of 'the Pryoresse of Stixwould'. A few years later, the husbandman Robert Tyllye, who had been born around 1540, still recalled the customs in the days of the Prior of Bath on whose former lands he lived in Gloucestershire, for 'he hath heard his father report' the same.[22] Equally, in the later seventeenth century, there were many ancient inhabitants who had lived through the tumultuous events of the the 1640s and 1650s and could recall the different world in the 'days before the wars'. Typically, in 1675, ten deponents averaging over 72 years of age from parishes adjoining the Forest of Kingswood near Bristol recounted the features of their community, its wildlife, cottages, coalmining, commons and enclosures, 'before the tyme of the late wars'.[23]

This, then, was the environment of memory and oral tradition in which custom had its existence, being imbibed from hand to mouth and transmitted by emulation and example over the generations. Yet, like so much oral tradition, customary law could be vague and ill-defined, subject to many subtle changes over time. Despite the claims, even in good faith, of ancient inhabitants to be recalling immutable practice during their lifetimes, 'and, by report, time beyond the memory of man', the reality was far less consistent. As studies of diachronic verbal communication reveal, imperceptible alterations in narrative, and the practices which structure it, gradually take place, adding up to substantial changes in the long run. Even if people remember their parents and grandparents with a degree of certainty, the value of testimony beyond personal contact can be highly variable and untrustworthy. It was often the case with customary memory that the 'report', faithfully invoked to demonstrate constancy since time immemorial, was based upon very little reliable knowledge.[24]

This lack of precision was of little consequence so long as customs remained free from contention. During the periods in which stable circumstances had given no occasion to question the rights and obligations of customary tenants, subtle changes in usage went unnoticed or unchallenged. However, when conditions arose in the late sixteenth and early seventeenth centuries which put a strain on traditional practice, a stricter and more exact definition of customs was suddenly very important and their indeterminacy became the occasion and the locus of much dispute. A number of factors, including both national and local political struggles, together with the demographic growth and rapidly rising prices which were such defining economic characteristics of this period, may have stimulated the many conflicts over customary rents and tithes, rights of common and of gleaning. Population increases resulted in shortages of both arable and pasture land which led, in turn, to attempts to assart the marginal land of forests, fens, marshes and heaths. As demands on common lands intensified, many landlords, including the Crown, tried to restrict access to them and to take them into their own hands through enclosure. In the face of high inflation, moreover, they sought to maintain their incomes by raising the rents on copyhold lands together with the fines and tributes payable upon its transmission which had hitherto been fixed by custom.[25]

Fixed rents and fines were, of course, greatly advantageous to customary tenants in inflationary circumstances and they fought hard to preserve them. Landlords, or their stewards and lawyers, on the other hand, began ransacking manorial rolls, leases and custumals in an effort to find evidence that the sums involved had varied at some time and were therefore uncertain. James I, motivated perhaps by his exalted view of the power of kings, was at the forefront of this movement in his attempts to replace customary rents and fines on the Crown lands with those at market rates in the early seventeenth century.[26] The resulting disputes which swelled the business of equity courts such as the Exchequer afford an opportunity to gauge the importance placed upon written record in such controversies, as both parties sought to find the valuable documentary corroboration which might prove the validity of the practices which they alleged. Indeed, this resort to legal process, with the premium which it placed upon evidence in writing, was largely instrumental in encouraging the transformation of much customary law, recorded in tradition and kept in memory, into a series of legal rulings set down in decrees and preserved as precedents.

IV

On 7 July 1607, a meeting took place in the chambers of Sir Francis Bacon, the solicitor-general, at Gray's Inn which took a form typical of many of the resultant disputes. Bacon was defending copy-holders from the manor of Great Gaddesden in Hertfordshire, of which Lord Chancellor Ellesmere was the lord. The tenants, headed by one of their number, Thomas Wells, were claiming 'a custom of certeyntye of fines upon dyscents and surrenders after the rate of fower pence an acre and to paye but one harryott onlye for severall copihoulde lands and tenements comeinge into one man's possession'. Ellesmere and his 'learned councell', on the other hand, had examined the manorial records and 'did finde by the . . . court rolles that the sayd fines . . . were uncerten, some-tymes more and sometymes lesse, at the lord's will and pleasure, and that the most of the other pretended customes weare not warranted by the sayde court rolles but meerelye contradicted the same'. At the meeting these rolls were produced, extending back from the reign of Elizabeth to that of Edward II, and they were read aloud. Unfortunately for the tenants, 'by continuall concur-rence of them, it appeared that the fines were uncertain'. They countered by claiming to have an 'ancient customarie' which would bear them out, but they could not produce it. They proffered instead 'a paper booke to prove the certainty of the said fines', but this indicated just as much variance. So it was concluded that the customs were 'therefore held suspitious' and the tenants were forced to concede.[27]

More successful, however, than the Great Gaddesden men were their neighbours, customary tenants of the king's manor of Hemel Hempstead. Exactly two years later, it was decreed by the Ex-chequer Barons that it was his Majesty's 'disposion not to interrupt the antient and setled customes and privileges of any his tenants but to suffer them to enjoy the same according to justice and equitie'. This victory was clinched by virtue of the copyholders being able to produce an award granted to them during the reign of Henry VIII when royal commissioners had settled a dispute between their forebears and the then lord of the manor, John Berkhampsted, also rector of the former monastery of Ashridge. On hearing all of the written and oral evidence, these commissioners had drawn up a deed of twenty-five articles confirming the ancient fines and heriots together with the rest of 'the true and laudable services and customes that hath been used of old tyme and and of right ought to be used in the said mannor', to which all parties had then given assent. Moreover, the subsequent court rolls bore witness to the fact that these customs had remained fixed and unwavering after the dissolution of Ashridge and for all the time since. In the face of such legitimate proofs, the Crown had no grounds on which to overide manorial custom in the quest for increased revenues.[28]

Clearly, access to the written word in such circumstances could be a source of considerable power, therefore. The individual or party who could control and manipulate the documentary evidence was in a position to invoke the authority which writing enjoyed as a standard of proof. Communities carefully guarded the valuable deeds, titles and copies preserved in the padlocked chest at the church or the manor court, while individuals kept their cherished 'evidences' in the family strong box at home. In times of dispute, considerable efforts could be made by both landlords and tenants to monopolise such records: court rolls mysteriously disappeared, custumals were tampered with and parish chests were robbed. For example, an inquisition at Wem, Shropshire, early in the seventeenth century, found that someone had erased and altered the custumal in an effort to validate the claims of the copyholders. Two generations later, however, it was the then landlord, Daniel Wytcherly, who was apparently appropriating all available documents and copies in his attempt to force up rents and fines. He was said to have removed 'a writing' from the penthouse adjoining the manorial court and to have stolen 'a roll, wherein the customes of the manor were expressed, kept in the parish church of Wem in a chest there', only to claim, when challenged, that they 'had beene lost and could not be gott or obtayned'. A similar theft appears to have occurred at Ottery St Mary, Devon, in the 1660s when, as 84-year-old Richard Channon later remembered, 'the court rolls, ledger bookes and other writinges' concerning the local customs suddenly vanished. Since the beginning of Elizabeth's reign they had been 'kept in a little roome within the church . . . under severall lockes and keys . . . for the safe keeping of the same and for the loan use of the lord and copyholders', who had always 'had free accesse to view the same as occasion required', being 'of great concernment to the copyholders and tenants . . . for defence of their titles to their . . . lands and the maintenance of their customes there'.[29]

If some customs such as the value of rents and fines were very likely to be well recorded in writing, other customary practices such as grazing and use rights on commons or waste ground were far less prone to be set down in all their complexity. They remained etched in the memories of commoners and continually rescored by repeated practice. When they came into question, therefore, the best guide to their antiquity, certainty and continuance was usually the oral tradition of the eldest inhabitants. In some cases, common rights may anciently have rested upon a grant or charter from a lord or landowner which had originally bestowed privileges on an ill-defined locality. If there remained a common memory of such a grant and evidence of it could be found, it might provide a reference of crucial significance to those concerned.

The tenants of Rodley in Gloucestershire, for example, claimed rights of common in the Forest of Dean by virtue of a charter dating from the reign of Henry II. In 1592, these rights came into question when villagers from neighbouring manors also tried to assert rights under the same warrant. The inhabitants of Minsterworth, Tibberton, Longhope and Bulley all made their bid 'by colour of the Charter of Rodleye'. Over forty years previously, it was recalled, some of them had gone to Christopher Yerworth, then a local bailiff, 'and produced unto the said bailiff (being learned) their Charter', but he had found that it 'contained no sufficient matter for their freedom of common in the Forest'. During an early seventeenth-century dispute over rights of common in the fens around Littleport, Isle of Ely, the tenants claimed their rights to cut turf and hedge on the authority of a licence granted to them in the thirteenth century by Bishop Hugh Northwold. They were able to produce the famous 'auncient coucher booke' of 1251, an 'ould

booke written in parchment . . . late remaining in the custodye of
the Deane of Elye, which doth expresse or declare . . . the boundes
of the fennes of Littleporte'. In the same way, when Sir Gervase
Clifton was seeking to enclose part of the great wood within his
large manor of Wakefield in the 1630s, the commoners tried to
defend their rights by invoking an ancient charter granted to them
by Earl Warren in the fourteenth century. Eighty-four-year-old
Thomas Somester testified that many times

> he hath seene a deed or charter in wrytinge from Earle Warren
> with a great seale thereto affixed and bound about with silver
> haveing an impression of the [Ex]chequer of the one side and a
> man on horse backe of the other side, made to the burgesses of
> Wakefield, by which the Earle did graunt comon unto them in his
> woods and wastes at Wakefield, excepting in his old parke and
> new parke and great meadowe,

which charter was safe in the parish church, 'being the place where
some evidences concerning the towne of Wakefield are usuallie
kept'.[30]

Such documents could assume iconic significance among commoners who looked upon them as symbols of their privileges and
bulwarks against their attack. The reverenced piece of parchment in the big chest at the church became a hallowed artefact, no
less so for the fact that most people could not read it themselves.
Such was the status of the indenture granted to the inhabitants of
the manor of Epworth in the Isle of Axholme, Lincolnshire, by their
lord, Sir John Mowbray, during the reign of Edward III. It guaranteed no further improvements to the commons there and was
invoked by the local people when repeated attempts were made to
undermine their rights during the seventeenth century. In 1649
Thomas Taylor, yeoman, related the history of the precious deed,
as 'hee hath heard it beene generally reported', and could remember that as a young boy, about fifty years before, he had once seen
it, 'kept in a great chest with barrs of iron in the parish church of
Haxey'.[31]

What was available to tenants was also available to their lords,
however, and they could equally draw upon any ancient documents
which might be recovered to defend their interests. When, for
example, the inhabitants of Thetford tried to claim rights of common in the manor of Westwick, Suffolk, at the beginning of the

seventeenth century, they were countered by the surveyor Robert Buxton who claimed to have seen, among various 'ancient evidences' in the church of All Saints, a 'wryting made in the time of Hamelyn, Earle Warren' and 'an old paper booke belonging to the monks of Thetford' dated 1337, from which he 'inferreth that this Westwick could be no common as is pretended'. The lawyers of the Earl of Devonshire, owner of the rectory of Tutbury, tried to settle some of the long-standing disputes involving bounds, commons and tithes in and around Needwood Forest by producing a charter from the reign of King John given by Lord Ferrers, the Earl of Derby, to the Priory of Tutbury, 'whereby the sayd Earle did grant tythes in the Forest of Needwood to the sayd Pryor and Pryorie of Tutbury in the county of Stafford'.[32]

The boundaries of parishes and manors, so important in defining the limits of commons and wastes, were imprinted upon the minds of community members by the traditions relayed and the demonstrations enacted in annual perambulations and rogations. But during the thirteenth century there had been many accounts taken of the boundaries around Crown lands and royal forests, and the records of these were known to be available to help in the settlement of later disputes. One such contest was heard by the court of Exchequer in 1678, for example, when the demarcation between the Forest of Exmoor in Devon and the commons belonging to its adjoining manors came into question. Many old men attested to the bounds dividing Exford Common from the Forest through a knowledge of the ancient markers which had been solemnly shown to them and imprinted on their memories in youth. Henry Stoke, a 68-year-old yeoman, could relate the 'mearstones' in vivid detail, recalling that:

above firty years since hee . . . did accompany the minister who then served the cure of the parish church of Exford and diverse of the inhabitants in a perambulation or procession which was then made about the bounds of the parish, and [he] doth well remember that in such their perambulacon they did take in and perambulate all of the said Common of Exford comeing up close home to the verge or bounds of the said forest divided by the mearstones or boundaries by [him] before described. And [he] doth well remember that at the time of the said perambulation their was one Silvester Gregory, being an antient inhabitant of the said parish of Exford, that did goe along . . . and if any of the said boundaryes or mearstones . . . were found to be in decay or fallen down, he . . . did take one of the boyes who went along with them following the said procession and lay him upon [it] and then give him some gentle blowes and pinches willing and bidding him to remember that that was an antient boundary or mearstone between the said Forest of Exmoor and Exford Common.

Corroboration was sought by the Exchequer commissioners, however, from 'a record remayning in the Tower of London giving an account of a certaine perambulation, made by comissioners in that behalf, authorized in the nyne and twentieth year of the reign of King Edward the First, of the Forest of Exmoor', together with a 'card or mapp' which showed the boundary markers between it and 'the country adioyning thereunto'. There were, in addition, 'the perambulation of diverse other forests conteined in the said record'. This document was also known to the local inhabitants, for Peter Howndell, yeoman of Exford, testified that he 'hathe seene and heard read unto him a certain paper coppy' of it, which, he claimed, agreed exactly with the course of the perambulation still practised, 'confirmed as well by his owne knowledge and experience as by the sayings of all antient people with whom [he] hath discoursed concerning the same'.[33]

Where they were to be found, therefore, ancient charters could provide vital proof of legitimate rights and liberties. Although they might demonstrate that such privileges had true foundation, however, they were rarely specific as to their precise nature. A medieval deed granting rights of common, for example, was unlikely to stipulate, in detail sufficient to be relevant to future generations, the intimate picture of exactly to whom these rights applied and under what circumstances. Such matters remained the preserve of prescription and usage, ever adapting and developing over the centuries, and only preserved in the memories and oral traditions of current practitioners. The lack of definition associated with such extant written records as there were, together with the inconsistency of verbal transmission, invited controversy over customary law.

V

It was in an effort to try to give precise and detailed fixity to customs that those whom they concerned sought increasingly to have them set down in writing during the sixteenth and seventeenth centuries. Both landlords and tenants in many manors and parishes began, sometimes for the first time, to transfer their customary usages from oral memory to written record. This creation of their own transcripts of custom was a reflection, perhaps, not only of the increased pressure put upon ancient practice by new social, economic and political conditions, but of an increasingly legalistic and documentary culture.

The precise nature and extent of this process of documentation may be established by further statistical analysis or by the detailed study of one particular community over time, but a preliminary survey suggests that the development was both quantitative and qualitative. The great proliferation of surveys, custumals and other similar records, which took place in the later sixteenth and early seventeenth centuries, represented a significant increase in the amount of written evidence available in such cases. 'Constant enquiery into the customs of manors and into the evidence of tenants' titles was', as one historian has put it, 'one of the outstanding features of Elizabethan and early Stuart times, as literally thousands of surviving documents testify'.[34] Moreover, the range of channels through which customs might be formalised and recorded seems to have become more varied and available at the same time, especially with the influence of central courts in local disputes.

Among the important facilitators in this respect were surveyors and manorial stewards, whose numbers were increasing greatly in the sixteenth century. For in their production of books of survey, valuation and assessment, derived from the available evidence in more and more jurisdictions, they compiled what were, in effect, custumals for subsequent reference. Some assessors or stewards drew up, and even had printed, schedules of customs in order to help them in their work and to apprise both present protagonists and future generations of their rights. In 1575, Francis Hinde, Robert Taylor and William Humberston were ordered by Exchequer commission to survey the queen's manor of Over in Cambridgeshire. Because the practices of commoning in this fen country 'have and dayly do alter' they could not 'set downe any custome certaine', but they compiled a list of rights and practices, nevertheless, for ratification at Westminster and preservation in the locality. Thus, it was hoped, the indeterminate and the mutable would be given fixity and permanence by writing. In the same year, officials from the Swanimote Court at King's Cliffe were ordered to survey the royal forests in Northamptonshire, with the result that sets of written orders were drawn up which codified rights of pannage and common in the woods. They were kept for subsequent reference, as was the survey of Rutland, compiled in the first year of Edward VI's reign by Thomas Heyes, which was produced again in 1603 to help establish the true customs of copyholders at the manor of Winge.[35]

The various local and manorial courts also had a crucial influence here. Oral presentments made before the homage or the steward and entered in the court books, gradually accrued into archives of written evidence. From this very process, tenants received education in their customary law as much as from the narratives of the ancients. Typically, the inhabitants of the manor of Farlington in Yorkshire went before the Justice in Eyre in the neighbouring Forest of Galtres in 1571 to recite their rights of common pasture and turbary therein. They were approved by the court and recorded by the steward who held them for safekeeping, being 'ingrossed in parchment conteyninge two or three skinnes, and sealed and subscribed'. In the same way, the husbandman Henry Rutter could relate in 1629 that the inhabitants of Purton Stoke had rights of common in Keynes Wood, Wiltshire, because they had 'made claym to such . . . at divers Justices Seats and Swanimote Courts held within the . . . Forest [of Braydon], which have been ratified there from time to time and allowed of'. The homages themselves often took the initiative in the business of documentation. When, in 1584 there was, at the court baron of the manor of Wigmore in Herefordshire, a jury of 'substanciall gents and yeomen . . . then impannelled', they made a presentment 'in writinge' directing 'that all and every of the auncyente tenants of Alston and Elston had and used to have their severall commons of pasture and estovers in Bringwood [Forest]'.[36]

Elsewhere, people acted independently of the courts in securing written copies of their customary practices and entitlements. Such action was inspired both by disputes between tenants and their landlords, and by conflicts between the tenants themselves. It was in response to the questioning of custom by their lord in 1563, for example, that twenty inhabitants of the manor of Bushey took it upon themselves to write out their customs, apparently citing them from memory since, as they claimed, 'we knowe not where the courte rolles, rentals, or customaryes of the manor are remayning or in whose custodye'. On the other hand, it was inter-community rivalry which lead the inhabitants of Great Wishford in Wiltshire to produce two charters of custom, in 1597 and 1603. The later, entitled 'The Sum of the Ancient Customs belonging to Wishford and Barford out of the Forest of Grovely', set out their common rights of plowbote, hedgebote, housebote and firebote in the Forest while rejecting the claims of their neighbours, of whom 'very many doe often resort into Grovely woodes and fetche fearne and wood there without any auethoritie for the doeing thereof'.[37]

Other statements of custom were the result of private agreements drawn up between contending parties in an attempt to settle the increasing strife caused by such matters. Thus in 1577 a 'schedule' of customs was drawn up for the copyholders of Chesterton, outside Cambridge, and the lord of the manor, Richard Brackyn, for 'finally ending' their 'sundry quarrels' over rents, fines and common rights. A few miles away at Milton, Henry Cooke compounded with his customary tenants to the same end in October 1591, producing another written covenant which was kept as a binding code of practice in the future. Like ancient charters, these documents could assume great significance in the minds of those who came to look upon them as bills of rights. Around 1565, for example, the copyholders of Bosham in Gloucestershire were granted an 'indenture of confirmation of their customs' by their landlord, Henry, Earl of Berkeley, and this 'they for the canonicalness thereof called Bosham bible'. Their bible lasted for over half a century until it was declared void by a decree in Chancery.[38]

As this case demonstrates, the records of decisions and agreements made locally could be superseded by the decrees of the central common law and equity courts to which increasing resort was being made in the sixteenth and seventeenth centuries. These judgments were not only handed down at the conclusion of legal process but those from the courts of Exchequer and Chancery, in particular, were also sought by parties as a means of ratifying a settlement already reached out of court. Thereafter, such decrees could act as precedents and copies of them were kept in estate offices and parish chests, or bound up by tenants in the form of 'a customary book' which was typically entrusted to one of the eldest and most sufficient amongst them. Where this was so, future disputants over custom were likely to base their claims at law as much upon documents of this sort as upon the memory of their elders. This development was to have significant effects upon both popular legal consciousness and general perceptions of the written word.[39]

In 1590, for example, a decree was issued in the court of Exchequer settling tithing customs in the parish of St Mary's, Whittlesey, in Cambridgeshire. Thereafter a copy of it, 'commonly called the customarye booke', was kept by the inhabitants of the parish, 'as a rule and direction for payment of theire tithes'. In February 1628, another Exchequer decree confirmed the rights of common in the Forest of Dean to existing commoners, either freeholders or tenants. Late in 1635 a further Exchequer suit over the same issue elicited several invocations of this document. John Bridgman of Littledean had 'seen a writing ingrossed in parchment purporting an exemplification of a decree under the seal of the Exchequer dated 4 February 3 Charles, concerning the claim of common and other privileges within the Forest of Dean by divers and several persons, townships, places and parishes'. Joseph White of Huntley, clothier, justified the grazing rights of the commoners of Westbury over Walmore Common with similar reference. It was with far less fondness, on the other hand, that many people in the Isle of Axholme looked upon the Exchequer decree of 1636 which ratified the enclosure of Epworth Common. Fifty years later ancient men could still remember how they were persuaded to sign away their rights, regarding the decree as a symbol of their loss.[40]

The authority of these judgments as legal precedents is evident and knowledge of, or access to, them could be of great importance. This was known very well by Mr Hunt, the parson of Lidford in Devon, early in the seventeenth century. One of his predecessors had lost a legal battle over tithes, 'the record whereof remained in the registers office of the Bishop of Exeter'. Hunt was alleged somehow to have appropriated the ruling, for he could boast that he would have his due, 'by reason he had gotten the said recorde into his owne handes'. Indeed, the preservation, or at least the popular memory, of these decrees could endure, like the memory of medieval charters, for many centuries. As late as the 1880s, the tenants of Cadnam and Winsor, adjoining the New Forest, saved their rights over Wigley Common from extinction when it was remembered that one of their number had a strong box containing an 'old paper'. Inside was found to be a Chancery decree of 1591 ratifying their custom. 'But for the big box', it was said, 'which impressed itself on the traditions of the tenants, as connected with their rights, the deed might have been lost.'[41]

VI

So it was that, in variously attempting to transmute oral or ill-defined customs into written and codified documents, people of all sorts attempted to provide themselves with what they believed to be the best means of defending and advancing their rights and interests. This mentality points to the ever greater importance attached to writing, in these circumstances at least, during the early modern period. In some senses, of course, the greater availability and use of texts at this time actually helped to undermine the power of the written word and the authority which it could command, reducing the likelihood of some texts assuming the iconic status which they had enjoyed in a less documentary culture. But as writing became more familiar and more understood it also became more depended upon and more trusted; documents were less likely to be objects of reverence or fear and more often media to be respected and utilised.

The extent to which this quickening process of documentation was then taking place may be exaggerated simply by a survival of records much in excess of that of former centuries. The greatly increasing business of the courts and the developments in legal practice which took place in the sixteenth and seventeenth centuries, however, suggests that many more 'evidences' and decrees were actually produced in these cases of disputed customs as in others. The place of writing in such suits may not be typical of the ways in which oral transmission and textual evidence were coming to be generally perceived at this time. The law, above all spheres perhaps, had long placed great store in the written word as witness, reference and proof. Nevertheless, as one part of the legal realm in which oral tradition was still required and respected, custom offers a revealing area for analysis. On the one hand, the depositions of witnesses provide insight into the working of memory in a partially literate society and, on the other, the evident struggles of all disputing parties to possess written testimony indicates that an appreciation of its value had penetrated deeply in society. Although the evidence is complex and often contradictory, the authority of writing was clearly growing in a number of different contexts at this time, and in a highly litigious age the law was an important agent in promoting documentary habits of mind.

NOTES AND REFERENCES

* I should like to thank Andy Wood for sharing with me his knowledge of the role of central equity courts in disputes over local custom and for his valuable criticisms of an earlier draft of this chapter, as for those of Carolyn Fox, Paul Griffiths, Steve Hindle, Brian Outhwaite, Steve Pincus and Keith Wrightson.

1. Among many works which discuss the implications of writing, see, in particular, J. Goody and I. Watt, 'The Consequences of Literacy', in J. Goody (ed.), *Literacy in Traditional Societies* (Cambridge, 1968), pp. 27–68; W. J. Ong, *Orality and Literacy: The Technologising of the Word* (London, 1982); B. V. Street, *Literacy in Theory and Practice* (Cambridge, 1984); R. Finnegan, *Literacy and Orality: Studies in the Technology of Communication* (Oxford, 1988); J. Goody, *The Logic of Writing and the Organisation of Society* (Cambridge, 1986); J. Goody, *The Interface Between the Written and the Oral* (Cambridge, 1987); R. Thomas, *Literacy and Orality in Ancient Greece* (Cambridge, 1992).

2. M. T. Clanchy, *From Memory to Written Record: England, 1066–1307*, 2nd edn (London, 1993), pp. 46–51. On the earlier use of writing, see S. Kelly, 'Anglo-Saxon Lay Society and the Written Word', in R. McKitterick (ed.), *The Uses of Literacy in Early Medieval Europe* (Cambridge, 1990), pp. 36–62. The wider European context is discussed in S. Reynolds, *Kingdoms and Communities in Western Europe, 900–1300* (Oxford, 1984).

3. 5 Elizabeth I c. 14 and 29 Charles II c. 3, in *Statutes of the Realm*, 11 vols (London, 1810–24), IV, pt. i, pp. 443–5 and V, pp. 839–42.

4. J. W. Salmond, 'The Superiority of Written Evidence', *Law Quarterly Review*, vol. 6 (1890), pp. 75–85; J. K. Weber, 'The Power of Judicial Records', *Journal of Legal History*, vol. 9 (1988), pp. 180–200.

5. W. Lambarde, *Eirenarcha: or, Of the Office of the Justice of Peace* (London, 1581), p. 71; J. Norden, *The Surveyor's Dialogue* (London, 1610), p. 22; J. Evelyn, *The History of Religion*, ed. R. M. Evanson, 2 vols (London, 1850), I, p. 425, quoted in K. V. Thomas, 'The Meaning of Literacy in Early Modern England', in G. Baumann (ed.), *The Written Word: Literacy in Transition* (Oxford, 1986), p. 112.

6. J. Hall, *The Olde Religion* (London, 1628), p. 167; J. Tillotson, *The Rule of Faith* (London, 1666), pp. 38, 50; Anon., 'A Calculation of the Credibility of Human Testimony', *Philosophical Transactions of the Royal Society*, vol. 21 (1699), p. 363; D. Defoe, *A Tour Thro' the Whole Island of Great Britain*, 2 vols (London, 1724–6), I, p. 257. Defoe also rejected tales about witchcraft on the grounds of 'oral tradition': *A System of Magick: or, A History of the Black Art* (London, 1727), p. 225. On the declining prestige of oral evidence in antiquarian scholarship, see D. R. Woolf, 'The "Common Voice": History, Folklore and Oral Tradition in Early Modern England', *Past and Present*, vol. 120 (1988), pp. 26–52.

7. Thomas, 'Meaning of Literacy', p. 113; D. R. Woolf, 'Speech, Text, and Time: The Sense of Hearing and the Sense of the Past in Renaissance England', *Albion*, vol. 18 (1986), pp. 173–8; D. F. McKenzie, 'Speech–Manuscript–Print', *The Library Chronicle*, vol. 20 (1990), pp. 87–109.

8. G. Markham, *The English Husbandman* (London, 1635), p. 9.

9. For some recent discussions of the many and varied contexts in which customary tenures and laws governed social and economic relationships, see C. E. Searle, 'Custom, Class Conflict and Agrarian Capitalism: The Cumbrian Customary Economy in the Eighteenth Century', *Past and Present*, vol. 110 (1986), pp. 106–33; R. W. Hoyle, 'An Ancient and Laudable Custom: The Definition and Development of Tenant Right in North-Western England in the Sixteenth Century', *Past and Present*, vol. 116 (1987), pp. 24–55; L. A. Knafla, 'Common Law and Custom in Tudor England: or, "The Best State of a Commonwealth"', in G. J. Schochet (ed.), *Law, Literature and the Settlement of Regimes* (Washington, 1990), pp. 171–86; E. P. Thompson, *Customs in Common* (London, 1991), ch. 3; A. Wood, 'Social Conflict and Change in the Mining Communities of North-West Derbyshire, *c.*1600–1700', *International Review of Social History*, vol. 38 (1993), pp. 31–58; T. Stretton, 'Women, Custom and Equity in the Court of Requests', in J. Kermode and G. Walker (eds), *Women, Crime and the Courts in Early Modern England* (London, 1994), pp. 170–89.

10. C. Calthorpe, *The Relation beteene the Lord of the Mannor and a Coppy-Holder his Tenant* (London, 1635), pp. 21–3; Sir E. Coke, *The Compleate Copy-Holder* (London, 1641), pp. 68–75; Sir W. Blackstone, *Commentaries on the Laws of England*, 4 vols (London, 1765–9), I, pp. 76–8; C. Watkins, *Treatise on Copyholds* (London, 1797), p. 15. For a recent discussion, see J. W. Wellwood, 'Custom and Usage', in *Halsbury's Laws of England*, 4th edn (London, 1975), XII, pp. 1–60.

11. For this definition, see, e.g., J. Cowell, *The Interpreter: or Booke Containing the Signification of Words* (Cambridge, 1607), sig. V4r; Coke, *Compleate Copy-Holder*, p. 68; R. Gough, *The History of Myddle*, ed. D. Hey (Harmondsworth, 1981), p. 64; R. B. Fisher, *A Practical Treatise on Copyhold Tenure* (London, 1794), p. 34.

12. S. Carter, *Lex Customaria: or, A Treatise of Copy-hold Estates*, 2nd edn (London, 1701), pp. 24–5; J. G. A. Pocock, *The Ancient Constitution and the Feudal Law* (Cambridge, 1957), pp. 32–3.

13. 'The Ancient Customes and Approved Usages of the Honourable City of London', in *The City Law* (London, 1647), p. 20 (I am grateful to

Craig Muldrew for this reference). *The City Law* was said to have been 'translated out of an ancient MS' in the bibliography of W. Camden, *Britannia*, ed. E. Gibson (London, 1695).

14. On the failure of written evidences to record the more complex reality of customary practice, especially concerning customs of common right, see J. Birrell, 'Common Rights in the Medieval Forest: Disputes and Conflicts in the Thirteenth Century', *Past and Present*, vol. 117 (1987), pp. 24–5; E. P. Thompson, 'The Grid of Inheritance: A Comment', in J. Goody *et al.* (eds), *Family and Inheritance: Rural Society in Western Europe, 1200–1800* (Cambridge, 1976), pp. 337, 342–3, 352; J. M. Neeson, *Commoners: Common Right, Enclosure and Social Change in England, 1700–1820* (Cambridge, 1993), pp. 77–80.

15. [P]ublic [R]ecord [O]ffice SP12/283A/80. On the parlous state of records relating to the royal estates, see D. Thomas, 'The Elizabethan Crown Lands: Their Purposes and Problems', in R. W. Hoyle (ed.), *The Estates of the English Crown, 1558–1640* (Cambridge, 1992), pp. 64–5; and on the poor condition of the public records in general, see R. B. Wernham, 'The Public Records in the Sixteenth and Seventeenth Centuries', in L. Fox (ed.), *English Historical Scholarship in the Sixteenth and Seventeenth Centuries* (London, 1956), pp. 11–30.

16. PRO SP12/283A/80. On each of these courts, see W. H. Bryson, *The Equity Side of the Exchequer* (Cambridge, 1975); W. J. Jones, *The Elizabethan Court of Chancery* (Oxford, 1967); L. M. Hill (ed.), *The Ancient State, Authoritie and Proceedings of the Court of Requests, by Sir Julius Caesar* (Cambridge, 1975); R. Somerville, *History of the Duchy of Lancaster* (London, 1953). On the way in which the common law had come to assume jurisdiction in copyhold cases during the sixteenth century, see C. M. Gray, *Copyhold, Equity and the Common Law* (Cambridge, Mass., 1963), chs 2–3.

17. Bryson, *Equity Side of the Exchequer*, pp. 16, 18–19, 33, 168–9.

18. PRO SP12/283A/80.

19. *The English Reports*, 176 vols (Edinburgh, 1900–30), XXI, p. 13, quoted in W. J. Jones, 'A Note on the Demise of Manorial Jurisdiction: The Impact of Chancery', *American Journal of Legal History*, vol. 10 (1966), pp. 306; Cowell, *Interpreter*, sig. V4r, quoted in D. R. Kelley, ' "Second Nature": The Idea of Custom in European Law, Society and Culture', in A. Grafton and A. Blair (eds), *The Transmission of Culture in Early Modern Europe* (Philadelphia, 1990), p. 138.

20. PRO E134/6 Chas 1/Trin 9; PRO E134/4 Chas 1/East 26. On the general importance of elders in societies with strong oral traditions, see Goody, *Interface Between the Written and the Oral*, pp. 150, 164; and in this context, see K. V. Thomas, 'Age and Authority in Early Modern England', *Proceedings of the British Academy*, vol. 62 (1976), pp. 233–4. It is testimony, no doubt, not only to the tardiness of legal process but also to the seniority of most witnesses in disputes over custom that the Exchequer Barons, in their not infrequent rulings to refer cases to the common law, would allow the depositions taken in their court to be used again at a future trial for the benefit of 'all such witnesses as shall be dead or not able to travel' by that time: see, e.g., PRO E126/5, fols. 48v, 54r, 60r, 162r, 207r, 262r.

114   *The Experience of Authority in Early Modern England*

21. PRO E134/7 Eliz/East 1; PRO E134/16 Eliz/East 6. In the later nineteenth century, Lord Hobhouse heard a dispute over common rights and concluded that 'the oral evidence', based upon 'what the old witnesses say of their own knowledge, and what in their boyhood have heard their grandfathers say, must go back for at least 100 years': G. J. Shaw-Lefevre, Lord Eversley, *Commons, Forests and Footpaths* (London, 1910), p. 107.

22. PRO E134/1 Jas I/East 3, m. 10; PRO E134/7 Jas I/Mich 12, m. 4. On popular memories of the days before the Reformation, see K. V. Thomas, *The Perception of the Past in Early Modern England*, Creighton Trust Lecture (London, 1984), pp. 11–23.

23. PRO E134/27 Chas II/Mich 29. Another case, eight years later, revealed more old men with these memories of Kingswood before 'the late troubles': PRO E134/35 Chas II/Mich 48, m. 3. For similar examples from elsewhere, see PRO E134/26 Chas II/Mich 23, m. 11; PRO E134/28 Chas II/East 20. Such reminiscences echo the memories of life 'before the civill warres' which John Aubrey repeatedly committed to paper: see, e.g., *The Remaines of Gentilisme and Judaisme*, ed. J. Britten, Folklore Society (London, 1881).

24. For various examples of the unreliability of oral transmission beyond first-hand experience, see J. Vansina, *Oral Tradition: A Study in Historical Methodology*, trans. H. M. Wright (London, 1965), pp. 101–2; M. T. Clanchy, 'Remembering the Past and the Good Old Law', *History*, vol. 55 (1970), pp. 166–7; D. P. Henige, *The Chronology of Oral Tradition* (Oxford, 1974), ch. 1; R. Thomas, *Oral Tradition and Written Record in Classical Athens* (Cambridge, 1989), pp. 125, 180, 283.

25. For some of these developments, see R. H. Tawney, *The Agrarian Problem in the Sixteenth Century* (London, 1912), pt ii; J. Thirsk (ed.), *The Agrarian History of England and Wales, vol. IV: 1500–1640* (Cambridge, 1967); E. Kerridge, *Agrarian Problems in the Sixteenth Century and After* (London, 1969), pp. 54–7; A. B. Appleby, 'Agrarian Capitalism or Seigneurial Reaction? The Northwest of England, 1500–1700', *American Historical Review*, vol. 80 (1975), pp. 574–94; R. B. Manning, *Village Revolts: Social Protest and Popular Disturbances in England, 1509–1640* (Oxford, 1988), ch. 6. Similar conditions were experienced in the late thirteenth and early fourteenth centuries: Reynolds, *Kingdoms and Communities*, p. 137; Birrell, 'Common Rights', pp. 22–3.

26. G. Batho, 'Landlords in England, 1500–1640', in Thirsk (ed.), *Agrarian History*, pp. 268–73; R. W. Hoyle, ' "Vain Projects": The Crown and Its Copyholders in the Reign of James I', in J. Chartres and D. Hey (eds), *English Rural Society, 1500–1800* (Cambridge, 1990), pp. 73–104; Hoyle, ' "Shearing the Hog": Reforming the Estates, c.1598–1640', in Hoyle (ed.), *Estates of the English Crown*, pp. 204–62.

27. Huntington Library, San Marino, California, Ellesmere MS. 233.

28. PRO E126/1, fols. 129v, 130r, 133–6.

29. Kerridge, *Agrarian Problems*, p. 56. PRO E134/26 Chas II/Mich 48; PRO E134/18 & 19 Chas II/Hil 13. For similar examples of the appropriation and corruption of written records, see PRO E126/1. fol. 46r; PRO E126/2, fol. 9r; PRO E126/5. fol. 206v; PRO E126/6, fols. 155v–56r,

Custom, Memory and the Authority of Writing — 115

204v–9r; Manning, *Village Revolts*, p. 137; E. P. Thompson, *Whigs and Hunters: The Origin of the Black Act* (London, 1975), p. 179; J. Martin, 'Private Enterprise versus Manorial Rights: Mineral Property Disputes in Eighteenth-Century Glamorgan', *Welsh History Review*, vol. 9 (1978), p. 171; C. E. Hart, *The Free Miners of the Forest of Dean and the Hundred of St Briavels* (Gloucester, 1953), pp. 137, 303–4. On the increasing number of parish chests from the sixteenth century, see W. E. Tate, *The Parish Chest: A Study of the Records of Parochial Administration in England*, 3rd edn. (Cambridge, 1969), pp. 37, 44–51.

30. PRO E134/34 Eliz/Hil 23, and quoted in C. E. Hart, *The Commoners of Dean Forest* (Gloucester, 1951), p. 14; [C]ambridgeshire [R]ecord [O]ffice P109/28/4; PRO E134/4 Jas I/Hil 14, m. 6 and PRO E126/1, fol. 46r; PRO DL4/94/46.

31. PRO E134/1649/Mich 11. On the iconic status of the Mowbray charter, see K. Lindley, *Fenland Riots and the English Revolution* (London, 1982), pp. 26–7; C. Holmes, 'Drainers and Fenmen: The Problem of Popular Political Consciousness in the Seventeenth Century', in A. Fletcher and J. Stevenson (eds), *Order and Disorder in Early Modern England* (Cambridge, 1985), p. 192.

32. PRO E134/1 Jas I/Trin 7, mm. 5–6; PRO E134/30 & 31 Chas II/Hil 5.

33. PRO E134/30 Chas II/East 21; see also PRO E134/30 Chas II/Mich 12. For the use of other perambulations from the reign of Edward I in Exchequer decisions, see PRO E126/1, fol. 184r; PRO E126/4, fol. 48v. The perambulation taken of Waltham Forest in 29 Edward I (1301) is printed in W. R. Fisher *The Forest of Essex: Its History, Laws, Administration and Ancient Customs* (London, 1887), pp. 393–9; and those of the Forest of Mendip for 1219, 1279, 1298 and 1300 are printed in J. W. Gough (ed.), *Mendip Mining Laws and Forest Bounds*, Somerset Record Society, vol. 45 (Frome, 1931), pp. 164–92. References to further thirteenth-century perambulations can be found in J. C. Cox, *The Royal Forests of England* (London, 1905), pp. 99, 125, 148, 151, 204, 229, 234–5, 247, 276, 284, 290–1, 336, 341.

34. Batho, 'Landlords in England', p. 304; and see M. Campbell, *The English Yeomen under Elizabeth and the Early Stuarts* (London, 1960), pp. 106–7; C. W. Brooks, *Pettyfoggers and Vipers of the Commonwealth: The 'Lower Branch' of the Legal Profession in Early Modern England* (Cambridge, 1986), p. 200.

35. CRO 258/M22; P. A. J. Pettit, *The Royal Forests of Northamptonshire: A Study in Their Economy, 1558–1714*, Northamptonshire Record Society (Gateshead, 1968), pp. 153–4; PRO E134/4 Jas I/Mich 1, m. 3. On the failure of other surveyors to establish certain customs in the face of conflicting oral evidence and ever changing practice, see PRO E134/28 Chas II/Trin 7, mm. 4–5; Campbell, *English Yeomen*, pp. 123–4. On the growing number of surveyors at this time and the documents that they produced, see Kerridge, *Agrarian Problems*, pp. 26–31; V. Morgan, 'The Cartographic Image of "The Country" in Early Modern England', *Transactions of the Royal Historical Society*, 5th series, vol. 29 (1979), p. 134; Brooks, *Pettyfoggers and Vipers*, pp. 198–203.

116   *The Experience of Authority in Early Modern England*

36. PRO E134/4 Chas I/East 26, m. 9; PRO E134/5 Jas I/East 12; PRO E134/5 Jas I/East 7. For a later example, see Thompson, 'Grid of Inheritance', pp. 352 n, 354–5.

37. Tawney, *Agrarian Problem*, pp. 126–8; R. W. Bushaway, ' "Grovely, Grovely, Grovely, and All Grovely": Custom, Crime and Conflict in the English Woodland', *History Today*, vol. 38 (May 1981), pp. 39, 42; and Bushaway, *By Rite: Custom, Ceremony and Community in England, 1700–1880* (London, 1982), pp. 209–11. On the conflicts within communities over who was entitled to customary rights, see B. Sharp, 'Common Rights, Charities and the Disorderly Poor', in G. Eley and W. Hunt (eds), *Reviving the English Revolution* (London, 1988), pp. 107–37.

38. CRO 399/E6; CRO L3/17/3; J. Smyth, *The Berkeley Manuscripts*, ed. Sir J. Maclean, 3 vols (Gloucester, 1883–5), II, p. 433; Kerridge, *Agrarian Problems*, p. 57.

39. On the 'growing authority accorded to decisions of the central courts' in such cases, see Jones, *Elizabethan Court of Chancery*, pp. 487–8; and Jones, 'Demise of Manorial Jurisdiction', pp. 315–18. For an example of the practice of keeping these decrees in the form of 'a customary book', see P. Large, 'Rural Society and Agricultural Change: Ombersley, 1580–1700', in Chartres and Hey (eds), *English Rural Society*, p. 123. There is also evidence that leading tenants might have such decrees or other judgments put into print in order to create multiple and accessible copies for the community: R. W. Bushaway, 'Rite, Legitimation and Community in Southern England, 1700–1850: The Ideology of Custom', in B. Stapleton (ed.), *Conflict and Community in Southern England* (Stroud, 1992), p. 113; and see the examples in chapter 8 below.

40. PRO E134/28 Chas II/Trin 7, m. 11; PRO E134/11&12 Chas I/Hil 2, and Hart, *Commoners of Dean Forest*, pp. 36–8; PRO E134/1&2 Jas II/Hil 25. A further Exchequer decree of 1638 sanctioned drainage and enclosure at Whittlesey: see PRO E134/27 Chas II/East 28; CRO 126/M88–90. On the enclosures at Epworth, see Lindley, *Fenland Riots*, pp. 27–33. The Exchequer Barons could deal harshly with anyone who challenged the authority of their decrees, but they themselves were quite prepared to revoke decisions made by the court in former times: see, e.g., PRO E126/1, fols. 76r–80r, 109v, 283; PRO E126/3, fols. 270v–72r.

41. PRO E134/3 & 4 Chas I/Hil 11, m. 6; Eversley, *Commons, Forests and Footpaths*, pp. 126–8; Thompson, *Customs in Common*, p. 159.

4 Separate Domains? Women and Authority in Early Modern England*

BERNARD CAPP

In 1602 Samuel Rowlands published a humorous story under the catchy title *Tis Merrie when Gossips meete*.[1] It describes how three London women (a widow, wife and maidservant) meet in the street one day and go off to a tavern, where they feast on sausages and claret and gossip for hours about marriage and men. Rowlands' story sets the scene for this chapter: it suggests how ordinary women could create their own social networks and their own social space, and hints at the potential implications for male authority. A Star Chamber case twenty years later offers a far more dramatic example of 'gossips' in action. Thomas Bulwer, a London apothecary, described how his former maidservant Joan Knipe had waged a war of revenge against his family ever since being turned away. It had climaxed one night in October 1622, after she and a female companion told their friends that Bulwer and his son were whoremongers, his daughters whores and his wife a witch. Around midnight Joan led an angry crowd to the Bulwers' house, where they pelted the door and windows with dirt and dung and screamed abuse at the occupants. She made similar attacks on other nights, and persuaded another friend, single and pregnant, to give out that Bulwer's son had fathered her child. Bulwer complained that the vendetta had damaged the family's good name and the marriage prospects of his children. Though Joan denied the charges, the case illustrates graphically the power that even a lowly maidservant might wield with the support of her friends.[2]

I

Female power and autonomy had no place in contemporary views of a well-ordered society. Women were seen as physically, morally and intellectually weaker, a view largely endorsed by scripture, classical antiquity and medical science. It followed that women should live obediently under the authority of the most appropriate male, whether father, master or husband. Commentators taught that the family was a miniature commonwealth in which the father was king. Every woman must obey her husband whatever his personal shortcomings, for subjects could have no right to resist. 'Ye are underlings, underlings, and must be obedient,' the Edwardian Reformer Hugh Latimer told his female auditors. Women could have no part to play in public life at any level; their lives belonged wholly to the domestic sphere. The Newcastle merchant Ambrose Barnes advised his daughters, in a memorable phrase, to model themselves on the tortoise – 'the emblem of a woman who should be a keeper at home, as the tortoise seldom peeps out of its shell'. Making the same point more conventionally, the Puritan Robert Cleaver stressed that the good wife was a housewife, 'not a streetwife, one that gaddeth up and down'.[3]

The deep-rooted patriarchal values of the period are too familiar to need rehearsing here. It is clear too that most women acknowledged the inferiority of their sex and to some extent 'colluded in their own oppression', as Judith Bennett has put it.[4] But relations between the sexes, both in theory and practice, were far more complex than any simple patriarchal model would suggest. Obedience to a father or master was very different from that owed by a wife to her husband. Puritan preachers and moralists insisted that a wife was the 'helpmeet' and partner of her husband, not a mere underling; he owed her respect as well as affection. The rule of a husband was by nature mild, the Puritan Richard Sibbes observed optimistically, 'though it be not a parity, yet it comes as near as can be'.[5] The obedience a woman owed to the magistrate or the king was different again, and not without its ambiguities. Though it was agreed that women (like children) had no place in the political sphere, being 'included' in their fathers or husbands, this belief rested on convention rather than law. And what of older spinsters and widows? The franchise was based on property rights, and several aristocratic widows took part in returning MPs on the strength of inherited status. Thus Lady Dorothy Packington, 'lord and owner of the town of Aylesbury', was able to return the rotten borough's two MPs to the Parliament of 1572. But when a group of less august widows tried to vote in a contest for Suffolk in 1640, the sheriff barred them on the grounds that their votes would be 'dishonourable' – not, we note, illegal.[6] The principle that women were included in their husbands for political purposes could raise problems of its own. If a husband's demands contradicted those of the magistrate, where did his wife's duty lie? – a problem which arose quite frequently in the religious sphere. It sometimes happened that a wife's beliefs differed from those of both husband and magistrate, in which case she had to balance her personal sense of duty to God against the claims of both private and public authority. The Henrician Protestant Anne Askew and the York recusant Margaret Clitheroe both chose to follow their consciences, and both paid the terrible price of martyrdom.

When we turn from theory to practice the position becomes still more complex. Even the basic principle that only men should bear rule was far from universally observed. The well-known achievements of a number of female monarchs, from ancient times to Elizabeth, raised questions which contemporaries were reluctant to pursue very far. Single or widowed women might be lords of the manor, wielding considerable power. On a much humbler plane, single women occasionally held parochial office where it rotated among local property owners.[7] At the level of the family itself, roughly 20 per cent of all households were in fact headed by women. Most were poor and elderly widows living alone, but by no means all; an increasing proportion of younger and better-off widows with children were remaining single from choice. In London and other ports, sailors' wives might have to support their families for months or years on end while their menfolk were away at sea, while at the bottom of the social pyramid there were many deserted wives forced to maintain themselves and their children by their own efforts. In all these families domestic authority was in practice matriarchal. And in some communities two or three poor, single women might even choose to live together in all-female families.[8]

'Conventional' families too might often show a significant gap between theory and practice. Men sensed that domestic authority was at best precarious, and the ballads, jestbooks, pamphlets and plays of the period are full of uneasy jokes about assertive, shrewish wives and hen-pecked husbands. In *The Merry Wives of Windsor* (II. i) Mistress Page is even shown vowing – if only in jest – to 'exhibit a bill in the parliament for the putting down of men'. Many contemporaries, convinced that female insubordination posed a serious threat, could see no cause for jests and lashed out savagely. Bishop Latimer complained that many women regarded male authority as a 'trifle' they could safely ignore; not so, he thundered, it was 'a matter of damnation and salvation'. The preacher William Whately insisted that a husband who failed to rule his wife was himself committing sin, while conceding that for men to maintain such rule was 'sooner said than done'.[9] The handful of embittered or violent wives who took domestic rebellion to the point of murder exerted a horrified fascination over contemporaries. At Myddle, Shropshire, townsfolk passed down for generations the chilling story of how three local women had once conspired to poison their husbands on the same night. Such 'unnatural' women featured far more often in ballads and news-pamphlets than wife-murdering husbands.[10]

Behaviour diverged from the prescribed patterns outside as well as inside the home. Women often showed little of the docility and submissiveness expected of their sex, resorting to abuse and sometimes blows against other women. Some harangued men too. If that was hardly new, the degree of male concern it provoked in this period is striking. David Underdown and Susan Amussen have argued that early modern England witnessed something of a moral panic over relations between the sexes. These fears, they suggest, can be attributed in part to the population explosion of the late sixteenth century, which brought in its wake inflation, greater social mobility, poverty and unemployment. Men who perceived society itself as under threat were hypersensitive to the stability of the family. Such fears naturally varied according to time and place, and Michael Roberts has pointed to particular tensions in late sixteenth-century London as young women from the provinces flocked to the capital to enter domestic service. The resulting casualisation of such work reduced social control over them, and led to fears that young women living 'at their own hands' would drift into prostitution or crime. Men responded to these perceived threats with a formidable array of weapons designed to curb the 'unruly woman': the cucking stool for scolds and shrews, the persecution of witches (often akin to scolds), mocking rhymes, and public shaming rituals such as 'rough music' and 'skimmingtons'. 'Loose women' might be despatched to Bridewell, and single young women living outside the immediate authority of a man might be arrested or expelled on those grounds alone. Any woman who stepped too far outside accepted norms of behaviour faced formidable and humiliating sanctions.[11]

The most striking examples of 'disorderly women' are to be found in riots over grain prices, enclosures, common rights and other issues. Women quite often took part in such riots, and some involved only women.[12] These episodes raise the question of female attitudes to male authority in the public sphere – and vice versa. Most riots were in effect demonstrations, designed to bring a local grievance to the attention of the magistrate and trigger his intervention. The presence of women in food riots is not really surprising, for they did much of the small-scale buying of grain and were most directly affected by sudden price increases or shipments out of the region. With a strong sense of fair prices and fair trading practices, they were natural champions of traditional rights and customs. But we can also find women rioting in very different and less obvious contexts. In August 1577, for example, some thirty women stormed the chapel at Brentwood, Essex, and barricaded themselves inside. They held off the sheriff and his men with pitchforks, bills, bows and arrows, a hatchet and kettles of boiling water, until the building was eventually retaken by storm. The sheriff, we note, was also the local squire; he had claimed the chapel as his inheritance and was intending to close it.[13] What needs explaining in such episodes is the surprisingly restrained response of the authorities to flagrant breaches of order and female propriety. In the Brentwood case the inhabitants had brought a suit in Chancery to prevent the chapel's closure, but probably feared the squire would demolish it before the case was resolved. The women's defiance proved highly effective: the Privy Council directed that any punishments were to be 'only for form's sake', and the chapel survived. The explanation may lie partly in the ambiguous position of women in the eyes of the law and the magistrate; some commentators held – mistakenly – that protests over food by women acting alone were not even covered by the law.[14] In certain circumstances such ambiguities could serve the interests of all parties, enabling the authorities to dismiss protests by women – by definition emotionally unstable – as misguided but not politically threatening. How could they be, when women did not exist politically? The magistrates could then intervene to remove the grievance, leaving authority intact with minimal loss of face. Had it been men storming the chapel at Brentwood, authority would probably have required a bloody retribution. Paradoxically, then, women could sometimes turn their inferior legal and political status to their own advantage and that of their menfolk.

Where rioters aimed at very limited change, the English Revolution brought about the overthrow of monarchy, episcopacy and Parliament. Though the Revolution was, of course, the work of men, contemporaries noted that women of all classes were playing more active roles in public than ever before, preaching, pamphleteering and demonstrating. Many men believed that the upheavals of civil war had seriously damaged authority within the family as well as in the State and society, and some feared that female activism posed a serious threat to the entire political, religious and social order.[15]

The most important of these developments was collective female petitioning. Early in 1642 there were mass petitions to Parliament denouncing episcopacy and protesting against the decay of trade. In the period 1646–53, women petitioners pressed for the release of imprisoned Leveller leaders, while 1659 saw a petition against tithes allegedly signed by 7000 Quaker women. Female activists were not necessarily radical in their politics or religion, however. In August 1643, for example, several thousand female petitioners lobbied Parliament, demanding peace. And in many cases the petitioners' behaviour was far more militant and shocking than the petitions themselves. The petitioners of August 1643 threatened to lynch John Pym, whom they blamed for the war, attacked the Trained Bands, and dispersed only when charged by mounted troopers with their swords drawn.[16] Mass petitioning was the nearest the English Revolution came to a protofeminist movement. Those involved were mainly concerned with limited and immediate objectives, but they were well aware of the novelty of their proceedings and the authorities were quick to remind them. One MP told petitioners loftily that 'the House could not take cognisance of their petition, they being women, and many of them wives, so that the law took no notice of them'. In 1643, women petitioners were told to leave matters of state to men, and 'go home . . . and meddle with your huswifery'.[17] Such snubs demanded a response, forcing the petitioners were forced to reflect on their actions and question the wisdom of centuries. Significantly, they offered no direct challenge to patriarchal assumptions, conceding that women were by nature inferior to men. Instead they argued from scripture that God might choose to work through 'the weaker vessel', and insisted that men and women were both created in God's image. Margaret Fell, the Quaker, demanded only spiritual freedom for women though she observed tartly that 'God hath put no such difference between the male and female as men would make'. Only on a very few occasions did the arguments move on to a secular plane. In 1649 Leveller women insisted that they had 'a proportionable share in the freedoms of this commonwealth', and the right to defend them independently. For women to claim a right to their own voice in public affairs, instead of being included in their menfolk, was a momentous step.[18]

The long-term effects of this civil war activity are much harder to establish. Female religious radicalism was to contribute little to women's subsequent emancipation. Radicals generally confined their claims to the religious sphere, and in the later seventeenth century the sects adopted an increasingly conservative stance on female preaching and prayer. Moreover, female militants, especially Quakers, provoked a backlash that may well have hardened male attitudes in the nation at large. Restoration women writers felt constrained to adopt a more cautious, defensive and conciliatory tone[19] – though it does not necessarily follow that ordinary women felt the same constraints in their everyday behaviour.

Any significant long-term gains from the civil war era were probably indirect. It is quite likely, paradoxically, that the acceptability of women on the Restoration stage owed something to the more visible roles women had played during the 'Puritan Revolution'. More important was the reduced power of the Established Church over the lives of ordinary people. For generations the Church had been the major vehicle for patriarchal teaching; after 1660 it had to compete with the Dissenters, and after 1688 it faced a world in which church attendance was in practice no longer compulsory. The significance of these changes for women – not altogether positive – is impossible to measure but we should not overlook it. Easier to quantify is the rise in the number of publications by women writers. The gains made here during the Revolution were maintained to the very end of the period.[20] Women had thus secured a platform for their ideas and interests, and some kind of implicit recognition of their right to a public voice – all the more important as female literacy rose in the late seventeenth century. And not all late Stuart women were conciliatory. In the Revolution of 1688 some women again wrote pamphlets, petitioned, and joined demonstrations. Among the first groups to lobby William of Orange on his arrival in England were fifty west-country women demanding vengeance against Judge Jeffreys for the Bloody Assizes of 1685.[21] Theirs was not a spirit of submission. Nor was that of Mary Astell and her circle. Astell was an overtly feminist writer, scornful of the male sex and its values. Her High Church, Tory convictions remind us that radicalism on gender issues was not confined to those of more general radical persuasion. Though Astell was not an activist and had few ideas on how society might be reshaped to offer women a better deal, she was certainly alive to the gender implications of contemporary politics. If James II had been driven out because arbitrary, absolute rule was unacceptable, she asked, how could men claim absolute rule over their wives?[22]

No consensus has yet emerged on the long-term changes in women's position over this period as a whole. The evidence is contradictory. In the economic sphere, guilds steadily tightened their controls in Tudor and early Stuart England, reducing opportunities for women; on the other hand, the importance of the guilds and of apprenticeship was declining by 1700, freeing the labour market for women at the lower levels. Most ordinary women in late Stuart London were engaged in paid work, and better-off women could find an economic niche as rentiers, money-lenders, land-ladies, retailers and so on.[23] More generally, Underdown and Amussen argue that the sense of gender crisis had weakened by 1700, as population pressure eased and the social and political order felt more secure. The law was now sufficient to contain any residual threats to order, Amussen suggests; insistence on order within the family to underpin social stability no longer seemed urgent. A concern with disorderly women and prostitutes is still evident in late seventeenth- century London, for example in So-cieties for the Reformation of Manners, but complaints against 'proud wives' now focused more often on indolence and luxury than rebelliousness.[24] In the religious sphere, the Reformation had in many ways a negative impact on the religious position of women, through the dissolution of convents and confraternities. Balancing this is the fact that early Protestantism, separatism, Dissent and Catholic recusancy each saw strong-minded women defying and even deserting their husbands in the name of obedience to God, and holding their own informal gatherings for prayer and discussion. These were for the most part short-lived developments, however, and traditional values on gender soon gained the upper hand within the new religious movements. Overall, we may conclude, what emerges most clearly throughout the period is the ability of patriarchy to adapt successfully to changing circumstances.[25]

II

The debate over women and authority, among contemporaries and historians alike, has mainly focused on the issue of submission or defiance. Any full analysis, however, would need to be conceived in much wider terms, for submission and defiance were not the only possible responses to male authority. 'Accommodation' or 'negotiation' offered an important and often preferable alternative. 'Accommodation', I will argue in the remainder of this chapter, is central to a proper understanding of gender relations in early modern England – as in very many other times and places.[26]

'Accommodation' here signifies women's ability to soften and sometimes bypass male authority without challenging it outright. The law, on the whole, was reluctant to intervene in domestic relations except in extreme circumstances, and in this sphere women possessed considerable leverage. Most men chose a wife at least partly for companionship, and while they expected to rule their families they were also looking for domestic harmony. Within the home the exercise of authority therefore reflected the interplay and balance of personalities. Other factors also came into play, including the wife's contribution to the family economy and the role of local opinion, in particular the readiness of friends, relations and neighbours to intervene if either partner strayed too far from accepted social norms. One important aspect of this was that many women had a circle or network of female friends, or gossips, who could bring pressure to bear in time of need as well as offering moral support and some degree of social autonomy. All these points need to be addressed; the role of female networks, still relatively unexplored, deserves special attention here.

The interplay of personalities leaves little mark in official records but features prominently in literary sources from ballads to drama, and can often be traced in personal documents such as diaries and memoirs. Thus William Stout tells how his easy-going brother Josias, a Lancashire farmer, married a younger but strong-minded wife and opted for a quiet life rather than trying to assert his authority. She was able to 'treat her friends at pleasure', William noted disapprovingly, 'more than would have been allowed by most of husbands'.[27] By contrast the Yorkshire yeoman Adam Eyre and his wife Susan were both obstinate people and their marriage was correspondingly stormy. When Adam came home late from an alehouse on 11 August 1647 he found himself locked out and Susan told him bluntly that 'she would be master of the house for that night'. Eyre's diary is a sad chronicle of marital strife.[28] Such friction was a common theme in popular ballads, many of which depict tough-minded women more than ready to stand their ground. The outcome varies, offering something for every taste: some ballad wives submit, others compromise, while a few are shown triumphant over their worthless partners. In *The Woman's Victory* [1684–95] a young wife tells how she eventually rebelled against an old, jealous and violent husband and beat him into submission. The ballad is addressed to young married women and presents its spirited heroine as a model for other wronged wives to follow. We should not necessarily take the message at face value, of course: the intention may have been rather to show the danger of such ill-matched marriages. None the less, we should be aware of the possible effect of such ballads in countering and perhaps subverting the patriarchal teaching of the Church.[29]

A second factor influencing the exercise of domestic authority was the wife's role as manager of the household. A husband needed cooperation as well as obedience from his partner, and compromise was the most likely means to secure it. The convention that men should bear rule was moreover balanced by a strong sense that each sex had its own responsibilities, on which the other ought not to trespass. Managing the household was seen as woman's work, and conduct-book writers warned husbands against meddling in it. This deep-rooted convention gave women some degree of autonomy within the household, as well as authority over the children and servants – including the right to inflict physical punishment on both.[30] A wife was thus in effect a subordinate magistrate within the miniature commonwealth of the family, a position which gave her some ability to 'negotiate' with its head. A weak, submissive wife would be a poor mistress of the household, lacking the authority to control the servants or to hold her own in the cut-and-thrust of market trading. The proverbial wisdom that it was 'better to marry a shrew than a sheep' sums up the recognition that a passive wife was a liability: beyond a certain point wifely submissiveness was against the interests even of the husband. This was even more important where the wife made a significant contribution to the family income, whether through helping her partner or by her own paid work. Women did much of the small-scale buying and selling at local markets, while many helped with seasonal tasks such as haymaking; in dairying regions they made and sold butter and cheese. Urban women took on paid work making and mending clothes, nursing, charring, laundering, and selling in the street or market-place. We find female witnesses in London church courts emphasising that they lived by their own earnings as well as their husbands'; one referred proudly to stocking-making as her 'profession'. In seventeenth-century Colyton, Devon, bone lace-making provided a well-paid craft for women quite separate from local patterns of male employment. It is surely significant that in London and elsewhere a woman's occupation might well be very different from that of her husband.[31] Female labour, if rarely well paid, thus brought some measure of social and economic independence and helped to reinforce the status of wives as partners rather than servants.

None of these considerations, of course, could guarantee a satisfactory marital relationship. Some wives inevitably found themselves trapped in domestic misery. In such a predicament their best chance of relief lay in winning the help and support of their 'gossips', and the exercise of authority within the household therefore needs to be set within the wider social context of the neighbourhood. In particular, we need to understand how such female networks came into being, and what part they played in women's lives. The first and obvious point is that women were never tied wholly to the home; their lives revolved equally around the street, the well and the market-place. In managing a household they had to visit neighbours to borrow food, utensils, money, or fire, fetch water from the well, take dirty clothes to the washing place and perhaps bread to the bakehouse, visit the pawnbroker, and so on. Such activities brought them into the company of other women on a daily basis. Female sociability found little place in the conduct-books, but it was central to female experience. A woman might linger to chat with her friends at the well, washing place, or bake-house. If working at home she would often prefer to sit in the doorway to spin or knit, rather than inside the house; at the door she could expect company as well as more light and room. Seven-teenth-century travellers often describe women working in com-pany, carrying distaffs and spinning as they strolled along the lane together, for example, or 'knitting four or five in a company under the hedges', as Celia Fiennes noted in Norfolk.[32] Court depositions offer a similar picture: women spinning together in the bakehouse while waiting for their bread to be baked, or assembling in a Durham churchyard in the 1570s to spin or bleach cloth.[33] In the case of street vendors and market-women, work, sociability and leisure were still more closely enmeshed. In 1623 Elizabeth Wilson of West Ham, market-woman, told a court how she would bring the family's produce to sell in the city; when business was done for the day in question, she and her gossips had repaired to the King's Head near Leadenhall to drink a pint or two of wine before setting off for home.[34] Female work thus brought women together in their own social networks, and created what was to some extent a separ-ate, female domain.

The parish church, perhaps unexpectedly, also contributed to the development of female networks. Though the church was a male-dominated institution, especially after the Reformation, men and women were usually required to sit apart, and such arrangements inevitably fostered a sense of collective gender identity. This could even cut across family ties. Husbands and wives did not always attend the same services, and when they did might not go together. Robert Cleaver complained that men often left their wives to follow them later, with the servants coming later still (if at all). A sense of collective female identity is apparent in the wide range of activities accepted as belonging to women alone. It was common in the fifteenth and early sixteenth centuries for the parish 'wives' or 'maidens' to assume responsibility for fundraising or maintaining specific religious furnishings. In Stanford in the Vale (Oxon.) two 'fontwives', elected annually, collected money for a church stock in a tradition which survived into the early seventeenth century. Widespread customs such as rush-bearing were recognised throughout the period as a female activity. The custom for rival bands of men and women to capture and extort money from members of the opposite sex on Hock Monday and Tuesday, to raise funds for the parish, is all the more striking in that the women's groups were far more successful.[35]

  There was a second and even more important link between religion and female sociability. The most common term for a woman's female friend in this period was 'gossip' – that is, god-sib, kin via baptism. Though in the religious sense 'a gossip' could be a godparent of either sex, the term in its wider sense was used almost invariably of women alone. This doubtless reflects the far more important part played by women in the rites of passage from childbirth to baptism and beyond. As Adrian Wilson has shown, usually only the midwife and married female neighbours attended a birth.[36] Once it was safely over, they shared in merry-making from which men were strictly barred. An unusual case at Great Tew (Oxon.) in 1633 shows how seriously this gender rule was applied: an inquisitive male servant put on women's clothes to gain admittance and then found himself prosecuted for indecency. The crossdressing is striking, but so is his recognition that only by such means could he ever hope to enter this female domain.[37] Women also dominated the other rituals linked to childbirth. It was women friends who took the new infant to be baptised a few days after its birth, while the mother herself still lay in childbed. The same friends might then attend her 'upsitting' and escort her a few weeks later to be churched, the ceremony which marked her return to society. Theologians might argue about the religious significance of churching, but David Cressy has shown that for the women involved it was primarily a social celebration for themselves and their friends, usually followed by a dinner or drinking in which women again played a central role.[38] Breaches of these customs were frowned upon. One Essex woman who went to be churched with her husband instead of her gossips was prosecuted for such unseemly behaviour.[39] The strength of custom had resulted here in the Church itself upholding the ties of gender over family.

  Many women thus enjoyed a supportive network of female friends, meeting in private houses, in the street, at the well and at church. These networks constituted a semi-separate domain outside the family structure and beyond male control. That is what made them significant – and so disturbing to men. The term 'gossip' often carried the pejorative connotations it has today, to describe a woman who spread idle, false or malicious tales. Men, of course, had their own networks, through guilds and alehouses, for example, and were just as ready to spread tales about their neighbours. But the term 'gossip' was very rarely applied to men in this context. Male companionship was more acceptable, and male assessment of their neighbours' behaviour an integral part of parochial order. Language itself thus worked to support male values, denigrating female sociability and pushing women back to the home as their only legitimate sphere. Yet most men were reluctantly aware that female sociability was too deep rooted to be challenged, and recognised also that it provided vital practical support and advice for their own wives on family and household care.[40] Many men were therefore ambivalent about female social networks. The preacher Robert Cleaver laid down only that the good wife 'must avoid gossiping, further than the law of good neighbourhood doth require'[41] – a significant qualification. Ambivalence is evident too in the usage of the term 'gossip' itself. In this period the word was by no means necessarily pejorative: it was frequently used in a neutral or positive sense to describe a woman's female friends and counsellors, and women are shown addressing each other as 'gossip' as a term of affectionate address.[42]

III

What roles might such networks play in the lives of their members? First, as already mentioned, they provided practical help and information on domestic matters and childcare. Second, they provided an important focus for recreation. Female leisure remains largely unexplored and was much less elaborate than its male equivalent, but many customs were clearly gender specific. Some were calendar based, especially those involving younger women: maids wassailed at Christmas, London milkmaids danced through the streets at Easter. Married women too might organise collective activities at particular seasons. We find the wives of one London parish celebrating Easter Monday 1557 by playing at barley-break with the parish priest, rounding off their day with drinking and feasting at a tavern;

their menfolk spent the day separately, at archery and other masculine pursuits. Less structured activities were equally important,
such as the visits married women paid to one another's homes.
Younger women and servants left at home on Sundays might seize
the opportunity for some fun together: four young women were
presented at Wisbech in 1638 for 'sporting at the bowling green in
time of divine service'. Sometimes the fun was more organised. In
1649, a Somerset girl took some malt to the local brewer to be made
into beer, announcing that 'she together with some other maidens
. . . had a desire to be merry together'.[43]

A third function of female networks, more central to this chapter,
was to give ordinary women some degree of social autonomy. Daily
social interaction fostered what we might call a 'female public
opinion', giving women an informal authority over their neighbours, especially their female neighbours. At the same time, it could
encourage a more complex response to male authority, helping
women to contain and negotiate male domination as well as providing a temporary refuge from it. The 'law of good neighbourhood'
was women's best weapon and protection, both as individuals and
collectively. Informal networks offered leverage and a *de facto* authority that has been little recognised.

For the most part this power was exercised over other women. At
the most basic level it consisted of gossip and insults on the conduct
and character of neighbours. Such gossip might spring from genuine moral concern about the good name of the neighbourhood,
or be used to pursue personal or family quarrels. In either case it
was a powerful weapon, for reputation – especially sexual reputation – was central to every woman's social position. Any individual
who fell under suspicion and failed to clear her name might well
face serious consequences – ostracism, dismissal, marital violence
and breakdown, and prosecution. Many charges of witchcraft originated in gossip spread by other women, and defamation cases in
church courts by women were as likely to be brought against female
as male slanderers.[44]

It was, of course, quite possible for women (or men) to deal with
suspected adulterers and fornicators by setting in motion the machinery of the church courts. In practice women (like men) often
preferred to act informally. Gossip was a speedy, free and powerful
sanction, controlled by themselves rather than officials. Men and
women might often act together against a particular offender, but

as much of a woman's everyday life was bound up with her female
neighbours, social pressure was very likely to have a gender dimension. Social ostracism, such as insults and the refusal of small gifts
or loans, would operate initially within the 'female domain'. If these
weapons proved insufficient, women (as well as men) could resort
to public shaming rituals. Female rituals were usually less elaborate
than the male-dominated skimmingtons and rough music, but far
more common; we often find women using raucous abuse in public
places to intimidate an offender and even drive her out of the
neighbourhood. These sanctions might sometimes assume a quasi-
judicial form. During this period it was common for courts to
empanel a 'jury of matrons' to examine female felons pleading
pregnancy, search an alleged witch, or pressurise an unmarried
mother to reveal the father's name; it is less well known that
ordinary women sometimes established informal 'juries' on their
own initiative. Their usual purpose was to examine or interrogate
pregnant girls, though they can be found in other circumstances
too. In 1584, for example, 'divers honest women' of Churchill,
Oxfordshire, subjected one of their neighbours to a humiliating
physical examination to determine whether she might have passed
on venereal disease to the vicar.[45] In such a case the search itself was
a cruelly shaming ritual, whatever its outcome. On a later occasion
a group of women at Wellow, Somerset, seized Mrs Mary Love 'and
in rude and shameless manner cast her upon the board and showed
her privy parts and afterwards washed the same with salt and water,
and then thrust her out of the company'. The salt symbolised her
sexual 'itch', cooled and cleansed by the ritual washing, while the
symbolic expulsion signified her rejection by the community.[46]
Women might thus take joint action on their own initiative over
suspected sexual offences, and similarly over petty thefts by female
neighbours or maidservants. They were in effect claiming the right
to choose – as men did too – between dealing with such offenders
informally and invoking the law.[47]

Gossip, insults and informal juries offer striking illustrations of
female power over other women. None of them posed a direct
threat to male authority. Indeed they were reinforcing the high
value men placed on female chastity, and it is likely that men often
connived at them. But a recent suggestion that female gossip simply
reinforced male supremacy tells less than the whole story.[48] Insults
and shaming rituals against a woman were quite likely to put pres-

sure on particular men too, and often deliberately so. One consequence of shaming a promiscuous woman, for example, was to limit
the sexual freedoms of her male neighbours. And when women
directed abuse at an adulterous wife they usually also intended to
put pressure on her weak or complaisant husband. Both sexes saw
cuckolds as offenders, not victims, and very often abuse was directed at both partners. Thus Elizabeth Mobbs stood at her door in
Bishopsgate one September evening in 1628 heaping invective on
her neighbours, the Tutchins: 'Get thee in, thou wittol, thou cuckold, and put on thy horns,' she taunted the husband, 'for thy wife is
a whore.' (A wittol is a complaisant cuckold.) Mobbs made a point
of identifying and ridiculing the wife's lover, mocking him as the
'town bull', and she added to the Tutchins' embarrassment by
blowing a horn to attract others to the scene.[49] This case and many
others show how easily women's actions could spill outside the
'female domain': Elizabeth Mobbs was shaming not only the alleged 'whore' Jane Tutchins but the two men also involved, the
feeble husband and the local stud. Her gesture was intended to
constrain the behaviour of them all.

In such cases women were not undermining *legitimate* male authority; they were shaming men who had abused or neglected that
authority. A protesting neighbour, moreover, was not challenging a
male with any direct authority over her. The position was far more
sensitive, however, when a wife felt herself seriously wronged and
wanted redress against a violent or adulterous husband. Conduct-
book writers accepted that she might plead with him, but gave her
no right to defy his authority. In extreme cases a wronged wife
could turn to the law. Some battered or frightened women turned
to a local magistrate, asking him to bind over a violent husband or
male neighbour to keep the peace towards her; this allowed tempers to cool, and was relatively informal and private.[50] It was rare,
however, for a wife to bring charges against her husband. Such a
step was bound to exacerbate tensions, and there was no guarantee
of a fair hearing. Even women suing for legal separation on the
grounds of marital cruelty knew they were likely to be branded as
shrewish and disobedient, and always took care to stress that their
own behaviour had been modest and dutiful.[51]

A wronged wife had one further option, however, and often the
most effective: she could fight back, alone or with her gossips, using
informal and indirect methods. The most common response of a

wife who found her husband involved with another woman was to confront her rival rather than the straying partner. Such a response minimised domestic conflict by avoiding any direct challenge to patriarchal authority. She might plead with the other woman to stay away, or beg the rival's kinsfolk to apply pressure of their own. If neither proved sufficient she might threaten physical violence, sometimes by vowing to slit the rival's nose – a shaming as well as disfiguring injury.[52] In desperation she might turn to shaming rituals of a still more public kind, several of which are documented in church court records. There was, for example, a commotion outside a lodging-house in Horn Alley, St Botolph's, Aldgate, one summer's evening in 1632. The landlady, investigating, discovered a female stranger shouting and scolding in the street, surrounded by a crowd of curious onlookers. The stranger heaped abuse on one Margaret Eddis, who had recently taken lodgings in the house, calling her a 'pocky whore' and 'hospital whore'. Margaret, she claimed, was having an affair with her husband, and she complained bitterly that he had pawned almost all the family's goods, even the children's clothes, for money to spend on her. Now she was fighting back. She had 'rousted' Margaret out of one place already, and she was determined to drive her out of these lodgings too. The strategy was plain: to whip up public outrage to shame Margaret into giving up the liaison or quitting London altogether.[53] Her outburst reminds us that infidelity could spell financial ruin for the whole family as well as destroying the emotional security of the innocent party.

In this episode, as often, the injured wife was acting alone, though her success depended on winning the sympathy and support of others. In a few cases, by contrast, we find wives resorting to more elaborate shaming rituals which also involved their friends and physical as well as verbal abuse. Possibly the most extreme, reported in a contemporary pamphlet by John Taylor, was played out in a baker's shop in Drury Lane in 1638. Convinced that her husband was having an affair with a former nursemaid, the baker's wife recruited her gossips for a brutal revenge. She lured the nurse back to her house, where the gossips were lying in wait; they seized and gagged her, tore off her clothes, and flogged her with birch rods. They had a razor and basin to hand too, apparently planning to shave her head as further humiliation; when her struggles rendered that impractical they dragged her into the street and ducked her under a pump till she was rescued by passers-by. Not surprisingly, the case made a considerable stir and was still remembered twenty-five years later.[54]

In the cases described above the challenge to male authority was oblique. Even the barber's wife and her friends had followed the convention of attacking the suspected rival, not the straying husband. In cases of marital violence, however, there was no female third party to confront and in these circumstances a wronged wife might sometimes resort to direct though highly discreet shaming rituals against the offender. John Taylor tells the story of a Southwark waterman's wife, beaten by her drunken spouse, who took her revenge a few days later by serving him some broth made with rope instead of eels; when he complained she observed tartly that she was only giving him what he had given her. That might sound like the product of Taylor's fertile imagination, but Flora Thompson describes a very similar episode in 'Lark Rise' in the late nineteenth century, and notes that such devices were a traditional and effective remedy against violent husbands.[55] Such mild reproofs, however, would obviously only work against less hardened offenders. In serious cases the wife's most promising strategy was once more to complain to her neighbours and kin. Susan Amussen has argued that most women rated wifely obedience as far less important than sexual honesty, so an abused wife might turn to her friends for moral and practical support. A bad husband might then find himself the target of hostile gossip and jeers. In one contemporary ballad a woman spurned by her drunken, wastrel husband resolves to go 'and to my neighbours make my moan'; in another two angry women agree that the local wife-beaters deserve to be hanged; and a third shows a worried husband complaining that his wife's gossips rail at him in the street about his behaviour towards her. It is likely that gossips would also discuss such matters with their husbands, who might then bring their own informal pressure to bear. And if a bad husband proved recalcitrant, the gossips or their menfolk – rather than the injured wife herself – might eventually decide to invoke the law by informing a churchwarden or constable.[56]

Women often had grievances, of course, against men other than their husbands. They might be propositioned, abused or cheated in the fields, the street or the market-place. In such circumstances they were often ready to stand their ground and trade insults, but such a response carried its own risks. In any serious confrontation the man would be likely to smear the woman's sexual reputation –

a weapon far more powerful than any at her own disposal. Though husbands were expected to stand by their wives in such cases, many a slandered wife felt she had no option but to bring a defamation suit to clear her name. The law offered little chance of redress for the original provocation. Married women often dared not even tell their husbands about sexual advances or assaults by other men: their position was too vulnerable, an 'honest' reputation too easily lost, a husband's response too unpredictable. And the courts themselves were far more likely to side with the male, so that a complaint might easily backfire.[57]

Here too then there was good reason for women to turn to their friends for support and protection. A single woman in dispute with a man was at a massive disadvantage, but women acting together might well be able to threaten his position. While gossip and jeers were the usual weapons, there is also some evidence of women taking more extreme measures against male offenders. In 1662, we find six Middlesex women joining together to bring charges of cruelty against a male neighbour after he had savagely beaten his maidservant.[58] There is some evidence too, if mainly literary, of offenders being subjected to physical retribution; the humiliation of the philandering Falstaff by the merry wives of Windsor is only the best known of many such stories. A few tales even describe wives and their gossips beating adulterous husbands and their paramours.[59] It would be very surprising to find such an episode paralleled in court records, but perhaps unwise to dismiss such stories out of hand. In 1563, for example, the chronicler Henry Machyn recorded the humiliation of a lecherous London priest in circumstances that recall Falstaff's own discomfiture. Machyn tells how the priest had offered money to a woman in return for sexual favours; she pretended to accept but also tipped off her friends, who then lay in wait at the rendezvous at the time appointed. When the priest arrived and stripped, they pounced.[60]

There is nothing implausible in Machyn's account. Neighbours felt a collective responsibility for the good name and well-being of their district, and women felt quite entitled to take independent action against any male who threatened it. Thus Richard Carew, the Elizabethan antiquary, tells of a Cornish hamlet which suffered an unfounded reputation for promiscuity, and how travellers passing through it liked to taunt the inhabitants. But the local women, he reports, would defend the honour of their community by flinging

the contents of their chamberpots at such rogues.[61] Nor were collective actions confined to issues of sexual honour. The Elizabethan
pamphleteer Robert Greene tells how a group of London women
seized and bound a coal-dealer who had repeatedly cheated them;
constituting themselves judge and jury, they condemned him to a
sound cudgelling and carried out the sentence with gusto.[62]
Women might also defend the religious honour of their neighbourhood. At Exeter in 1536 angry women attacked workmen ordered
to demolish the rood-loft of a local priory, while in 1547 militant
Catholic women in Stepney allegedly conspired to murder a Protestant zealot they saw as defiling the purity of their neighbourhood.[63]
A sense of collective responsibility, once implanted, might be trans-
ferred to almost any situation.

IV

Much of this chapter has been concerned with women's actions in
a domestic context. Earlier, however, we saw that women sometimes
took a very active part in riots and civil war demonstrations. Is there
a link? And what can riots and demonstrations tell us about women
and male authority in the public sphere?

We should note, first, that boundaries between the private and
public spheres were blurred. A domestic problem might concern
the neighbourhood, and neighbourhood action could easily raise
issues of public order and authority. Greene's story of the cheating
coalman raised precisely this issue, as he was well aware. Housewives
were expected to resolve their own domestic problems, but the
maintenance of proper trading standards surely belonged to the
magistrate. Greene's own comments reflected the ambiguities of
such a case: magistrates ought to stamp out such abuses, he observed, but in the meantime other wives would do well to take
similar direct action.[64] It was only a short step from beating a
dishonest collier to rioting against a profiteering grain dealer.

Second, it is clear that women's respect for authority in the public
sphere was by no means total or automatic. We can find many
individuals expressing indifference or contempt in a wide variety of
circumstances.[65] As we saw earlier, women had no recognised standing in the public sphere, and therefore no formal place in the
hierarchy of public authority. In any clash between the interests of

the family and the claims of public authority, women would often choose the former without hesitation. There are numerous examples of wives (and daughters) showering abuse and sometimes blows on constables, bailiffs and tax collectors trying to distrain their family property. We can find similar defiance inspired by religious passions. A York woman summoned before the town council in 1576 for recusancy told the messenger bluntly that she had better things to do than attend the mayor; her husband, we note, was also a recusant.[66]

In the case of female riots and demonstrations the most intriguing question is whether the women had been set on by their menfolk, as the courts generally suspected, or had acted on their own initiative, as the women often claimed.[67] There are instances of both. In most cases women who took independent action probably did so in the knowledge that their menfolk would approve. The fact that magistrates were likely to look more leniently on female protest must have influenced the thinking and behaviour of men and women alike. When an overzealous official arrested a minister in Co. Durham one Sunday in 1629, for example, the local bailiff declared angrily that 'it had been well done of the *wives* of the town to have joined together and have stoned him forth of the town'.[68] He knew that such action by men would have been classed as seditious, whereas by women it might well have been condoned. The question of initiative is, however, to some extent a red herring. Whether or not women acted independently, the success of any protest depended on their solidarity and determination in action.[69] The militant demonstrations over the Brentwood chapel in 1577 or outside Westminster Hall in the 1640s were possible only because there was social cohesion among the demonstrators, a cohesion rooted in the tradition of informal social interaction.

In food and enclosure riots women knew they would have at least moral support from their menfolk. In a handful of episodes, however, there is the suggestion of a specifically female response to events in the public sphere. Many London women, for example, appear to have judged the marital behaviour of Henry VIII by private rather than political criteria, viewing Catherine of Aragon as an innocent wife unfairly cast aside. In October 1531, the Venetian Ambassador reported, 7–8000 women had marched out of London to waylay and kill her usurper, Ann Boleyn. Their action, we note, was reproducing the common response of a wronged wife and her friends – to confront the other woman rather than the adulterous husband.[70] Also remarkable, on a much smaller scale, is the story of a maidservant hanged for infanticide at Oxford in 1658. After being taken down from the gallows she revived, only to be seized from her friends during the night and hanged again from a tree; Anthony Wood records that 'the *women* were exceedingly enraged at it, cut down the tree whereon she was hanged', and hurled abuse at the bailiff responsible whenever they met him in the street.[71] These episodes, unlike many demonstrations, cannot be explained as appeals to a higher authority: they suggest, rather, contempt and perhaps a sense of dissociation from public authority. Could it be that women, largely excluded and viewed with disdain by the State and the law, might sometimes respond in kind, preferring their own values to those of the magistrate?

V

This chapter has ranged widely in both time and space, seeking broad patterns at the expense of local or temporary variations. I have argued that ordinary women in early modern England were not the helpless, passive victims of male authority, despite the barrage of patriarchal teaching fired at them throughout the period. Far from being confined to a narrowly domestic sphere, as many commentators wished, they enjoyed a lively public life in the street, at the market and at church. Their networks of friends or 'gossips' offered some measure of support, independence and even power. There was in effect a semi-separate female domain, a subculture which existed uneasily and at times almost invisibly alongside the dominant, masculine culture of the age. In some contexts, male and female networks were defending values common to both; in others, their interests were in conflict. Though women never demanded equality, their networks provided a refuge from patriarchal authority and a means to contain and accommodate it. In the right circumstances, whether a local food crisis or the upheavals of civil war, this subculture could generate dramatic and sometimes violent behaviour in sharp contrast to the traditional, submissive stereotype. E. P. Thompson once remarked that eighteenth-century female rioters 'appear to have belonged to some pre-History of their sex before its Fall . . . unaware that they should have waited for some two hundred years for their Liberation'.[72] The role of female networks helps us to make sense of that 'pre-History': demonstrations by women were not a bizarre anomaly but could grow quite naturally from everyday sociability and cooperation. It *was* merry when gossips met, as Samuel Rowlands observed, but 'gossiping' also helped to mould the social character of early modern England.

NOTES AND REFERENCES

* This is a revised version of papers given at Birmingham, the Institute of Historical Research (London), Nottingham Trent and Warwick. I am grateful to the participants, and also to the editors, for their comments.

1. Reprinted in S. J. G Herrtage (ed.), *The Complete Works of Samuel Rowlands* (London, 1880), vol. I.

2. Public Record Office STAC 8/56/17.

3. G. E. Corrie (ed.), *Sermons by Hugh Latimer*, Parker Society, vol. 16 (Cambridge, 1844), p. 253; W. H. D. Longstaffe (ed.), *Memoires of the Life of Mr Ambrose Barnes*, Surtees Society, vol. 50 (Durham, 1867), p. 69; R. Cleaver, *A Godly Forme of Household Government* (London, 1614), sig. 06v. For surveys, see, e.g., I. Maclean, *The Renaissance Notion of Women* (Cambridge, 1980); S. Amussen, *An Ordered Society: Gender and Class in Early Modern England* (Oxford, 1988); D. H. Coole, *Women in Political Theory: From Ancient Misogyny to Contemporary Feminism* (Brighton, 1988).

4. J. Bennett, 'Feminism and History', *Gender and History*, vol. 1 (1989), p. 263. For a striking case study, see N. H. Keeble, ' "The Colonel's Shadow": Lucy Hutchinson, Women's Writing and the Civil War', in T. Healy and J. Sawday (eds), *Literature and the English Civil War* (Cambridge, 1990), pp. 227–47.

5. See, e.g., A. Fletcher, 'The Protestant Idea of Marriage in Early Modern England', in A. Fletcher and P. Roberts (eds), *Religion, Culture and Society in Early Modern Britain* (Cambridge, 1994), pp. 161–81; Amussen, *Ordered Society*, pp. 41–7; M. J. M. Ezell, *The Patriarch's Wife: Literary Evidence and the History of the Family* (Chapel Hill, 1987). For Sibbes, see C. Hill, *The World Turned Upside Down* (Harmondsworth, 1975), pp. 309–10.

6. J. E. Neale, *The Elizabethan House of Commons* (London, 1949), pp. 182–3; D. Hirst, *The Representative of the People? Voters and Voting in England Under the Early Stuarts* (Cambridge, 1975), pp. 18–19.

7. C. Bridenbaugh, *Vexed and Troubled Englishmen* (Oxford, 1968), pp. 247–8; R. Thompson, *Women in Stuart England and America* (London, 1974), p. 223.

8. J. Boulton, *Neighbourhood and Society: A London Suburb in the Seventeenth Century* (Cambridge, 1987), pp. 128–9; B. Todd, 'The Remarrying Widow' in M. Prior (ed.), *Women in English Society, 1500–1800* (London, 1985), pp. 54–92; P. Sharpe, 'Literally Spinsters: A New Interpretation of Local Economy and Demography in Colyton in the Seventeenth and Eighteenth Centuries', *Economic History Review*, 2nd series, vol. 44 (1991), pp. 46–65;

R. Wall, 'Woman Alone in English Society', *Annales de Demographie Historique* (1981), pp. 303–17.

9. Corrie (ed.), *Sermons by Hugh Latimer*, p. 253; W. Whateley, *A Bride-Bush: Or, A Directive for Married Persons* (London, 1623), pp. 97–9.

10. J. A. Sharpe, 'Domestic Homicide in Early Modern England', *Historical Journal*, vol. 24 (1981), pp. 29–48; F. E. Dolan, 'Home-Rebels and House-Traitors: Murderous Wives in Early Modern England', *Yale Journal of Law and the Humanities*, vol. 4 (1992), pp. 1–31; R. Gough, *The History of Myddle*, ed. D. Hey (Harmondsworth, 1981), pp. 148–9.

11. D. Underdown, 'The Taming of the Scold: The Enforcement of Patriarchal Authority in Early Modern England', and S. Amussen, 'Gender, Family and the Social Order, 1560–1725', both in A. Fletcher and J. Stevenson (eds), *Order and Disorder in Early Modern England* (Cambridge, 1985), pp. 116–36, 196–217; D. Underdown, *Revel, Riot and Rebellion* (Oxford, 1985); M. Roberts, 'Women and Work in Sixteenth Century English Towns', in P. Corfield and D. Keene (eds), *Work in Towns, 850–1850* (Leicester, 1990), pp. 86–102; J. M. Beattie, 'The Criminality of Women in Eighteenth-Century England', *Journal of Social History*, vol. 8 (1974–5), pp. 103–7. On single women 'at their own hands', see the contribution of Paul Griffiths to this volume, Chapter 5 below. The idea of a crisis in gender relations has recently been questioned by M. Ingram, ' "Scolding Women Cucked or Washed": A Crisis in Gender Relations in Early Modern England?', in J. Kermode and G. Walker (eds), *Women, Crime and the Courts in Early Modern England* (London, 1994), pp. 48–80.

12. J. Walter, 'Grain Riots and Popular Attitudes to the Law: Maldon and the Crisis of 1629', in J. Brewer and J. Styles (eds), *An Ungovernable People: The English and Their Law in the Seventeenth and Eighteenth Centuries* (London, 1980), pp. 47–84; R. B. Manning, *Village Revolts: Social Protest and Popular Disturbances in England, 1509–1640* (Oxford, 1988), pp. 96–8; R. Houlbrooke, 'Women's Social Life and Common Action in England from the Fifteenth Century to the Eve of the Civil War', *Continuity and Change*, vol. 1 (1986), pp. 176–86. Cf. E. P. Thompson, *Customs in Common* (London, 1991), pp. 192, 233–4, 305–36; and R. Malcolmson, *Life and Labour in England, 1700–1780* (London, 1981), pp. 117–18 for female rioters in the eighteenth century.

13. *Acts of the Privy Council, 1577–78*, pp. 12, 34–5; A. C. Edwards, *English History from Essex Sources, 1550–1750* (Chelmsford, 1952), pp. 56–7; *VCH Essex*, vol. VIII, pp. 100–1.

14. Manning, *Village Revolts*, pp. 96–7.

15. K. V. Thomas, 'Women and the Civil War Sects', *Past and Present*, vol. 13 (1958), pp. 42–62; Hill, *World Turned Upside Down*, ch. 15; C. Durston, *The Family in the English Revolution* (Oxford, 1989); P. Crawford, *Women and Religion in England, 1500–1720* (London, 1993), esp. chs 7–8; P. Crawford, 'The Challenges to Patriarchalism', in J. Morrill (ed.), *Revolution and Restoration: England in the 1650s* (London, 1992), pp. 112–28; P. Mack, *Visionary Women: Ecstatic Prophecy in Seventeenth-Century England* (Berkeley, 1992).

16. P. Higgins, 'The Reactions of Women', in B. Manning (ed.), *Politics,*

Religion and the English Civil War (London, 1973), pp. 179–222; B. Reay, *The Quakers and the English Revolution* (London, 1985), p. 83.

17. Higgins, 'Reactions', pp. 203, 207–8, 211.

18. Ibid., pp. 208–17; M. Fell, *Womens Speaking Justified* (London, 1666), p. 3.

19. E. Hobby, *Virtue of Necessity: English Women's Writing, 1649–88* (London, 1988), pp. 11, 18 and chs 4–6.

20. P. Crawford, 'Women's Published Writings, 1600–1700', in Prior (ed.), *Women*, pp. 212–14.

21. L. G. Schwoerer, 'Women and the Glorious Revolution', *Albion*, vol. 18 (1986), pp. 195–218.

22. M. Astell, *Reflections upon Marriage*, 3rd edn (London, 1706), quoted in B. Hill (ed.), *The First English Feminist* (London, 1986), p. 76.

23. P. Earle, 'The Female Labour Market in London in the Late Seventeenth and Early Eighteenth Centuries', *Economic History Review*, 2nd series, vol. 42 (1989), pp. 328–53.

24. Amussen, *Ordered Society*, ch. 6; on Societies in London, see R. B. Shoemaker, *Prosecution and Punishment: Petty Crime and the Law in London and Rural Middlesex c.1660–1725* (Cambridge, 1991), ch. 9; on 'female idleness', see P. Earle, *The Making of the English Middle Class* (London, 1991), pp. 163–6.

25. Bennett, 'Feminism and History', p. 264.

26. See, e.g., L. Gordon, *Heroes of Their Own Lives: The Politics and History of Family Violence: Boston, 1880–1960* (New York, 1988).

27. J. D. Marshall (ed.), *The Autobiography of William Stout of Lancaster, 1665–1752*, Chetham Society, 3rd series, vol. 14 (Manchester, 1967), p. 159.

28. A. Eyre, 'A Dyurnall, or Catalogue of All My Accions', in C. Jackson (ed.), *Yorkshire Diaries and Autobiographies in the Seventeenth and Eighteenth Centuries*, Surtees Society, vol. 70 (Durham, 1877), p. 54.

29. *The Woman's Victory* begins 'Young married women, pray attend/ To these few lines which I have penned/ So will you clearly understand/ How I obtained the upper hand.' See further N. J. Raistrick, 'Seventeenth Century Broadside Ballads and the Portrayal of Women' (unpublished University of Warwick MA thesis, 1992), chs 3–4; J. Wiltenburg, *Disorderly Women and Female Power in the Street Literature of Early Modern England and Germany* (Charlottesville, 1992), pp. 90–1 and chs 6–7.

30. See, e.g., Cleaver, *Godly Form*, sig. A7, B2; W. Gouge, *Of Domesticall Duties* (London, 1634), pp. 255–6.

31. Guildhall Library, London, MS 9189/1 (Examinations, 1622–23), fol. 51; see generally L. Duffin and L. Charles (eds), *Women and Work in Pre-Industrial England* (London, 1985); Roberts, 'Women and Work'; Earle, 'Female Labour Market'; Earle, *Making of the English Middle Class*, pp. 158–74; M. D. George, *London Life in the Eighteenth Century* (London, 1966), pp. 425–8; K. Snell, *Annals of the Labouring Poor: Social Change and Agrarian England, 1660–1900* (Cambridge, 1985), chs 1 and 6; Sharpe, 'Literally Spinsters', p. 55 and passim.

32. 'Thomas Baskerville's Journeys in England, *temp.* Car. II', *Historical*

Manuscripts Commission: Portland MSS, Vol. II, p. 266; C. Morris (ed.), *The Journeys of Celia Fiennes* (London, 1947), p. 150.

33. J. Raine (ed.), *Depositions and Other Ecclesiastical Proceedings from the Courts of Durham,* Surtees Society, vol. 21 (Durham, 1845), pp. 295–7; for bakehouses see, e.g., 'Baskerville's Journeys', p. 303.

34. Guildhall Lib. MS 9189/1, fol. 74.

35. M. Aston, 'Segregation in Church', in W. J. Sheils and Diana Wood (eds), *Women in the Church,* Studies in Church History, vol. 27 (Oxford, 1990), pp. 237–94; Cleaver, *Godly Forme,* sig. C2–C3; R. Whiting, *The Blind Devotion of the People: Popular Religion and the English Reformation* (Cambridge, 1989), pp. 6, 105; E. Duffy, *The Stripping of the Altars: Traditional Religion in England 1400–1580* (New Haven, 1992), pp. 147–8, 150; *Stanford-in-the-Vale Churchwardens' Accounts, 1552–1728,* transcribed V. M. Howse (Stanford-in-the-Vale, 1987), pp. 27, 44, 147 and passim; R. Hutton, *The Rise and Fall of Merry England: The Ritual Year, 1400–1700* (Oxford, 1994), p. 26.

36. A. Wilson, 'The Ceremony of Childbirth and its Interpretation', in V. Fildes (ed.), *Women as Mothers in Pre-Industrial England* (London, 1990), pp. 68–107.

37. [O]xfordshire [A]rchives [O]ffice Oxford Archdeaconry Papers c. 12 (Act Book 1633–4), fol. 75.

38. D. Cressy, 'Purification, Thanksgiving and the Churching of Women in Post-Reformation England', *Past and Present,* vol. 141 (1993), pp. 106–46.

39. Wilson, 'Ceremony of Childbirth'; F. G. Emmison, *Elizabethan Life: Morals and the Church Courts* (Chelmsford, 1973), pp. 160–1.

40. See, e.g., the remarks in *Tis Not Otherwise: Or, The Praise of a Married Life* [1626–36], in H. E. Rollins (ed.), *A Pepysian Garland: Black-Letter Broadside Ballads of the Years, 1595–1639* ([1922], repr. Cambridge, Mass., 1971), p. 359.

41. Cleaver, *Godly Forme,* sig. F7. The phrase appears to have been formulaic: see Houlbrooke, 'Women's Social life', p. 173.

42. For example, by Jonson, Rowlands and balladeers.

43. J. G. Nichols (ed.), *The Diary of Henry Machyn,* Camden Society, old series, vol. 42 (London, 1842), p. 132; W. M. Palmer (ed.), *Episcopal Visitation Records of Cambridgeshire* (Cambridge, 1930), p. 69; G. R. Quaife, *Wanton Wenches and Wayward Wives: Peasants and Illicit Sex in Early Seventeenth-Century England* (London, 1979), pp. 66–7.

44. L. Gowing, 'Language, Power and the Law: Women's Slander Litigation in Early Modern England', in Kermode and Walker (eds), *Women, Crime and the Courts,* pp. 26–47; J. A. Sharpe, *Defamation and Sexual Slander in Early Modern England: The Church Courts at York,* University of York, Borthwick Papers no. 58 (1980); M. Ingram, *Church Courts, Sex and Marriage in England, 1570–1640* (Cambridge, 1987), ch. 10; Amussen, *Ordered Society,* pp. 101–4; J. A. Sharpe, 'Witchcraft and Women in Seventeenth-Century England: Some Northern Evidence', *Continuity and Change,* vol. 6 (1991), pp. 179–99; C. Holmes, 'Women: Witnesses and Witches', *Past and Present,* vol. 140 (1993), pp. 45–78.

45. E. R. Brinksworth (ed.), *The Archdeacon's Court: Liber Actorum, 1584,*

Oxfordshire Record Society, vol. 22 (Oxford, 1942), p. 64; cf. L. Gowing, 'Gender and the Language of Insult in Early Modern London', *History Workshop Journal*, vol. 35 (1993), p. 8. For a recent discussion of 'juries of matrons' in witchcraft and other cases, see Holmes, 'Women', pp. 65–75.

46. Quaife, *Wanton Wenches*, p. 170; on the sexual symbolism of salt and water, see OAO Archdeaconry Papers c. 118 (Depositions 1616–20), fol. 50–50v; J. M. Rosenheim (ed.), *The Notebook of Robert Doughty, 1662–1665*, Norfolk Record Society, vol. 54 (Norwich, 1989), p. 64.

47. G. Walker, 'Women, Theft and the World of Stolen Goods', in Kermode and Walker (eds), *Women, Crime and the Courts*, pp. 81–105.

48. M. Chaytor, 'Household and Kinship: Ryton in the Late Sixteenth and Early Seventeenth Centuries', *History Workshop Journal*, vol. 10 (1980), p. 49.

49. Greater London Record Office DL/C/231, Consistory Court Depositions 1627–30, fols. 47v–49.

50. M. Hunt, 'Wife Beating, Domesticity and Women's Independence in Eighteenth-Century London', *Gender and History*, vol. 4 (1992), p. 18; see, e.g., Rosenheim (ed.), *Notebook of Robert Doughty*, pp. 53, 59; C. Z. Wiener, 'Sex Roles and Crime in Late Elizabethan Hertfordshire', *Journal of Social History*, vol. 8 (1974–5), pp. 43–4.

51. Hunt, 'Wife-Beating', p. 15; Wiener, 'Sex Roles', pp. 43–4; Beattie, 'Criminality of Women', pp. 86–7; cf. L. Roper, *The Holy Household: Women and Morals in Reformation Augsburg* (Oxford, 1989), ch. 5.

52. OAO Archdeaconry Papers c. 118, fol. 265v; Gowing, 'Gender', p. 10, Gowing, 'Language, Power and the Law', p. 32; M. Parker, *Well Met Neighbour* [c. 1640], in W. M. Chappell (ed.), *The Roxburghe Ballads*, vols. I–III, The Ballad Society (London, 1871–80), III, p. 100; cf. Quaife, *Wanton Wenches*, p. 26.

53. Guildhall Lib. MS 9057/1, Archdeaconry Court Depositions 1632, fols. 10–13. A 'hospital whore' had been treated there for venereal disease. See also Gowing, 'Gender', pp. 14–15.

54. J. Taylor, *Stripping, Whipping and Pumping* (London, 1638); for related episodes, cf. *The Cony Barber* [?c.1670], in Chappell (ed.), *Roxburghe Ballads*, III, pp. 572–5; A. Raine (ed.), *York Civic Records*, vol. VIII (York, 1953), p. 58; OAO Archdeaconry Papers c. 118, fols. 34–35.

55. [J. Taylor], *The Women's Sharp Revenge* (London, 1640), pp. 200–2; F. Thompson, *Lark Rise to Candleford* (Harmondsworth, 1984), pp. 75–6.

56. Hunt, 'Wife Beating', pp. 21–2; Amussen, *Ordered Society*, pp. 117–22; Wiener, 'Sex Roles', pp. 44; *The Merry Gossips Vindication* [1672–95], brs; A. Halliarg, *The Cruel Shrow* [sic] [c.1640?] in Chappell (ed.), *Roxburghe Ballads*, vol. I, p. 97; *Well Met Neighbour*, in Chappell (ed.), *Roxburghe Ballads*, vol. III, pp. 98–103; J. A. Sharpe, 'Plebeian Marriage in Stuart England: Some Evidence from Popular Literature', *Transactions of the Royal Historical Society*, 5th series, vol. 36 (1986), p. 80.

57. Beattie, 'Criminality of Women', 87; Quaife, *Wanton Wenches*, pp. 139–40; Gowing, 'Gender', p. 8; Gowing, 'Language, Power and the Law', pp. 37–9; Hunt, 'Wife Beating', pp. 14–16, 18.

58. J. C. Jeaffreson (ed.), *Middlesex County Records* (London, 1886–92), vol. III, p. 318; Gowing, 'Gender', p. 8.

59. T. Dekker, *The Ravens Almanacke* [1609] in Dekker, *Non-dramatic Works*, ed. R. B. McKerrow ([1885] repr. London, 1963), vol. IV, pp. 243–65; cf. a parallel story in T. Harman, *A Caveat or Warning for Common Cursitors* [1567] in A. V. Judges (ed.), *The Elizabethan Underworld* (London, 1930), pp. 101–5.

60. Nichols (ed.), *Diary of Henry Machyn*, p. 310. The original MS is damaged, and the gender of the friends is unclear. Cf. Gowing, 'Gender', p. 6.

61. R. Carew, *The Survey of Cornwall* [1602], ed. F. E. Halliday (London, 1969), p. 177; cf. J. Taylor, *Part of This Summers Travels* (London, 1639), pp. 1–2.

62. Greene, *A Notable Discovery of Coosenage* [1592] in Judges (ed.), *Elizabethan Underworld*, pp. 146–8. It may be significant that nothing is said of their husbands.

63. Whiting, *Blind Devotion*, p. 75; S. Brigden, *London and the Reformation* (Oxford, 1989), p. 431.

64. Greene, *A Notable Discovery*, p. 148.

65. For example, in April 1646 six women from Ware disrupted the Quarter Sessions at Hertford by brawling in open court; the outraged magistrates sent them back to Ware under guard to be ducked on the next market day as a warning to other women. In 1662 Mary Greene, a Middlesex woman, was indicted for declaring, 'A pox on all kings!' She had explained that 'she did not care a turd for never a king in England, for she never did lie with any'. W. le Hardy (ed.), *Hertfordshire County Records*, vol. 5 (Hertford, 1928), pp. 368–9; Jeaffreson (ed.), *Middlesex County Records*, vol. III, p. 327.

66. A. Raine (ed.), *York Civic Records*, vol. VII (York, 1950), pp. 136–7; for attacks on constables, etc. see, e.g., Beattie, 'Criminality of Women', pp. 85, 88.

67. On the difficulty of establishing male involvement, see Manning, *Village Revolts*, pp. 97–8, 115–16, 281; Houlbrooke, 'Women's Social Life', pp. 181–5.

68. W. H. D. Longstaffe (ed.), *The Acts of the High Commission Court of the Diocese of Durham*, Surtees Society, vol. 34 (Durham, 1857), pp. 18–19 (my italics).

69. For a good example of a female riot instigated by men but dependent on solidarity among the women, see Malcolmson, *Life and Labour*, p. 118.

70. A. Clark (ed.), *The Life and Times of Anthony Wood* (London, 1891–2), vol. I, pp. 250–1 (my italics).

71. Brigden, *London*, p. 208.

72. Thompson, *Customs in Common*, p. 234.

5 Masterless Young People in Norwich, 1560–1645*

PAUL GRIFFITHS

In June 1623, Jane Sellars was discovered idle on the streets of Norwich and promptly dispatched to the town's Bridewell to be put to work 'till she be reteyned in service'. This was the first in a long string of offences which was to give Sellars the rather dubious distinction of being one of the most prosecuted individuals in late Jacobean and early Caroline Norwich.[1] In April 1624, she was again found 'livinge idely' in the city. In Michaelmas 1625, Thomas Robinson of Yarmouth retained her for one year, but she broke her covenant and ran back to Norwich where the beadles discovered her 'vagrant' in April 1626. After the statutory whipping, the bench issued a pass and told her to return to Robinson, but Sellars never left Norwich and was back in Bridewell a few days later. At her discharge in August she was allowed two days to leave the city. Typically Sellars ignored the order, and was discovered 'vagrant and out of service' in October 1626 and was once again committed to Bridewell 'till she be reteyned in service'. She was probably discharged without such employment, however, for she was picked up idle in November 1626 and confined in Bridewell 'till further order'. In 1627, she ran away from two different masters, and in October found herself back inside the now familiar walls of Norwich Bridewell where she also celebrated Christmas 1628. In 1629, Sellars was whipped for 'ill rule' and 'michery'[2] – her first recorded theft. Her first appearance at Quarter Sessions was in April 1630, when she was charged with stealing six pairs of stockings. By now she had an illegitimate child who was 'put' to a wife of St Swithin's parish in the following month. Eight months later Sellars was 'punished at the post' for 'lewdness and ill rule', and again prosecuted for 'ill rule' at the close of the same month. In April 1631, she was acquitted of petty larceny, and in August was returned to Bridewell

146

with Blanch Fryer (another regular young offender) for begging. A few days later Sellars was branded for 'felony under x shillings'. She was discharged in October and promised the court that she would go 'forthwith to Yarmouth to gett . . . a service'. An entry in the Sessions' minute book for December 1631 simply states, 'Jane Sellars to be executed'. This could refer to an outstanding action or it may be a reference to a verdict reached elsewhere. Sellars makes no further appearances in any later Norwich records. Perhaps she chose to remain in Yarmouth or perhaps the limited patience of the civic magistrates had finally been exhausted, and the hangman's noose provided the final twist in an eight-year long tale in which Jane Sellars had proved to be a sharp thorn in the side of Norwich's civic body.[3]

Sellars belonged to one of early modern England's marginal groups – the masterless young. That is, young people who were *perceived* to have stepped outside the well-marked boundaries of the socialising process by not being under the charge of an older householder and who were labelled by magistrates as part of a definitional process of criminal regulation, which was intended to publish and punish their nonconformity. They were masterless by definition, though often by choice. It is well known that the stigmatisation of deviance is one concern of magistrates, and Howard Becker has commented that 'the attack of hierarchy begins with an attack of labels and conventional conceptions' of inclusion and exclusion.[4] Early modern people, for example, were expected to comply with a number of connected roles, which were allocated according to age, gender, class and work.[5] Marginality can be interpreted as *a lack of participation*, and the selected labelling of groups represents a collision between the authorities and the values of alleged deviants.[6] By naming and prosecuting crime, governors seek to clarify the shape of the social order and its ordering principles.[7] This aspect of the expression of authority in this period has been relatively little explored. Contemporary governors were resolute nomenclators, and they issued an intimidating array of labels which placed people who corrupted their ideas of order on the margins of society. Their opening stratagem was often to label unsavoury groups with a badge like 'vagrant' or 'lewd' which advertised their suspicions. One underused point of entry to the history of English crime is the examination of thinking about crime and the provenance of tactical labels.

This chapter explores the history of two labels, being 'out of service' and 'at their own hand' in Norwich in the period 1560–1645. It seeks to explain what governors had in mind when they used such epithets to communicate their understanding of experiences which stirred suspicions. This social language drew attention to young people who appeared to have few points of contact with formal service. We must consider why suspicions were first aroused and upon whom they fell. The first section of this chapter constructs an explanatory model for the study of masterless youth, which incorporates the symbolic meaning of service – the typical experience of plebeian youth. Anxieties tend to rise and fall in cycles which hamper linear readings. The timing of arrests for being 'out of service' and 'at their own hand', therefore, will be closely related to Norwich's changing socio-economic fortunes. Having introduced a problem and recovered a trend, later sections will explore the social milieu of masterless young people, including gender, criminality, patterns of residence and sociability, and finally, the responses of authority at a time of deep socio-economic difficulty. But it is with the politics of service that we will begin.

I

Youth has been identified as a major characteristic of marginal groups in former centuries as in our own.[8] Indeed, youth itself was in some respects a marginal stage of life in which people were being prepared for full participation in adult society; a 'dark' age in the words of contemporary moralists, which had to be steered towards a virtuous course. Parental responsibility, full participation in a trade, and the growth of appropriate wisdom and maturity provided a series of stages by which people passed into full independent adulthood.

Moralists and magistrates had a clear set of expectations, they circulated accounts of conforming pious youth and orderly generational progress, though most young people grew up in very different ways from the image of temperate and chaste youth which was recycled in conduct literature or the indenture of apprenticeship. In fact, the social history of youth provides a good illustration of the ambiguity of conventional patterns of authority in early modern society. Of equal significance to the codes of the authorities was the independence and creativity of youth, which was rarely (if at all) an inevitable or passive experience; a procession of ideal types and paper figures. Young people actively contributed to their maturation, seeking formative experiences and peer association, and in so doing they helped to make their own history.[9] We should be cautious, therefore, about proposing a functional interpretation of life-cyclical progress, which tends towards the attitudes and requirements of adults in places of authority and employment. Nevertheless, we are still told that the household and socialisation were daunting twin towers hovering over the lives of early modern youth, stretching out their oppressive grips, and pulling young people back within the 'safe compass' of authority structures. Even the most recent interpretations have presented the nature of experiences of youth at this time in negative and colourless terms, Mitterauer presents early modern youth as a time of 'comprehensive subordination'; while Ben-Amos suggests that 'the lack of a marked spatial and temporal segregation of the young and old' 'undermined' formative experiences of youth.[10] The institutional and ideological setting constructed by adult males was of great consequence for the lives of early modern youth. Yet we must not relegate their story to that narrated by the requirements and rules of dominant ideologies and institutions alone. That is merely one possible side of youthful experiences. We must retain interpretative flexibility and a measure of imagination in our approach to sources and ideas, and seek to free historical youth from the grip of prescriptive ideologies and institutions when it is appropriate to do so.

Young people in former centuries did in fact make choices, and some of them chose to work at home or to enter service on their own terms and in their own time. They are one subject of this chapter. Again, youth was not a passive experience in early modern society, and young people responded in different ways to the pressures of the socialising process – they were obedient, indifferent, meek, sometimes keen or mutinous. One significant aspect of the transition from childhood to youth and full membership of adult society was an alteration in attitudes towards work, time and play; a reordering of priorities. Youth was a time of transitional training for the adult world of work in which people were expected to digest appropriate notions of time and labour discipline. The majority of early modern people were introduced to the fresh rhythm of work in youth, and one of the perennial tensions in the socialisation process was the dispute about time. Contemporary moralists claimed that the apparent spontaneity and freedom of young people was one uncomfortable token of a 'dangerous age' which thirsted after licentiousness and spurned restraint. It was held that the whims of youth often contradicted concerns with place, order, property, time and work; they induced a series of generational collisions which were sometimes referred to the courtroom. It was hoped that in youth people would adjust to fresh rhythms of time and work. Youthful independence was considered to be quite simply a waste of time in the study, pulpit and courtroom.

Squabbles about time, work and order helped to raise the spectre of masterless young people. Perceptions of youthful independence derived from contemporary notions of what young people were thought to be evading. Peter Laslett has described service as being the 'characteristic' experience of early modern youth, and we possess some striking statistical and literary proofs.[11] More recent surveys have questioned the universality of service, and even suggest that in some cases it was the preserve of particular groups like orphans or migrants.[12] Yet even if some allowance is made for the differing experiences of town and country, or the variable impact of local economic and social structures, it still appears that the majority of plebeian youth, at least, entered service in another household and that young servants composed the largest single body in the workforce.[13] The successful completion of service (and the 'perilous' period of youth) was vital to social order more generally since age-relations were one aspect of contemporary theories of order. The desire to mould sober citizens and Christians from very unpromising raw materials in this period of service was a political impulse of a society in which age was a principle of authority.

Young people, therefore, were pushed into service. Structured work (and time) promised one solution to the threat of youthful disorder. It was claimed that 'the bringing up of apprentices of both sexes' was 'very profitable in the commonwealth and acceptable and pleasing to almightie God'. The smooth running of service would reduce the number of executions and the 'multitude of enormities' and sins.[14] The idea that tutored work could be provided both by service and Bridewells was given a statutory footing in 1576, so that 'youth may be accustomed and brought up in labour and work, and then not like to grow to be idle rogues'.[15] It was hoped that these institutions would tame the energy of youth and channel it towards productive purposes. Thus residents of Norwich who were prosecuted as vagrants, scolds or filchers,[16] or who were found 'out of service' or 'idle' were often presented with the option of a spell in Bridewell or entering service. Magistrates naturally related service to good order. In their reply to the Privy Council's inquiry about the impact of the Book of Orders (1631), the Essex justices reported that pressuring young people to enter service 'doth exceedingly prevent both disorders and poverty'.[17] Thus the failure to implement effectively a policy of regular service was felt to be a principal source of disorder. In a petition of the 1630s the Sheffield gentry argued that the meaning of the Poor Law of 1601 'was not for the education of boys in arts but for charity to keep ym and relieve ym from turning to roguery and idleness'.[18] Governors in turn kept a check on masters. In Norwich it was ordered that nobody was to take servants 'unles he or she bee able and shall kepe and bring [them] upp honestly without begging'.[19] It was held that outside the regulatory reach of competent adults, young people easily if not naturally slipped into disorder.

The language which was coined by contemporaries to label youth-ful independence expressed the disciplinary aspects of service. Young people who strayed outside the political compass of adult regulation were said to be 'masterless', sometimes 'vagrant', 'out of service', or 'at their own hand'.[20] Such titles had a strategically vague character; a spectrum of possible meaning to satisfy magiste-rial sentiment, individual biography, occasion and circumstance. They belonged to a highly manipulative vocabulary which articu-lated in clear and easy terms suspicions which were the very nerve end of conventional theories of authority. This social language must be approached with care because it is *age-related* rather than *age-specific.* In fact, service could imply any form of work and was not the exclusive property of youth, so that being 'out of service' could mean being 'out of work'.[21] In the Norwich Census of the Poor (1570), however, the language used to depict 129 cases of adult unemployment does not feature service – the preferred terms being 'work' in 115 cases (89.2 per cent), and 'occupation' in thirteen others.[22] In contrast, when the clerk of the Mayor's Court noted ages in cases of being 'out of service' or 'at their own hand' they all fell within the 14–26 age-range. On a further sixty-five occasions offenders were given a significant age-title, and they all inferred youth – 'servant', 'singlewoman', 'daughter', 'son', 'wench', 'lad' and 'maid'. Service was not age-specific, though it was clearly age-related in this period.

In resorting to such language contemporaries had in mind a good deal more than the regulation of labour supply and wages which has received most coverage in discussions of the legislation governing service.[23] William Hunt has commented that cases of 'being out of service' in Essex were brought by parishes concerned to push young people into service to produce a steady stream of labour, and to help in the task of 'fairly allocating scarce employment'.[24] The governors of Norwich also pursued such strategies, but to contain interpretation within an economic straitjacket is seriously to misread contemporary mentalities. It should be remembered that the Statute of Artificers of 1563 which remained on the statute books until 1814 was also intended to curb the 'licentious manner of youth'.[25] Political and economic concerns were woven in an explanatory framework. Parishes were concerned that young people 'out of service' would prove 'burdensome' *and* 'dangerous'. They would only be raised in 'idleness and disordered kynde of lyfe, to their utter overthrow and to the great prejudice of the whole commonwealth'.[26] Governors treated limited participation in service as evidence of immorality and even resistance. An early life spent drifting in and out of service, therefore, was interpreted not only as an absence of subordination, but also as an opportunity to claim independence and display invention.[27]

'At their own hand' is also a term with several meanings but the common thread is again political and economic independence, which permits us to treat both terms in the same interpretative process. (Maidstone's elite related the policing of 'out of service' and 'at their own hand' to 'good government'.)[28] It implied working alone outside the reach of regulatory institutions, and a freedom to impose ideas about the quality of product and fair wages.[29] But on occasion it certainly meant much more than this. 'At their own hand' also incorporated a chosen course of life; gaining a living in an untutored and by extension probably improper way. Most offenders in the Norwich records are said to be *living* rather than working 'at their own hand', though the two meanings naturally inform each other. Consider this episode from Manchester in April 1584 when the Leet Jury complained that

whereas gret unconvenyence ys in this town in that senglewomen
being unmarried be at ther owne hands and doe bake and brewe
and use other trades to the great hurte of the poore inhabitants
havinge wieffe and children. As also in abusing themselves with
younge men and others *havinge not anny man to controle them* to the
gret dishonor of God and evell ensample of others. In consider-
accon whereof [the jury ordered] . . . that noe senglewomen un-
maried shalbe at ther owne hands, or keepe any house or
chamber within this towne. (Emphasis added).

This order was reissued in 1589 and on at least one other later
date.[30] Dubious conduct was tied to the fair allocation of scarce
structured work, and common to both was the uneasy state of
independence.

Work, then, was a moral category. It was, however, gendered also,
and one further dimension of these cases must be emphasised.
While they are not gender-specific they are certainly gender-
related. Of the 263 cases of being 'out of service', 212 involved
women (80 per cent). Cases of being 'at their own hand' were
entirely gender-specific before as late as 1632 when the only male
was prosecuted. Sixty-one of the sixty-two cases concerned women
(98.4 per cent). We have a series of arrests which are clearly related
to issues of gender. In 84 per cent of prosecutions it was women who
appeared at the Mayor's Court. This gender bias was less sharp
before 1600,[31] though it was striking in the 1600s, and most visible
in periods which witnessed peaks in the number of arrests like
1609–11, when fifty-one of fifty-six cases involved women. It sprang
from ideas which closely associated structured work with order,
purity and honesty, and casual work or unemployment with their
opposites, confusion, corruption and pollution.

This contrast affected the lives of both sexes but not in equal
measure, and in Norwich *c.* 1560–1645 it was singlewomen and
female servants who suffered the accusations of the authorities in
far greater numbers. They attracted a great deal of speculation
about their reputation and character.[32] Merry Wiesner has recently
argued that the figure of the independent woman was a potent
symbol of disorder at a time when religious reformers were placing
much greater emphasis upon the authority of husbands, parents
and masters, and describing marriage as a 'natural' state for
women. Moreover, 'the early modern period was a time of increas-

ing suspicion of masterless persons', and 'the most mistrusted' group were 'unmarried women working and living on their own'. Wiesner also suggests that such problems were more visible in the towns.[33] Cases of being 'out of service' and 'at their own hand' clearly imply that the 'problem' of youth in urban society had particular gendered aspects regarding conceptualisations of work, character and criminality.

These epithets were usually reserved for young *residents* of Norwich, though this was not a completely tidy distinction. Young *outsiders*, however, were an imported problem, and the responsibility for their reintegration belonged to another community. They were, therefore, whipped and handed a pass to send them on their homeward passage.[34] Yet both residents and outsiders were suspect because of their masterless condition. The language which was used to identify them belonged to a pliable vocabulary of social discipline which was coined to conceptualise social situations in which the principal characters were typically young. Moving with apparent ease across the border dividing Norwich from the nearby countryside and conventional society from its marginal fringe, masterless youth inhabited a shady quarter of urban society which has been little penetrated by historians hitherto. We will follow this group in the records of the Norwich Mayor's Court (the principal court for the regulation of everyday life and petty disorders in the city)[35] and try to sketch the rough contours of their world. We will also follow them through time, and the next section will trace the rate of prosecution of cases of being 'out of service' and 'at their own hand'.

II

Young people living 'out of service', 'at their own hand' or 'vagrant' were a perennial source of concern in the period 1500–1700, but these problems were sharper in particular years and places. One interesting aspect of the rate of prosecution in Norwich is its changing frequency, which merits close investigation. Prosecutions proceeded at a trickle, but gathered pace and became a stream in certain periods. The timing of cases is one guide to the falling and rising concern with masterless youth in governing circles. There were periods of relative tranquillity and greater tolerance, and other more anxious moments when unease was elevated to a pitch which could only be resolved by arrests. Attaching labels to alleged crime is not a casual or mercurial exercise, but a calculated process of monitoring with specific contexts and concerns. We can trace the fortunes of Norwich to examine the situations in which the 'problem' of masterless youth became more visible in the sources.

The turn of the seventeenth century was a time of socio-economic difficulty, one highly visible consequence of which was a rising tide of vagrants, most of whom were young people in their teens and twenties.[36] Service was as vulnerable as any other institution (including the family) to the harmful effects of rising population, unemployment, inflation, land shortages, deeper poverty, and the keen instinct to safeguard present employment. Justices in early seventeenth-century Wiltshire, for example, 'expressed alarm at the growing number of masters . . . who refused to take apprentices bound to them by the parish authorities', or who 'abandoned . . . apprentices in the midst of training'. Debt and poverty had a part to play in the economy of service.[37] Two principal potential problems interfered with the smooth running of service at this time. It was more difficult to gain entry into service, and master–servant relations were more fragile. Peter Clark has commented that masters were 'unable to cope in periods of rising population and mounting unemployment'.[38] Young people who encountered difficulties in obtaining a foothold in service raised problems for the authorities. The age structure of the population tipped towards the young in this period and Beier has suggested that a result of the coincidence of this demographic condition with socio-economic strain, despite high levels of infant and child mortality, was that 'the problem of great numbers of unproductive youngsters was greatly intensified'.[39] One response to a lack of opportunity at home was to move in search of service. Indeed, Salerno has discovered that many Wiltshire folk who crossed the ocean to the New World were recently 'out of service'. More generally, a majority of emigrants were male, single and young.[40] However, most displaced young people kept their feet on English soil and joined in the drift to the towns and wood-pasture regions.

All of this may have resulted in problems of absorption in English towns. The nature of urban society at this time is, of course, a much debated question. The impact of high levels of in-migration upon order and criminality, for example, have stirred much discussion.[41]

Some recent scholarship has stressed the basic stability of urban society,[42] though other contributions draw attention to the strategies by which rulers pursued stability.[43] Some of these studies arguably rely too much on evidence relating to the more stable and integrated sections of urban life, thereby focusing disproportionately upon more functional aspects of urban experiences like social mobility, poor relief, neighbourhood, guilds, office-holding and the life-cycle. Yet a surface gloss of stability should not disguise 'dysfunctional' aspects of urban society, A more rounded interpretation would investigate the milieux of criminal groups and their points of contact with more 'orthodox' political, occupational and residential structures. Much can be gleaned about rhetorics of order in encounters between elite typecasters and 'labelled' criminals. This study does not elevate disorder at the expense of institutions and officers charged with the task of pursuing stability. I simply hope to draw attention to one group – masterless young people – who are difficult to accommodate within the tidy interpretations proposed by Pearl and Rappaport, for example, in which alleged social equalisers like poor relief or social mobility rendered the majority patient, and even content in the slender comfort of present relief or the contemplation of future aspirations. A more complete view of urban society would incorporate other people and groups who whether by choice or force of circumstance found themselves, if only for a brief moment, at the margins of society. Significantly, the drift to the towns was in large part a movement of youth. Not only did service create problems of household discipline,[44] the 'pull' of service also mustered a wave of migrants, some of whom were less successfully integrated into the urban economy and political structure.

A 75 per cent rise in Norwich's population in the period 1580–1620 is directly attributable to the quickening pace of in-migration.[45] John Patten has commented that 'the years between 1500 and 1700 were a time of great stability for East Anglian towns'. There were 'no major social disruptions' and 'no urban disasters'.[46] It is true that despite the best efforts of Robert Kett the city's walls never came tumbling down, but Patten's interpretation of urban disorder – disasters and major disruptions – is misleading and exaggerated because it neglects more commonplace aspects of the 'problem' of order, including petty crime, which were a persistent nuisance. Norwich's rulers had to wrestle daily with questions of law and order, and we can also identify periods when stability seemed to be under greater threat.

Historians of urban 'crisis' tend to channel their energies into the 1590s. Norwich had its problems in that decade, though one sensitive indication of urban anxieties, vagrancy prosecutions, draws attention to the period 1615–30 as a time of strain. Figure 5.1 presents figures for the number of vagrants brought before the Mayor's Court in the period 1590–1645 who were *not* residents of the city. The timing of prosecutions was marked by peaks in 1600–1, 1609–11, 1615–17 and 1622–3. The fall in numbers after 1623 was still distinguished by notable increases in 1630–1 and 1634–6.[47] In Norwich, as elsewhere, vagrants were characteristically young. In the period 1595–1609, 72 per cent of arrested vagrants were under 21 and 52 per cent were under 16 years of age.[48] Young people took to the road for all sorts of reasons, though in most cases the principal concern was that they had fled from a master or parent. The chance to find a service, to beg, hide or steal carried young East Anglians to their regional capital. Either on the road or at large in the city they were perceived to be outside the compass of appointed authority.

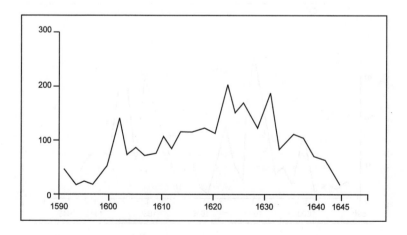

Figure 5.1 *Vagrancy in Norwich, 1590–1645, by two-year periods*

This first group of *immigrant* masterless young people were joined by a second, consisting of young *residents* of Norwich who were found vagrant, 'out of service' or 'at their own hand'. Here the accusation of independence turned on the correspondence between service and the control of work and youth. Three groups of residents were targeted by governors – children or servants who had run away from a parent or master; others who remained at home but 'out of service' with a master (a contemporary perception related idleness to young people who chose to remain at home rather than enter service);[49] and young people who had independently taken lodgings. These groups of migrant and resident masterless youth converged in time. Cases of being 'out of service' and 'at their own hand' among residents peak in much the same years that witnessed rises in vagrancy prosecutions. The combined totals for the first two offences are presented in Figure 5.2. Prosecutions peak in the 1630s, but the timing of cases is again distinguished by clustering. The 'problem' of independence among young residents was most acute in years of rising vagrancy like 1609–11, 1630–1 and 1634–6, when 134 of the 313 recorded cases of being 'out of service' and 'at their own hand' in the period

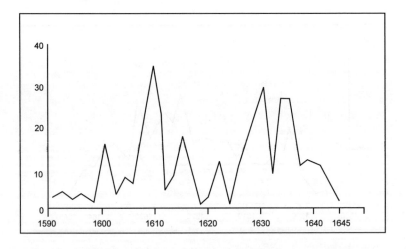

Figure 5.2   *'Out of service' and 'at their own hand' in Norwich, 1590–1645, by two-year periods*

1590–1645 (42.8 per cent) were prosecuted. Lesser peaks in 1600, 1617, 1623, 1626 and 1628 also coincided with rises in the numbers of vagrants arrested in the city.[50]

Cases of being 'out of service' and 'at their own hand' were not confined to the years after 1590. There were eleven prosecutions in the period 1560–89. This language was by no means chronologically specific, though it was rarely heard before 1600. There were six more cases in the single year 1609 than in the forty-year period 1560–99. In contrast, the expression 'at their own hand' belonged to the turn of the century. The first case in the city sources was in December 1599.[51] The turn of the century witnessed a sharp intensification of the gender bias, and the appearance of a language of social discipline which was age-related and first coined to describe an exclusively female social situation – 'at their own hand'. These expressions were not the exclusive property of Norwich's elite. They were heard at different times in different places.[52] But in this East Anglian city the 1600s mark the point at which the 'problems' raised by youthful independence, and especially female independence, could only be resolved by going to court with much greater regularity.

III

Life in early seventeenth-century Norwich was punctuated by campaigns against masterless young people, which were part of a broader concern with social discipline and included the closer policing of alehouses, deeper poverty, begging and inmates.[53] The Mayor's Court steered these drives against unshackled youth. It was here that strategies were discussed, beadles and marshals were appointed, and powers of search granted to aldermen in their wards. Policy characteristically took the form of round-ups of pairs or small groups of masterless youth, who were either discovered pacing the streets with no particular place to go or at home 'out of service'. In March–May 1601, for example, searches turned up a pack of young residents who were found begging on the streets and sent in to Bridewell at much the same time as the Mayor's Court expelled a number of young vagrants who had tramped to the city.[54] We know that migrants were usually whipped and returned home. In some cases, the authorities ordered that a beadle, parent or master should escort young rogues back home. Edward Burges was returned to Yarmouth by a craftsman 'who hath occasion to goe to Yarmouth'.[55] One London master tracked his apprentice to Norwich, though he is a solitary example of an amateur sleuth.[56] Young residents were invited to choose between a spell in Bridewell or a fixed period in which to find a service. In these cases magistrates hoped that the fear of Bridewell with its dark cells and tough labour discipline would be sufficient to frighten them into finding a master. In thirty-seven of the seventy-eight cases for which we possess information (47.4. per cent), the time allowed to find a place in service was two weeks, in thirty-two others it was one week (41 per cent). Other young people were permitted ten days (two cases), three weeks (two cases), one month (four cases), and two months (a single case).

The records reveal very little about how such young people were expected to find work in service, and the few snapshots we possess disappointingly identify the individual rather than the precise method. In a few cases responsibility rested with a parent – the mother in eight cases[57] and father in four.[58] Nor was the bench slow to introduce the threat of committal proceedings against wavering parents.[59] But in the majority of cases in which young people were not ferried to Bridewell, the records simply report that the court ordered them to find a place in service. Overseers and justices occasionally intervened, though their role is again obscured by the bare information recorded in the courtbooks. In 1634, for example, Cecily Robinson, being 'out of service', was told to either stay in Bridewell 'or be reteyned in service before some justice of the peace of this citty', and in November 1600 one Frances Key was ordered to be 'put to service by the overseers'.[60]

In most cases, however, offenders were not permitted the liberty of remaining at home to obtain employment, and rather than rely upon mere fear the court issued a committal order. The typical sequence of events in these proceedings, as in the case of Martha Johnson who was alleged to be of 'lewde life' and was 'wandring abroad idely', was that offenders were 'set on worke in the howse of correccon' until they 'be reteyned in service'.[61] They were given a short and sharp introduction to the world of structured work and usually held in Bridewell for days, weeks or, less often, months.[62] We tend to lose sight of young people once they are inside Bridewell, and the methods by which they were expected to find a master are largely lost to us. In some cases the authorities issued a committal order with a master in mind. Other evidence implies that they sometimes attempted to find a service, but we cannot be sure whether this was routine or a final resort. Anne Saffrey, for example, who was 'not settled in a good service', was set on work 'till she shalbe provided of a master'. In another case an artisan acted as job-hunter. John Hallawaye was told 'to remayne in Bridewell till Mr Maior can send William Morris a taylor . . . to see if he can gett him a mayster'.[63] We can assume that there was talk with Bridewell craftsmen, and that family, friends and neighbours would have helped some young people to be placed in service.

The gaps in the sources mean that any impression of success or failure can only be at best preliminary. We know that some young people were retained[64] and that others were accepted for a trial period upon a 'liking',[65] though potential masters may have been less cooperative in periods of strain when arrests increase. Still others who make a single appearance in the records had a brief historical moment, a fleeting taste of marginality, only to sink without trace into the anonymity of daily life upon their return to conventional structures of socialisation. In contrast, we also know of some young people who were found 'at their own hand' or 'out of service' on more than one occasion. Their case histories provide a sign of the enduring nature of this urban marginal fringe. The regular coincidence of peaks in prosecutions with a rising tide of vagrancy was a sober thought for the authorities who associated youthful independence with disorder. Nor were such anxieties without good foundation. Patten stresses the basic stability of urban society, but he also writes that in a town like Norwich the poor must have 'collected in great number, regulated and sometimes supported by better-off citizens. Pickpockets, thieves and prostitutes', he continues, 'must have flourished in urban society.'[66] It is well known that marginal groups grow and prosper in towns.

In Norwich vagrants who were typically young begged and stole their way along the streets, always trying to keep one step ahead of officers. They were found drunk and playing unlawful games, having sex, extending 'ill rule', and committing other offences gathered under a catch-all like misdemeanour, misbehaviour, or idle.[67] These migrants only added to the problems raised by those clearly resident, who robbed orchards, smashed windows, abused officers, and stole anything they could get their hands on – clothes, money, food, lambs, ducks, dogs, horses and hens.[68] The changing fortunes of urban economies as well as domestic tensions provided a steady procession of new recruits into the masterless group, and helped to create a 'problem' of youth in the towns. Young Norwich folk joined the migrants on the streets, gathering at markets and fairs, adding to the cast of misfits, begging here, stealing there, who exercised the wits of officers. They included Dorothy Sadlington who was noted for 'commonly begging in the streets'; John Foster, apprentice with Whinney the tailor, who was picked up 'living idely about the city'; and Edward Bushel, a boy, who 'would be carefully looked unto . . . [for] he ys a very bad one'.[69]

Crime among the masterless young tended to be opportunistic – petty theft and begging to get food and drink. The sources convey a very real sense that they were an enduring subgroup in Norwich, though in number and personnel they were fluid. One problem is the silence of the sources in periods of few or no arrests. Is this apparent calm an illusion springing from a reduction in anxieties in periods of greater stability, or does it represent a fall in numbers of masterless and vagrant youth? I shall return to these questions shortly. Despite this there emerged some people who spent the greater part of their youth moving in and out of this urban basement. We first catch sight of Joanne Weeting, for example, in March 1630 when she was 'branded for felony' at Quarter Sessions, given a pass, and told to return to her master, John Thaxter of Hanworth. But it seems that she never left the city. In August she was discharged from Bridewell, being 'nowe desirous to goe to Holland'. However, Weeting did not venture outside the gates of the city, preferring her present life to foreign travel. In September 1630, she was convicted of petty larceny with Dennis Powell, another doyen of the masterless group, and ordered to be 'whipped about the markett' and confined until she could be returned to her master. Back on the streets she was quickly rearrested for ripping up the pass 'signed by Mr Maior and Mr Jermy'. A second pass was issued for 'conduccon of her' to Hanworth, but she was discovered in Norwich at the close of of the same month and returned to Bridewell. In January 1631, Weeting was ordered to remain there 'till she be reteyned in service'. Further confining orders were issued in April, May and June. We then lose sight of her until July 1632 when she was again sent in to Bridewell 'till she shall be reteyned in service', though she was probably set free without such employment. At large in the city she returned to theft and was whipped in December 1632 for petty larceny and set on work once again. Weeting was also pregnant with an illegitimate child at this time, as she was back in Bridewell in May 1634 'for havinge a bastard'. Yet she did not serve the statutory year, for the bench was satisfied with 'her affirmacon that she shall goe oversea to Holland'. Weeting had fooled the court with the same promise four years earlier, and on this occasion also her feet remained firmly on English soil. In fact, she never left the city, and in September 1634 we find her committed to Bridewell for 'ill rule' with one Butters of Norwich, her final appearance in civic materials.[70]

Weeting displays many of the attributes of the masterless group which upset the authorities – slipping in and out of Norwich; disregarding the magistracy almost as a matter of course, committing petty crime, and refusing to play the part in which they were cast by patriarchal ideologies. Like Jane Sellars who began this story, she drifted with apparent ease along East Anglia's roads. Similar case histories can be traced for other young people who ran to Norwich. In June 1604, William Jackson and Robert Mayer, 'two boyes', were sent in to Bridewell for 'cuttinge of purses'. A few days later Jackson was ordered 'to retorne to Colston in Norfolk where he was borne'. Mayer was found vagrant in August 1605 when he was 16 years of age, whipped, and given a pass to return to his village, Forncett in Norfolk. However, he was wandering in Norwich two months later, when he was again whipped and handed a pass. Mayer chose to taunt the authority of the court as he was picked up 'roging and begging' in November with Robert Simpson of Lincolnshire aged 12. The pair were whipped and expelled, though Mayer was at large in Norwich in January 1606, and he was whipped for a fifth time in March for 'myching' with Peter Lynes, another boy. April saw the return of Jackson who was whipped and given a pass. He was found 'roginge' in September, when he was twelve years old.[71] James Goldsmith, a boy aged xiii years [was] taken begging' in January 1608, whipped and sent home. Nevertheless, he was picked up begging in February 1609 and twice more in October 1610. Robert and Margery Gedg were presented in November 'for receiving Gouldsmith and Webb, two leawd boyes, and giving them almost a weeks lodging'. They asked the pair to steal fowls for them. A few days later Goldsmith was whipped for vagrancy. But the whip was clearly no deterrent in his case, for he was was again discovered vagrant in January 1611.[72]

In Norwich, therefore, the correspondence between masterless youth and petty crime is well established. Contemporary sources sometimes show that they wandered, stole and begged in small groups and pairs.[73] There were a number of assembly points in Norwich – public sermons, fairs and the market-places attracted the pilferers, pickpockets and cutpurses who were active in the city.[74] It was also thought that sanctuary could be found in the cathedral grounds. In January 1600, the beadles complained 'that rogishe boyes and beggars escape from them [and] runne into the liberties of Christe's Churche where they are harbored and not punished, and in the evenings they goe abroad in the citie begging'. In October 1632, a baker was presented 'for counsellinge the apprentices in London that run from their masters to fly to Christ Church being a priviledged place that they might not be followed'.[75] A number of alehouses and lodging houses offered a room and refreshment. Robert Morgan, for example, was prosecuted for 'lodging and harboring young and ydel vagrants', and told that he would lose an ear if he sheltered any other young strays. While John More was arrested for lodging 'cutpurses and other lewd persons . . . from tyme to tyme'.[76] The White Horse, the Cardinal's Hat and a few other alehouses were safe ports of call for masterless young people.[77] Others less fortunate who could not afford a few pence to get a room for the night were forced to sleep as best they could 'in the streets', barns and cellar windows.

A steady stream of young people tripped in and out of Norwich and across the nearby countryside. Some of them ignored the wishes of governors as a matter of course, and they provide a clue to the structural inadequacies of a system of law enforcement which often relied upon the good faith and participation of masterless young people and their families. Some parents refused to cooperate with the court. In September 1634, for example, the Mayor's Court received word that widow Moore's daughter who had been told to find a service a month earlier had not yet been 'retayned' because her mother had persuaded her to ignore their order.[78] A number of young migrants seem to have drifted in and out of Norwich without any concern for the threats of the magistrates. William Miller, for instance, 'a boye of xii years of age' from Seething in Norfolk, was picked up 'roginge and begging' in 1596, having been 'divers tymes heretofore commaunded oute of the citie'. While Margaret Utting was ferried to Bridewell in 1598 'to dwell and remayne for ever', but this did not stop her from embarking upon a decade of vagrancy and theft.[79] It is as if we are witnessing a theatre of rehearsed responses, a clandestine return follows quickly on the heels of an involuntary removal. But despite the perhaps inevitable flaws in civic strategies, the city preserved an orderly image. Yet beneath this surface gloss of managed order the 'masterless seam' cut deep, and was laying strong roots in a period of rising in-migration. However, the timing of cases of being 'out of service' and 'at their own hand' is decidedly uneven, and we must try to explain why anxieties sharpened in certain periods – in particular, we must explore the 'peaks' of 1609–11, 1630–1 and 1634–6.

IV

The cycle of cases closely shadows the timing of dearth, plague and deeper poverty when visible death and distress elevated concern with rhetorics of inclusion and exclusion. Severe plague cast a shadow over the city in 1603–4 and 1625–6,[80] and cases of vagrancy and being 'out of service' increased. Yet the more prominent peaks occurred a few years after these grave epidemics as fresh reports of plague coincided with deeper poverty, higher in-migration in the wake of chronic plague (the jobs of the dead had to be filled and Norwich's population quickly regained its pre-plague levels)[81] and, in 1630, bitter dearth. In 1609–10, there was a fresh crop of infections which were more than an echo of 1603–4.[82] This helped to raise fears which were still strong in recent memory. Poverty cut deeper. In January 1608, the Mayor's Court was passing orders 'in regard of the hardness of the tymes'.[83] In 1610 a rumour rushed around the city that 100 apprentices in the textile trades planned to strike until all non-apprenticed labour was dismissed.[84] Thus the light plague of 1609–10 played its part in bringing anxieties into sharper focus, with the result that rulers were left brooding about the grim coincidence of plague, deeper poverty and rising vagrancy.

Much the same sequence of events can be traced in the next peak of arrests in 1630–1, and rising concern with masterless young people should be contextualised against a social canvas of lingering plague, dearth, deeper poverty and problems in local textiles, including unemployment. The severe plague of 1625–6 was followed by further infections in 1630–1. The court noted fresh plague cases in April 1630 and appointed a 'searcher for the infected' and watchmen at the pesthouses.[85] There was a notable rise in vagrancy in 1630 when 111 individuals were arrested – the second highest annual total in the period 1581–1646. A marshal was appointed 'for the taking up of rogues and idle persons' in June, and two 'able and sufficient men' were appointed in each ward in July 1631 to check rogues, beggars and other disordered persons. The 'very miserable' state of the poor was attributed to the present 'scarcity and dearth of all manner of victualls', and the 'want of worke' and 'all things necessary for the maintenance of life'.[86] There was a steady procession of measures on behalf of the poor in 1630–1, including the fair allocation of grain, reassessments of contributions to the poor rate, and orders to put the resident poor to work. Further cases of plague were reported in April 1631, at the same time as grumbling about unemployment and the shortage of work in some parts of the textile trades reached the ears of magistrates.[87] Dearth and disease seem to have retreated in 1632–3 but concern with masterless young people again sharpened in 1634 at much the same time as orders regulating poor relief, begging, inmates, alehouses, and further complaints about unemployment were entered in the sources.[88] 'Country journeymen' who 'filled' the city were the subject of 'dayly' complaints from 'out of worke' resident journeymen to 'Mr Maior' in 1634. They also arranged a meeting at The Unicorn under cover of choosing '4 feastmakers' to 'consent how they might draw their . . . masters to give greater wages'.[89] A slight lull in magisterial activity in 1635 was followed by further plague measures and detailed orders for the poor in 1636.[90]

John Walter has demonstrated that in dearth years magistrates attempted to strike up a rallying communal tune; an emotional sense of what he calls 'the myth of the community'. They followed their paternal role with vigour distributing relief to protect the poor from hunger and to still the threat of disorder which hung over the community.[91] By playing the 'commonweal tune',[92] the authorities restated civic identity, thereby casting outsiders in a darker and more suspicious hue. Plague also assisted in the framing of policies of exclusion (and inclusion) and a rhetoric of community. It was ordered that the infected should be shut up and prohibited any communication with the healthy civic body. A watch was set at the approaches to the city to turn back suspicious characters. Vagrants were popularly believed to carry plague, leaving behind a trial of misery as they drifted across the land. In fact, marginal groups – and young people – suffered high death rates.[93] The reintegration of young misfits and the expulsion of risky outsiders had a close correlation with cycles of socio-economic difficulty. In these grim times greater pressure was applied to push young people into formal service.[94] Nevertheless, the coincidence of two peaks of arrests for vagrancy and youthful independence in times of dearth, plague, and deeper poverty, and the fall into crime of some masterless young people, which partly confirmed elite labelling, will not explain the striking gendering of cases of being 'out of service' and 'at their own hand'. We can recover an ideological context to discuss anxieties; that age, for example, should tame the rash temper of youth. Yet the usual sequence of events placed a young woman before a male-dominated courtroom. Perhaps the rulers of Norwich were spurred on by a concern with the place of women in their city?

In 1985 David Underdown alerted us to the possibility of a 'crisis' in gender relations in England *c.*1560–1640. His argument turns on the alleged convergence in time of three gender-related offences – witchcraft, being 'out of service', and scolding.[95] Norwich had its cucking stool by 1562, though that usual barometer of gender tensions, cases of scolding, remained steady hovering at one, two or three prosecutions each year. In fact, there were no cases in seventeen years of the period 1581–1640. If there was a gender 'crisis' in Norwich it was not a crisis of tongues.[96] At first sight, the tempting timing of cases of being 'out of service' and 'at their own hand' would appear to offer support for a gender 'crisis'. Yet we have seen that these offences are gender-related rather than gender-specific. While the concept of 'crisis' with its strong connotations of a rapid fall into confusion may not provide the most helpful way of depicting gender relations at this time. We need to know, for example, what levels of magisterial activity represented more 'ordinary' and 'routine' periods. The idea of 'routine' raises other complications. The study of one part of Underdown's threefold interpretation in a single city suggests that we must distinguish more tense moments within his alleged 'crisis' period. In fact, it is more helpful to interpret a heightened sensation of gender as part of a broader concern with order at this time. Nevertheless, in Norwich the generalised concern with fetching young people within the regulatory reach of service was to become more narrowly focused on gender issues as investigations turned up a greater number of women living independently. We can precisely fix a turning-point in the wave of arrests in 1609–11. In June 1609, the Mayor's Court ordered overseers to search for 'maydes and singlewomen' who 'lyve at their owne handes'.[97] As the gender bias intensified the gendering of prosecutions may have become a near self-fulfilling prophecy.

There is no simple answer to this question of the prominent role of gender in the drive to push young people into formal service. We in fact require a complicated explanatory model with several strands to explain both the timing and gendering of prosecutions. Conditions in Norwich provide one part of the model for the timing of arrests, but as we shall see the activities of central government also had a part to play. The issue of gender was one of work, residence, and the suspicions hanging over the independent woman. It may also be a question of numbers. We are told that larger towns had 'a disproportionately high number of women', one reason being the pull of domestic service.[98] I have consulted the registers of seven 'poor' and four 'medium' wealthy Norwich parishes to compare sex ratios of births and burials in two decades, 1610–20 and 1710–20.[99] Following the usual ratio of 104 male to 100 female baptisms, there was a slight preponderance of women in the earlier period when the sex ratio of baptisms was 103.6 and burials 102.3. It seems that growing numbers of women were making journeys to Norwich in the seventeenth century because the sex ratio of baptisms in 1710–20 hovered at 104.0, while the burial ratio clearly tipped towards women, 96.6.[100] The population of early Stuart Norwich was in this respect more 'balanced', though further work may well uncover a more difficult situation towards the close of the seventeenth century if the pace of female in-migration was rising as fast as burial figures would seem to indicate. Yet in Norwich numbers alone are not an adequate explanation.

Being 'out of service' and 'at their own hand' in Norwich, however, were chiefly perceived and prosecuted as the transgressions of independent young women. One answer may be that young men were more likely to travel in search of work or service. Another, is that they had a greater prospect of being in service in their home community, formally apprenticed or otherwise. One might expect to discover a higher number of women living and working at home, perhaps being taught skills by a relative.[101] This twilight world of casual work and informal training in which young women boosted the family economy of widows[102] or unemployed men[103] was more egalitarian than the ordinance-ridden world of the guilds.[104] But it is an aspect of Norwich life which is seldom mentioned in the records I have consulted. The Census of the Poor (1570), however, offers one window, and in its 'tour' of poor households we can observe women working at home, usually assisting in the manufacture of textiles. It is well known that women had no public or formal role in the guilds, widows being the exception, and that ideas about occupational careers were largely confined to young men. Casual work took opportunities away from apprenticed labour and householders, who in theory earned a wage to provide for their families and keep them from turning to poor relief. The allocation of work was *prioritised* in favour of resident males, especially in times of unemployment and work shortages. A further concern was that women should have been at work in formal service, earning wages which were considered to be appropriate by the authorities.

Michael Roberts has recently argued that the nature of women's work in urban society was changing *c.* 1570–1650, 'sharing [to a limited extent] in that general proliferation of occupational roles with which these later years [of the sixteenth century] have been identified'. Growing opportunities for female work 'of all kinds' uneasily coexisted with the unequal share of freedom given to men and women in political and occupational spheres, especially in stressful times when competition sharpened. So, Roberts has also argued that 'what might almost be called a late sixteenth century urban "crisis of gender" ' offered a 'significant challenge' to civic rulers.[105] Again, 'crisis' infers a leap into severe instability and may be inappropriate here. But Roberts has identified structural changes in patterns of work, and if he is correct they may help to explain the timing of cases. Thus rising numbers of arrests may have resulted from attempts to regulate the greater participation of women in work at a time when female independence was viewed with suspicion. In tough conditions like those in 1609–10 and 1630–6, elites intervened to help secure the life-chances of householders by more closely regulating wages and labour supply. Outsiders of all sorts were one target.[106] Another, were resident women like Rose Nelson, a single woman who was presented for 'not [being] in service for wages', and who, like Joanne Norton, a 'singlewoman lyveing wholly at her own handes', was free to plot her own course.[107] These cases belonged to the same concern which spurred on the would-be strikers in 1610 and 1634 – marginal and foreign workers – the difference being that they resulted from the responses of governors. To the concern with reintegrating masterless youth in times of dearth, plague and economic difficulty, we can add the prioritising of work in favour of resident men in the same conditions.

For work was a moral category. Young women like Martha Johnson, one of 'lewde life', who was found 'wanderinge abroade idely' and confined in Bridewell 'till she be reteyned in service'; Jane Humeston, who was picked up 'roginge about the towne and not abyding in any service', living 'very suspiciously and disorderly in lewdness of her body'; Katherine Prostwick, 'one who keepeth at her owne hande', and who had committed 'filthines'; and Jane Palsy, 'a yonge wench of 24 years goeinge at hir owne hand and frequentinge the alehouse', provided some confirmation of the connection between untutored time and immorality.[108] A significant number of masterless young women were also charged with suspected or actual sexual offences.[109] A singlewomen taking private chambers stirred suspicions. It is clear that youth was seen as a troublesome stage of life. Masterless young people raised anxieties, but a particular gendered discourse elevated suspicions about independent young women. In May 1605, for instance, Grace Kerrison, a 'singlewoman' and 'one who lyved very suspiciously' at Stephen Warnfrey's alehouse, was expelled for 'ill rule'. In the same year, Grace Sketch was ordered to depart the city 'unless she shall be retained in service with some honest man not beinge an inholder'. While Margaret Thackwell and her companion, 'beyng young women . . . out of service', were sent to Bridewell for 'taking chambers' in March 1592.[110]

These half-expressed suspicions connecting alehouses, immorality, freedom and private work can help us to conceptualise the magistrates responses. Patriarchy looms large over these events. In 1561, for example, Margaret Watt was punished for 'ill rule' and told 'not to dwell in the town unless she shall fortune to marry some honest man'. While Elizabeth Claxton was given two weeks to find a service 'with some sufficient man'.[111] 'Honest' and 'sufficient' clearly implied correct morals, hard work and the ability to provide; yet another sign of the correspondence between issues of economics and morality. In these cases masterless young women were to be disciplined by marriage and the regulated rhythm of work with 'sufficient' men. Significantly, the chances of a woman being presented for a habit of independence alone without being charged with an additional offence were higher – 79.4 per cent of women were only labelled with a title like being 'out of service'; the figure for men was 59.6 per cent. Singlewomen raised anxieties, and like their Manchester cousins many of them had 'not any man to controle them', which raises issues of family structure, and in particular the presence of a male householder.

We can partly reconstruct the households of thirty women who were discovered at home 'out of service', and ten others who were 'at their own hand'.[112] There is no visible pattern in cases of being 'out of service'. Nine women were living with their widowed mothers at the time of the search, and five others with their mothers who may have been widowed. But sixteen others were reported to be living with their fathers when they attracted the magistrates attention. Not one of these fathers was deemed unfit to keep his daughter. In contrast, Alice Stubbs was judged to be an incompetent tutor and provider; she was 'not fit' to care for her daughter. While widow Bensley was considered 'not able to keepe' her daughter who was found 'out of service' in December 1628 and December 1630, and 'at her own hand' in 1634. Widow Bensley herself had been presented for 'lewdnes and ill rule', 'for frequenting the companye of the bearers of the infected', and for lodging masterless people.[113] Cases of being 'at their own hand' reveal a clearer pattern, and the potentially tenuous position of female heads of household is much more apparent. Only one daughter was living at home with her father at the time of her arrest. While another eight households were headed by women (three of whom can be positively identified as widows). One other woman was living with her sister at the time of the search.[114]

V

The ambiguous position of widows returns us to the question of chronology and the cyclical pattern of arrests. Widows were fully responsible for ninety-four families in the Census of the Poor, and it was recorded that those households contained at least 171 young people.[115] It is quite likely that prosecutions for being 'out of service' would have swiftly followed such revelations in early Stuart Norwich, but a paltry two cases were brought in the period 1570–5. An order was issued by the Norwich Assembly in 1577 to apply the Statute of Artificers – 'that no maydes [being able to serve] maye hyer chambers' or 'be harbored in eny mans howse'. Young women 'refusing to serve' were to be promptly dispatched to 'prison or bridewell'.[116] Yet no wave of arrests followed this decree, there is only significant silence in the records. In addition, a number of severe plagues swept through the city in 1579,[117] 1584–5 and 1589–92, and a light plague, sufficient to cause scares and many deaths, was reported in 1597–9.[118] It is well known that the 1590s were a bleak time of dearth. Nor did the cycle of economic difficulty which left a blemish on the city's fortunes leave any notable trace upon the timing of prosecutions before the turn of the seventeenth century. Nevertheless, these were the very conditions which raised the spectre of masterless young people in subsequent decades. In fact, there was a greater or equal number of cases of being 'out of service' or 'at their own hand' in each of nine single years in the period 1600–36 than in that whole 'crisis' decade of 1590–9. Yet this social language was part of civic vocabulary before 1600, though it was not widely used. We can find it in Norwich materials, but a single mention is sometimes followed by years of silence.

Thus the first years of the seventeenth century mark the point at which either the tensions contained in this social language cut deeper, or concern was elevated to a pitch resulting in a sequence of clampdowns. The timing of cases is related to the close correspondence between these explanations; between perceptions and realities, ideology and the material environment. But there is a third layer of explanation which has the value of directing attention to the period when arrests were rising fast. The Poor Laws of 1598 and 1601 did not provide the occasion to issue labels, but they provided a further statutory endorsement of forced service, and drew attention to 'outsiders' who charted an alternative course of life. A firm identification of the marginal fringe was made in the 1601 Act – it was ordered that people who 'use no ordinarie and dailie mode of lief to get their livinge by' should be put to work. A later Act of 1610, 'for erecting and buylding of howses of correction' and punishing vagrancy, encouraged an institutional solution to problems raised by the 'idle and wandring life', and offered another statutory justification for issuing manipulative labels by describing pliable categories such as vagabond, rogue, disorderly and idle.[119] The Assembly order of 1577 had little impact on the rate of prosecution, which proceeded at a faint trickle. The Assembly issued a further set of articles in 1600, however, 'to be inquired upon by the churchwardens and overseers' of each parish, which asked 'what maids or singlewomen keepe chambers by themselves beynge under the age of xl years and goe to their owne hands', as part of a broader moral thrust which also included the closer regulation of inmates, 'naughty packs' with child, suspected houses, unlawful games, country journeymen and vagrant and idle folk, as well as ordering that 'any pore folkes children' should be placed in service at age 14 for boys and 15 for girls.[120] This drive ushered in the first peak of prosecutions for being 'out of service' and 'at their own hand' in 1600–1.

This significant sequence of central and civic legislation not only encouraged a particular interpretation of outsiders, but also proposed clear strategies which if not entirely new were gathered under a single statutory seal. It should also be remembered that the 1610 Act articulated a far harsher line on illegitimacy. While the infanticide Act of 1624 bitterly condemned 'lewd women'. The background to this interpretative climate which raised anxieties about outsiders and female sexuality is beyond the scope of this chapter, though it requires attention. It is true that none of these perceptions or problems belonged exclusively to the early seventeenth century, but their statutory form at that time is surely significant.

A more complete picture of the mental world of Norwich's governors would also explore other lines of communication between the city and central government, including the registers of Privy Council.[121] Another line of inquiry is offered by the beliefs of magistrates in the Mayor's Court. Does the changing rate of prosecution reflect religious tempers or perhaps new policing strategies? Are we witnessing yet another wave of reforming manners discussed by Martin Ingram in this volume, and which he in fact partly relates to the concern with educating youth? Yet these lines of inquiry will probably add only another dimension to the idea that masterless youth were more tightly policed in particular conditions. A heightened sensation of godliness, however, could be a neglected aspect of this study. It is well known, for example, that magistrates and ministers tended to dwell on sin in plague sermons and orders, and that they 'mistrusted' singlewomen.[122]

In fact, magistracy and ministry had a long association in Norwich which can be traced as far back as the 1570s.[123] Interestingly, it has been argued that the 'Puritan movement in Norwich exhibited considerable strength in the 1620s and 1630s', and that in the same period 'city government decisively committed itself to the protection of the godly cause'. New figures emerged, and some of them were 'imbued with strong religious ideals'.[124] Puritans 'were always in the minority', but the corporation was sympathetic, and 'was of great utility in sponsoring Puritan lectureships and in enacting and enforcing local ordinances regulating the desired moral and social behaviour'. The Mayor's Court played a prominent part.[125] Yet the social rhetoric being studied here is not often associated with elevated piety or reforming manners. Moreover, Norwich was an early reformed city, and we must still explain the puzzling reluctance to use this language before 1600. Nevertheless, active piety is one potential layer of a much broader explanation, which must also explore how the interpretative climate of the early seventeenth-century and socio-economic conditions in Norwich sharpened concern with the masterless condition, youth, work and gender. It is unlikely that casual work, the preference for working at home, or drifting in and out of service were the product of difficult times alone. Vagrancy increased and perhaps theft in time of need. But the problems raised by masterless youth do not sit dormant for a few years and then spring into life when summoned. One key to the clustering of prosecutions is elite perceptions, which were already finely tuned by the interpretative climate of the early seventeenth century and the rise in the size of the city. Legislation did not create such concern, but clearer strategies and identifications were certainly being proposed, and they could be treated as one sign of elevated concern with their principal subjects.

Yet these Acts can only explain the pursuit of the *resident* young. To pursue coincidences we can turn to the as yet little explored problems regarding entry into service in this difficult period, and the growing number of people coming to Norwich towards the close of the sixteenth century. Rising in-migration contributed to the city's population explosion, but it also had some unpleasant side-effects elevating poverty, economic competition and the threat of disorder. In-migration at this rate could have altered the 'shape of service as a form of work' and caused a multiplication of casual work.[126] This may partly explain why arrests increased after 1600. The articles of that year, therefore, were one response to alterations in the fabric of the city resulting from rising in-migration and changes in occupational structures.[127] Thereafter the cycle of prosecutions reveals a sequence of prominent clusterings, punctuated by a few sudden falls; the timing of cases is one sign of how concern with civic order, unshackled youth, gender and work peaked in certain conditions. Suspicions about masterless young people and the regulation of work were more clearly articulated and prosecuted in 1609–10, for example, 1630–1 and 1634–6.

There were also some relatively tranquil periods when troubles apparently eased and a semblance of tolerance settled on Norwich. Casual and domestic work or the connection between female independence and disorder did not cease to operate in less stressful times, but we could argue that magisterial concern (as expressed in the historical record) was dampened. The courtbooks therefore do not disclose the true extent of the problems raised by masterless youth; tensions festered and then broke forth in a fresh crop of arrests. This clustering of prosecutions possesses ideological significance above that of mere numbers. Gender and youth are timeless problems which touch all societies in some form. Yet no principle of order is ever experienced as a historical constant; ideologies are redefined or reanimated, and anxieties can sharpen. In early Stuart Norwich a number of factors isolated one conspicuous group – singlewomen. The wounds that they inflicted upon patriarchal feelings were expressed in a label which was also age-related – 'at their own hand'. Another term, 'out of service', which before 1600 revealed no striking gender trend, was to become primarily a badge of female independence in the new century.

The provenance and meaning of such labels has received little attention hitherto. Yet they were a dynamic aspect of the articulation of authority and process of law enforcement and caught a multitude of 'suspicious' situations and characters within the wide circumference of their supple meaning. The social language being studied here captured a spectrum of tensions, but uppermost in the minds of governors as they applied their labels was the concern that young people should remain within the compass of their master's authority in tutored work (and time). This concern took on a gendered character which was in large part derived from particular suspicions about female independence and enterprise. Masterless young people appeared free and restless. Some of them worked at home in casual labour or informal training and became more visible in difficult periods. Others followed an 'idle and wandring life', taking lodgings and drifting from service or home. They shared the common thread of *perceived freedom* and had a tenuous and sometimes distant relationship with formal structures of authority and work.

Slipping in and out of service, Jane Sellars, Joanne Weeting, Robert Mayer and others moved between competing statuses of 'masterless' and 'servant', thereby blurring the fine distinction between socialisation and the impulses of youth, which defined conformity and opposition in strategic polarities. They did not follow the 'ordinarie and dailie mode of lief'. In fact, they clarified the implications of their inferiority in different ways from the image of civil youth, which was defended in prosecutions and further communicated in indentures of apprenticeship, government decrees, catechisms, sermons and conduct books. Moreover, with the steady decline of service and apprenticeship in later centuries,[128] and the rise in the size of towns, the proletariat and casual work, difficulties raised by the control of youth may have sharpened. Tutored work and time became more contested issues.[129] Adam Smith mourned the gradual loss of indoor apprenticeship in which young people were in theory confined within the compass of their master's authority.[130] In the first decade of the nineteenth century, the master clothiers and workers in the west of England thought that the proposed repeal of the Statute of Artificers was 'one of the most awful propositions ever submitted to the legislature'. They argued that apprenticeship was 'both a moral and political institution', and 'a custom which has prevailed time out of mind'.[131] Opposing the repeal of the Statute in 1814, one MP drew upon an age-old concern with dissolute youth, declaring that its loss would be 'ruinous to the morals of youth'. His was not a lone voice and he was joined in the House by Mr Searjant Best, who argued that 'it was much better that young people should not be left without some controle'.[132] Thus the concern with masterless youth stretches across centuries, and already Adam Smith could sit at his desk in the second half of the eighteenth century and glance back to a fading 'golden age' when young people were tightly bound to their master's household.

NOTES AND REFERENCES

* I must thank John Beattie, Bernard Capp, Peter King, Brian Outhwaite, Roger Schofield, Paul Slack, Keith Wrightson and my fellow editors for their very helpful suggestions in the preparation of this chapter. My earlier thoughts on this subject were given to seminars in Cambridge, London, Oxford, Toronto and Warwick, and I am very grateful for the constructive comments of the participants.

1. This comment is based upon evidence from the surviving records of [N]orwich [C]ity [Q]uarter [S]essions and the [N]orwich [M]ayor's [C]ourt, the principal sources for this chapter, which, along with the [N]orwich [A]ssembly [M]inute Books, are housed in Norwich and Norfolk Record Office in Norwich.

2. A form of petty theft.

3. Sellar's case history can be followed in NMC 15, fols 428v, 524; 16, fols 88v, 89, 109, 115v, 120v, 137, 166, 221, 264v, 266, 280, 315v, 316, 357v, 363; NCQS 'Sessions Boke 1630–38', fol. 55; minute book 1629–36, fols 38v, 42v, 53.

4. H. Becker is quoted by R. V. Ericson, *Criminal Reactions: The Labelling Perspective* (Lexington, 1975), p. 112.

5. Cf. G. Germani, *Marginality* (New Jersey, 1990), p. 50.

6. Germani, *Marginality*, pp. 54, 64–5; D. L. Potter and J. B. Roebuck, 'The Labelling Approach Re-examined: Interactionism and the Components of Deviance', *Deviant Behaviour*, vol. 9 (1988), pp. 19–32, esp. 23–24, 27, 29; D. Downes and P. Rock, *Understanding Deviance: A Guide to the Sociology of Crime and Rule Breaking*, 2nd edn (Oxford, 1988), pp. 178–9; P. Rock, 'The Sociology of Crime, Symbolic Interactionism and Some Problematic Qualities of Radical Criminology', in D. Downes and P. Rock (eds), *Deviant Interpretations* (Oxford, 1979), pp. 69–70; Ericson, *Criminal Reactions*, pp. 34, 38, 83, 95–6; P. Burke, *Sociology and History* (London, 1980), p. 58.

7. Downes and Rock, *Understanding Deviance*, p. 150; S. Box, *Deviance, Reality and Society* (London, 1971), pp. 31, 39–41, 49.

8. For example by B. Geremek, *The Margins of Society in Late Medieval Paris* (English trans., Cambridge, 1987), pp. 121, 286, 288.

9. This is a principal theme of my new book about early modern youth. See P. Griffiths, *Youth and Authority: Formative Experiences in England, 1560–1640* (Oxford, 1996).

10. M. Mitterauer, *A History of Youth* (English trans., Oxford, 1993), pp. 115, 131; I. Krausman Ben-Amos, *Adolescence and Youth in Early Modern England* (New Haven, 1994), pp. 205–6.

11. P. Laslett, *Family Life and Illicit Love in Earlier Generations* (Cambridge, 1977), p. 44. Much of the recent research has been conveniently sum-

marised in G. Mayhew, 'Life-Cycle, Service and the Family Unit in Early Modern Rye', *Continuity and Change*, vol. 6 (1991), pp. 201–26.

12. See especially Mayhew, 'Life-Cycle, Service and the Family Unit'; R. Wall, 'Leaving Home and the Process of Household-Formation in Pre-Industrial England', *Continuity and Change*, vol. 2 (1987), pp. 77–101.

13. See A. Kussmaul, *Servants in Husbandry in Early Modern England* (Cambridge, 1981), p. 3; A. L. Beier, *Masterless Men: The Vagrancy Problem in England, 1560–1640* (London, 1985), p. 23.

14. 7 James I c. 3; J. Rushworth (ed.), *Historical Collections*, 8 vols. (London, 1721), vol. II, p. 358.

15. 18 Elizabeth I c. 3. Cf. T. Hitchcock, 'Paupers and Preachers: The SPCK and the Parochial Workhouse Movement', in L. Davison *et al.* (eds), *Stilling the Grumbling Hive: The Response to Social and Economic Problems in England, 1689–1750* (Stroud, 1992), pp. 145–66.

16. Another form of petty theft.

17. Quoted in W. Hunt, *The Puritan Moment: The Coming of Revolution in an English County* (Cambridge, Mass., 1983), p. 250.

18. Quoted by I. Pinchbeck and M. Hewitt, *Children in English Society, Volume I: From Tudor Times to the Eighteenth Century* (London, 1969), p. 235.

19. NAM 4, fol. 139v. Cf. E. M. Leonard, *The Early History of English Poor Relief* (London, 1965), p. 244.

20. In Italy, young female migrants were described as being 'out of place'. See S. Cohen, *The Evolution of Women's Asylums Since 1500: From Refuges for Ex-Prostitutes to Shelters for Battered Wives* (New York, 1992), pp. 62, 79.

21. Cf. K. S. Martin (ed.), *Records of Maidstone Being Selections From Documents in the Possession of the Corporation* (Maidstone, 1926), p. 23.

22. The source is J. F. Pound (ed.), *The Norwich Census of the Poor, 1570*, Norfolk Record Society, vol. 40 (Norwich, 1971).

23. For example, by D. Woodward, 'The Background to the Statute of Artificers: The Genesis of Labour Policy, 1558–1563', *Economic History Review*, 2nd series, vol. 33 (1980), pp. 32–46.

24. Hunt, *Puritan Moment*, p. 65.

25. R. H. Tawney and E. Power (eds), *Tudor Economic Documents, Vol. III: Pamphlets, Memoranda and Literary Extracts* (London, 1924), pp. 345, 356, 363.

26. 7 James I c. 3; B. H. Cunnington (ed.), *Some Annals of the Borough of Devizes* (Devizes, 1925), p. 83. Cf. the fears expressed by the Wiltshire Bench in 1655 discussed by A. Fletcher, *Reform in the Provinces: The Government of Stuart England* (New Haven, 1986), p. 220. It has been argued that cases of being 'out of service' were part of a dual concern to 'keep wages down' and to assert patriarchal authority. See J. Innes, 'Prisons for the Poor: English Bridewells, 1555–1800', in F. Snyder and D. Hay (eds), *Labour, Law and Crime: An Historical Perspective* (London, 1987), p. 48.

27. Including the opportunity to pursue alternative sources of income. See M. Roberts, ' "Words They Are Women and Deeds They Are Men": Images of Work and Gender in Early Modern England', in L. Charles and L. Duffin (eds), *Women and Work in Pre-Industrial England* (London, 1985), p. 157.

28. Martin (ed.), *Records of Maidstone*, pp. 123, 72.

29. Cf. NAM 4, fol.139.

30. J. P. Earwaker (ed.), *The Court Leet Records of the Manor of Manchester . . . 1552 to . . . 1686*, 6 vols (Manchester, 1884–90), vol. I, p. 241; vol. II, pp. 37, 43.

31. In this period eight of the twenty-three cases (23.8 per cent) involved males.

32. Cf. Geremek, *Margins of Society*, p. 221, on suspicions of immorality with respect to single women of the 'popular and plebeian classes' who lived 'outside the context of the family'; E. P. Thompson, *Customs in Common* (London, 1991), ch. 2, esp. p. 501; P. J. P. Goldberg, *Women, Work and Life-Cycle in a Medieval Economy: Women in York and Yorkshire, c.1300–1520* (Oxford, 1992), pp. 299–300; Cohen, *Evolution of Women's Asylums*, pp. 62, 79.

33. M. E. Wiesner, *Women and Gender in Early Modern Europe* (Cambridge, 1993), pp. 62, 23, 99, 62, 89; Goldberg, *Women, Work and Life-Cycle*, p. 299.

34. There are, however, some examples of outsiders being presented. The residential pattern in 325 cases is as follows: 285 (87.7 per cent) can be positively identified as Norwich residents, twenty-five (7.6 per cent) were outsiders, while a further fifteen cannot be positively placed. In turn, the resident young were sometimes labelled as 'vagrants': see, e.g., NMC 13, fol. 387; 14, fols. 46, 183, 268v.

35. The operation and character of the Mayor's Court is examined in greater detail in J. F. Pound, *Tudor and Stuart Norwich* (Chichester, 1988), ch. 9; J. T. Evans, *Seventeenth-Century Norwich: Politics, Religion and Government, 1620–1690* (Oxford, 1979), pp. 58–9, 85. The City Quarter Sessions were used less frequently for these sorts of petty disorders, though as we shall see, a few masterless youths were prosecuted there. The records of the Mayor's Court, however, survive in an unbroken series for the entire period 1560–1645, and this permits us to quantify and tabulate with some confidence.

36. See A. L. Beier, 'Vagrants and the Social Order in Elizabethan England', *Past and Present*, vol. 64 (1974), pp. 9–10; P. Slack, 'Vagrants and Vagrancy in England, 1598–1644', *Economic History Review*, 2nd series, vol. 27 (1974), reprinted in P. Clark and D. Souden (eds), *Migration and Society in Early Modern England* (London, 1987), p. 54; Ben-Amos, *Adolescence and Youth*, chs 2–4. Cf. Goldberg, *Women, Work and Life-Cycle*, pp. 282, 292, 294.

37. A. Salerno, 'The Social Background of Seventeenth Century Emigration to America', *Journal of British Studies*, vol. 19 (1979), p. 38. The difficulties in placing parish apprentices can be partly followed in the State Papers. See, e.g., Public Record Office SP 16/239/6, 16/240/35, 16/250/2, 16/250/10, 16/259/15, 16/266/72. See also P. Slack, *Poverty and Policy in Tudor and Stuart England* (London, 1988), p. 142; T. G. Barnes, *Somerset, 1625–1640: A County's Government During the 'Personal Rule'* (London, 1961), p. 200; Fletcher, *Reform in the Provinces*, p. 216.

38. P. Clark, *The English Alehouse: A Social History, 1200–1830* (London, 1983), p. 139.

39. A. L. Beier, *Masterless Men: The Problem of Vagrancy in England, 1560–1640* (London, 1985), pp. 20, 47, 55.

40. Salerno, 'Social Background', p. 38. Cf. D. Souden, ' "Rogues, Whores and Vagabonds?" Indentured Servant Emigration to North America, and the Case of Mid-Seventeenth-Century Bristol', *Social History*, vol. 3 (1978), p. 27; Beier, *Masterless Men*, pp. 161–3; D. Cressy, *Coming Over: Migration and Communication Between England and New England in the Seventeenth Century* (Cambridge, 1987), pp. 63, 68.

41. The best recent summary of research is D. M. Palliser, *The Age of Elizabeth: England Under the Late Tudors*, 2nd edn (London, 1992), ch. 7. See also J. Barry, 'Introduction', in Barry (ed.), *The Tudor, and Stuart Town 1530–1688: A Reader in English Urban History* (London, 1990), pp. 1–34. Cf. Beier, *Masterless Men*, pp. 39–40.

42. See, e.g., V. Pearl, 'Change and Stability in Seventeenth-Century London', *London Journal*, vol. 5 (1979), reprinted in Barry (ed.), *Tudor and Stuart Town*, pp. 139–65; S. Rappaport, *Worlds Within Worlds: Structures of Life in Sixteenth-Century London* (Cambridge, 1989); J. Boulton, *Neighbourhood and Society: A London Suburb in the Seventeenth Century* (Cambridge, 1987).

43. See I. Archer, *The Pursuit of Stability: Social Relations in Elizabethan London* (Cambridge, 1991); P. Clark, 'A Crisis Contained? The Condition of English Towns in the 1590s', in Clark (ed.), *The European Crisis of the 1590s* (London, 1985), pp. 44–66.

44. See Griffiths, *Youth and Authority*, ch. 6.

45. P. Corfield, 'A Provincial Capital in the Late Seventeenth Century: The Case of Norwich', in P. Clark and P. Slack (eds), *Crisis and Order in English Towns, 1500–1700: Essays in Urban History* (London, 1972), pp. 263–310; Evans, *Seventeenth-Century Norwich*, pp. 4–5.

46. J. Patten, *English Towns, 1500–1700* (Folkestone, 1978), pp. 294–5.

47. The sources are NMC 11–16 and 20. I have excluded people who were expelled without being prosecuted for vagrancy. Banishment was imposed upon residents, but we can be sure that an unknown number of outsiders were within their ranks. However, the trend presented here would remain if we included the banished people.

48. Beier, *Masterless Men*, p. 54.

49. See W. Gouge, *Of Domesticall Duties* (London, 1622), p. 535; H. Cunningham, 'The Employment and Unemployment of Children in England c.1680–1851', *Past and Present*, vol. 126 (1990), p. 126. A recent study of women and gender in early modern Europe has noted that 'authorities at times even tried to prevent grown daughters from continuing to live with their parents, arguing that parents gave them too much freedom which causes "nothing but shame, immodesty, wantonness and immorality", with their idleness leading to "tearing hedges, robbing orchards, beggaring their fathers" ', Wiesner, *Women and Gender*, p. 99.

50. The sources are NMC 12–16 and 20. Of the 313 cases, 61 were prosecuted for being 'at their own hand' and 252 for being 'out of service'. The chronology of prosecutions for both offences follows the same pattern. See P. Griffiths, 'Some Aspects of the Social History of Youth in Early

Modern England, with Particular Reference to the Period, *c.*1560–*c.*1640'
(unpublished University of Cambridge Ph.D. thesis, 1992), p. 353 (table
6.3).

51. NMC 13, fol. 387.

52. For example at the parish vestries of Finchingfield and Braintree in
Essex, F. G. Emmison (ed.), *Early Essex Town Meetings* (Chichester, 1970),
pp. 9, 15, 23–4, 46, 57–8, 63, 65, 78, 92, 115–16, 122, 126; in Maidstone,
Martin (ed.), *Records of Maidstone* pp. 23, 72; in Dorchester, D. Underdown,
Fire from Heaven: Life in an English Town in the Seventeenth Century (London,
1992), p. 82; and in Bedworth (Warwickshire), S. C. Ratcliff and H. C.
Johnson (eds), *Warwick County Records,* 5 vols (Warwick, 1935–9), vol. V, pp.
212, 217. For London cases, see Guildhall Library (London) Courtbooks
of London Bridewell, vol. 4, fols 153, 186, 278, 312v, 320, 348v, 349, 356,
363, 370, 374,; vol. 5, fols 61v, 80, 111, 118, 130, 168v, 308v; [C]orporation
of [L]ondon [R]ecord [O]ffice Journals of Common Council [hereafter
Jour.] 29, fol. 20v; 32, fol. 319; Repertories of the Court of Aldermen, 34,
fol. 288. Interestingly, the gender bias was equally pronounced in these
dispersed locations. Cf. Roberts, ' "Words They Are Women", pp. 157ff;
R. Thompson, *Sex in Middlesex: Popular Mores in a Massachusetts County,
1649–1699* (Amherst, 1986), pp. 89, 91–2; Thompson, 'Adolescent Culture
in Colonial Massachusetts', *Journal of Family History,* vol. 9 (1984), p. 134.
The tensions under review here also affected late medieval towns. See M.
D. Harris (ed.), *The Coventry Leet Book: Or Mayor's Register Containing the
Records of the City Court Leet or View of Frankpledge AD 1420–1555,* 4 parts,
Early English Text Society, original series, nos 134, 135, 138, 146 (London,
1907–13), part II, pp. 545, 568.

53. See NMC 13, fol. 177; 14, fols. 256v–57v, 257–9; 16, fols. 291, 314v,
316, 317; 20, fols. 9, 11–11v, 32–32v, 132. Fuller references to types of cases
and civic procedure described here are to be found in Griffiths, 'Social
History of Youth'; Griffiths, *Youth and Authority.*

54. NMC 13, fols 568–71, 572–82.

55. NMC 15, fol. 247v.

56. NMC 15, fol. 332.

57. NMC 8, fol. 193; 15, fol. 22v; 16, fol. 211; 20, fols 9v, 17v, 22, 279v,
488.

58. NMC 15, fols 84, 489; 20, fols 12v, 322.

59. See, e.g., NMC 20, fols. 17v, 22.

60. NMC 20, fol. 12v; 13, fol. 307.

61. NMC 20, fol. 210. The records reveal 144 cases in which young
people were confined in this way. This is nearly double the number of cases
(78) in which offenders were first returned home and given a fixed period
in which to find a master.

62. Cf. Innes, 'Prisons for the Poor', pp. 54, 57, 76; J. M. Beattie,
Crime and the Courts in England, 1660–1800 (Oxford, 1986), p. 562 (table
10.6).

63. NMC 15, fol. 429; 20, fol. 276v.

64. See, e.g., NMC 15, fols 114, 501; 16, fols 219, 225; 20, fols. 17v, 309,
347.

65. See NMC 16, fol. 255v; 20, fol. 347.

66. Patten, *English Towns*, p. 265.

67. For full archival references, see Griffiths, 'Social History of Youth', pp. 365–7.

68. For full archival references, see ibid.

69. NMC 16, fol. 414v; 14, fols 344, 246. See Griffiths, 'Social History of Youth', p. 368.

70. NMC 16, fols 298v, 303v, 305, 316, 331v, 337v, 347, 400v, 479v; 20, fols 3, 14, 21; NCQS Minute Book 1629–36, fols 21v, 30, 74; 'Sessions Boke 1630–1638', fols 1v, 30.

71. NMC 14, fols 38v, 39, 101v, 108, 110, 115v, 123v, 125v, 127v, 148.

72. NMC 14, fols 231v, 234, 304, 304v, 306, 306v, 313.

73. As well as some of the evidence presented here, see NMC 14, fols 38v, 110, 123v, 206v; 16, fols 424v, 430; 20, fols 123, 156v; NCQS Minute Book 1629–36, fols 38v, 71, 87v, 113v, 117v.

74. See NMC 12, fols 488, 595, 745, 820; 13, fols 132, 133, 139 (two cases), 387, 674 (three cases); 14, fol. 38v; 16, fol. 19; 'Sessions Boke 1630–1638', fol. 27.

75. NMC 13, fol. 399; NCQS 'Sessions Boke 1630–1638', fol. 27.

76. NMC 7, fol. 588; 14, fol. 359.

77. NMC 13, fols 508, 524.

78. NMC 20, fols 18, 22. Cf. Roberts, ' "Words They Are Women" ', pp. 159–60; Cunningham, 'Employment and Unemployment of Children', p. 106.

79. NMC 13, fols 23, 182.

80. The chronology of plague in Norwich can be followed in P. Slack, *The Impact of Plague in Tudor and Stuart England* (London, 1985), pp. 126–43.

81. Cf. Ibid., pp. 126–43 and ch. 7.

82. Ibid., p. 131.

83. NMC 14, fol. 196.

84. *Calendar of State Papers Domestic, 1603–1610*, p. 611.

85. NMC 16, fols 280, 290v–91, 332, 334, 337v. The light plague of 1630–1 and socio-economic difficulties at that time are discussed in Slack, *Impact of Plague*, pp. 132–3, 194.

86. NMC 16, fols 291, 351; NCQS Minute Book 1629–36, fol. 35.

87. See NMC 16, fols 290v, 314v, 317, 320v–21, 322–22v, 325–26v, 327–28, 329–29v, 348v, 351v–52, 366v; NCQS Minute Book 1629–36, fols 27–27v, 30v–31, 35, 53; 'Sessions Boke 1630–1638', fol. 16; NAM 6, fol. 91.

88. NMC 16, fols 470v, 475v; 20, fols.9, 11–11v.

89. NMC 16, fol 470v; NCQS 'Sessions Boke 1630–1638', fol. 60.

90. Slack, *Impact of Plague*, p. 278; NMC 20, fols 128, 132.

91. J. Walter, 'The Social Economy of Dearth in Early Modern England', in J. Walter and R. S. Schofield (eds), *Famine, Disease and the Social Order in Early Modern Society* (Cambridge, 1989), pp. 126–8. Cf. Slack, *Impact of Plague*, chs 10–11; Slack, *Poverty and Policy*, pp. 143–5; Pound, *Tudor and Stuart Norwich*, pp. 116, 122.

92. Quoting Slack, *Poverty and Policy*, p. 145.

93. Slack, *Impact of Plague*, pp. 181–4, 188; R. S. Schofield and E. A. Wrigley, 'Infant and Child Mortality in England in the Late Tudor and Early Stuart Period', in C. Webster (ed.), *Health, Medicine and Mortality in the Sixteenth Century* (Cambridge, 1979), pp. 61–95, Cf. CLRO Jour. 26, fol.172.

94. Cf. P. Sharpe, 'Poor Children as Apprentices in Colyton, 1598–1830', *Continuity and Change*, vol. 6 (1991), pp. 259–60 who finds large rises in the number of pauper apprentices in times of 'specific distress' like dearth, high prices, the Dutch Wars and related trade depression. In Colyton, the year of the highest number of apprenticeships (1647) was a year of plague and high prices.

95. D. Underdown, 'The Taming of the Scold: The Enforcement of Patriarchal Authority in Early Modern England', in A. Fletcher and J. Stevenson (eds), *Order and Disorder in Early Modern England* (Cambridge, 1985), pp. 116–32. Sadly Underdown confines his thoughts about being 'out of service' to a single sentence (p. 119). Further, he simply assumes that these cases are gender-specific without investigating the sex ratio of offenders, or indeed, the precise tensions which lay behind them.

96. Ibid., pp. 123–4. However, my figures are only drawn from civic judicial sources. They reveal a total of ninety-five prosecuted scolds in the period 1581–1640. Interestingly, the only period in which there was a regular run of cases at about three or four each year was the troubled period 1629–32.

97. NMC 14, fol. 250v.

98. J. A. Sharpe, *Early Modern England: A Social History, 1550–1750* (London, 1987), p. 80.

99. I am following the categorisation of 'poor' and 'medium' parishes given in Slack, *Impact of Plague*, pp. 135, 138 (tables 5.4, 5.5). The parishes studied are the 'poor' parishes of All Saints, St Julian, St James, St Augustine, St Margaret, St Benedict and St Peter Parmentergate, and the 'medium' parishes of St Gregory, St Giles, St Lawrence and St John Timberhill.

100. I have followed the discussion of sex ratios in E. A. Wrigley and R. S. Schofield, *The Population History of England, 1541–1871: A Reconstruction* (Cambridge, 1981), pp. 224–6. Cf. D. Souden, 'Migrants and the Population Structure of Late Seventeenth Century Provincial Cities and Market Towns', in P. Clark (ed.), *The Transformation of English Provincial Towns, 1660–1800* (London, 1984), pp. 99–132; Pound, *Norwich Census of the Poor*, appendix 1.

101. Cf. Ben-Amos, *Adolescence and Youth*, ch. 6; Ben-Amos, 'Women Apprentices in the Trades and Crafts of Early Modern Bristol', *Continuity and Change*, vol. 6 (1991), pp. 227–52; Sharpe, 'Poor Children as Apprentices', p. 259; M. Roberts, 'Women and Work in Sixteenth Century English Towns', in P. Corfield and D. Keene (eds), *Work in Towns, 850–1850* (Leicester, 1990), p. 91.

102. See, e.g., Pound (ed.), *Norwich Census of the Poor*, pp. 39, 42, 44, 49, 51, 56, 57, 59, 60, 62, 64.

103. See, e.g. ibid., pp. 33, 34–5, 38, 41, 43, 45, 50, 55, 57. The informal

training of young women in this period is more fully explored in Ben-Amos, *Adolescence and Youth*, pp. 145–50.

104. Cf. S. Wright, ' "Churmaids, Huswyfes and Hucksters": The Employment of Women in Tudor and Stuart Salisbury', in Charles and Duffin (eds), *Women and Work*, pp. 104–5.

105. Roberts, 'Women and Work', pp. 91, 93–4, 95.

106. See NMC 16, fols 279–79v, 334v–35, 335, 337, 338–40, 341v, 364v–65, 366, 379; 20, fols. 30, 96v; NCQS 'Sessions Boke 1630–1638', fol. 8.

107. NMC 14, fols.257v, 235.

108. NMC 12, fols 910, 918; 14, fol.175; 16, fol.211; 20, fol.210.

109. See, e.g., NMC 14, fols 121v, 426; 15, fol.63; 16, fols 271, 379; 20, fols, 6v, 9v, 184.

110. NMC 14, fols 83, 46; 12, fol. 640. Cf. R. A. Houston, *Social Change in the Age of the Enlightenment: Edinburgh, 1660–1760* (Oxford, 1994), pp. 80, 139, 181–2.

111. NMC 7, fol. 494; 20, fol.148.

112. Sadly, we only possess information about two males who were both found 'out of service': 'John Furrys, the sonne of Furrys the dummer', who finally took him into his service; and William Palsy, 'a boy' of 18 years of age, who was living at home with his mother in the parish of St Martin's-in-the-Palace. See NMC 20, fols 64–64v, 66v;16, fol. 211.

113. NMC 16, fols 31v, 224v, 311v, 338v, 359; 20, fols 9, 17v. Cf. M. E. Wiesner, *Working Women in Renaissance Germany* (New Brunswick, 1986), pp. 88–9.

114. The combined total for both offences is forty. A male householder was resident in seventeen cases (42.5 per cent). Twenty-three households were headed by women, and twelve of them can be positively identified as widows.

115. Pound (ed.), *Norwich Census of the Poor*, p. 18 (table 7).

116. NAM IV, fol. 139.

117. The 1579 plague was 'the greatest mortality in the town's history after the black death'. Slack, *Impact of Plague*, p. 129.

118. This 'light' plague may partly explain the rise in prosecutions in 1600–1.

119. 43 Elizabeth I c.2; 7 James I c.4, Cf. R. B. Shoemaker, *Prosecution and Punishment: Petty Crime and the Law in London and Rural Middlesex c.1660–1725* (Cambridge, 1991), pp. 168–70.

120. NAM 5, fol. 45.

121. Cf. Evans, *Seventeenth-Century Norwich*, pp. 63–4.

122. See, e.g., Slack, *Impact of Plague*, esp. ch. 2; M. Healy, 'Discourses of the Plague in Early Modern London', in J. A. I. Champion (ed.), *Epidemic Disease in London*, Centre for Metropolitan History Working Papers Series (London, 1993), pp. 19–34.

123. See Evans, *Seventeenth-Century Norwich*, pp. 84–6, 96–7; Pound, *Tudor and Stuart Norwich*, p. 87; P. Collinson, *The Religion of Protestants: The Church in English Society, 1559–1625* (Oxford, 1982), pp. 141–5; Slack, *Poverty and Policy*, p. 119.

124. Evans, *Seventeenth-Century Norwich*, p. 96; Pound, *Tudor and Stuart*

Norwich, p. 85. The emergence of new groups is fully examined in Evans, *Seventeenth-Century Norwich*, chs 2–3; and Pound, *Tudor and Stuart Norwich*, pp. 78–82. One indication of this shift in the distribution of influence in municipal politics was the number of disputed elections in this period; another was the controversy about the appointment of lecturers; see Evans, *Seventeenth-Century Norwich*, pp. 66–79, 84–96; Pound, *Tudor and Stuart Norwich*, pp. 88–90; P. King, 'Bishop Wren and the Suppression of the Norwich Lecturers', *Historical Journal*, vol. 11 (1968), pp. 237–54. 'By the 1620s Puritanism was a socially respectable movement with deep roots and its leaders were among the towns élite' – Evans, *Seventeenth-Century Norwich*, p.102.

  125. Evans, *Seventeenth-Century Norwich*, pp. 97, 103. Evans has argued that the Puritans were 'only a determined hard-core minority in the Court of Aldermen', but that they were 'supported by an overwhelming number in the Common Council'. Both historians of the city call the Mayor's Court a 'moral policeman': Evans, *Seventeenth-Century Norwich*, p. 85; Pound, *Tudor and Stuart Norwich*, p. 88.

  126. Roberts, 'Women and Work', 92.

  127. We require much further work on aspects of urban history and migration before changes in urban occupational structures *c.*1570–1650 are fully established, and then related to the type of problems discussed in this chapter. First, we require closer study of the character and extent of inmigration to the towns in this period, and in particular, sex ratios should prove significant. Second, the timing of prosecutions for the sort of offences under review here requires further study in other towns. The concerns behind labelling (and the history of other labels) need to be established. Third, we need to further explore the policing of casual labour and employment more generally in times of stress. It would also be of great value to relate prosecutions for being 'out of service' and 'at their own hand' to occupational structures by gleaning more evidence about the occupational histories of offenders than the Norwich sources I have consulted so far have permitted. The home parish (when appropriate) of offenders would also help us to build up a picture of the provenance of labels. Finally, one missing (and important) dimension in this chapter has been the socio-economic conditions in the countryside and the study of 'push' factors in migration patterns. I have tended to assume that many of the reasons for in-migration can be related to the demand for labour in the towns and other attractions the town could offer, though the possible correspondence between the demands of the town and problems in its hinterland may be significant. Cf. Goldberg, *Women, Work and Life-Cycle*, p. 291.

  128. Though this decline was gradual and more rapid in certain trades; others retained tight control over entry through service. See. C. Brooks, 'Apprenticeship, Social Mobility and the Middling Sort, 1550–1800', in J. Barry and C. Brooks (eds), *The Middling Sort of People: Culture, Society and Politics in England, 1550–1800* (London, 1994), pp. 54–62. Cf. K. Snell, *Annals of the Labouring Poor: Social Change and Agrarian England, 1660–1900* (Cambridge, 1985), chs 2 and 5; Kussmaul, *Servants in Husbandry*, chs 2, 6 and 7.

129. E. P. Thompson, *Customs in Common*, pp. 36–42, 352–403. See also the contribution of John Rule to this volume, Chapter 9 below; and M. J. Wiener, *Reconstructing the Criminal: Culture, Law and Policy in England, 1830–1914* (Cambridge, 1990), pp. 17–19, 51.

130. Smith's position is discussed in H. Hendrick, *Images of Youth: Age, Class and the Male Youth Problem, 1820–1920* (Oxford, 1990), pp. 15–16.

131. Quoted by A. J. Randall, *Before the Luddites: Custom, Community and Machinery in the English Woollen Industry, 1776–1809* (Cambridge, 1991), p. 243.

132. *Hansard* (1813–14), pp. 879, 892–3.

6 Disruption in the Well-Ordered Household: Age, Authority, and Possessed Young People

J. A. SHARPE

I

Authority in early modern England ran along various channels, and operated within a spectrum of spheres of concern. At one end of that spectrum lay the authority most familiar to the historian and the general reader, the authority of the monarch and central government. At the other, lay that bundle of social norms and conventions, often imperfectly grasped and articulated by contemporaries, which constituted, in the broad sense of the term, the 'authority' within which people lived their everyday community and family lives. In between these there lay a number of webs of authority. Some, like the authority inherent in the social structure, have been much studied by historians as they have attempted to reconstruct social hierarchies or analyse languages of social description. Others, like the authority which structured gender relations, have come to attract considerable attention from historians over the last few years. Yet others, like the problems of authority implicit in the relationships between different age groups which form the background to this chapter, although now the subject of an important new book by Paul Griffiths, have been little studied hitherto.[1] This is odd, since, even when due allowances are made for the stereotyped social complaint of contemporary didactic literature, it is evident that concern over the age hierarchy, over the problems of maintaining appropriate behaviour in different age groups, and of ensuring the authority of older people over younger ones were all firmly embedded in Tudor and Stuart social comment. Jacques's speech in *As You Like It* is only the most familiar example of a considerable, and usually highly conventionalised, body of 'Ages of Man' literature.

The writers and readers of this literature, whether they were aware of it or not, were living in an age whose demographic regime had created distinctive age structure. Currently, in Western Europe and North America, populations are ageing, and contain what is, historically, an abnormally high proportion of elderly people. In early modern England a bouyant birth rate meant that, despite the ravages of child mortality, a very high proportion of the population was young. Estimates vary, but it seems likely that some 40 per cent of the people living in England in 1600 were aged less than 21.[2] It is thus hardly surprising that a large number of writers were concerned with the problems of bringing up children and of instilling proper conduct in adolescents. Indeed, there was a wide body of opinion in print which held that adolescence, or 'youth' as it was normally termed (a period most frequently thought to lie roughly between an individual's fourteenth and twenty-eighth birthdays) was a peculiarly difficult period. Although the writers rarely attributed undesirable characteristics solely to any specific age group, it was generally held that young people were likely to be unusually prone to bad behaviour which, if uncurbed, would impede both their own spiritual development and the running of an orderly Christian Commonwealth: sensuality, disobedience, levity, wantonness, idleness, excess, envy, ambition, and mocking of elders or authority more generally, were numbered among the sins to which youth was prone.

It is hardly surprising that one of the standard views of this stage in the life-cycle was that it constituted something of a metaphorical battleground between good and evil. Youth was, like childhood, seen as a formative period, in which individuals would be shaped by good or bad influences which might normally be expected to leave a decisive impression upon their characters for the rest of their lives: unlike childhood, the imminent prospect of the acquisition of adult status leant a certain urgency to the need to form characters correctly. Thus Richard Burton, in his *Apprentice's Companion* of 1681, could describe youth as 'the season of [the individual's] greatest trial, wherein nature will soon discover itself; whether filthiness or holiness; the righteous commands of God, or the wretched lusts of the flesh shall be dearer to him'. The writer of an earlier moral handbook for apprentices could contrast two ways of life, one 'a religious profession . . . in which the liberties of the flesh and blood may be restrained', and another, 'the way of death', in which 'liberty and full head' was given to 'youthful affections and lusts of the flesh'. 'Wherefore', he advised his intended audience, 'let every young man beholding these two ways, choose that which leads unto eternal life in heaven'.[3] Certainly, from the Reformation onwards, writer after writer warned of the necessity to bring youth up correctly to be a fully socialised member of household and commonwealth.

Thus historians of early modern England, as they continue in their attempts to deepen their understanding of that society, must recognise that age is one of the variables to be built into their models of social relations. If they are to do so, it is evident that issues revolving around the age hierarchy will crop up in a number of rather unexpected places. Contemporary views on such matters can be found in a number of contexts, in the allocation of local office, for example, where men of maturity were preferred, or in the language of insult, where 'boy' was an epithet which was resented by the grown men at whom it was hurled in anger. A list of such contexts might expand to take in such headings as clothing, church seating, and precedence in local civic processions. Paul Griffith's work, we must reiterate, demonstrates how concern over the age hierarchy was one which permeated early modern life.

Once this is realised, it comes as less of a surprise to find age as a very germaine issue in witchcraft accusations. Despite the attention which witchcraft as a historical phenomenon in Europe has attracted over the last century or so, there is still a certain sense that we are still in the process of establishing the relevant social contexts which surrounded it. But it seems safe to affirm that if the age hierarchy in general, and problems of youth more particularly, have been little studied in the early modern world, the same can hardly be said of witchcraft. Since the immediate aftermath of the last European executions for witchcraft, the subject has attracted the attention of a large body of writers, among them a core of serious scholars and historians are now accustomed to looking at witchcraft accusations not as the mere evidence of the 'ignorance' or 'superstition' of earlier ages, but rather as serious phenomena which were set firmly in a social and cultural context. Part of that context is provided by the position of the accused and the accuser in certain social hierarchies: work on English witchcraft, to move towards our immediate concerns, has placed the witch and her accuser firmly in the context of social relationships and social hierarchies within the village community, while more recent work has explored the problem of witchcraft accusations and gender relationships.[4] Thus the importance of the familiar dichotomies of rich and poor, male and female, have been fully established by historians of early modern witchcraft. What is also becoming evident is that age – and perhaps that other basic dichotomy between old and young – needs to be built into the equation. It is my intention to demonstrate this point by examining one of its more important aspects, the supposed possession of young people by witchcraft, this most frequently taking the form of their bodies being entered by demons sent by the witch.

The presence of young people as victims of alleged witchcraft or as the accusers of supposed witches can be traced in a number of early modern cultures. Thus in one of the most celebrated witch crazes of all, that at Salem, Massachusetts, in 1692, a group of young girls lay at the centre of a web of accusations which brought in over 200 suspected witches.[5] The period of intense witchcraft prosecutions in Sweden, occurring between 1668 and 1676, saw a heavy involvement of child and adolescent accusers, while one of the features of late trials in south western Germany, an area of heavy persecution, was the prevalence of child accusers.[6] In England, likewise, most relevant bodies of archival evidence suggest the presence of children and adolescents as victims of witchcraft, and as accusers of witches. Indictments on the Home Circuit of the assizes between 1610 and 1659 reveal 192 accusations of witchcraft, in which the alleged witches were supposed to have killed or harmed sixty-one adults and forty-four children. Documentation relating to the mass trials in East Anglia between 1645 and 1647 allows us to reconstruct details of the accusations against 110 of the accused witches, of which thirty-six involved harming or killing adults, and fifty-six children. In a body of twenty sets of assize depositions relating to Yorkshire accusations over the second half of the seventeenth century, twelve involved the harming or killing of children and adolescents.[7] Thus most bodies of evidence which are capable of being analysed statistically suggest that the age hierarchy was one of the factors in operation in English witchcraft accusations.

Qualitative evidence may be set against such exercises in quantification. As one reads into the fuller narratives of witchcraft provided by the longer contemporary printed accounts of cases and the better documented manuscript evidence, it becomes obvious that the bewitchment of children and adolescents was a recurring phenomenon. This frequently took the form of the infliction of strange illnesses on them, which were then diagnosed as evidence that they were possessed by demons sent by witches. Close reading of these accounts shows how the possessed child or adolescent frequently lay at the centre of a complex network of fears about witchcraft, suspicions of witchcraft, and witchcraft beliefs. They also show how the young person's role as a victim of possession permitted a means for effecting a series of temporary subversions of the age hierarchy. The youthful victim of possession, the centre of attraction as he or she writhed on the sickbed, posed a number of challenges to traditional concepts of how the young should behave.

The subject of this chapter would, therefore, seem to be a promising one. There are, however, two issues which must be addressed at this introductory stage. First, it has proved unprofitable, in what is essentially an exploratory piece, to enter too deeply into how different sub-groups within the general category of 'young people' might have reacted to possession. One variant is age, especially that crucial dividing line, coming at 14 or so, between childhood and youth. Contemporaries had a clear sense of a division here, and it is obvious (especially given our awareness of modern psychology) that puberty would be a very relevant factor. Most of the cases discussed here involved teenagers or people in their early twenties, although a number, which have been indicated, concerned younger persons. One point that is worth stressing is that in a number of cases (for example those involving the Starkie, Throckmorton and Fairfax households) younger children seem to have developed symptoms of possession in line with older ones, showing how the border between youth and childhood might be crossed. Indeed, if we may look across the Atlantic to the group of possessed girls at Salem, we find an age range that stretches from 9 to 20. Gender is another variable. Unfortunately, the materials defy quantification, but the sources upon which this chapter is based do create the impression that young women were more likely to be involved in these cases than were young men. This must, however, retain the status of an impression until further investigation can allow us to be be categorical on the point.

Second, the source materials themselves need scrutiny. As we shall argue, the behaviour described in possession cases was very stereotyped and patterned. There is, of course, the risk that this patterning was created by the authors of the pamphlets and tracts from which so much of our evidence comes. Many of these tracts were anonymous, which makes it difficult to be too certain about the intentions or ideological positions of their authors. What is evident, however, is that many of them could be seen as falling into a literature of 'example'.[8] These narratives of the evil done by the devil's agents on earth could obviously be turned to a didactic purpose: indeed, the witchcraft literature in general of the period was often cast in such a mould. The battle between good and evil was a major theme within a theme, while it was obvious that those of the possessed who resisted satan and his agents as they writhed in their fits were worthy examples of godliness to others. Yet while we must be alert to such problems, I would contend that these tracts are (within the parameters of contemporary perceptions) factual accounts rather than fictionalised moral tales. Manuscript evidence is reassuring on this point. The lengthy manuscript accounts of Anne Gunter's sufferings or the possession of the Fairfax children read very like the tracts. And another early manuscript source, a case of the possession of a son of the gentry in Yorkshire from the beginning of the seventeenth century, although short, describes all the standard symptoms.[9] Despite the stereotyped rhetoric in which they were cast, these descriptions of possession do reflect a genuine social phenomenon.

II

The belief in the possibility of diabolical possession was a natural consequence of the belief in the existence of the devil, and in his hostility to mankind. The origins of the notion that incarnate spirits can enter into living human bodies, and animate or control them, was long established by the late sixteenth century, and indeed has been found in cultures other than those in the early modern Christian West. We are, of course, with our modern knowledge of hysteria, psychology and psychosomatic behaviour, now able to give 'rational' scientific or medical explanations of the symptoms of possession. Moreover, practically every well-documented case of the time includes references to physicians being called in, while some of the incidents became a contested field between those who adduced medical explanations and those who preferred supernatural ones. What is obvious is that demonic possession was a widely accepted explanation of unfamiliar illness, that the behaviour of those thought to be possessed followed a set cultural pattern, and that, in England at least, possession was, by the late sixteenth century, frequently attributed to the influence of witches rather than directly to the devil. 'It seemeth to be a matter very pertinent to the dignity of the exorcist', wrote the sceptical Samuel Harsnett in 1599, in the wake of a series of well-publicised cases of possession, 'that he be able to declare who sent the devil to his patient'.[10]

That the pattern of such cases was well established by the mid-Elizabethan period is demonstrated by a case of feigned possession, allied to malicious accusations of witchcraft, which arose in London in 1574. Two teenage girls, Agnes Briggs and Rachel Pinder, admitted to simulating possession, and of having falsely accused a woman named Joan Thornton of bewitching them. What is obvious, however, is that a number of the elements which were to recur in later and better documented cases were already present: the fits and trances suffered by the two girls, the way the devil spoke through them in strange voices, their vomiting of foreign bodies, the eagerness with which Protestant ministers of the hotter sort organised prayer meetings around them as they suffered.[11] Within fifty years, possession was a phenomenon so widely recognised that it was thought possible to stage it as a commercial enterprise. In 1621 Elizabeth Saunders, a yeoman's wife living at West Ham in Essex, confessed during an investigation by Star Chamber to having taught a young married woman named Katherine Malpas how to stimulate possession, in 'expectation & hope that much money would be given unto her . . . by such persons as should come to see her in pity and commiseration'. Malpas, when first instructed by Saunders, had proved a 'fit and apt' student, who in due course proved able to add elaborations of her own to her pretended possession. Yet, clearly, these two women were confident that possession of this type would be widely recognised, and knew how to simulate it.[12]

That possession should be a recognised cultural phenomenon by the 1620s was hardly surprising: there had been a series of well-publicised cases involving possession and subsequent accusations of witchcraft which must have done much to inform both educated opinion and the beliefs of the population at large. In 1589–93, one of the formative English witchcraft cases had occurred, involving the children of the Throckmorton family of Warboys in Huntingdonshire, an incident which formed the basis both for a lengthy tract and a ballad, the latter now lost, and was commemorated in an annual sermon against witchcraft. At the end of the sixteenth century the activities of a young exorcist named John Darrell prompted a major scholarly debate. Darrell had apparently achieved some reputation in the Midlands and the north of England, and had been involved in the dispossession of seven members, most of them children or adolescents, of the Starkie household in Lancashire, of a teenage girl named Katherine Wright, of a teenage boy named Thomas Darling, and of a 19-year-old apprentice called William Somers. In 1602, London was disrupted by the possession of Mary Glover, the 14-year-old daughter of a wealthy shopkeeper. In 1606, the alleged possession of Anne Gunter, the teenage daughter of a Berkshire gentleman named Brian Gunter, attracted the attention of King James I and was subsequently investigated by Star Chamber. And, a few years later in 1621, the possession of two of the daughters of a Yorkshire gentleman named Edward Fairfax prompted the worried parent to write a lengthy manuscript account of his daughters' sufferings. All of these cases led to allegations of witchcraft, all of them involved adolescents or children, most of them involved the families of the gentry or of people, like the Glovers, who were well connected in their community.[13]

Taking these and other, less well-documented, cases together, a standard narrative of possession by witchcraft emerges, one which forms a contrast to the standard narrative of village *maleficium*, revolving around refused alms and neighbourly tensions, constructed twenty-five years ago by Alan Macfarlane. A young person falls ill, exhibiting a set of symptoms which are thought to lie outside the normal range of sickness experienced by young people. Doctors are called in, and either prescribe remedies which prove useless, or confess that the condition of the suffering young person defies their skill and knowledge. The parents are nonplussed and persist in attributing the problems to natural causes, even though various people (often the afflicted themselves, but sometimes doctors, or interested parties like relatives or local clergymen) begin to suspect witchcraft. Eventually, the weight of parental and community opinion accepts this explanation. The sufferers claim to see the spectres of women, often with a pre-existing reputation for witchcraft, in their fits, or they remember an incident in which they, or somebody else in their household, may have offended such a woman.

The fits and other afflictions continue and the afflicted become the centre of attention. People, some friends or relatives of their families, others driven merely by curiosity, come to see them. Prayer meetings are organised around their sickbeds, often involving the participation of a number of clergy from the area. Doctors, some drawn from outside their immediate area, might continue to attend them, while the local gentry would visit to help lend support to members of their social stratum suffering misfortune. The parents, most frequently of a godly frame of mind, would struggle with their consciences as they considered turning to such dubious remedies as resorting to cunning men or scratching the supposed witches to draw blood. Most dramatically, the suspected witches would be brought before them, and confrontations would ensure which constituted a public struggle between good and evil. In a certain sense, we return to that problem of representation of the symbolic significance of these accounts of contests between good and evil, in which the bodies of youthful people (and the fact that the sufferers were youthful makes the contest all the more meaningful) are invaded by evil influences. It is difficult, without extensive quotation, to convey the dramatic intensity of some of the accounts of possession. It is no accident that the Shakespeare scholar Stephen Greenblatt has recognised this quality, and argued that much of the intensity of the accounts derives from the invasion of the familiar world by 'a fearful visitation of the perverted spiritual presences of the other world'. 'For,' he writes, 'if the demons were exotic tormentors with weird names, the victims were neighbors enduring their trials in altogether familiar surroundings.'[14] And, sometimes after a lengthy period of intense drama, the witches would be tried before a court of law, although the outcome of this process varied: those accused of bewitching the Throckmorton children were executed, for example, while those supposedly bewitching the daughters of Edward Fairfax were acquitted.

So in studying these cases of possession we are not looking at a series of random events: here as elsewhere, beliefs about witchcraft fall within culturally determined parameters and, while making all due allowance for unique events and individual variations, tended to reproduce a number of recurring cultural motifs. In the early 1970s, Alan Macfarlane and Keith Thomas established that the village witchcraft accusations of this period, so easy to write off as the random consequences of peasant credulity, were patterned, had a social function, a cultural meaning, and made sense in the context of their time.[15] It would now seem worthwhile to examine the rather wider evidence of beliefs and practices furnished by these possession cases, and see what cultural significance can be drawn from them. Arguably, they provide an important avenue into early modern English witch beliefs. For our immediate purposes, however, we shall focus our attention on one of the most striking recurring features of these narratives of possession, the youth of those allegedly suffering from the hostility of the witch. In so doing, we shall find ourselves confronting some of the potential fault lines in the age hierarchy of the period.

III

At the centre of all the narratives were the young, all of them described as suffering from alarming symptoms. Consider 14-year-old Mary Glover, possessed in 1602:

> She was turned round as a hoop, with her head backward to her hips; and in that position rolled and tumbled, with such violence, and swiftness, as that their pains in keeping her from receiving hurt against the bedstead, and posts, caused two or three women to sweat; she being all over cold and stiff as a frozen thing. After she had been thus tossed and tumbled in this circled roundness backward, her body was suddenly turned round the contrary way, that is, her head forward between her legs, and then rolled and tumbled as before. And certain days spent in the fits, she came to have exceeding wide gapings, with her mouth, during the which, there did fly out of her mouth a venomous and stinking blast.[16]

These fits, in which the body and face of the sufferer would undergo the most severe contortions, might alternate with periods of trance or coma in which the sufferers appeared to be insensible, or during which they might claim to see visions of the suspected witches, or the demons thought to be possessing would speak to onlookers, or commence a dialogue with the afflicted. As we have noted, modern doctors or psychologists might find much of interest in these accounts, and would probably be able to reduce most of what appears to have happened to the categories of modern medicine. To contemporaries, such an explanation was only one of the possibilities. Some might suggest medical causes, but others could refer to the growing body of knowledge about possession and witchcraft, knowledge which was underpinned by scripture. As John Darrell noted in one of his justifications of his practices as an exorcist, scripture contained numerous references to the symptoms of possession, 'as crying, gnashing the teeth, wallowing, foaming, extraordinary and supernatural strength, & supernatural knowledge, with sundry others to the number of 18'.[17]

And, again as we have noted, given the rather more public nature of everyday life in the period, those suffering these fits would normally find themselves to be the object of widespread attention. It is easy to caricature the repressive nature of childhood and youth in the sixteenth- or seventeenth-century godly gentry household, but there can be little doubt that most parents, outside certain prescribed contexts, wanted their offspring, if they were to be seen and heard, to present themselves in as disciplined and comely a way as possible. The writhing and screaming children at the centre of a possession case immediately subverted these ideals by becoming a major centre of attraction. Narrative after narrative attests to the public nature of their suffering. One account of the sufferings of Mary Glover recorded that 'it was a usual thing, daily, in times of her ordinary fits, to have many beholders, coming in and going out, sometimes by troops of 8 or 10 at once; and persons of worship and honour, which had way made for them'. During the possession of the Starkie family in Lancashire in 1595–7, 'the honest neighbours near about coming in, the room filled apace, some holding and tending the sick possessed, & some sitting by'. Indeed, such cases could have a didactic role in spreading ideas about witchcraft. When, in 1669, a Hertfordshire girl aged about 20 fell into fits after being bewitched, people came from the adjacent villages to see her some out of pity, to help and comfort her, others out of curiosity to be ascertained of the truth of these relations, and some who were diffident to such things as witchcraft or conjurations, who being fully satisfied in the truth of what is here set down, went home fully convinced of their errors.[18]

The afflicted person was not merely a passive spectacle: he or she regularly entered into a dialogue with those in the sick-chamber, again emphasising how their sufferings gave them a temporarily privileged role. Let us turn to the account of the sufferings of another daughter of the gentry, Elizabeth Mallory, daughter of Lady Mallory of Childley Hall, near Ripon in Yorkshire. Elizabeth, aged 14 or so, suffered in 1656, allegedly after being bewitched by a married couple, William and Mary Waide. She went through the usual fits, convulsions and vomitings, while the account of her torments, lodged among the depositions of the northern assize circuit, shows how the possessed might interact with their audience. At one point, Elizabeth was in a fit while those around the bed called the names of possible suspects to her. When the name of Mary Waide was mentioned, Elizabeth 'shrieked & cried out she comes, she comes. & now she sits yonder in the window like a cat'. When Mary Waide was brought in to confront her supposed victim, Elizabeth, 'though immediately before her limbs were drawn up that she could not stir', declared that she was well, 'and walked upon the bed, but presently after the said Mary Waide denied that she had done her wrong, whereupon the said Elizabeth said if she denied it I shall be ill again', and promptly fell into her fits. Another witness deposed how at an earlier point those around her bed asked her to describe what she saw in her fits, and whom she suspected. She said that she suspected nobody, 'but only trusted in God, and desired them to pray with her, which this informer and the rest of the company did accordingly'.[19] In the case of Anne Gunter, such fits attracted the attention successively of her village, the surrounding area, the Fellows of Exeter College, Oxford, where she was taken for examination, the local ecclesiastical authorities, and the monarch and the court.[20] This was a fair achievement for the daughter of an obscure Berkshire gentleman.

But being afflicted not only made these adolescents the centre of attraction: it also gave them a licence for bad behaviour. The decent and comely behaviour which the writers of conduct books recommended as the norm for youth was clearly blown aside by the possessed. They could do and say things which would not otherwise have been tolerated. At one level, this misbehaviour could be minor: one of the children in the Warboys case, for example, is shown, at the instigation of the spirit possessing her, playing with her food, the spirit 'making her miss her mouth, whereat she would sometimes smile, and sometimes laugh exceedingly'. Slightly more conventional affronts were offered to godly respectability by Margaret Hurdman, aged 14, afflicted in the Starkie household. She began by speaking out against 'the proud women of our times' in her fits, and to castigate pride in attire. Unfortunately, the spirit possessing her then took control and she, in the spirit of teenage girls, asked it for fashionable clothing: a smock of silk, a petticoat of 'the best silk that is', 'a French body, not of whalebone, for that is not stiff enough, but of horn . . . it shall come low before, to keep in my belly', a 'French farthingale', and a gown and cap of black velvet.[21] On a more serious level, as we shall see, and as contemporaries would feel appropriate in those possessed by devils, the misbehaviour amounted to blasphemy.

Sometimes the behaviour attributed to the supposedly possessed tells us a great deal about contemporary expectations of conduct in young people. This becomes clear if we continue with the very full contemporary account of the sufferings of the Throckmorton children at Warboys. At one point, one of the children had 'merry fits', when she was 'full of exceeding laughter (as they were all often times in their fits)', during which they laughed 'so heartily and excessively, that if they had been awakened, they should have been ashamed thereof, being also full of trifling toys, and some merry jests'. At another point, the narrative noted 'the exceeding hearty and immodest laughter in some of her fits, and such indeed as the child's modesty would have blushed at, and could not have permitted, if she had been well'. One wonders what exactly the bounds of the immodest were among the daughers of the gentry in Elizabethan England.[22] These spells of 'exceeding laughter' would be balanced by other periods when she would display behaviour which would have been found equally reprehensible under normal circumstances, becoming 'heavy and droopy', so that 'she could not sit in her chair, but would cast herself on the ground, and so lie with a cushion or pillow under her head half the day together'.[23]

The possession of the Throckmorton children in fact provided them with the opportunity of inverting normality and chiding adults. In one of their conversations with mother Sawyer, the most active of the suspected witches in this case, they warned her of the hell fire which awaited her if she did not confess her witchcraft, and then 'they rehearsed likewise unto her, her naughty manner of living, her normal cursing and banning of all that displeased her', singling out as specially reprehensible 'her negligent coming to God's Service' and 'her lewd bringing up of her daughter, in suffering her to be her dame, both in controlling of her, and beating of her'. The daughter herself, Agnes Sawyer, also came in for a verbal critique, this time from Elizabeth Throckmorton, aged about 13:

> Oh that thou hadst grace to repent thee of thy wickedness, that thy soul might be saved: for thou hast forsaken thy God, and given thyself to the devil. Oh that thou didst know what a precious thing thy soul was, thou wouldst never then so lightly have parted with it: thou hadst needs to pray night and day, to get God's favour again, otherwise thy soul shall be damned in hell fire for ever . . . thou art a wicked child.

Elizabeth continued by advising this 'wicked child', in fact a young woman several years her senior, on the need for heartfelt prayer.[24]

Even if they did not cheek adults, the conviction that they were suffering from witchcraft might give adolescents the courage of their convictions when contradicting them. An instance of this is provided by the case of the two daughters of another Yorkshire gentry family, the Corbets of Burton Agnes. The girls' afflictions began in 1660, and continued until 1664, and are remarkable in that the parents took so long a period to attribute their illness to witchcraft. From the start the children were adamant that they suffered through the malevolence of two local women, Alice Huson and Olive Bilby, the former at least having an existing reputation for being a witch. Their parents thought that they suffered from a natural disease, called in doctors from Hull, York and Beverley, and sent the girls to stay with relatives at Pickering in hopes that the air in that part of the county would do them good. One of the girls, clearly put out by such parental obduracy, declared that 'all the doctors and physick in the world could do no good, as long as those two women were at liberty; they would have her life, and she would be contented, since she could not be believed'. The parents' final acceptance, in the spring of 1664, that the girls were bewitched must have seemed to them to be a considerable vindication of their arguments, even if Huson and Bilby did escape execution.[25]

For most parents and other contemporary observers, however, the most disturbing form of misbehaviour must have been the tendency for the youthful possessed to reject right religion. The notion that the household was a basic unit of religious instruction, a microscopic godly commonwealth where future Christians would be socialised into correct belief and proper behaviour, obviously made the rejection or mocking of religion especially worrying. When the Starkie children went into their fits, 'thus they continued all afternoon, 3 or 4 of them gave themselves to scoffing and blasphemy, calling the holy bible being brought up bible bable bible bable and this they did aloud and often all or most of them joined together'. One of them, John, so an account of their case informs us, began 'nicknaming every word in the Lord's prayer, so far as we went in it. For when we perceived such horrible blasphemy, we durst not proceed but gave over.' The Throckmorton children, when prayed for by the local minister, Doctor Dorrington, shrieked when he began the prayers, but desisted when he finished, and went through a similar performance when the Bible was read to them. Anne Gunter, surrounded by Oxford clerics and physicians when she was lodged in Exeter College, made fun of one of the clergymen present, punning on his name.[26]

A broad spectrum of accounts of the possession of adolescents confirms that this abhorrence or mocking of religion was a recurring theme. At one point Helen Fairfax 'threw herself backward, and fell into a deadly ecstasy, and so continued very long' when her father tried to read the Bible to her. A Norfolk gentleman's daughter, suffering in 1688, exhibited symptoms very like those of the children at Warboys nearly a century previously: she was stricken blind when she was asked to read the Bible, and fell senseless when a local clergyman who was taking an interest in her condition mentioned it at family prayers. John Barrow, a Southwark youth possessed with evil spirits in the early 1660s, when in his fits, 'if any other did take the bible, and mention the word of God or Christ in his hearing, he would roar and cry, making a hideous noise'. Hannah Crump of Warwick, possessed in 1664, struck and spat at those who prayed around her.[27]

As we have noted, at least some contemporary commentators saw youth as a period when the individual's propensity for good or evil might be determined, so that youth might be interpreted as a metaphorical battleground between these two forces. To the parents or other interested parties struggling to aid the possessed, this metaphorical battleground became a literal one: they honestly believed that they were involved in a contest in which the physical and spiritual well-being of the young people in question was at stake. Edward Fairfax clearly felt this as he worried about how best to aid his teenage daughter Helen. One of the peculiarities of her case was the frequency with which she went into trances where she saw not only the spectres of the women thought to be bewitching her and their familiars, but also of more exotic beings. Most pertinently, on several occasions she saw the visions of shining ethereal creatures who tried to convince her that they were God. The spiritual energies of her father and the rest of her family were mobilised to dissuade her on that point. After seeing one such vision, 'all that night she was persuaded this was God, or some angel sent to comfort her, and could not be removed from that opinion; but next morning, with some difficulty we persuaded her to the contrary, by such reasons and scripture as our small knowledge could afford'.[28] This assistance proved successful. When spectres appeared to her again, Helen, in her trances, was heard to call out against them, saying on one occasion, 'thou callest me and I am nought, but I had rather have thy evil word than they good word', her resistance this time being stiffened by one of her brothers reading a psalm.[29]

So at least some of those afflicted could, in the course of their personal struggle against evil, with the assistance of those supporting them, escape from the blasphemous mocking of religion into reaffirming their faith in defiance of the forces of evil. Perhaps the clearest example of this type is provided by Thomas Darling, a Derbyshire youth who suffered after being bewitched in 1597. Darling, despite his tender years, was clearly one of the godly: when he thought himself near to death in his torments he expressed the wish that he 'might have lived to be a preacher to thunder out the threatenings of God's word'. In the intermissions between his fits he asked those around him to read scripture to him, which they could not do 'for weeping to behold his misery'. When unable to speak during his firts, he made signs of praying with his hands, 'sometimes lifting them up, and sometimes striking them upon his breast'. He also seemingly entered into a dialogue with the devil in his fits, on one occasion crying out:

> Avoid, Satan. I will worship the Lord only, Dost thou say thou wilt mitigate my torments if I will worship thee? Avoid Satan, I will worship none, save only the Lord God my saviour, my sanctifier, my redeemer . . . do thy worst Satan, my faith standeth sure with my God, at whose hands I look for succour.

Darling's interpretation of what was happening to him was clearly structured by his having been exposed to, and his having internalised, godly ideas: at one point, indeed, he treated his listeners to a lively description of hell, where he claimed to have been taken.[30]

Another exemplary performance was mounted by one of the Starkie children. In his fits he cried out against the 'strange sins of the land committed in all estates & degrees of people, and denounced the fearful judgements of God due unto them'. He then exhorted his parents and the other adults there to repent (again, another inversion of how religious inculcation normally ran), 'that they might avoid all those grievous plagues, and wishes that all the whole land might do the like'. After this his uttered 'a most excellent prayer' for the church, for the queen's long life and the confounding of her enemies, for peaceable government, for the gospel, for all true ministers of Christ, for all those in authority, and for his parents. This prayer took two hours. Further evidence that religious ideas were widely disseminated among the teenage children of the gentry was demonstrated by Anne Gunter, who, on the evidence of the depositions about her case, had not been brought up in a markedly godly atmosphere. Yet even she was able to ask Thomas Holland, the Professor of Divinity of the University of Oxford, when preaching in her parish church, to make a sermon 'saying that although the devil had power to keep from her food for her body, yet he had no power to take from her the food of her soul'.[31] The contemporary fear that possession cases were evidence of the devil's desire to subvert the Christian Commonwealth must have been assuaged by such tokens that, even when Satan was trying to subvert the young, the world might well be staying the right way up.

IV

The American historian John Demos, in his analysis of accounts of possession in seventeenth-century New England, accounts which are for the most part identical to those we have considered here, commented:

> They present a picture that is almost clinical in substance and tone: comparison with psychiatric case reports in our own time does not seem far-fetched. There is, in short, no better window on the inner world of mental and emotional structures that supported the belief in witchcraft in colonial New England.[32]

Arguably, these accounts of a personalised battle between good and evil in the individual young person, and of the reaction of the immediate family and the wider society to them, also tell us a great deal about expectations of youthful behaviour, and of how young people reacted to the family authority in which they found themselves. For although some of these cases of possession were clearly simulated, others involved genuine symptoms. Even some of those cases which began as simulation, in an attempt to attract attention for example, must have become 'real' as the supposed sufferer became sucked into the logic of the situation and developed 'symptoms' along the culturally known and approved lines. Considering what those known and approved lines were, however, leads us into some interesting areas of speculation.

On one level, what the subject of early modern possession needs is a full-scale examination by modern medical doctors and psychologists. This is not the place at which to enter such an examination, but it is noteworthy that a number of students of witchcraft as a historical phenomenon have been attracted by the possibilities of applying the concepts of modern psychoanalysis to their materials. Marion Starkey, author of a once influential study of the Salem which craze, was heavily influenced by Freudian ideas in her analysis of the behaviour of the possessed girls. Her interpretation has been overtaken by more modern ones, but it remains clear that, in her focus on the girls' behaviour, she was at least asking some important questions.[33] More recently, John Demos has analysed one of the best documented New England cases, that of a 16-year-old girl named Elizabeth Knapp. In her sufferings, Demos detected signs of such modern psychoanalytical symptoms as exhibitionism, dependency (on the clergyman attempting to 'treat' her) and anger. Without doubt, analysing some of the English evidence, notably that of the Warboys case, along these lines would prove rewarding. Similarly, Demos's comments on this New England case seem very pertinent to the English ones: 'the danger implicit in Elizabeth's fits came through to her audience in many ways. Cherished values, affectionate relationships, established routines – not to mention life and limb itself – were immediately at risk'.[34]

Cherished values, affectionate relationships, established routines: the very stuff, if you like, of family life. And, for the student of authority in early modern England, the family, in that society as in most others the basic unit of socialisation, is of central importance. That possession cases were to involve young people apparently in revolt against the established routines, and certainly the normal disciplines, of family life, is hardly surprising. Anthropological studies of possession in cultures far removed chronologically and geographically from early modern England have commented on how the phenomenon tends to occur most frequently among the least powerful groups of any given society: possession makes people who do not normally possess much power into centres of attention, and also, if only temporarily, gives them prestige.[35] Teenagers in godly Tudor and Stuart households, caught in a liminal phase between childhood and adulthood, between the two life stages of puberty and marriage, were doubtlessly subjected to a number of stresses as they endured parental control and were instilled with a sense of their own sinfulness by religious instruction.

As has been suggested, parent–child relations in this period should not be dismissed as purely repressive. Without doubt, most parents were, by their own standards, loving and caring, and hoped to raise well-adjusted children. Occasional clues, however, lead us to believe that all was not perceived to be well between the parents of children suffering in possession cases and their offspring. A number of witnesses in the case of Anne Gunter commented that before her possession her father did not seem to care for her, and had left her badly provided for in his will. Edward Fairfax (who in his account of his daughters' sufferings shows himself to have been a very caring and loving parent) noted that a number of people thought that the girls simulated possession so that he would cherish them more.[36] And even when no particular tension was present, the normal emotional and spiritual rigours of a godly upbringing provided a sufficient basis for fears of demonic possession to flourish. It was noted of a Norfolk knight's daughter, supposedly possessed in 1688, that she was 'a person of very good decency, & great ingenuity, and appears to have had a religious education, & to make conscience of her duty, & to have repented regularly'.[37] Arguably, it was exactly young people of this type who were most likely to undergo the torments of possession: as Keith Thomas has commented: 'an intense regime of religious observance could thus provoke a violent reaction. In France the best known cases of possession occurred in nunneries for the same sort of reason.'[38]

It is no surprise, therefore, that when possession provoked symptoms of youthful rebellion in England, it should most often do so in the form of blasphemous and irreligious behaviour. It is striking that there seems to have been very little evidence of what, since Freud, we might have expected to have been present, sexual misbehaviour. Perhaps some of the 'immodest' or 'undecent' behaviour referred to in contemporary accounts had sexual overtones, but there is little by way of direct reference. Perhaps the clearest comes in the case of the Starkie children. These 'for the most part delighted in filthy and unsavoury speeches, very agreeable to the nature of the unclean spirit which then dwelled within them', while one of them, 'Though she was a maid' was heard 'to utter openly in the hearing of the people, such filthy uncleanness, as is not to be named'.[39] More intensive research might reveal similar instances, but it currently seems that the central terrain of conflict was interpreted as the maintenance of godliness: and this maintenance of godliness, given the tendency to see youth as disputed terrain between good and evil, was crucial to the control of young people. Perhaps an appropriate area of comparison here would be with that other form of peculiar behaviour whose symptoms were practically indistinguishable from demonic possession, religious ecstasy. Students of the Salem trials, for example, have commented on how the behaviour of the bewitched girls was very like that of young people undergoing intense religious experiences during periods of evangelical activity in eighteenth-century America, while some of the English narratives of possession read very like the ecstatic conversions undergone by many in the early stages of methodism.[40] Here, too, one feels that extreme behaviour is felt to be more appropriate to young people.

By way of illustration, if we may use an example involving somebody slightly too young to be classified as a 'youth' in contemporary terminology, let us examine the case of William Withers, an 11-year-old boy from Walsingham in Suffolk, who on 24 December 1580 went into a trance, not unlike those allegedly suffered by young people supposedly afflicted by demonic possession. At the end of his trance, Withers began to speak of God's glory and to warn his listeners to lead a holy life. Just as in cases of possession, ministers and 'divers worshipful gentlemen' repaired to the boy's home to 'behold this rare token of God's singular love and severe justice set forth in this child'. The boy moved from his general comments on the need for godliness to making some more personal comments on the adults who attended him. Thus he reproved one man for his 'great and monstrous ruffs', and went on to tell him 'it were better for him to put on sackcloth & mourn for his sins, than in such abominable pride to prank up himself like the devil's darling'. One suspects that many 11 year olds would have liked to talk to adults like that, but few had the opportunity to. Here, as in cases of possession, immersion in what was interpreted as a religious experience provided a normally subordinate young person with the occasion to effect a temporary inversion of normal authority.[41] The intellectual framework and rhetoric supplied by godliness was usually deployed by adult authority to socialise the young away from youthful lusts into the pathways of obedience and godliness: it is perhaps no accident that this framework and rhetoric should also provide the context within which so many of their challenges to that authority were mounted. Indeed, here as elsewhere, the territory of control effectively becomes the arena of revolt. And within that arena, the elements of authority and disobedience can be represented or inverted through symbolic actions or speech, while normal behaviour and reactions can be manipulated by abnormality. Not all children, of course, were being brought up in godly households. Our sample of cases, it must be reiterated, is drawn largely from those levels in the social hierarchy whose experiences were likely to be well documented. Whether the children of lower social groups experienced a similar discipline awaits further research, while the fact that so many children of sub-gentry families would be resident in households other than their parents', as servants or apprentices, raises a further complication. Intriguingly, however, many cases involving children and adolescents from the lower orders supposedly suffering from witchcraft show symptoms very similar to those suffered by the Throckmorton children, Mary Glover, Anne Gunter or the Fairfax girls. It is doubtful that these children were subjected to the same spiritual rigours as those raised in godly gentry households, and the fact that they too were seen to writhe, contort, vomit foreign bodies and see the spectres of the witches tormenting them in their fits is evidence of the widespread cultural dispersion of notions of possession. That such notions were so widespread raises another set of problems, again too complex to be treated deeply here: namely, the involvement of young people in that world of gossip and story-telling which must have played so large a part both in spreading and refining ideas about witchcraft and in confirming the reputation for ill-doing of particular local women thought of as witches. Just over half a century after William Withers' godliness made his a centre of adult concern, another 11-year-old (if we may go a little down the age range once again), Edmund Robinson, of Newchurch in Lancashire, also became the focal point of considerable attention, including that of central government in Westminster. He initiated a number of witchcraft accusations which nearly took off into being a major craze. Hauled down to London, the boy retracted his original accusations, among them allegations that witches had transported him to the sabbat. He had been late coming home with the cattle, and had made up the stories about being bewitched to avoid being chastised by his mother. His story, he said, was all 'false and feigned, and has no truth at all, but only that he has heard tales and reports made by women, so he framed his tale out of his own invention'. He later gave details of the stories he had heard about individual women, and confessed that his account of the sabbat was based on accounts he had heard of the meeting of the 1612 Lancashire witches at the Malking Tower.[42] Robinson, like Anne Gunter before him, achieved a notoriety which attracted the attention both of local society and central authority, while his case shows how children and the young had easy access to that adult, perhaps largely female, world of gossip and story-telling. Reading between the lines, it is obvious that both the Throckmorton and Fairfax girls had spent an amount of time listening to 'tales and reports' about witchcraft in their localities.

The challenges to authority offered by possessed adolescents were, therefore, like so many such challenges in the early modern period, short-lived and doomed to failure. And, again like so many such challenges, they were unable to break out of current frames of thought and modes of expression, and hence, in their disorder, showed considerable order. They do, however, provide a body of evidence about that most rarely documented of phenomena, licensed disorder by young people initially in a family, then within a wider context. Their conduct attracted the attention of many agents of 'authority': parents, clergymen, doctors, local justices of the peace, and the involvement of such people in possession cases reminds us that 'authority' in early modern England was a widely diffused entity. Indeed, that much of this demonically inspired disorder, except in obviously simulated cases, was taking place on a subconscious level, leads us to an important conclusion about the nature of authority: namely, that the most important forms of authority were and are those which have been internalised, and affect us as we go about our day-to- day business. It is a pity that this type of authority leaves so little by way of historical evidence. Here as elsewhere, the phenomenon of witchcraft, so extraordinary and alien, helps throw light on the ordinary and the normal.

NOTES AND REFERENCES

1. K. V. Thomas, 'Age and Authority in Early Modern England', *Proceedings of the British Academy*, vol.62 (1976), pp. 205–48. The issue of youth is discussed fully in P. Griffiths, 'Some Aspects of the Social History of Youth in Early Modern England, with Particular Reference to the Period, *c.*1590–*c.*1640' (unpublished University of Cambridge Ph.D. Thesis, 1992); and in P. Griffiths, *Youth and Authority: Formative Experiences in England, 1560–1640* (Oxford, 1996).

2. E. A. Wrigley and R. S. Schofield, *The Population History of England, 1541–1871: A Reconstruction* (Cambridge, 1981), pp. 528–9 (table A3.1).

3. Richard Burton, *The Apprentice's Companion* (London, 1681), pp. 88–9; W. P. *The Prentises Practise in Godlinesse and His True Freedom* (London, 1613), sigs. 3v–4.

4. On social hierarchy and English witch trials, see K. V. Thomas, *Religion and the Decline of Magic: Studies in Popular Beliefs in Sixteenth and Seventeenth Century England* (London, 1971), esp. ch. 16 ('The Making of a Witch'); and A. Macfarlane, *Witchcraft in Tudor and Stuart England: A Regional and Comparative Study* (London, 1970). On gender, see J. A. Sharpe, 'Witchcraft and Women in Seventeenth-Century England; Some Northern Evidence', *Continuity and Change*, vol. 6 (1991), pp. 179–99.

5. The Salem trials have attracted a considerable literature, the most

useful work being perhaps P. Boyer and S. Nissenbaum, *Salem Possessed: The Social Origins of the Salem Witch Trials* (Cambridge, Mass., 1974). For a more recent discussion of this episode, set firmly in the context of magical and related beliefs, see R. Godbeer, *The Devil's Dominion: Magic and Religion in Early New England* (Cambridge, 1992), ch. 6 ('The Rape of a Whole Colony: The 1692 Witch Hunt').

6. B. Ankarloo, 'Sweden: The Mass Burnings (1688–76)', in B. Ankarloo and G. Henningsen (eds), *Early Modern European Witchcraft: Centres and Peripheries* (Oxford, 1990), pp. 285–318; H. C. E. Midelfort, *Witch Hunting in South Western Germany, 1562–1684: The Social and Intellectual Foundations* (Stanford, 1972), p. 140. It should be noted that these Swedish and German cases involved children as alleged witches as well as accusers.

7. The calculations for the Home Circuit are based on materals printed in C. L. Ewen, *Witch Hunting and Witch Trials* (London, 1929), pp. 200–52; for the East Anglian trials, see J. A. Sharpe, 'The Devil in East Anglia: The Matthew Hopkins Trials Reconsidered', in J. Barry *et al.* (eds), *Witchcraft in Early Modern Europe: Studies in Culture and Belief* (Cambridge, 1996); for the Northern Circuit, see Sharpe, 'Witchcraft and Women', 189.

8. For two essays touching on this literature, see N. Smith, 'A Child Prophet: Martha Hatfield as *The Wise Virgin*', and G. Avery, 'The Puritans and Their Heirs', both in G. Avery and J. Briggs (eds), *Children and Their Books: A Celebration of the Work of Iona and Peter Opie* (Oxford, 1989), pp. 79–94, 95–118.

9. British Library Add. MS 32496, fol. 42v.

10. S. Harsnett, *A Discovery of the Fraudulent Practices of John Darrell Bachelor of Artes* (London, 1599), p. 36.

11. *The Disclosing of a Late Counterfeited Possession by the Devyl of Two Maydens Within the Citie of London* (London, 1574), passim.

12. [P]ublic [R]ecord [O]ffice STAC 8/32/12.

13. For the Warboys case, see *The Most Strange and Admirable Discoverie of the Three Witches of Warboys Arraigned, Convicted and Executed at the Assizes at Huntingdon* (London, 1583). The works relating to Darrell's activities are listed and discussed in C. H. Richert, *The Case of John Darrell: Minister and Exorcist* (Gainsville, 1962). Materials relating to Mary Glover are collected in M. MacDonald (ed.), *Witchcraft and Hysteria in Elizabethan London: Edward Jordan and the Mary Glover Case* (London, 1990). Anne Gunter's simulated possession is discussed in C. L. Ewen, *Witchcraft in the Star Chamber* (privately pub., 1938), ch. 6 ('A Berkshire "Demoniac" '), while the Star Chamber investigation of the case is in PRO STAC 8/4/10. For the sufferings of the Fairfax children, see William Grainge (ed.), *Daemonologia: A Discourse on Witchcraft as it was Acted in the Family of Mr Edward Fairfax of Fuyston in the Younty of York, in the Year 1621. Along With the Only Two Eclogues of the Same Author Known to be in Existence* (Harrogate, 1882). There are a number of modern works dealing with the phenomenon of demonic possession in this period, of which D. P. Walker, *Unclean Spirits: Possession and Exorcism in France and England in the Late Sixteenth and Early Seventeenth Centuries* (Philadelphia, 1981) constitutes perhaps the most useful discussion. For a more recent discussion of possession in its Elizabethan English

context, see F. W. Brownlow, *Shakespeare, Harsnett and the Devils of Denham* (Cranbury, N. J., 1993).

14. S. Greenblatt, *Shakespearean Negotiations* (Oxford, 1988), p. 103.

15. Macfarlane, *Witchcraft in Tudor and Stuart England*; Thomas, *Religion and the Decline of Magic.*

16. MacDonald (ed.), *Witchcraft and Hysteria*, pp. 5–6.

17. J. Darrell, *A Briefe Apologie Proving the Possession of William Somers* (London, 1599), p. 9.

18. MacDonald (ed.), *Witchcraft and Hysteria*, p. 67; G. More, *A True Discourse Concerning the Certain Possession and Dispossession of 7 Persons in One Family in Lancashire* (London, 1600), p. 59; *The Hartford-Shire Wonder: Or, Strange News From Ware* (London, 1669), p. 6.

19. PRO ASSI 45/5/3/132–3.

20. PRO STAC 8/4/10, passim.

21. *Discoverie of the Three Witches of Warboys*, sig. C2v; More, *True Discourse*, p. 27.

22. *Discoverie of the Three Witches of Warboys*, sigs.C3v, E1.

23. Ibid., sig.D2.

24. Ibid., sigs.G3–G3v, L4v–M1.

25. Matthew Hale, *A Collection of Modern Relations of Matter of Fact Concerning Witches and Witchcraft Upon the Persons of People* (Part I, London, 1693), pp. 52–9.

26. J. Darrell, *A True Narration of the Strange and Grevous Vexation by the Devil of 7 Persons in Lancashire, and William Somers of Nottingham* (London, 1600), pp. 9, 56; *Discoverie of the Three Witches of Warboys*, sig.C1v; PRO STAC 8/4/10, m.14v.

27. Fairfax, *Daemonologia*, p. 53; Oxford Bodleian Library Tanner MS 25, fol. 161v; *The Lord's Arm Stretched Out in Prayer: Or, A True Relation of the Wonderful Deliverance of James Barrow, the Son of John Barrow of Olaves Southwark, Who Was Possessed With Evil Spirits Near Two Years* (London, 1664), p. 7; *A True Relation of the Wonderful Deliverance of Hannah Crump, Daughter of John Crump of Warwick, Who Was So Afflicted By Witchcraft, For the Space of Nine Months* (London, 1664), pp. 19–20.

28. Fairfax, *Daemonologia*, p. 63.

29. Ibid., p. 65.

30. J. Denison, *The Most Wonderfull and True Storie, Of a Certain Witch Named Alse Goderidge of Stapen Hill, Who Was Arraigned and Convicted at Darbie at the Assizes There* (London, 1597), pp. 2, 12, 31.

31. More, *True Discourse*, p. 25; PRO STAC 8/4/10, m. 208.

32. J. Demos, *Entertaining Satan: Witchcraft and the Culture of Early New England* (New York, 1982), p. 99. In addition to Demos's work on colonial America, a number of historians have turned their attention to the psychiatrical and broader medical aspects of possession cases. See e.g. David Harley, 'Mental Illness, Magical Medicine and the Devil in Northern England, 1650–1700', in R. French and D. Wear (eds), *The Medical Revolution of the Seventeenth Century* (Cambridge, 1989), pp. 114–44; M. MacDonald, 'Religion, Social Change and Psychological Healing in England, 1600–1800', in W. J. Sheils (ed.), *The Church and Healing*, Studies in Church

212   *The Experience of Authority in Early Modern England*

History, vol. 19 (Oxford, 1982). pp. 101–25; and Ronald C. Sawyer, ' "Strangely Handled in All Her Lyms": Witchcraft and Healing in Jacobean England', *Journal of Social History*, vol. 23 (1988–9), pp. 461–86.

33. M. L. Starkey, *The Devil in Massachusetts: A Modern Enquiry into the Salem Witch Trials* (London, 1952). For a more recent discussion of the possible usefulness of modern psychoanalytical ideas in the study of early modern witchcraft, see L. Roper, 'Witchcraft and Fantasy in Early Modern Germany', *History Workshop Journal*, vol. 32 (1991), pp. 19–43. Dr Roper's ideas on this subject are developed further in Lyndal Roper, *Oedipus and the Devil: Witchcraft, Sexuality and Religion in Early Modern Europe* (London, 1994). Further light on this approach will doubtlessly be shed by Miranda Chaytor's research in progress on north eastern English sources.

34. Demos, *Entertaining Satan*, pp. 116–23.

35. For a good recent discussion, see I. M. Lewis, *Ecstatic Religion: A Study of Shamanism and Spirit Possession*, 2nd edn (London, 1989), ch. 4 ('Strategies of Marginal Attack: Protest and its Containment').

36. PRO STAC 8/4/10, m. 94; Fairfax, *Daemonologia*, p. 124.

37. Bod. Lib. Tanner MS 28, fol. 161v.

38. Thomas, *Religion and the Decline of Magic*, p. 573.

39. More, *True Discourse*, p. 45.

40. Boyer and Nissenbaum, *Salem Possessed*, pp. 215–16. On methodism, see the references to possession in Bristol in 1739, and the events at Everton in Bedfordshire in 1759; N. Curnock (ed.), *The Journal of the Rev. John Wesley*, 8 vols (London, 1909–16), vol. 11, pp. 180, 190, 299–301; vol. IV, pp. 333–42.

41. J. Philip *The Wonderfull Worke of God Shewed Upon a Chylde, Whose Name is William Withers, Being in the Town of Walsam, in the Countie of Suffolk* (London, 1581), sigs B1–B2.

42. *Calendar of State Papers Domestic, 1634–35*, p. 141.

7 The Keeping of the Public Peace*

STEVE HINDLE

I

'The history of a society is also the history of a clash that exists between its instinct for survival and desire for union and collaboration with its taste for destruction and ashes.'[1] This ambiguous relationship between stability and conflict was particularly marked in early modern England, a society whose obsession with order is axiomatic, yet one where tension, dispute and litigation were common enough. Fundamentally, the community politics of this society entailed the resolution of social conflict, the keeping of the public peace. Pacification appealed to an extensive value system of neighbourly relations, especially to aspirations of charity and harmony. In practice, however, the 'moral economy of the early modern community' might be less than consensual, the meaning of charity might fluctuate, and the keeping of the peace might involve public processes of constraint or coercion as well as private injunctions to mutuality and forgiveness.[2] In this sense, pacification and litigation enjoyed a particularly problematic relationship, one that is much commented upon, although not yet fully resolved, in the historiography of the period. It will be argued here that this 'culture of reconciliation' depended upon far more than ideals of neighbourliness.[3] Ultimately, pacification involved the injection of some measure of public authority into the 'disputing process', and it is with the experience of that authority that this chapter is concerned.

Both historians and anthropologists have identified the salient features of the processes of dispute and reconciliation in past societies.[4] Ideally, it has been argued, initiatives of force, aggression or malice should be curtailed through extra-curial settlements, usually private composition or third-party mediation, which might foster amicable social relationships thereafter. In practice, however, disputing parties often eschewed pacification, pursuing satisfaction through the 'waging of law'. Even then, the issuing of writs was not infrequently intended as a means of precipitating an out of court settlement. 'Societies being weaned from habits of private revenge always turn to the law with intemperate enthusiasm', and litigation, initially promoted as a solvent for violent self-assertion, was gradually found to be corrosive of social harmony.[5] Casting the 'utterly uncertain dice of pleas' resulted not only in 'troble and charge', it raised the stakes of conflict, propelling dispute into the public arena.[6] Bills and brawls were equally abhorred as symptoms of the breakdown of harmony. In this light, the preference for quasi-formal or arbitrated settlement is easily understood. Arbitration countered both the fear of violence on the one hand, and the fear of litigation on the other, and was revered as 'such redress as would best stand with the quiet of the country'.[7] These were the parameters of tolerance within which social conflict was perforce resolved.

There was, therefore, a structured ambiguity about the role of law in this disputing process: was litigation intended to resolve or to further dispute? Broadly speaking, historians have answered this question in two ways. On the one hand, litigation has been regarded as characteristic of an environment racked by socio-economic tension, anxious about its own stability, and ridden with endemic petty conflict. This school of thought can conveniently be divided into two hypotheses: the 'hard'; and the 'soft'. Lawrence Stone has proposed the crudest variant, arguing that litigation was fuelled by a general 'decline of neighbourliness', a monolithic trend concomitant on 'The Reformation' which steam-rollered community values in the onward march of individualism. Stone envisages a 'dog-eat-dog' world characterised by high levels of dispute and violence: a place where inter-personal behaviour was often unrestrained, and in which even 'respectability' did not imply self-control. With characteristic hyperbole, Stone writes of 'social anomy', the 'breakdown of consensual community methods of dealing with conflict', and 'ethical and economic fissures opening up' in communities 'filled with malice and hatred'.[8] John Beattie, Keith Wrightson and David Levine, and Jim Sharpe might be taken as spokesmen for the second 'soft' hypothesis, in that each recognises the dynamics and ambiguities inherent in any given social situation. Beattie and Wrightson are particularly sensitive to the subtleties of changing attitudes in the past, while Sharpe's focus on the enduring orderliness of Stuart society is tempered by his sophisticated understanding of the complex social significance of litigation.[9] Both hypotheses, however, are vulnerable to the criticisms that they generalise about the nature of social control, and that their evidence is drawn exclusively from the archives of complaint, prosecution and litigation.[10]

On the other hand, Cynthia Herrup has portrayed a fundamentally stable society, obsessed with order, and infused with a keen sense of Christian charity. In her stress on orderliness and participatory legal responsibility, Herrup echoes Alan Macfarlane's views that 'there is scarcely any evidence that people used physical threats or brutal attacks to punish each other', and that the law was a resource to be used for doing 'good'.[11] This understanding of charity is arguably a very traditional one, focusing exclusively on the ideal of loving one's neighbour. The ideal of parochial harmony carried enormous ethical weight, and could be potent. But ultimately, as Eamon Duffy reminds us, it was just that – an ideal.[12] The consensus approach, therefore, is equally flawed, most obviously because it underestimates the practical difficulties of managing 'social relations in motion',[13] but also because it fails to take account of incremental social change, in particular the cultural shifts resulting from the interacting processes of increasing economic differentiation and of Reformation, especially at the turn of the sixteenth century.

The extent to which these processes constituted a cultural watershed during which social identities and relationships were significantly reshaped is, of course, hotly debated.[14] None the less, the impact of economic and cultural change on the conception of charity in particular has recently been investigated by Felicity Heal. Her study of hospitality constitutes an analysis of continuity and change in the quality of social relations. She argues that during the early modern period both the ideal and the practice of hospitality, the 'vision of neighbourliness', became fragmented and marginalised. The 'experience of economic and demographic crisis in the sixteenth century led to a reconceptualisation of forms of beneficence, both of the worthiness of the recipient and of the best apportionment of resources'. Moreover, the transition from private to public charitable relief, itself underpinned by an intensification of the social gulf that existed between the needy and their benefactors, 'completed the separation of hospitality to the prosperous and alms to the poor that had always been latent' in English culture.

These changes, though not necessarily linear, amounted to a more calculating and discriminating concept of Christian charity.[15] Such conclusions echo John Bossy's analysis of the impact of 'the disintegration of traditional Christianity' on the changing connotations of 'venerable' words in this period. In 1400, he argues, 'charity' meant 'the state of Christian love or simple affection which one was in or out of regarding one's fellows; an occasion or body of people seeking to embody that state'. By 1700, however, it merely 'meant an optimistic judgement about the good intentions of others; an act of benevolence towards the poor or needy; an institution erected as a result of such an act'. This individual 'migration' of meaning, he suggests, was symptomatic of a larger social process, the transition from an ethics of solidarity to one of civility. Furthermore, the 'moral arithmetic' of transforming seven sins into ten commandments produced an ethical code which was 'narrower on obligations to the neighbour'.[16] By definition, these modifications fostered a more distanced, more circumscribed, perception of social obligation. Although, therefore, the vocabulary of charity persisted throughout our period, its meaning was neither static nor unambiguous.

These sophisticated readings of cultural change are enormously significant for our understanding of social relations in general, and the disputing process in particular. First, while they supersede linear conceptions of the 'decline of neighbourliness', they retain a dynamic perspective on the history of social values. Since the neighbourhoods of early modern society were 'moral communities', 'founded upon the expectation of adherence to conventional standards of both public and private behaviour', modifications of the meaning of charity had significant practical implications.[17] Second, in demonstrating that ideals themselves were continually adjusted and readjusted to changing social realities, they demand far greater sensitivity to the fluidity of social interaction, and especially to the constant jostlings and realignments of community and neighbourhood. In a social environment where neighbourliness was continuously fractured and reconstituted, changing images of charity, hospitality and Christian duty inevitably ramified in different ways.[18] Patterns of sociability, familiarity and community were therefore crucially dependent on local social and economic circumstances. In hard times, parochial harmony and charity might be less forthcoming, as even charitable minds found their resources of compassion exhausted. During years of dearth in particular the nature of social responsibilities might be renegotiated, perhaps even resulting in the short-term revival of such traditional values such as reciprocity, paternalism and reluctance to prosecute, though entitlement to all of these presupposed membership of a community.[19] Such renegotiation was often beyond the direct control of élites, and might moreover manifest itself very differently in the large and scattered parishes, the 'back-to-back' communities, of upland England, than in the 'face-to-face' nucleated parishes of the south and east with which historians are more familiar. It is, for example, much more difficult to walk away from conflict with those with whom you live in very close proximity: the more intense the locality, the more complex relations become.[20] From the perspective of Heal and Bossy, therefore, the model of a consensual society constructed by Herrup seems somewhat idealised, implying that old-fashioned, static values permeated English society well into the seventeenth century. The suggestion that 'the attributes of a good life – love of God and monarch, belief in obedience and neighbourliness – were the traits that ensured social quiet', is not only normative rather than descriptive, it also fails to do justice to social change.[21]

These ambiguous relationships between charity and conflict are perfectly illustrated by the popularity of quasi-formal processes of dispute settlement. This chapter explores these ambiguities by discussing the technique of binding over, one mechanism through which public authority was integrated into the multilateral process of pacification. Binding over, it will be suggested, acted as a non-aggression pact, initially precluding any further physical self-assertion, and subsequently allowing a cooling-off period during which negotiation, either 'informally' (through mediation) or 'quasi-formally' (through arbitration), might restore disputing parties to the condition of charity. This analysis therefore addresses four specific problematics in the increasingly complex historiography of law and society in early modern England. First, it emphasises the significance of binding over, a practice gradually becoming recognised as crucial to the governmental process.[22] Second, it implicitly reconstructs the 'ideology of order', a phenomenon usually investigated through consideration of its obverse.[23] Third, following Edward Thompson's suggestion that the 'violence we have lost debate' is best located within a total context 'which assigns different values to different kinds of violence' (whether physical, verbal, or symbolic), this discussion argues that violence was the product of a wider system of attitudes and mentalities, and seeks to trace them over time.[24] Fourth, it raises important questions both about the quality of social relations and about the nature of the early modern State, the mechanics of its growth and of the 'civilising process', some of which are considered in a concluding discussion of the relationship between authority, arbitration and State formation. It will be suggested that the public peace was guaranteed less by governors' initiatives of coercion and control, than by the widespread exercise and experience of authority by middling sorts of people within the populace at large.

II

How was the public peace best kept in early modern England? The significance of magistrates' contributions to early modern governance under the revised Commission of the Peace of 1590 has long been evident to historians.[25] But recent scholarship has suggested that magistrates' labours would have been fruitless without the active cooperation of inferior officers and sections of the public at large.[26] Both the massive growth of civil litigation and extensive popular participation in the criminal and administrative aspects of the legal system, suggest a general familiarity with, and desire to use, judicial structures and processes. Striking demonstration of such 'popular legalism' is provided by the widespread practice of appearing before magistrates to swear the peace, to request that an opponent be bound over.[27] Binding over refers to a magistrate's power to bind an individual over in a fixed sum, or recognisance, and for a fixed period, to keep the peace and/or to be of good behaviour irrespective of conviction for a criminal offence.[28] If the person bound over was subsequently found to have breached the peace and/or failed to be of good behaviour during that period, he or she was liable to have the recognisance 'estreated' or forfeited to the Crown. The practice has underpinned the structures of authority in English society for almost ten centuries.

Although binding over probably originated with Anglo-Saxon attempts to combine suretyship with local self-policing, the first 'commissions of the peace', empowering magistrates to hear and determine criminal cases, were issued in 1328. A statute of 1361 enjoined justices 'to take of all them that be [not] of good Fame . . . sufficient surety and Mainprise of their good Behaviour towards the King and his People'. This statute has formed the basis of magisterial powers to bind over ever since, and several legal commentators, including William Lambarde and Michael Dalton in the late sixteenth and early seventeenth centuries, William Blackstone in the late eighteenth, and contemporary Law Commissioners, have devoted considerable energy to explaining them. Blackstone noted in the 1760s that

> a man may be bound to his good behaviour for causes of scandal, *contra bonos mores* [against good behaviour], as well as *contra pacem* [against the peace]; . . . or for words tending to scandalise the government, or in abuse of the officers of justice, especially in the execution of their office. Thus also a justice may bind over all nightwalkers; eavesdroppers; such as keep suspicious company, or are reported to be pilferers or robbers; such as sleep in the day and wake in the night; common drunkards; whore masters; the putative fathers of bastards; cheats; idle vagabonds; and other persons, whose misbehaviour may reasonably bring them within the general words of the statute, as persons not of good fame.[29]

Throughout these developments, discretion has been both the strength and weakness of the system. While breach of the peace has always had a 'surprising lack of authoritative definition', the limits of 'good behaviour' extend even more vaguely to activities which are neither strictly criminal nor even dangerous, but are simply distasteful to the magisterial establishment and those that have its ear. Although the Law Commissioners of 1994 recommended the abolition of binding over, on grounds of 'uncertainty' and 'natural justice', they noted that the power was most fervently supported by those responsible for its practical application.[30] From a contemporary perspective this reminds us of the distinction, particularly marked in the early modern period, between legal theory and legal practice. Historians of early modern law enforcement agree not only that 'common law' might differ from 'common practice' but also that the fabric of criminal justice was shot through with discretion at every level.[31]

Binding over in early modern England can be divided into three broad categories: first, to keep the peace, either towards a named individual or to the community at large; second, to be of good behaviour, likewise either to particular persons or in general; and third, to perform specified activities or to refrain from performing others. Early modern justices' handbooks devote lengthy sections to the warrants and sureties through which recognisances were administered.[32] Dalton's *Country Justice* (1618), for instance, explained that a 'surety for the peace' was a measure of 'security' because 'the party that was in fear is thereby the more secure and safe'. Justices could demand sureties either 'as a minister, commanded thereto by a higher authority', or 'as a judge'. In the latter case, Dalton distinguished between powers exercised by a magistrate 'of his own motion and discretion', and those executed 'at the request and prayer of another'. These categories overlapped slightly in that a justice might persuade one party to desire the peace against another.[33] Of the sixteen offences identified by Dalton for which 'discretionary sureties' might be commanded, six were transgressions committed in the justice's presence: assault upon the magistrate himself; assault on others; threats of assault, wounding, or arson; 'contending in hot words (for from thence often times do ensue affrays and batteries, and sometimes mayhems, yea manslaughters and murders)'; riding with unusually numerous attendants, including any servant or labourer bearing arms; and suspected inclination to breach the peace'.[34] Justices were also empowered to bind over any person arrested by a constable for threatening assault; for suspicion of imminent breach of the peace; or for participation in a domestic dispute into which a constable had intervened, even 'by breaking open the doors' of a house. Those reported to have made affray could be bound by discretion, and in cases of wounding, both parties were to be bound 'until the wound be cured and the malice be over'. Constables were empowered to arrest and secure the binding before a justice of any who rode armed, rioted or committed barratry.[35]

Although Dalton described magistrate's discretionary powers in some detail, he emphasised that binding over depended upon popular participation. To a far greater extent than either Blackstone or the Law Commissioners of 1994, he stressed the role of private initiatives in causing justices to bind others over. Magistrates usually commanded the finding of sureties upon complaint by a third party. Such requests had to be validated by an oath that the party stood 'in fear of his life or of some bodily hurt', thus ensuring that the peace was not craved lightly, or 'for any private malice, or for vexation, but of very fear, and for the needful safety of body or houses'.[36] 'Breach of the peace' therefore constituted an offence against the person rather than against property, and recognisances could not protect 'cattle, servants, or other goods'.[37] They were, moreover, concerned solely with present or future danger, and could not be used retrospectively. Almost any individual could therefore be bound before a magistrate if their opponent could both afford the legal fees and was prepared to swear that they had been threatened.[38] Only peers of the realm could not be bound over, Dalton argued, because the law 'conceived an opinion of the peaceable disposition of noblemen', whose word of honour was considered sufficient.[39] But otherwise, the technique was of virtually unlimited applicability: sureties could, for instance, be demanded both of local office-holders, and between members of a family.[40] In practice, then, the smokey, wainscotted parlours of gentry seats were to be filled with local yeomen and husbandmen swearing oaths that they feared for their lives, as magistrates' clerks filled in the relevant documents.

The oath not only deterred the perpetuation of feuds in the law, it also represented the sanction of spiritual violence that was inherent in the judicial process, in that the oath-taker was required, voluntarily, to imperil his or her soul. This spiritual and psychological threat was legitimated by the law, which harnessed its coercive potential for the good of the commonwealth. In this *symbolic* sense, authority worked through the ordering of violence: a 'rite of violence' presided over by a magistrate regulated the right of violence.[41] The *practical* virtue of the system for those in authority, however, lay in the justice's discretionary power 'to appoint and allow the number of sureties, their sufficiency in goods or lands, the sum of money wherein they shall be bound, and to limit the time how long the party shall be bound'.[42]

So much, then, for binding over to keep the peace. Dalton described 'surety of good behaviour' as 'of great affinity with the peace, and ordained chiefly for the preservation of the peace', although he argued that 'there is more difficulty in the performance [of good behaviour], and the party so bound may sooner fall into the danger of it'.[43] Whereas 'affray, battery, assault, imprisoning or extremity of menacing' merely constituted breach of the peace, both 'the peace' and 'the good behaviour' could be infringed by the attendance of an extraordinary number of people; by carrying arms; by issuing threats tending to the breach of the peace; or by any activity which 'put the people in dread or fear'.[44] Whereas the surety of the peace was 'usually granted at the request of one, and for the preservation of the peace towards one', 'good behaviour' was usually granted 'to provide for the safety of many' upon complaint from several 'very honest and credible persons'.[45] This explains why warrants for good behaviour were usually ordered after Quarter Sessions Benches received petitions from the 'better sort' of people.[46] In this way, five types of delinquents were likely to be bound for their good behaviour: barrators, quarrellers and disturbers of the peace; rioters; those who lay in wait to rob or assault; suspected highway robbers; and those with intent to commit murder.[47] But here, again, the discretionary powers granted to the justices were very broad: such warrants could be awarded against 'any of evil name and fame generally', including 'suspected persons who live idly and yet fare well, or are well apparelled having nothing whereon to live'.[48]

Behaviour tending to breach of the peace was, therefore, extremely broadly defined, while warrants of good behaviour could be ordered against an almost infinite range of transgressors. Those categorised as anti-social included many (quarrellers, fornicators, nightwalkers, drunkards, idlers) whose actions might not have been strictly criminal. 'The peace' was, therefore, on the one hand, a flexible and powerful *instrument* of authority which empowered the magistracy to suppress conduct perceived to be anti-social; and on the other, a *resource* of authority available for private individuals to protect themselves from aggression. In this sense, binding over was attractive to magistrates and disputing parties alike. For justices, it operated as an early modern 'sus-law', with all the discretion and flexibility that implies. To the actual or potential victim of crime, swearing the peace offered protection without the trouble and charge of indictment for assault, or civil litigation.

Analysis of both the extent and the operational significance of binding over is fraught with difficulty. In the first place, recognisances were evidently certified to courts whose records do not survive, or, even more significantly, were never certified at all.[49] Second, 'discretionary' bonds are difficult to distinguish from those secured upon private complaint, a task further complicated by the 'dark figure' of warrants which never succeeded in bringing defendants before magistrates. Third, by the turn of the seventeenth century, recognisances were apparently taken in disputes which, strictly speaking, did not involve threats to the person. Both Beattie and Bob Shoemaker have demonstrated that Restoration justices used recognisances in cases relating to vice, to the Poor Law, and to property and regulatory offences.[50] By the turn of the seventeenth century, binding over apparently formed part of the matrix of social control in the metropolitan campaign for the reformation of manners, and was frequently used by justices who heard large numbers of cases of vice in which defendants were frequently poor.[51] Shoemaker distinguishes three patterns of judicial preference in the handling of misdemeanour prosecutions, which he characterises as 'ideal types' of magisterial activity: 'mediating', 'law and order' and 'social control'.[52] The 'mediating' justices who frequently issued recognisances did so because binding over facilitated quasi-formal arbitrated settlements.[53]

Shoemaker's analysis is invaluable in two respects. First, it clarifies the inordinately complex relationship between recognisances and indictments, and therefore between binding over and prosecution. Second, it emphasises the importance of magistrates' idiosyncracies, especially in a system which granted them enormous discretion. It does, however, have certain limitations. The validity of its conclusions depends upon the quantification of data whose integrity he defends at great length, yet the complexities of real life are often sacrificed to the demands of this heavily statistical methodology. Furthermore, in focusing on magistrates' strategies, rather than plaintiffs' priorities, it illuminates the exercise, rather than the experience, of authority. Shoemaker regards recognisances as a governmental tool, to be used as and when magistrates saw fit. To put it another way, he is more concerned with binding over than with the swearing of the peace that caused it. Finally, his analysis entirely ignores the question of violence, and treats both oath-taking and threats of physical harm as if they were legal fictions.[54] Finally, he fails to address the changing social dynamics of binding over: how did the practice of, and attitudes towards, swearing the peace change over time?

Although medieval evidence is scarce, the Cheshire archive provides the largest and most complete set of bonds for any county in the fifteenth century.[55] In the period 1442–85, Dorothy Clayton counted 1069 mainprize bonds, and a further 1717 recognisances, to keep the peace. Given that these bonds were certified in the country court rather than at quarter sessions, these statistics are of limited comparative value.[56] For the early modern period, however, the picture is much fuller. Surviving quarter sessions records for mid-seventeenth-century Essex contain almost 1700 recognisances for the peace or good behaviour in a sixty-year period, an annual average of twenty-eight.[57] Shoemaker himself identifies 2392 defendants prosecuted by recognisance in Middlesex and Westminster between 1661 and 1725.[58] Of these, 2092 had not previously been indicated, and of them only 1148 (55 percent) were involved specifically in offences against the peace.[59] The changing purposes of binding over therefore render the quantitative analysis of long-term trends in the use of recognisances extremely hazardous.

The following discussion thus seeks to illuminate changing attitudes towards contention, litigation and violence through a medium-term analysis of the priorities of those who sought to have opponents bound over in late sixteenth- and early seventeenth-century England. Much of the evidence is drawn from Cheshire, a county whose abundant records have been relatively little studied by historians.[60] At the very least, discussion of social relations in this 'far distant place of the realm', in an environment relatively unfamiliar to those historians preoccupied with the small-scale, closed communities of lowland 'incorporated' England, might encourage comparative analysis. It is not suggested here that the north-western marches of the realm were necessarily more lawless than the Home Counties. None the less, the dynamics of authority, neighbourliness and conflict were bound to ramify according to the 'politics' of each individual 'parish'.[61] Furthermore, the nature of the Cheshire archive facilitates both quantitative and qualitative analysis.

In the first place, administrative records provide impressionistic evidence of the increasing frequency of swearing the peace during the course of the seventeenth century. Various county benches modified their procedures relating to recognisances: increasing business was visibly placing strains on the system, and intervals between court appearances for those bound over were extended in order to ease pressure on quarter sessions' agenda.[62] This impression is confirmed by a count of recognisances for the peace and for good behaviour certified in the Cheshire quarter sessions order books, 1590–1609. A total of 4120 persons, or an average of 206 each year, stood bound to the peace or for good behaviour during these two decades. Moreover, the numbers bound were increasing over time. The average number bound at each sessions in the period 1605–9 was almost sixty-four, an increase of over 80 per cent on the average for 1590–4.[63] The increasing popularity of petitioning to have an opponent bound for good behaviour is demonstrated by a doubling of the proportion of all recognisances which were entered for good behaviour from forty-three or 2.7 per cent (1590–9), to 136 or 5.3 per cent (1600–9). This picture is confirmed by a count of warrants issued upon petition to quarter sessions: over the same period, the number of warrants for good behaviour ordered by the Bench increased from fourteen to ninety-six. At a 'time of troubles', during which a combination of social, economic and cultural tensions were at work in village communities, the recognisance for good behaviour was 'an ideal instrument of social control' in that it helped the better sort of the inhabitants of English parishes, especially those holding local power, to 'enforce standards of behaviour which they considered appropriate and conducive to social well-being upon all members of the community'.[64]

This late sixteenth-century intensification of craving the peace was not confined to Cheshire. Of the twenty-three interpersonal disputes which resulted in recognisances to keep the peace in the Essex village of Terling during 1560–1699, sixteen arose in the period 1599–1612. This concentration of business has been taken as evidence of 'a high degree of conflict amongst villagers of middling status', conflict bitter enough to result in threats, fear, and requests for formal arbitration.[65] This suggestion is confirmed by analysis of the changing social profile of peace-swearers. Clayton argued that 'the vast majority of people involved in Cheshire recognisances made in the second half of the fifteenth century were gentlemen'.[63] The late sixteenth-century evidence suggests that binding over was far more frequently requested by those of much lower social status. In a sample of 244 recognisances filed at eight Elizabethan Cheshire Quarter Sessions, eighty-six of those swearing the peace can definitely be classified as yeomen, and a further forty-two as husbandmen. These two groups therefore account for almost two-thirds of all those of known social status who swore the peace in this period. The 'middling sort' were the most frequent swearers of the peace in late Elizabethan England.[67] Such a conclusion is significant in two respects. First, it chimes with Shoemaker's view that while recognisances were cheaper than indictments, they were still prohibitively expensive for the poorer sort of the parish. The bare minimum cost of prosecution by recognisance (the fee for a warrant for the peace) was two shillings, at a time when a Chester labourer might earn between six and eight pence per day.[68] Second, it suggests that middling-sort respectability first found expression in changing attitudes towards violence, threatening language and contention.[69]

Recognisances illustrate both the nature and extent of these forms of social tension in the past. In the first place, the reporting of threats to the peace implies that conflict was endemic, and attempts have been made to relate the frequency of binding over to the experience of social change in local communities. In Terling, for example, Wrightson and Levine argue that demographic pressures at the turn of the sixteenth century created new patterns of social and economic differentiation within the middling ranks of parish society, resulting in a sharp concentration of interpersonal disputes concerning property issues.[70] Although economic tensions may well have been at play there, wider issues were clearly at stake in other communities, especially since violence was both a cause and a symptom of conflict. In the second place, the fact that recognisances were secured at all, often in preference to indictments, suggests that, whatever its causes, conflict was often highly mediated.[71] This perspective helps explain other contemporaneous trends in the use of the law, including the complex networks of petitioning and counter-petitioning to which magistrates were subjected; the increasing concern of Grand Jurors with anti-social behaviour; and the redefinition and punishment of sedition at every social level.[72] This was evidently a period in which larger processes of social change created new forms of conflict and necessitated novel means of control. Binding over for an increasingly wide range of activities was merely one expression of this trend, and because it reflects the extent of potential rather than actual lawlessness in this period, it serves as a valuable index of both contention and resolution.

Binding over therefore reflects two facets of early modern social relations: on the one hand, the ubiquitous threat of violence; on the other, notorious legal-mindedness. While the widespread use of recognisances is *prima facie* evidence of participation in the legal process, this particular form of 'quasi-litigation' was ostensibly appropriate only when threats of violence had been issued. These two apparently contradictory trends can, however, be reconciled. As Phillipa Maddern has argued, there is 'little chance of understanding the purposes and progress of . . . litigation and arbitration without analysing the role of violence'.[73] Indeed, the tendency to place violence and the law at opposite moral poles is arguably a very modern one, which ignores the extent to which they might operate in tandem to establish and protect divinely ordained social and political order. Binding over perfectly embodies this complementary relationship between violence and litigation. Recognisances were popular not simply because they were authoritative, but also because they coerced antagonists to desist from violent acts. The frequency of swearing the peace might be taken as evidence of an increasing tendency to litigate, but it was also characteristic of an environment in which even the most respectable members of a community could be provoked into offering insults, or uttering threats of violence. While it is true, therefore, that the proliferation of recognisances reflects a great deal more about life in early modern England than its tendency to become violent, the threat of violence necessarily underpins it. The widespread finding of sureties at the turn of the sixteenth century was arguably a decisive phase of what John Beattie describes as

> a very-long-term transformation of the place of violence in English society, from a period in the late Middle Ages when violence was less restrained either by the State or by men's attitudes, to what has come to be the broad disapproval and control of private violence in the modern world.[74]

The demanding of the peace suggests that the line dividing acceptable from unacceptable conduct was not hard and fast, and implies a gradually emerging sense of abhorrence, especially amongst middling social groups, of deeds and words that had once been so commonplace as to cause little concern.[75]

It is, therefore, into the contexts of both 'warring' and 'lawing', of both 'pistols' and 'process', that the cultural preference for pacification must be placed. Evidence from the Cheshire archive demonstrates the complex relationship between litigation, violence and binding over. Several of those bound over in late Elizabethan and early Stuart Cheshire were guilty of issuing threats of violence. They included George Richardson of Rushton whose 'foul words'

228 The Experience of Authority in Early Modern England

included the threat to 'stick that old queen' widow Addishead; John Gill of Aston-near-Minshull who promised to put that 'cuckoldly knave' William Gibbons 'in a sack and beat him'; William Fallowes of Chelford who offered 'twentie nobles' to have that 'arrant knave' William Burges 'cunningly knocked'; Robert Bancroft of Hulme who tempted James Taylor with £20 to 'knock out the brains of his master'; Richard Tue of Buerton who conspired with Thomas Dayes, 'one of the conningest men in all England', to murder Thomas Massy of Wrenbury; and Thomas Day of Tibbe Green who had maliciously 'lain in wait to have grieviously wounded and assaulted' Robert Audley.[76]

But recognisances were also employed to preclude the institution-alised vengeance of litigation, by bringing the force of authority 'to remedy that that otherways seems to be remedyless'.[77] The Cheshire magistrate Sir Richard Grosvenor, for example, was furious with his son's insistence on litigation during a property dispute. Although a neighbour had 'propounded divers ways of peace' in a 'difference for makinge a diche' between their lands, the younger Grosvenor would 'proceed noe way but by a . . . Jury'. His father urged him to 'to gayne and keep the love of your neighbours, without which I had rather not be. Differences may arise betwixt the nearest friends; but it is a Christian part to try all faire way to decide them before extremity be used.' Grosvenor urged his son to enter a recogni-sance, to 'yield to a reference and try to make choice of one to end the cause'.[78] His analysis of the disputing process was at once moralistic yet intensely practical. Litigation, he explained, 'for the most parte concludes doubtfully and ends costly'. A willingness to attempt a 'fair and friendly way of composure' was crucial to the pacification of quarrells. Even when confronted with obdurate opponents, Grosvenor advised clemency: 'a seasonable gentler usage may have power to charme, when rigour helpeth to enrage'. Reconciliation should be sought in every case. 'None can dislike this Christian way', he wrote, 'but men of froward dispositions and turbulent spirits' who sought 'to glutt themselves in revenge, and to delighte in the misery of their neighbours'. Only as a final event-uality, when attempts at mediation and arbitration had proved unsuccessful, would he sanction institutional retaliation: 'then may a man justly seeke for his owne by law . . . you are then blameless before God and man, and may justly defend yourself with weapons answerable to those wherewith you are assaulted'.[79]

Grosvenor's air of resignation seems well justified in the context of the massive increase in litigation in late Tudor and early Stuart England.[80] Whatever the ideals of charity and forgiveness, the 'furious words, threats and taunting recriminations' that Grosvenor feared were common enough, and men of 'base sperits' used the law with alacrity.[81] One dispute in Waverton, in 1597, captures this trend perfectly, the parson informing the Bench that although he and his neighbours had 'endeavoured to compound variance and dissension' between two parishioners, they had 'prevailed nothing therein, neither is there any likelihood that persuasion might hereafter prevail, but more malice and evil will is like to be showed' by 'molesting either other by suits and charges in law'. Although one party was 'willing that all such matters be laid away so as they might live in love and charity as becomes good Christians', his opponent refused to yield 'unto this Christian reconciliation, being in very deed of wayward and wrangling nature'.[82] Such mediation often failed precisely because mediators were usually selected with hard bargaining in mind. Grosvenor noted that even where mere 'trifles and toyes' were at stake, disputants sought out mediators 'so fast knit and tyed unto' them that they could be trusted to prosecute their interests rigorously.[83] The desire for authoritative arbitration therefore led to a substantial increase in quasi-formal dispute settlement during the late sixteenth and early seventeenth centuries, without which the increase of litigation would have been even more marked.

Arbitration was crucial in almost every jurisdiction in early modern England. Three examples from the Cheshire archive demonstrate the centrality of quasi-formal settlement at every level of the legal system. In 1620, the Privy Council appointed a Chester Exchequer commission to settle 'all questions and controversies' among Crown copyholders during the enclosure of Macclesfield common. When certified that substantial exceptions still remained, a second Commission was issued 'to mediate a peaceable and friendly atonement' if one might 'be conveniently effected'. In 1607, Lord Chancellor Ellesmere referred a 'debate' to the Justices of Chester 'for the settling of quietnes' between the cathedral and city authorities there. In 1594, a property dispute in Hurleston was referred by the Kinderton court leet to the arbitration of a local yeoman, who subsequently certified the end of 'controversie and discord'.[84] The Quarter Sessions Bench likewise stepped into this role, frequently delegating individual magistrates to arbitrate in specific disputes, urging reconciliation rather than rigorous prosecution. The Chester Diocesan Chancellor was ordered in 1594 to sequestrate a pew disputed by two Knutsford parishioners and to mediate between them; a Hurleston Yeoman was compelled to accept the order of two magistrates 'concerning all matters in variance' in 1597; another magistrate was delegated to mediate between a 'poor man' and his landlord during a rack-renting dispute in Mobberley in 1608; and in 1617 Sir Urian Leigh arbitrated a settlement between four disputing husbandmen in Macclesfield Forest.[85]

Some of these arrangements could be complex. When two petitioners who had been 'grieviously troubled and vexed' by riot indictments prosecuted 'upon unjust and untrew suggestions' pleaded for mediation by 'some gentlemen of Macclesfield hundred', the Cheshire Bench referred them initially to the 'arbitrament and ending' of two magistrates, and ultimately to an 'umpire indifferently chosen betwixt them'.[86] Ideally, arbitrators should not only carry sufficient authority to be impartial, they ought to be familiar with the personal circumstances of the parties. Local magistrates or landlords were, therefore, very frequently ordered to enforce reconciliation. 'Differences' within the Tomlinson family, for example, were regarded as 'fittest to be determined by such justices as live near' them because 'they understand and know best [their] qualities', while 'oppressions and injuries' between Sir Thomas Smith's tenants were referred to their landlord.[87] Arbitrators were not even necessarily required to certify the conclusion of their hearings: Sir Richard Wilbraham was ordered to certify his opinion only if he failed to end an apprenticeship dispute. If litigation was inevitable, the Bench might dictate its terms: 'all the controversies touching trespasses betwixt' two parties in Macclesfield were 'to be tried between them, and not by way of indictment'.[88]

Recognisances were particularly useful in this regard, since by referring disputes to arbitration, they might preclude further private initiatives. Their role was ambiguous. Recognisances might sometimes be suspended pending arbitration, or actually made conditional on composition. Recognisances against two parties in Nantwich were 'stayed for that the controversy is referred to the ending of William Lord Brereton'. Good behaviour was to be granted in favour of petitioners from Partington only if those appointed to 'end the controversie' failed. Because the Bench referred 'controversies' in Nantwich to two magistrates 'not doubting that [they] will take paynes for the ending thereof', warrants of good behaviour were 'ceased and none hereafter to be granted forth'. Equally, binding over could defuse tension pending further investigation: Sir Richard Wibraham was delegated to 'order' a dispute in Nantwich while the parties were continued bound to their good behaviour.[89]

How effectively, then, were positive attitudes to 'a fair and friendly way of composure' fostered? How did early modern Englishmen and women react when they were bound to the peace? Although binding over might actually have constrained further vexation or violence, it seems to have been growing less effective over time, perhaps as a consequence of the decreasing social status of those involved. Among Clayton's largely gentlemanly late medieval participants in the practice, 'there is little evidence that Cheshire peace bonds were broken'. In Shoemaker's Restoration and Hanoverian sample, however, 'close to a third of all recognizances did not lead to satisfactory conclusions'. Perhaps as many as 15 per cent of recognisances issued by Westminster justices were actually estreated, while process for forfeiture was initiated in a further 11 per cent of cases.[90] In early seventeenth-century Cheshire, the data do not lend themselves to systematic quantification, but there is sufficient impressionistic evidence to demonstrate the matrix of social and cultural pressures which constituted the experience of being bound over.

Some of those subject to bonds were simply contemptuous. Most obviously, the very poorest members of the community, 'people of low and desperate fortunes' as they were later called, had little to lose if they defaulted.[91] Ralph Ashes feared that his opponent was 'the rather emboldened' to break the peace because he and his sureties were 'all men of very weak estate, and have not wherewithall to satisfy His Majesty of any forfeiture'. William Baker of Calcott allegedly regarded the forfeiture of his recognisance 'but lightly'. In other cases, rage, fury and the desire for revenge were sufficiently intense to outweigh any financial or judicial imperatives. John Bradshaw threatened to 'be loose' and to 'be remembered upon' those who had sworn against him. Before a fracas in Stockport in 1602, one of the rioters initially remarked that 'we are bound to the peace and therefore dare not stir', but his grieving father swore that he 'would be in no place quiet' towards his son's murderers. Other offenders were simply incorrigible. Thomas Sale of Weaverham had beaten his wife so badly that 'for fear of her life', she fled to live with Sale's sister. When he threatened them with arson, magistrates affirmed that they 'had formerly bound [Sale] to the peace and good abearing which he did infringe'. Similarly, although the Jenkyn brothers of Wigland were 'very lewd persons, common quarrellers, and barretors, common defamers and slanderous of their neighbours, [and] common drunkards' who had repeatedly been bound to their good behaviour, they had nevertheless 'continued their usual and wonted course of life in quarrelling, brawling, defaming and slandering of their neighbours'. In a third instance, Randle Farrer remarked that he 'neither cared for the warrant [of the peace] nor for the King', and threatened to kill the vicar of Weaverham. Such contempt often resulted in physical violence: Michael Millington committed an assault in Wybunbury churchyard 'wherein he broke a bond of £40'. Some officers were not above reproach either. Although the constable of Broxton was bound to the peace, he incited his wife to assault a bailiff, promising to 'bear her out if she was in danger of law'.[92] For these and others, the threat of financial penalties for them and their sureties was neither sharp nor even meaningful, and their participation in the law was a downward spiral of binding over, imprisonment and indictment.

Pacification, then, was not always easily achieved, least of all when recognisances were secured vexatiously. The frequency and geographical spread of references to vexation have led Jim Sharpe to conclude that launching suits on slight or malicious grounds was a national problem.[93] Swearing the peace was no less vulnerable to abuse, and evidence suggests that malicious binding over was relatively common. If litigation constituted a breach of proper neighbourly relations, binding over at least tended to one's discredit within the community, and implied guilt, unless a counterwarrant was procured. Being bound over also entailed considerable trouble and charge, since the minimum cost of defending a recognisance was four shillings and four pence in fees to clerk and court.[94] Since a warrant cost two shillings to secure, both prosecutors and magistrates might have motives for abusing the system. Sir Richard Grosvenor reminded his fellow magistrates to 'prize not the clerks fee before the peace and quiet of your neighbours'.[95] Malicious oaths, like vexatious litigation as a whole, illustrate what might be termed 'unpopular legalism', the use of the law to further feuds.

Several laconic references to malicious recognisances suggest that men of a 'wayward and wrangling nature' were all too common. When composition was suggested by Clement Starky's opponent after both were bound over, for example, Starky replied that 'he had him fast and would keep him fast' so long as he lived. Robert Sponne of Warmincham was alleged to have 'upon mere malice and knavery' sworn the peace against his neighbours 'whom he knew to be men well stayed and of good government [who] never purposed or intended any hurt against him'. Henry Mainwaring prayed for the release of another recognisance because both parties 'are labourers and are poor and the man has been kept long enough under no great charge rather upon malice than matter'. Thomas Marbury perceived that the warrant procured against John Shaw, yeoman of Rosthorne, was 'rather upon malice than upon cause'. A shoemarker who 'upon meere malice' swore the good behaviour against the mayor of Stockport was whipped through the market there in 1621.[96] For some individuals, swearing the peace was apparently a habitual, even a professional, activity. William Baker of Calcott retaliated to his neighbours' complaints by maliciously binding them to the peace 'until they give him money for composition, when he himself has spent nothing at all'. Agnes Stonyer allegedly 'made a living of swearing her dread of bodily harm and thereupon procuring warrants of the peace' and 'taking money to dispense with' them, to a total of thirty-six shillings from seven neighbours.[97]

Grosvenor warned his fellow magistrates that recognisances were wide open to such vexatious abuse: the demanding of the peace from one another by neighbours was, he wrote, 'too common a way of revenge upon the least unkindness'.[98] Dalton had anticipated this tendency, warning that 'if a man will require the peace because he is at variance with his neighbour, it shall not be granted'.[99] The issue depended on the magistrate's ability to distinguish between 'matter' and 'malice'. If the justice perceived vexation, he may 'safely deny' the request for a warrant. He accepted that this could be a frequent occurrence:

Where A shall upon just cause come and crave the peace against B and have it granted to him; when B shall come before the

justice, B will likewise crave the peace against A, but yet will
nevertheless be content to surcease his suit and demand against
A so as A will relinquish to have the peace against him.

Placed in this difficult situation, it was the magistrate's responsibility to arbitrate. If B took the oath, then the justice was obliged to
grant the peace against A, but Dalton warned justices 'not to be too
forward in thus granting the peace', but rather 'to persuade with B'
and 'show him the danger of his oath'.[100]

Grosvenor, however, doubted the efficacy of the threat of spiritual violence implied by the oath. Although he warned the Cheshire Grand Jury that oathtaking was 'a most sacred action which is
not to be sleighted as a matter of base form but to be accounted of
great weight and moment', he feared that 'custome in often taking
an oath may with some irreligious persons lessen their esteem
thereof'.[101] Grosvenor knew that perjury was endemic where sworn
testimony was ubiquitous, and he would certainly have heard comments like those of Peter Norris of Middlewich who allegedly remarked in 1604 that 'oathes were but wordes, wordes were but
wynde and wynde is mutable', and that it was merely 'a chyldishe
tricke to make account of an oathe'. Norris was more concerned
with the physical rather than the spiritual danger of his oath: 'if I
forsweare me I shall lose but my eares'.[102] For some, it seems, a
cropping at the pillory was, even in the early seventeenth century,
more potent a threat than the smell of brimstone.[103]

Both malicious binding over and perjury indicate that participation in the legal system, so often regarded as a positive advantage,
might have negative consequences. Vexatious swearing of the peace
(the 'brabbles and discurtesies', for example, that were exhausting
the patience of the Cheshire Bench by the mid-1630s) is a potent
reminder that litigation was not invariably beneficial.[104] Making the
system work, and striving to make the system work for you were very
different enterprises, and some of those who employed the mechanism of binding over did both. Indeed, arbitration could be coercive, and historians should be more sensitive to the contours of the
power structures which are all too often levelled by indiscriminate
use of the term 'arbitration'. Sir Richard Grosvenor's injunctions to
reconciliation might well have been, at least in part, class specific,
noting that amongst gentlemen 'the most noble soules are beawti-
fied with the raies of clemency', and implying that only the wealthy

were 'armed with power as with will to revenge' their enemies at law. His comments were, moreover, explicitly justified on the grounds of 'pollicye'. These reservations are especially pertinent with respect to binding over: where magistrates sought to reconcile antagonists, they often denied poor disputants access to the protection offered by the formal mechanisms of the law, and enforced them to submit to recognisances that might be beyond their means. Neither injunctions, nor unilateral willingness to consent, to arbitration should, therefore, necessarily be read as indices of altruism or public spirit.[105]

It would, however, be both churlish and misguided to deny that in practice 'a gentle answer pacifieth wrath'.[106] Swearing the peace frequently did smooth the passage to amicable composition. In these cases, it was probably the pacifying influence of sureties, themselves vulnerable to financial penalty if the recognisance was forfeit, that prevailed. The coercive potential of the bond restrained several would-be pugilists. George Clayton, against whom the peace had been sworn by Richard Stapleton, could only threaten his opponent that 'if he were not bound, he would beat him'. Although the sureties for Thomas Rawlinson's good behaviour 'made great braggs that they would do much', the magistrate who had bound him over was confident that they would be 'tamer before he be released'.[107] Although 'a suddayne falling out between the vicar of Plemstow and his neighbour' resulted in 'some bodily hurt', soon afterwards the two parties 'in verie loving manner reconcyled themselves' before two magistrates 'and did then become and do still continue perfect friends'. Two days before the sessions at which he had bound Roger Bennett to appear, George Barrett travelled to Adlington and released his opponent of a recognisance taken before Thomas Leigh. Ralph Rutter informed the Bench that 'all quarrels controversies and unkyndnesses betwixt' him and John Malbon were 'ended, pacified and friended', and asked for the recognisance to be cancelled. Thomas Aston certified 'upon [his] creditt' that two of his tenants were agreed before the sessions. Henry Delves similarly certified that Thomas Waddington and his wife Elizabeth had composed their differences and that she had released him of the peace.[108] For those bound by magisterial discretion, the cooling-off period could be similarly effective: for twelve months after 'dissension and breach of the peace' in Middlewich had caused Thomas Venables to bind two

quarrellers for their good behaviour, they had 'honestly and pea-
ceably behaved themselves towards their neighbours and others
with whom they had occasion to deal', and Venables released them
without further action.[109] A substantial proportion of recognisances
were intended to precipitate this type of settlement. The number of
recognisances which were released within a day or two of the
coming sessions lends further weight to this argument. Of 244
recognisances to keep the peace towards a named party surviving in
eight Cheshire quarter sessions files, at least eighty (30.5 per cent)
were relaxed before the sessions at which the bound party was to
appear.[110] Once an individual was made to appear, however, he was
almost certain to be bound over for a further appearance. Almost
two-thirds of all those who found sureties of either type were continued bound over, to allow tempers to cool.[111]

Sometimes, therefore, binding over was abused or manipulated
by disingenuous adversaries to harass or intimidate their opponents; more frequently, it constrained the contentious or recalcitrant; quite regularly, it facilitated an arbitrated or negotiated
settlement between parties in dispute; most often, it formed part of
the litigation strategies of enemies seeking short-term advantage
over one another. In all these circumstances, a recognisance might
serve as a 'sword of Damocles' hanging over the head of a defend-
ant, though its efficacy depended both upon the sharpness of the
threat of forfeiture and upon the attitudes of sureties.[112] The public
peace was not always kept, and in a society where governmental and
judicial resources were unprofessional and relatively shallow, contention was the thin end of the wedge of malice, disorder and
violence.

III

The divergent analyses of the 'conflict' and 'consensus' schools of
thought on early modern English social relations are only, then, to
be reconciled by an awareness that each reflects the ambiguities
and ambivalences of a social reality: that whatever its claims, the
State enjoyed no monopoly of violence in early modern England.[113]
Such ambiguities had, of course, to be managed in practice. Hence
the significance of binding over: it represented a way of mediating

between the ideal of social harmony and the realities of social conflict. Its widespread use owed much to its marvellous flexibility. The very broad applicability of swearing the peace, and the subtly coercive potential of binding to the good behaviour, were precisely what made them attractive to contemporaries. In this regard, recognisances had three main merits. First, they shared several of the characteristics of formal action, even of coercion: they were in many ways as effective as a prosecution. Second, they could be highly sensitive to individual needs and circumstances. Recognisances could be released easily and cheaply without loss of face, and with the threat of further 'prosecution' unimpaired. Third, from the point of view of those in authority, they were a splendid instrument for defusing tension and encouraging restraint. It is not coincidental that historians of the administration of central government have made so much of the use of recognisances as an innovative 'policy of financial terror' against the late medieval nobility; and of the Cromwellian régime's use of binding over by the 'commissioners for securing the peace of the commonwealth' in the 1650s.[114] In all these respects, swearing the peace was an almost infinitely adaptable apparatus of containment. Binding over curtailed head-on conflict, and encouraged the 'civilising process', without itself bringing social and political relationships to crisis point.

Recognisances could, and did, cope admirably with various forms of social tension. But bonds and their sureties also had a creative role to play in that they subtly reinforced the early modern obsession with order. In attempting to preclude the violent settlement of dispute, binding over injected public authority into the regular communion of conflict, thus symbolically edging forward the boundaries of the State. Recognisances therefore illustrate the participatory nature of State formation in the English context. Social theorists have drawn attention to the increasing emphasis on 'civilisation', 'discipline' and the 'management' of disorder in early modern Europe, suggesting that the initiative for 'normative pacification' lay with governors and with the State, and that cultural values shifted under the pressures of constraint imposed 'from above'.[115] Such analyses arguably ignore, or at least overlook, the extent to which order and authority did not merely 'trickle down' but 'welled up' within society itself. In this sense, analysis of the experience of authority facilitates an understanding of the fashion-

ing of the forms and processes of governance 'from below', especially by the 'honest' or 'better sort' of inhabitants of English
parishes. The early modern English State in particular grew as
structures of authority, especially those of the law and administration, were participated in, and experienced, by sections of the
population at large. The central role of the middling sort in such
participation and experience in the sixteenth and seventeenth
centuries arguably prefigured later more structured developments
in the transformation of the 'public sphere'.[116] In this sense, binding over provides an invaluable insight into the wider processes of
social and political development in early modern England. The
very increase of governance meant that the recognisance was quite
simply more available to the populace, especially those holding
local power, wealth and influence, for their own purposes. For the
governed as well as their governors, binding over restrained conflict
without rechannelling it into other forms, and demonstrated that
the law might be manipulated and adjusted to local needs. Arbitration was the most effective mechanism of adjustment, enabling the
law to function as an instrument both of the State, to secure 'order',
and of the individual and his or her community, to achieve 'settlement'. The often contradictory impulses of authority and amity
could be reconciled precisely because, when dealing with recognisances, magistrates were required to arbitrate. Sir Richard
Grosvenor was explicit on this point, enjoining his fellow magistrates to

> Be a Chancellor rather than a Justice among your neighbours,
> who are tow apt to fale into contentions, and count it an honour
> if you can compose theire differences and keep them from that
> pick-purse lawinge . . . If your neighbours demand from you the
> peace one against another . . . before you grant it persuade and
> move them to a reconciliation; such an end will be lasting and
> begett heavenly peace.[117]

The practice of binding over is, therefore, one manifestation of the
capacity of the Tudor and Stuart State to mould local society by
providing it with an instrument of authority that served local social
needs and yet simultaneously promoted the interests of government. As such, it served rather than challenged the existing power
structures of society. The simple recognisance, that laconic, much
neglected, and undramatic instrument of law enforcement, was

arguably crucial to the keeping of the public peace at every social level.

NOTES AND REFERENCES

* This is a revised version of an essay which was awarded the John Nicholls Prize by the University of Leicester Department of English Local History in 1995. The paper has been read to seminars in Cambridge and Manchester, and I would like to thank the participants for their comments. I am also grateful to Mike Braddick, Adam Fox, Craig Muldrew, John Walter and Keith Wrightson for reading drafts of the text.

1. A. Farge, *Fragile Lives: Violence, Power and Solidarity in Eighteenth Century Paris* (English trans., Cambridge, 1993), p. 285.

2. P. Collinson, 'The Cohabitation of the Faithful with the Unfaithful', in O. P. Grell *et al.* (eds), *From Persecution to Toleration: The Glorious Revolution and Religion in England* (Oxford, 1991), p. 71.

3. C. Muldrew, 'The Culture of Reconciliation: Economic Disputes and Their Settlement in Early Modern England', *Historical Journal* (forthcoming). I am very grateful to Dr Muldrew for the opportunity to read his paper in advance of publication.

4. S. Roberts, *Order and Dispute* (Harmondsworth, 1979); J. Bossy (ed.), *Disputes and Settlements: Law and Human Relations in the West* (Cambridge, 1983); W. Davies and P. Fouracre (eds), *The Settlement of Disputes in Early Medieval Europe* (Cambridge, 1986); E. Powell, *Kingship, Law and Society: Criminal Justice in the Reign of Henry V* (Oxford, 1989), ch. 4.

5. L. Stone, *The Crisis of the Aristocracy* (Oxford, 1965), p. 240.

6. M. Clanchy, 'Law and Love in the Middle Ages', in Bossy (ed.), *Disputes and Settlements*, p. 47.

7. Quoting the inhabitants of the Cheshire township of Calcott in 1605. [C]heshire [R]ecord [O]ffice QJF 33/1/24. Arbitration itself has been most intensively studied by medievalists. See Edward Powell, 'Arbitration and the Law in England in the Late Middle Ages', *Transactions of the Royal Historical Society*, 5th series, vol. 33 (1983), pp. 49–67; Powell, 'Settlement of Disputes by Arbitration in Fifteenth-Century England', *Law and History Review*, vol. 2 (1984), pp. 21–43; L. B. Smith, 'Disputes and Settlements in Medieval Wales: The Role of Arbitration', *English Historical Review*, vol. 106 (1991), pp. 835–60; L. Attreed, 'Arbitration and the Growth of Liberties in Late Medieval England', *Journal of British Studies*, vol. 31 (1992), pp. 205–35; and B. R. McCree, 'Peacemaking and Its Limits in Late Medieval Norwich', *English Historical Review*, vol. 109 (1994), pp. 831–66.

8. L. Stone, 'Interpersonal Violence in English Society, 1300–1980', *Past and Present*, vol. 101 (1983), p. 32; Stone, *The Family, Sex and Marriage in England, 1500–1800* (Oxford, 1977), pp. 95, 98.

9. J. M. Beattie, 'The Pattern of Crime in England, 1660–1800', *Past and Present*, vol. 62 (1974), pp. 47–95; Beattie, *Crime and the Courts in England, 1660–1800* (Oxford, 1986), chs 3, 8, 11; K. Wrightson and D. Levine,

Poverty and Piety in an English Village: Terling, 1525–1700, 2nd edn (Oxford 1995), chs 5, 7; K. Wrightson, *English Society, 1580–1680* (London, 1982), chs 2, 6; J. A. Sharpe, 'Such Diasgreement betwyx Neighbours: Litigation and Human Relations in Early Modern England', in Bossy (ed.), *Disputes and Settlements*, pp. 186–7; Sharpe, 'The People and the Law', in B. Reay (ed.), *Popular Culture in Seventeenth Century England* (London, 1985), pp. 262–5; Sharpe, 'Debate: The History of Violence in England: Some Observations/A Rejoinder', *Past and Present*, vol. 108 (1985), pp. 212–13.

10. M. Spufford, 'Puritanism and Social Control?', in A. Fletcher and J. Stevenson (eds), *Order and Disorder in Early Modern England* (Cambridge, 1985), p. 43; C. B. Herrup, 'Crime, Law and Society: A Review Article', *Comparative Studies in Society and History*, vol. 27 (1985), p. 170.

11. Professor Herrup's study of the administration of criminal justice in East Sussex forms the basis of the current paradigm: see C. B. Herrup, *The Common Peace: Participation and the Criminal Law in Seventeenth-Century England* (Cambridge, 1987); Herrup, 'Law and Morality in Seventeenth-century England', *Past and Present*, vol. 106 (1985), pp. 102–23. Cf. A. Macfarlane, *The Justice and the Mare's Ale: Law and Disorder in Seventeenth-Century England* (Cambridge, 1981), pp. 1–26, 173–99, quoting p. 194; Macfarlane, *The Culture of Capitalism* (Oxford, 1987), ch. 3. The conclusions of these studies have, broadly speaking, been supported by research on the activities of the ecclesiastical courts: see M. Ingram, *Church Courts, Sex and Marriage in England, 1570–1640* (Cambridge, 1987).

12. E. Duffy, *The Stripping of the Altars: Traditional Religion in England, 1400–1580* (New Haven, 1992), p. 95.

13. W. G. Runciman, *A Treatise on Social Theory, II: Substantive Social Theory* (Cambridge, 1989), p. 123.

14. The literature on these topics is immense. The best introduction to the debates over economic and religious influences on late sixteenth-century cultural polarisation are Wrightson, *English Society*, chs 5–7; M. Ingram, 'Religion, Communities and Moral Discipline in Late-Sixteenth- and Early-Seventeenth-Century England: Case Studies', in K. von Greyerz (ed.), *Religion and Society in Early Modern Europe, 1500–1800* (London, 1984), pp. 177–93; and P. Collinson, *The Birthpangs of Protestant England: Religious and Cultural Change in the Sixteenth and Seventeenth Centuries* (London, 1988), chs 4, 5. But see now K. Wrightson, 'Postscript: Terling Revisited' to the reissue of the Terling study. Wrightson and Levine, *Poverty and Piety*, ch. 8.

15. F. Heal, *Hospitality in Early Modern England* (Oxford, 1990), pp. 392–3, 402.

16. J. Bossy, *Christianity in the West, 1400–1700* (Cambridge, 1985), pp. 168–9; Bossy, 'Moral Arithmetic: Seven Sins into Ten Commandments', in E. Leites (ed.), *Conscience and Casuistry in Early Modern Europe* (Cambridge, 1988), p. 217.

17. D. Levine and K. Wrightson, *The Making of an Industrial Society: Whickham, 1560–1765*, (Oxford, 1991), p. 280.

18. Cf. the discussion of the 'primacy of neighbourhood' in David

Garrioch, *Neighbourhood and Community in Paris, 1740–90* (Cambridge, 1986), ch. 1.

19. P. G. Lawson, 'Property Crime and Hard Times in England, 1559–1624', *Law and History Review*, vol. 4 (1986), pp. 95–127, Cf. J. Walter, 'The Social Economy of Dearth in Early Modern England', in J. Walter and R. S. Schofield (eds), *Famine, Disease and the Social Order in Early Modern Society* (Cambridge, 1989), pp. 107–13, 122–3, 127.

20. Collinson, 'Cohabitation', p. 73. A. P. Cohen, *The Symbolic Construction of Community* (Chichester, 1985), quoted in C. Carpenter, 'Gentry and Community in Medieval England', *Journal of British Studies*, vol. 33 (1994), p. 355.

21. Herrup, *Common Peace*, p. 4.

22. See, e.g., J. Samaha, 'The Recognizance in Elizabethan Law Enforcement', *American Journal of Legal History*, vol. 25 (1981), pp. 189–204; Norma Landau, *The Justices of the Peace, 1679–1760* (Berkeley, 1984), ch. 6; R. Paley (ed.), *Justice in Eighteenth-Century Hackney: The Justicing Notebook of Henry Norris and the Hackney Petty Sessions Book*, London Record Society, vol. 28 (London, 1991), pp. xvi–xxii; R. B. Shoemaker, *Prosecution and Punishment: Petty Crime and the Law in London and Rural Middlesex, c.1660–1725* (Cambridge, 1991), chs 2, 5; Shoemaker, 'Using Quarter Sessions Records as Evidence for the Study of Crime and Criminal Justice', *Archives*, vol. 20 (1993), pp. 145–57.

23. Most of the essays in the three prominent recent collections on the general theme of order and disorder have been concerned with the latter. J. Brewer and J. Styles (eds), *An Ungovernable People: The English and Their Law in the Seventeenth and Eighteenth Centuries* (1980); Fletcher and Stevenson (eds), *Order and Disorder*; P. Slack (ed.), *Rebellion, Popular Protest and the Social Order in Early Modern England* (Cambridge, 1984). But see J. Walter and K. Wrightson, 'Dearth and the Social Order in Early Modern England', *Past and Present*, vol. 71 (1976), pp. 22–42; and K. Wrightson, 'Two Concepts of Order: Justices, Constables and Jurymen in Seventeenth-Century England', in Brewer and Styles (eds), *An Ungovernable People*, pp. 21–46.

24. Quoting E. P. Thompson, 'Folklore, Anthropology and Social History', *Indian Historical Review*, vol. 3 (1977), p. 255. N. Z. Davis, 'The Rites of Violence: Religious Riot in Sixteenth-Century France', *Past and Present*, vol. 59 (1973), reprinted in *Society and Culture in Early Modern France* (Stanford, 1975), p. 187; M. E. James, 'English Politics and the Concept of Honour, 1485–1642', *Past and Present* (Supplement no. 3, 1978), reprinted in James, *Society, Politics and Culture: Studies in Early Modern England* (Cambridge, 1986), pp. 310–14; M. Keen, *English Society in the Later Middle Ages, 1348–1500* (London, 1900), ch. 8; and I. Gilmour, *Riot, Risings and Revolution: Governance and Violence in Eighteenth-Century England* (1992), 'Introduction: A Violent Society?', pp. 1–20, make similarly perceptive insights. For the violence debate itself, which has generally assumed rather than explained the link between litigation, violence and mentalities, see Macfarlane, *Justice and the Mare's Ale*; J. A. Sharpe, 'Domestic Homicide in Early Modern England', *Historical Journal*, vol. 24 (1981), pp. 29–48; Stone, 'Interpersonal Violence'; J. M. Beattie, 'Violence and Society in Early

242   *The Experience of Authority in Early Modern England*

Modern England', in A. N. Doob and E. L. Greenspan (eds), *Perspectives in Criminal Law: Essays in Honour of John Ll. J. Edwards* (Toronto, 1984), pp. 36–60; Sharpe and Stone, 'Debate: The History of Violence in England'; Beattie, *Crime and the Courts*, ch. 3; J. S. Cockburn, 'Patterns of Violence in English Society: Homicide in Kent, 1500–1985', *Past and Present*, vol. 130 (1991), pp. 70–106; and S. Amussen, 'Punishment, Discipline and Power: The Social Meanings of Violence in Early Modern England', *Journal of British Studies*, vol. 34 (1995), pp. 1–34.

25. The best introductions to an enormous literature are J. H. Gleason, *The Justices of the Peace in England, 1558–1640* (Oxford, 1969); A. Fletcher, *Reform in the Provinces: The Government of Stuart England* (New Haven, 1986); and Landau, *Justices of the Peace*.

26. See Wrightson, 'Two Concepts of Order'; A. Fletcher, 'Honour, Reputation and Local Officeholding in Elizabethan and Stuart England', in Fletcher and Stevenson (eds), *Order and Disorder*, pp. 92–115; Sharpe, 'The People and the Law'; J. R. Kent, *The English Village Constable, 1580–1642: A Social and Administrative Study* (Oxford, 1986); Fletcher, *Reform in the Provinces*, chs 7, 8; and Herrup, *Common Peace*.

27. Quoting D. M. Hirst, 'Local Affairs in Seventeenth-Century England', *Historical Journal*, vol. 32 (1989), p. 438.

28. For a brief summary, see Shoemaker, *Prosecution and Punishment*, pp. 25–7.

29. The best summaries of the history of binding over are in M. Hale, *Historia Placitorum Coronae: The History of the Pleas of the Crown* (London, 1778), vol. I, p. 23 n. (n); and in Justice Avory's judgment in an action before the King's Bench in 1914. See *Lansbury vs. Riley* [1914] 3 KB 229, pp. 235–7. For the statute of 1361 (34 Edward III c. 1), see *Statutes of the Realm*, 11 vols (London, 1810–24), vol. I, pp. 364–5. For contemporary legal commentators, see W. Lambarde, *Eirenarcha: Or, Of the Office of the Justices of Peace*, 7th edn. (London, 1592), pp. 189–205, 299–349; M. Dalton, *The Countrey Justice Conteyning the Practise of the Justices of the Peace out of Their Sessions* (London, 1618), pp. 127–64; and W. Blackstone, *Commentaries on the Laws of England*, new edn (London, 1811) vol. IV, pp. 256 ff, quoting p. 256. Following Blackstone's broad construction of 'infamy', binding over is still ordered in the contemporary criminal justice system against those suspected of an enormous variety of offences against public order, causing annoyance or distress, or provoking neighbourhood and domestic disputes, even where the offender has been neither charged with, nor convicted of, any crime. For binding over in the late twentieth century, see the Law Commission Working Paper, no. 103, *Criminal Law: Binding Over: The Issues* (London, HMSO, 1987), p. 5 [para. 2.2]; and the Law Commission (LAW COM. no. 222), *Binding Over: Report on a Reference Under Section 3(1)(e) of the Law Commissions Act 1965* (London: HMSO Cm 2439, February 1994), Schedule to Appendix D (Examples of Cases in Which Binding Over Powers Were Used).

30. G. L. Williams, 'Arrest for Breach of the Peace', *Criminal Law Review* (1954), p. 578; LAW COM. no. 222, pp. 4, 6, 30–1, 34, 41 [esp. paras 1.18(5), 4.3, 4.4, 4.14, 4.31].

31. This problem of 'legal pluralism' is addressed in Wrightson, 'Two Concepts of Order'; A. L. Erickson, 'Common Law *versus* Common Practice: The Use of Marriage Settlements in Early Modern England', *Economic History Review*, 2nd series, vol. 43 (1990), pp. 21–39; and P. J. R. King, 'Gleaners, Farmers and the Failure of Legal Sanctions in England, 1750–1850', *Past and Present*, vol. 125 (1989), pp. 116–50.

32. The clearest, although not the fullest, treatment is Dalton, *Countrey Justice*, pp. 127–64; but see also Lambarde, *Eirenarcha*, pp. 189–205, 299–349. The following critique draws largely on Dalton, citing Lambarde's various conflicting interpretations where relevant.

33. Dalton, *Countrey Justice*, p. 127.

34. Ibid., p. 128.

35. Ibid., pp. 128–9.

36. Ibid., p. 130.

37. Ibid.

38. Ibid., p. 131.

39. Ibid., pp. 131–2. For the lawlessness of late Tudor aristocrats, see Stone, *Crisis of the Aristocracy*, pp. 225–34. Cf. James, *Society, Politics and Culture*, pp. 375–83.

40. Dalton, *Countrey Justice*, p. 134.

41. Cf. Davis, *Society and Culture*, p. 187. Oathtaking and perjury are neglected subjects, although preliminary discussions include P. Zagorin, *Ways of Lying: Dissimulation, Persecution and Conformity in Early Modern Europe* (Cambridge, Mass., 1990); J. Spurr, 'Perjury, Profanity and Politics', *The Seventeenth Century*, vol. 8 (1993), pp. 29–50; and J. Oldham, 'Truth-telling in the Eighteenth-Century English Courtroom', *Law and History Review*, vol. 12 (1994), pp. 102–7.

42. Dalton, *Countrey Justice*, p. 141.

43. Ibid., p. 158. Cf. Lambarde, *Eirenarcha*, p. 115, where the two sureties are virtually indistinguishable. Lord Chief Justice May noted in 1883 that 'Burn and all the ancient writers on the subject treat sureties for the peace and sureties for the good behaviour as of near affinity, and scarcely distinguishable', *Seymour vs. Davitt* [1883] 15 Cox CC pp. 242, 250–1.

44. Dalton, *Countrey Justice*, p. 158.

45. Ibid., p. 159.

46. For an analysis of such petitions, see S. Hindle, 'Aspects of the Relationship of the State and Local Society in Early Modern England, with Special Reference to Cheshire, c.1590–1630' (unpublished Cambridge University Ph.D. thesis, 1992), ch. 4. i. Cf. S. Amussen, *An Ordered Society: Gender and Class in Early Modern England* (Oxford, 1988), p. 166.

47. Dalton, *Countrey Justice*, p. 160.

48. Ibid., pp. 161–2.

49. The possibility that large numbers of agreed recognisances were never certified is raised in Landau, *Justices of the Peace*, pp. 184–90.

50. Beattie, *Crime and the Courts*, pp. 61–3; Shoemaker, *Prosecution and Punishment*, pp. 96–7 (table 5.1).

51. Shoemaker, *Prosecution and Punishment*, pp. 230–3 (esp. table 8.6).

52. Ibid., p. 228.

244   *The Experience of Authority in Early Modern England*

53. Ibid., pp. 93, 237.
54. Ibid., p. 27.
55. D. J. Clayton, 'Peace Bonds and the Maintenance of Law and Order in Late Medieval England', *Bulletin of the Institute of Historical Research*, vol. 58 (1985), pp. 133–48; and Clayton, *The Administration of the County Palatine of Chester, 1442–85* (Manchester, 1990), ch. 6, esp. pp. 240–1.
56. Clayton, *Administration of the County Palatine*, pp. 242, 245.
57. J. A. Sharpe, *Crime in Seventeenth-Century England: A County Study* (Cambridge, 1983), pp. 116–17.
58. Shoemaker, *Prosecution and Punishment*, p. 50.
59. Ibid., pp. 96–7 (table 5.1).
60. For a sketch of the jurisdictional, economic and cultural contexts, see Hindle, 'State and Local Society', ch. 1. v. For the administrative structures of the county, see T. C. Curtis, 'Some Aspects of the History of Crime in Seventeenth-Century England with Special Reference to Cheshire and to Middlesex' (unpublished Manchester University Ph.D. thesis, 1973); Curtis, 'Quarter Sessions Appearances and Their Background: A Seventeenth-Century Regional Study', in J. S. Cockburn (ed.), *Crime in England, 1550–1800* (London, 1977), pp. 135–54; G. P. Higgins, 'County Government and Society in Cheshire, c.1590–1640' (unpublished University of Liverpool M. A. thesis, 1973); Higgins, 'The Government of Early Stuart Cheshire', *Northern History*, vol. 12 (1976), pp. 32–52; J. S. Morrill, *Cheshire, 1630–60: County Government and Society During the 'English Revolution'* (Oxford, 1974); Morrill, *The Cheshire Grand Jury, 1625–1659: A Social and Administrative Study* (Leicester, 1976); and T. Thornton, 'The Integration of Cheshire into the Tudor Nation State in the Early Sixteenth Century', *Northern History*, vol. 29 (1993), pp. 40–63.
61. See the contribution of Keith Wrightson to this volume, Chapter 1 above.
62. The Cheshire orders at the turn of the sixteenth century are CRO QJB 1/3, fols. 128, 164v; 1/4, fol. 7v; and [C]hester [C]ity [R]ecord [O]ffice Grosvenor MS 2/32. For the modification of procedures in other counties, see Fletcher, *Reform in the Provinces*, pp. 89–90.
63. Based on an analysis of CRO QJB 1/2, fols. 162v–199v; 1/3; 1/4, fols. 1–20v.
64. Quoting (in turn) W. Hunt, 'Spectral Origins of the English Revolution: Legitimation Crisis in Early Stuart England', in G. Eley and W. Hunt (eds), *Reviving the English Revolution* (London, 1988), p. 307; (Tim Curtis, cited in) Fletcher, *Reform in the Provinces*, p. 81; and M. K. McIntosh, *A Community Transformed: The Manor and Liberty of Havering, 1500–1620* (Cambridge, 1991), p. 2, n. 2.
65. Wrightson and Levine, *Poverty and Piety*, p. 122.
66. Clayton, *Administration of the County Palatine*, p. 261.
67. The relevant Sessions Files are CRO QJF 29/1–4; 31/1–4. On the 'middling sort' and the social order, see K. Wrightson, 'The Social Order of Early Modern England: Three Approaches', in L. Bonfield *et al.* (eds), *The World We Have Gained: Histories of Population and Social Structure* (Oxford, 1986), pp. 177–202; Wrightson, 'Estates, Degrees and Sorts: Chang-

ing Perceptions of Society in Tudor and Stuart England', in P. Corfield (ed.), *Language, History and Class* (Oxford, 1991), pp. 30–52; and Wrightson, ' "Sorts of People" in Tudor and Stuart England', in J. Barry and C. Brooks (eds), *The Middling Sort of People: Culture, Society and Politics in England, 1550–1800* (London, 1994), pp. 28–51.

68. Shoemaker, *Prosecution and Punishment*, pp. 117, 277, 280–1. D. Woodward, 'The Determination of Wage Rates in the Early Modern North of England', *Economic History Review*, 2nd series, vol. 47 (1994), p. 40.

69. Cf. D. T. Andrew, 'The Code of Honour and its Critics: The Opposition to Duelling in England, 1700–1850', *Social History*, vol. 5 (1980), p. 434; V. A. C. Gatrell, *The Hanging Tree: Execution and the English People, 1770–1868* (Oxford, 1994), ch. 7; and J. Stevenson, 'An Unbroken Wave?', *Historical Journal*, vol. 37 (1994), p. 695.

70. Wrightson and Levine, *Poverty and Piety*, p. 123.

71. The relationship between recognisances for the peace and indictments for assault is ambiguous, and it is far from clear that the ratio of recognisances to indictments for assault is meaningful. For what it is worth, the ratio in Essex (1620–80) appears to have been about 3:1, in Middlesex and Westminster (1661–1725) about 9:1, and in Cheshire (1610–19) about 14:1. These ratios are calculated from Sharpe, *Crime in Seventeenth-Century England*, pp. 116–17; Shoemaker, *Prosecution and Punishment*, pp. 50, 130; Curtis, 'Aspects of the History of Crime', pp. 56–7; and (Tim Curtis, cited in) Fletcher, *Reform in the Provinces*, p. 81.

72. For a discussion of these related trends, see Hindle, 'State and Local Society', ch. 4. i. For a microhistorical study of their interaction, see S. Hindle, 'The Shaming of Margaret Knowsley: Gossip, Gender and the Experience of Authority in Early Modern England', *Continuity and Change*, vol. 9 (1994), pp. 391–419.

73. P. C. Maddern, *Violence and Social Order: East Anglia, 1422–42* (Oxford, 1992), p. 227.

74. Beattie, *Crime and the Courts*, p. 138. Cf. Macfarlane, *Justice and the Mare's Ale*, pp. 185–9.

75. For a subtle and astute analysis of a not entirely dissimilar long-term attitudinal shift, see K. V. Thomas, *Man and the Natural World: Changing Attitudes in England, 1500–1800* (London, 1983).

76. CRO QJF 32/4/11; 26/3/23–4; 27/2/2; 29/1/35; 29/2/30; 30/3/26. The use of the legalistic terminology in this last example hints that petitioners often borrowed the legal formulae of recognisances in order to make their case more persuasive.

77. Quoting the petitioners soliciting magisterial intervention in a dispute in Waverton, Cheshire in 1597. CRO QJF 27/2/44.

78. CCRO Grosvenor MS 2/24. Grosvenor's personal papers are replete with references to litigation, arbitration and reconciliation. For a study of his social and political attitudes, see R. P. Cust and P. G. Lake, 'Sir Richard Grosvenor and the Rhetoric of Magistracy', *Bulletin of the Institute of Historical Research*, vol. 54 (1981), pp. 40–53.

79. CCRO Grosvenor MS 2/22, fols. 48–9.

80. C. Brooks, *Pettyfoggers and Vipers of the Commonwealth: The 'Lower*

Branch' of the Legal Profession in Early Modern England (Cambridge, 1986), ch. 4; Brooks, 'Interpersonal Conflict and Social Tension: Civil Litigation in England, 1640–1830', in A. L. Beier *et al.* (eds), *The First Modern Society* (Oxford, 1989), pp. 357–99; C. Muldrew, 'Credit and the Courts: Debt Litigation in a Seventeenth-Century Urban Community', *Economic History Review*, 2nd series, vol. 46 (1993) pp. 23–38; and Hindle, 'State and Local Society', ch. 1. i. 3.

81. The phrases are Grosvenor's. CCRO Grosvenor MS 2/22, fols. 48–9.

82. CRO QJF 27/2/44. On the settlement of conflict as the primary social task of the ministry, see J. Bossy, 'Blood and Baptism: Kinship, Community and Christianity in Western Europe from the Fourteenth to the Seventeenth Centuries', in D. Baker (ed.), *Sanctity and Secularity: The Church and the World*, Studies in Church History, vol. 10 (Oxford, 1973), pp. 129–43. For the mechanics and ideals of reconciliation, see Duffy, *Stripping of the Altars*, pp. 94–5, 125–9.

83. Grosvenor was referring to privately chosen arbitrators (mediators) in this context. CCRO Grosvenor MS 2/19.

84. [P]ublic [R]ecord [O]ffice CHES 38/28/7; CCRO Grosvenor MS 2/2; CRO Vernon of Kinderton MSS DVE Kinderton Manor Court Book 2/3, fols. 222–3.

85. CRO QJB 1/3, fols. 7, 56v, 270v; 1/4, fols. 168v–69.

86. CRO QJB 1/5, fol. 32.

87. CRO QJB 1/5, fol. 221.

88. CRO QJB 1/5, fols. 204, 85.

89. CRO QJB 1/5, fols. 121v, 122, 130v, 224v.

90. Clayton, *Administration of the County Palatine*, p. 268; Shoemaker, *Prosecution and Punishment*, pp. 111, 113–14. Whether estreats were actually collected is another matter, and one rendered more problematic by the poor survival rate of Sheriff's accounts.

91. Thomas DeVeil, *Observations on the Practice of a Justice of the Peace* (1747), quoted in Shoemaker, *Prosecution and Punishment*, p. 113.

92. CRO QJF 32/4/5; 33/1/24; 32/4/5; 31/2/56v. PRO CHES 24/109/1/2, unfol. 'Chief Justice's Warrant for the Apprehension and Good Behaviour of Thomas Sale'; CHES 24/109/4/2, unfol. 'Petition of John Parker of Wigland to the Chief Justice of Chester'. CRO QJF 33/3/82; 26/3/31; 32/3/99. Cf. the attitude of Thomas Holman quoted in Wrightson and Levine, *Poverty and Piety*, pp. 124–5.

93. Sharpe, 'Such Disagreements betwyx Neighbours', pp. 169–70. Cf. Paley (ed.), *Justice in Eighteenth-Century Hackney*, pp. xxix–xxx. For a full-scale study of malice at law in the later period, see D. Hay, 'Prosecution and power: Malicious Prosecution in the English Courts, 1750–1850', in D. Hay and F. Snyder (eds), *Policing and Prosecution in Britain, 1750–1850* (Oxford, 1989), pp. 343–95.

94. Shoemaker, *Prosecution and Punishment*, p. 117.

95. CCRO Grosvenor MS 2/22, fol. 53. This concern with judicial extortion long predates the mercenary activities of trading justices. Cf. Landau, *Justices of the Peace*, pp. 184–6.

96. CRO QJF 27/2/43; 31/2/67; 29/3/18; 32/4/4. CRO QJB 1/5, fol. 51.

97. CRO QJF 33/1/24; 26/4/20.

98. CRO Grosvenor MS 2/22, fol. 53.

99. Dalton, *Countrey Justice*, p. 131.

100. Ibid.

101. CCRO Grosvenor MS 2/52, fols. 2v–3.

102. PRO STAC 8/288/16, mm. 35, 16.

103. Cf. D. Hay, 'Property, Authority and the Criminal Law', in D. Hay *et al.*, *Albion's Fatal Tree: Crime and Society in Eighteenth-Century England* (London, 1975), p. 29. It has recently been suggested that, by the eighteenth century, oathtaking was largely ritualistic, and that prosecution for perjury was a 'largely impotent threat'. Oldham, 'Truth-telling', 103.

104. CRO QJB 1/5, fols. 424v–25.

105. CRO Grosvenor MS 2/22, fol. 49.

106. CCRO Grosvenor MS 2/22, fol. 49. Grosvenor's allusion was to Solomon in Proverbs 15:1.

107. CRO QJF 40/1/21; 27/1/30. Cf. the attitude of John Vincent quoted in Herrup, *Common Peace*, p. 88.

108. PRO CHES 24/112/1, unfol., 'Petition of John Batteriche of Barrow'. CRO QJF 24/2/47; 26/4/26; 27/1/30; 28/3/23. For printed examples of such agreements, see Paley (ed.), *Justice in Eighteenth-Century Hackney*, pp. 6 (no. 26), 47 (no. 260), 48 (no. 267), 52 (no. 291).

109. CRO QJF 25/2/43.

110. The Sessions Files on which these calculations are based are CRO QJF 29/1–4; 31/1–4.

111. This would suggest that the party who had sworne the peace would almost always prefer to release his opponent locally before the nearest resident magistrate rather than attend a distant quarter sessions. Of the 4120 individuals who stood bound in the period 1590–1609, 1549 (38 per cent) were released at each sessions. Cf. the view that 'most of the recognizances entered at the [East Sussex] Quarter Sessions were discharged without further action', Herrup, *Common Peace*, p. 88.

112. Cf. Herrup, *Common Peace*, p. 88.

113. This Weberian definition of the State is arguably implicit in the notion of the King's peace. Those bound by recognisance were expected to keep the peace to 'the King and all his liege people'. See Dalton, *Countrey Justice*, p. 127; and the legal *formulae* for Jacobean recognisances surviving as CRO QJF 32/1/55. On Weber's definition, see A. Giddens, *The Nation-State and Violence* (Cambridge, 1985), pp. 18–19.

114. See J. R. Lander, 'Bonds, Coercion and Fear: Henry VII and the Peerage', in Lander, *Crown and Nobility, 1450–1509* (1976), pp. 267–300; S. B. Chrimes, *Henry VII* (1972), pp. 212–16; P. Williams, *The Tudor Regime* (Oxford, 1979), pp. 393–4; Morrill, *Cheshire*, pp. 280–3; D. Underdown, *Revel, Riot and Rebellion: Popular Politics and Culture in England, 1603–60* (Oxford, 1985), pp. 199–206.

115. In different ways, the works of Elias on manners, of Foucault on surveillance, and of Bakhtin on Rabelaisian carnival converge in a portrait

of the mechanics of the enforcement of 'cultural order'. N. Elias, *The Civilising Process*, 2 vols ([1939] English trans., Oxford, 1981–2); M. Foucault, *Discipline and Punish* ([1975] English trans., Harmondsworth, 1979); M. Bakhtin, *Rabelais and His World* ([1965] English trans., Bloomington, 1984). For a treatment of some of these themes, see P. Burke, *History and Social Theory* (Cambridge, 1992), pp. 147–58.

116. Few historians have acknowledged the early modern antecedents of the expansion of the 'public sphere'. See, e.g., J. Innes, 'Representative Histories: Recent Studies of Popular Politics and Political Culture in Eighteenth- and Early-Nineteenth-Century England' *Journal of Historical Sociology*, vol. 4 (1991), pp. 182–211; and D. Wahrman, 'National Society, Communal Culture: An Argument About the Recent Historiography of Eighteenth-Century Britain', *Social History*, vol. 17 (1992), pp. 43–72. For a fuller development of this criticism, see Hindle, 'State and Local Society', ch. 8. ii. Cf. J. Barry, 'The State and the Middle Classes in Eighteenth-Century England', *Journal of Historical Sociology*, vol. 4 (1991), pp. 82–3; M. J. Braddick, 'An English Military Revolution?', *Historical Journal*, vol. 36 (1993), p. 974; and Wrightson, ' "Sorts of People" ', pp. 44–50, all of whom argue for the decisiveness of the mid- seventeenth-century crisis in the development of English political culture.

117. CCRO Grosvenor MS 2/22, fol. 53.

8 Custom, Identity and Resistance: English Free Miners and Their Law *c.*1550–1800*

ANDY WOOD

Recent historical interpretations of the role played by the law in early modern English society have tended to emphasise its incorporative and consensual nature. While some historians have chosen to stress the hegemonic qualities of the law, whereby the ruled were reconciled to their station through a legalistic and libertarian discourse which emphasised the inalienable 'rights of the freeborn Englishman', while actually operating in the interests of a ruling class,[1] in more recent interpretations the law has been seen to stand outside society and class relations, as a neutral arbit-rating force.[2] In its practical operation, the criminal law has been seen as a force for social harmony and consensus in a society undergoing rapid structural change.[3] Access to legal redress, it has been argued, was available to all inhabitants of early modern so-ciety, while litigation allowed for an equality between rich and poor before the law.

In a wide-ranging and important essay, Jim Sharpe has described the significance of the law in the popular culture of the early modern period.[4] He argues that through their involvement in legal offices and institutions, as parish officers, jurors and constables, 'members of the popular classes' did not merely gain an under-standing of legal process, but actively assimilated that under-standing into their responses to and understanding of the nature of authority. Thus the law became 'a part of popular culture, at least for those plebeian strata above the labouring poor'. Although 'popular consciousness formulated its own ideas about the law', the central tenets of state law were 'accepted at a very early date' by ordinary people. Sharpe recognises the importance of plebeian

249

understandings of the law in their experience of authority, and from this he draws the conclusion that 'the law was . . . a powerful cement of society, virtually omnipresent in human affairs'. In Sharpe's account, the law comes to 'permeate' popular culture from 'outside'; the central tenets of the law were then 'internalised' by popular culture.[5] In consequence 'popular culture' was remodelled in the interests of the ruling elite through the medium of the law.[6] Sharpe persuasively demonstrates that 'popular culture' was directly influenced by contact with 'the law' in the early modern period. He asserts that this encounter helped to cement a profoundly unequal social order. But central to his narrative is the assumption that at some unidentified point 'the law' entered a predetermined 'popular culture' and reworked its understanding of authority; having done the dirty deed, 'the law' then 'removed' itself.[7] Moreover, not only does Sharpe implicitly assume that 'the law' was itself a homogeneous unit, but his focus upon the literate and seemingly rational operation of the criminal law leads him to address early modern concepts of legality and order in terms of homogeneity and incorporation.[8] His essay is largely concerned with the operation of the criminal law. The equity courts of Westminster and the multiplicity of local manorial courts and customary laws receive little attention.[9] Although recognising that 'the operation of the law might, under certain circumstances, constitute a form of disorder',[10] the possibility that different conceptions of legality, order and authority might be articulated by different social groups through different legal or quasi-legal institutions is not addressed.

In this chapter I shall suggest that for at least one significant and growing section of Sharpe's 'popular classes' of early modern England – the free miners of ancient mining areas – there existed a rather different, yet highly sophisticated, understanding of 'the law' from that articulated by society's rulers (Figure 8.1). While the customary element of common and equity law was being challenged by statute law, and by the sometimes arbitrary interventions of royal authority, free mining law retained a much stronger and more obvious customary component. Moreover, and unlike the common law, its jurisdiction was localised and specific in nature. I shall follow Sharpe's suggestion that the miners' understanding of their laws was indeed a central determinant of their culture. But the existence of local free mining law, far from reconciling the miners

1. Alston moor lead deposits
2. Durham lead deposits
3. Yorkshire lead deposits
4. Derbyshire High Peak lead deposits
5. Derbyshire Wapentake of Wirksworth lead deposits
6. Forest of Dean coal and iron deposits
7. Mendip calamine and lead deposits
8. Cornish tin deposits
(N.B. This is by no means a definitive guide to those areas in which free mining rights were claimed or exercised.)

Figure 8.1 *English free mining areas mentioned in the text*

to the exercise of elite authority, in fact sharpened their sense of collective identity and proved to be an enabling force in the miners' resistance to their rulers' wishes. A study of English free miners and their law, therefore, might shed new light upon the responses of one section of the 'popular classes' to elite authority, and of some aspects of the nature of plebeian perceptions of law, property and social order.

I

Over the course of the early modern period, English extractive industries were growing in their economic significance. In terms of the overall output of metallic ores and coal, as well as in terms of the number of people employed, mining was becoming increasingly important. As markets expanded for both coal and metals, the possibilities for profit amongst entrepreneurs and investors increased. In many mining areas, conflict developed between the independent miners and smallholders who had traditionally dominated English extractive industries, and a series of manorial lords, crown lessees and entrepreneurs who were anxious to capitalise on England's mineral wealth. This conflict was largely expressed through differing interpretations of law and property, as customary rights to coal and ore were challenged by lords and industrialists, in favour of individual property rights.

This conflict over mineral rights was a part of a broader struggle over customary law in the early modern period. Under local customary law, tenants and inhabitants of a given manor or locality laid claim to a series of common rights: for instance, to timber, furze, game, grazing and gleaning rights or access across fields. Such rights were contested both physically and legally by lords, lessees of rights and other authorities. It is difficult to say at what point this conflict began, or at what point it finished. Communal access to material resources was a hot issue between lord and tenant in the medieval period, and access to bridle paths and the open moors, or the ownership of mineral rights, remain contentious issues to this day.

The long-running and often intense conflict over the issues of customary law and common right has only recently begun to reassert itself as an issue of interest to social historians after almost half a century of near neglect.[11] David Levine has suggested that it forms one of the essential continuities in English history;[12] certainly the issue lies at the heart of debates over the emergence of capitalism in England.[13] Common rights and customary laws were often tenaciously defended by those who benefited from them. Such actions were frequently successful, preventing enclosures of common fields by decades or even centuries, or sustaining access to turf, wood and game. While attacks on common right and common land periodically resulted in crowd disturbances on the part of defenders, these were typically preceded by months of litigation and petition. Careful local research has suggested that while it is possible to detect a gradual hardening of attitudes on the part of equity and common law courts to customary law over the course of the early modern period, litigation in such courts frequently resulted in the successful defence of common right. The most important work on the defence of custom has centred on the eighteenth century, the period in which historians of customary law have located the principal attacks upon the bases of that law.[14] Certainly the combined effects of parliamentary enclosure, the developing elite antipathy towards notions of 'moral economy', and the resolution of certain key legal cases against the interest of common right in the second half of the eighteenth century had a dramatic effect in the decisive marginalisation of customary law. But in the long war of attrition over such issues, major engagements had already been fought, and with varying outcomes. Nowhere is the ambiguous place of customary law within the early modern English legal system more clearly revealed than in the contests fought in ancient mining areas between independent miners and those who sought the abolition of the miners' rights.[15]

The reasons for the intensity and longevity of disputes over mineral rights in ancient mining areas are multifarious, but two aspects of early modern mining industries and communities seem of particular significance. First, within those parts of the country where mining had always been an important source of employment, many mining workforces had developed their own local laws and courts which regulated industrial activity. These, I shall argue, granted a peculiar autonomy and sense of collectivity to free miners which made them unusually assertive of their rights. Second, although large capitalised mine workings were of developing importance between 1550 and 1800, even at the end of the period many miners in ancient mining areas remained independent, working in mines which they partly or wholly owned. Both the economic and legal bases for continuing conflict were therefore present in free mining areas throughout the early modern period. The conflicts in many ancient mining areas between free miners and lords and entrepreneurs were not merely most typically fought out through the law, but in the process of that conflict both the free miners and their contestants came to a clearer sense of their opposing interests.

II

Given the elite stereotypes of industrial workers in general, and of miners in particular in this period, it is ironic that the political culture developed by English free miners in response to attacks upon their rights was so deeply legalistic. Miners were generally thought by their would-be rulers to be lewd in their manners, profligate in their spending and irreligious in their habits.[16] Gentlemen often found the manners of miners worrying, their dialect incomprehensible and their culture itself 'opake'.[17] Such attitudes ran through the early modern period. The mayor of Bristol founded his claim that the Kingswood colliers were 'very desperate fellows' upon the fact that to him and his social world, they were 'but little known'.[18] Miners were considered by their superiors to be 'the arrantest knaves in nature', as one employer described his Lancashire colliers; 'never man had such rogues to deal with' complained another gentleman of the Forest of Dean free miners.[19] In part, gentry observers of mining communities assumed that the miners' supposedly rebellious manners were the product of their ecological and material environment. The Forest of Dean, for instance, was considered to be a 'forlorn, disowned piece of ground', the inhabitants of which were so defiant that 'a Regiment of Soldiers would scarce effect a reformation'.[20] The lack of gentry supervision of such areas, it was thought, allowed for the growth of alehouses and cottages, and the development of frightening and subversive ideas.[21] From such perceptions flowed hysterical accounts of the 'lawless' and 'ungovernable' nature of the early modern miner.[22] Miners, then, were presented in elite descriptions as a culturally degenerate and socially subversive isolated mass, cut off from normal society: the archetypal 'many-headed monster', inhabiting the 'dark corners of the land'.[23] Where the miners attempted to defend their laws through litigation or direct action, they were stereotyped by elite outsiders as anarchistic levellers, or as 'Robin Hoods'.[24] Some historians have latched on to these stereotypes and have addressed early modern miners in almost exactly the same terms. Thus, David Underdown has written of the Mendip miners' 'brawling, riotous independence'; their historian J. W. Gough considered them to be 'as unruly as their fellows all the world over'; Robert Malcolmson writes that eighteenth-century miners 'lived in communities which were culturally . . . isolated . . .

apart from other men'. In their account of the dominant nature of official ideas of the law, Anthony Fletcher and John Stevenson explicitly exempt 'pockets of persistent disorder' from their model, including those mining areas such as the Forest of Dean and Kingswood which made up something called 'the proto-industrial "frontier" '.[25]

Three points need to be made here. First, many of the descriptions offered by gentry outsiders of mining communities reveal not only a sense of class hostility towards what they perceived to be unruly industrial workers; they are also the accounts of *outsiders* to such communities. The houses of nearby aristocrats were protected from the 'sinking and poor neighbourhood[s]' beyond by towers and gates to keep out the 'rabble' of the mining villages. No doubt they felt, like Defoe, that miners were 'subterranean wretches' to be kept at a discreet distance. They had little direct intercourse with such people, save only on 'calculated occasions of popular patronage' and charity, such as the Earl of Rutland's traditional Christmas dole of tuppence from the gates of Haddon Hall to the poor of the surrounding mining villages.[26] The accounts of such outsiders tell us little about the realities of miners' lives and attitudes in this period, and rather more about contemporary elite perceptions.[27] Second, the opinions of outsiders such as Defoe or of the local nobility may well not have been representative of all sections of the local gentry. The less wealthy gentry, who dwelt within villages and small towns in which mining was the key employer in the period, often possessed an understanding of the miners' culture which was rather different. Miners were typically poor men; but they were also the neighbours, associates and sometimes friends of the humbler gentlemen and gentlewomen of their communities. There is little evidence to suggest that the local lesser gentry felt themselves to be living in communities dominated by a threatening 'race apart' of proto-Bolsheviks. In the course of disputes over mining rights, or over the exaction of certain manorial dues or tithes, or in the representation of a mining community's case to the authorities, such gentlemen and women can be found actively pleading the case of the miners or helping with legal advice. Conflicts between lesser gentry and their mining neighbours did occur, for instance over the ownership of a given mine or the reclamation of certain debts, but these disputes were significantly less intense than those between free miners and outside entrepreneurs or 'oppressive' lords of manors.[28] Third, it is difficult to characterise early modern English miners in general, and free miners in particular, as the inhabitants of a lawless proto-industrial 'frontier'. Careful research needs to be carried out on the relative criminal tendencies of miners and non-miners in given areas from court records before sweeping judgements concerning miners' 'lawlessness' can be accepted. But in the meantime, it is evident from the complaints lodged before Westminster equity courts by miners claiming the infringement of their customary rights and laws, and from the records of courts established to administer the mining industries of free mining areas that, far from being outside the law, such workers in fact possessed a highly developed consciousness of their legal rights.

III

Just as with all other issues of customary or common right, the right of miners, inhabitants or tenants to dig for coal or ore was subject to enormous local and regional variation. Within classic free mining areas, such as the King's Field lead mining area of Derbyshire or the Forest of Dean, the miners laid claim to and for the most part enjoyed the 'free libertie' to minerals found anywhere within a given manor or lordship. Although the legal basis of the Dean and Derbyshire miners' rights were increasingly coming under question over the course of the early modern period, it was widely recognised even by their opponents that both by statute and custom the free miners' claims were strong. One gentleman who took a case against the Dean miners' right was advised by his attorney to drop the proceedings on the basis of the strength of the miners' 'ancient custom'; another local gentleman admitted his personal antipathy to the miners' rights, but explained that he could not find 'any legal way to hinder them'.[29] Matthew Hale responded to claims that the Derbyshire miners' laws were 'a kind of levelling custom' with the argument that free mining laws were 'good to encourage to make the most of the Kingdom's treasure'.[30]

In those territories where mining activity was recent in origin, or where the tenants' liberties were traditionally weak, lords found it very much easier to oppose popular claims to mineral rights. This was in part a consequence of the fact that in such areas miners did not possess the same sense of collectivity and independence as those in free mining areas; but it was also due to the weaker basis of such claims in law. The absence of local mining courts meant that tenants or miners were more likely to turn for redress to the Westminster equity courts where they had less chance of receiving a favourable hearing, or to direct physical action.[31]

The particular strength of early modern free mining law in part had its origins in the successful defence of those rights in earlier centuries. From the thirteenth century onwards, manorial authorities and the Church periodically complained to the Crown that miners were invading their estates and digging for minerals.[32] The Crown sought to take on the role of a neutral arbitrating force in such quarrels, and on a number of occasions issued proclamations or granted charters which for the first time set down the precise nature of the miners' rights. Such charters typically codified and confirmed existing free mining rules, and provided a legitimate basis for the operation of a multiplicity of local courts and offices which had been created for the regulation of the industry. These royal charters did not therefore represent grants of rights from a beneficent Crown, but rather should be taken as indicators of the early influence and prominence of free miners in given communities. By the early modern period, the rights and liberties enshrined in royal charters had come to be looked upon as inviolate and 'ancient'.[33] Moreover, the fact that such rights had been confirmed by a long dead monarch or Prince created the impression that the right of free mining was the creation of royal authority and the object of royal aid, rather than merely the codification of pre-existent popular practice. This allowed the miners, in their complaints to higher authorities, to cast attacks upon their rights as assaults upon royal justice. Those Derbyshire miners who worked within the parts of the lead field held by the Crown in its right as Duke of Lancaster described themselves in complaints to the courts, the Privy Council or to Parliament as the 'King's Miners' working in the 'King's Field' wherein any of the monarch's 'liege people' might work. In laying claim to the origins of their laws in royal grants and decrees, and in emphasising the fealty owed to the Crown by the miners in return, the miners were seeking to defuse the claims made against them by their gentry opponents that theirs were 'levelling' customs which threatened order, government and property. The miners were thus able to employ the rhetoric of elite legal culture in order to serve their own ends.

Free miners' concern for order in their industry, however, was more than a rhetorical trick with which to win the sympathy of their social betters. Mining courts and the laws they maintained became increasingly sophisticated over time. In particular, the early modern period saw a number of major innovations in the organisation and administration of local mining law. From the late sixteenth century, for instance, 'great' mining courts in the larger free mining areas met twice yearly to lay down new by-laws for the regulation of the industry and the defence of the miners' customary rights, while 'small' courts met more regularly to consider the day-to-day affairs and disputes thrown up between the miners. Mining courts laid down new by-laws dealing with (amongst other issues) smelting, the quality control of smelted ores, waged labour, apprenticeship, drainage, share transactions, miners' service in other trades, and the raising of common purses to defend the miners' interests at law.[34] In Derbyshire, the barmote mining courts dealt with disputes concerning the ownership of particular mines or shares, breaches of contract, debt and, as the industry became increasingly capitalised, with wage disputes. The Forest of Dean Mine Law courts also concerned themselves with slander and with apprenticeship into the 'mystery' of mining.[35] The jurisdiction of most mining courts strayed into the territory of the criminal law, assuming the right to punish acts of theft from mines. The punishments such courts doled out varied as much as the areas of jurisdiction they laid claim to. There is no evidence from the early modern period that Derbyshire barmotes ever carried out any of the violent punishments they were entitled to inflict for theft; rather, acts of theft or trespass were punished with fines, or by the confiscation of mineshares. The Mine Law court in the Forest of Dean also employed fines and confiscations as punishments, together with periodic imprisonments, while the Minery Courts of the Mendips could prohibit thieves from mining activity. It was not only free miners who appeared as litigants before mining courts; many gentlemen who held shares in the larger mineworkings which began to appear from the early seventeenth century also took cases there, both against free miners and against one another. Although there was a growing tendency over the period upon the part of such wealthier individuals to transfer cases away from local mining courts to the assizes or Westminster equity courts, it is significant that frequently they chose to do so only after having been frustrated in their litigation in mining courts.

The capacity of mining courts to act as institutions for the main-tenance of a sense of autonomy and collectivity amongst free miners varied from one area to another. In Derbyshire, barmote courts could occasionally be packed by the gentlemen who control-led the office of barmaster, the overseer of the Crown's interest in the mines which brought with it the rights to both exact manorial dues upon the miners' production and to choose barmote juries. It is difficult to characterise courts such as the barmote or the Forest of Dean Mine Law court as the purely autonomous institutions of the free miners. The local gentry could, on occasion, manipulate decisions in the Mine Law court to fit their interests; leading gentlemen were periodically granted the honorary title of 'Free Miner' by the miners, allowing them to take an active role in the administration of the industry. Such gentlemen often had shares in mines in the Forest. Moreover, from the early seventeenth century, attorneys can be found advising miners or mineowners in cases taken before mining courts, or directly pleading such cases.[36] But on the whole, both barmote courts and those in the Forest of Dean were successfully used to defend and advance the miners' inter-ests.[37] The relative autonomy of the Derbyshire barmotes can be contrasted with the Stannary courts which regulated the tin indus-tries of Devon and Cornwall. While the Stannaries were keen to protect the tinners' access to ore across the whole of both counties at least up to the middle of the seventeenth century, they had long ceased to be a court run by and in the interests of the 'poor tynner', that is, the independent producer. Since the late Middle Ages, the Stannaries and their offices had been occupied by leading tin merchants and mine investors, chosen by the mayors of the nearby towns. Moreover, their autonomy was severely restricted by the ability of the Crown to intervene directly to reorder or suppress customs considered inimical to the royal interest.[38] Similarly, the Somerset lead miners of Mendip were governed by Minery courts which, although the jurors were mostly miners, came under rather closer scrutiny and control from the lord of the manor than was the case in the Forest of Dean or most barmote courts in Derbyshire.[39]

Similar variations existed in the extent to which the officers of mining courts operated directly in the interest of free miners. It has already been noted that the overseer of the Crown's interest in the Derbyshire lead mining industry, the barmaster, was generally recruited from amongst the local gentry or nobility. Large profits accrued to gentry households from the possession of the post, together with considerable potential power over the miners. However, from the early seventeenth century, gentlemen barmasters chose to rely upon 'under-barmasters' recruited from amongst the miners themselves for the administration of barmote law and the collection of dues. While in certain circumstances such men could bring popular opprobrium upon their heads from their fellow miners for corrupt or irresponsible behaviour, in other instances they emerged as leaders of resistance to attacks on the miners' interests. Moreover, the Derbyshire miners recognised the importance of taking control of the key office of the mining industry, and argued for many years that the barmaster should be elected from amongst their own number. Similarly in the Somerset Mendips, miners and tenants contested their lords' claims that the office of lead reeve, equivalent to the Derbyshire barmaster, was 'ministeriall or servile' to the lord, instead insisting that the office was 'elected' from amongst the 'homage' of the manor.[40] In mining areas where small-scale independent workings took place at the will of the lord, rather than by the custom or right of the miners, it is significant that very often there were no mining courts in existence, and that mining officers came under the direct supervision of the manorial authorities.[41] The maintenance of mining courts by the miners, and their contests with the authorities over the right of appointment of officers, involved wider issues than merely the control of a particular court or office. Their control by free miners created an institutional space for the articulation of the interests of a section of the ruled which was unusual in early modern society. Control of such offices and courts allowed the miners to maintain local systems of justice and to regulate the affairs of the industry in which they worked.

Experience in the formulation and execution of mining law fostered a sense of rights and an understanding of legal process amongst free miners. The deputy barmasters of Derbyshire and their equivalents in the Forest of Dean and the Mendips were regularly chosen to give evidence to Westminster equity courts concerning the customs and laws of the miners.[42] Members of mining court juries were also prominent as deponents in cases concerning mining rights, or in leading and organising extra-legal resistance to attempts to undercut their customs. The very basis of the jurisdiction of many mining courts allowed for a certain equality between lord and miner which stood in contrast to the inequalities of power and wealth in early modern society. In the Mendips, the Minery courts claimed jurisdiction over all mining matters, 'as well betweene the lord of the soile and workmen as between workmen and workmen'; the Forest of Dean Mine Law court claimed the right to try all cases between 'miner and miner, and miners against all other men'.[43]

In the long-running conflict between mining courts and elite legal institutions, one sense of good order, legality and property was counterpoised against another.[44] In spite of accounts of the miners' alleged lawlessness, the English free miners who made up mining court juries appear to have been keen to establish careful rules and by-laws for the efficient and peaceful running of their industry. The theme of order continuously resurfaced in charges to mining court jurors, and in the proclamations and by-laws of the courts. The Minery Court jurors of the Mendips were enjoined to 'Examine all Abusses and Offences Comitted or done by any workmen against the Laws and Customs of this Occupation . . . [and] Uprightly [to] Behave your selves as Well Between the Lord and workmen as Between workman and workman.'[45] The Minery Court periodically issued orders against swearing and theft, expressing concern for the 'disOrderly striking of Groves [ie. mines] . . . notwithstanding many good and laudable laws'. The court took an interest not only in the immediate affairs of the industry, but also sought to regulate the behaviour and discipline of those children and servants who laboured on the surface of the mines. This concern for order and good government in mining industries allowed mining courts to define themselves against both the poor and landless semi-vagrant 'cavers' or 'cobblers' who worked for free miners as surface labourers, and also those gentlemen who sought to remove mining cases to other courts. The miners were able to present both the poor and the gentry as threats to order and the law. The former were described as 'Audacious Rogues' who 'Picke and Steale' from the miners' works; the latter were presented as 'malicious and turbulent persons' for removing mining cases to equity courts.[46] In contrast, the miners flattered themselves that their courts were designed 'for the most part for the settling of peace'. Unlike the miners' experience of litigation against powerful opponents in Westminster courts, of which they complained they found expensive, difficult and sometimes 'terrifying', cases taken before mining courts were resolved swiftly and cheaply, process was in vernacular English, and access easy.[47]

By-laws which were passed through mining courts were often specifically designed to maintain the identity of the free miner and to protect his independence. Many Derbyshire barmote courts passed laws restricting both the size and the number of mines an individual could hold; Mendip Minery Courts laid down and enforced guidelines which specified the accepted depth of legal mine-workings, so preventing unskilled 'cobblers' from laying claim to shallow ditches as legitimate mines. In both Cornwall and Derbyshire, mining courts specified that toll and tithe gatherers could not approach legal workings until allowed to do so by the miners; similarly, Derbyshire barmote laws prevented unskilled 'cavers' from approaching mineworkings, or from digging over rubbish tips for scraps of lead ore, without the miners' permission. In the Forest of Dean, where the miners sought to restrict entry to the trade to those who had been 'bred and brought up in the mystery or craft of mining', and to those skilled workers who had laboured in the industry for six years, the landless poor 'cabbiners' were further disadvantaged by a requirement that their apprenticeship should be extended by an extra year than normally required.[48]

A close interrelationship existed between the miners' rights, the institutions developed to maintain those rights, and the other key determinants of the miners' collective identity: skill, gender and work. In most free mining areas, an informal system of apprenticeship existed whereby boys and youths would be gradually introduced to work in the industry, first as surface workers, then as underground carriers, and finally as skilled face workers owning shares in the enterprise as a free miner.[49] In the Forest of Dean, their apprenticeship was itself formally regulated by the Mine Law court. But in all free mining areas, this hierarchy of age and skill was reinforced by the mining courts. Mining court juries tended to be selected from amongst 'old and wise' miners whose memory and experience of mining law was the most extensive. Such men were careful to protect their 'rights' and 'privileges' which formed the basis for the 'Art or "Mistery of Mining"'. Free miners saw a real distinction between themselves and those 'servants' or 'hirelings' who worked only for day wages in capitalised mines. Even where free miners were recruited to work in gentry-owned mines, the miners were careful to protect their identity as skilled men, contracting in as self-organised gangs paid on high piece rates. In many cases they assumed responsibility for the maintenance of labour discipline amongst underground carriers, and hired their wives and children to mineowners as surface labourers. This hierarchy of skill and gender was explicit in the miners' self-definition as collectivities. Miners felt that they were a part of a 'fraternity' or 'Fellowship' of 'Free miners'; they were 'stout, able-bodied men' whose masculinity derived in part from their skill and independence. This sense of a male identity was reinforced through the agency of the mining court, from which women were excluded, the Mendip Minery Court going so far as to stipulate that 'neither Infants, Woeman, Ideotts or unservicable persons' were to serve on such juries.[50]

In some respects, mining courts fulfilled similar functions to friendly societies. The Forest of Dean Mine Law court assumed the rights to set wage rates for free miners working in gentry-owned works, to regulate entry to the trade, and throughout the seventeenth and early eighteenth centuries raised common purses both to defend the miners' interests at law and to provide a fund for sick or injured miners. Similarly, the Derbyshire miners' habit of raising common 'purses' as legal funds through barmote courts in the seventeenth and early eighteenth centuries had distinct similarities to the 'Club' of miners which in 1777 withdrew the benefit of its 'Box' from those miners who continued to work while others were on strike.[51]

Mining courts thus provided an institutional focus which allowed for the maintenance of those rights which guaranteed the miners their peculiar independence. They helped to maintain a sense of continuity and of history amongst miners which stood them in good stead in their conflicts with the opponents of their rights.

IV

From an early date the jurisdiction of mining courts over extractive matters came under threat from those legal institutions which lay more fully in the hands of the gentry and nobility. The court of Star Chamber had insisted upon its right to hear appeals from Stannary courts since the early sixteenth century; the first Derbyshire lead mining case brought before a Westminster equity court other than the Court of the Duchy of Lancaster was in 1562 and set off a flood of litigation by opponents of the miners' rights; similarly, the courts of Chancery, King's Bench, Requests, Exchequer and Common Pleas, together with the institutions of the common law, chose to intervene with increasing regularity from the late sixteenth century in the affairs of mining courts.

In the complaints they set before the Westminster courts, gentle and noble litigants sought to deny the existence of a legitimate basis to free mining law. Sir Edward Winter complained to the Star Chamber in 1608 that the Dean miners' customs were 'pretended customes and liberties' which existed only in 'the myndes of the vulgar sort'. Twenty-nine years later, the Privy Council ordered the Justices of Gloucestershire to intervene against 'certain people of base and mean condition' who were 'intruding and taking unto themselves a right to dig coal and grindstone . . . without colour of reason to justify their actions'. In 1661, the authorities were once again seeking to prosecute miners for trespass, for having entered freehold land in the Forest of Dean to dig for coal and iron ore. By 1680, Crown Commissioners sent to survey Dean forest were still couching their descriptions of the miners' rights in the same terminology, noting the miners' claim to take wood with which to timber their works, 'which they pretend an ancient right [to] by prescription'. The Dean miners' claims to wood remained a lasting source of conflict throughout the following century and a half.[52] In Derbyshire, the miners' right to take wood proved an intermittent irritant for some three centuries. In 1610, the miners were announcing their right to 'wood where wood is growinge'; by the 1630s Sir William Armyn was having miners who 'pilfered' wood from his land whipped, while as late as 1815 Derbyshire gentlemen were describing the miners' claim as 'This free-booting sort of practice'. In Cornwall, where the Stannaries fell rather more under the influence of elite groups than was the case with other mining courts, the process of the redefinition of mining law in favour of the interests of the gentry and nobility could be effected through the Stannaries themselves. As early as 1525 the Stannary courts, therefore, were engaged in the suppression of 'certain doubtfull Customs' and were advancing the interests of that class of merchants and gentlemen who made up the juries.[53]

The Crown played an ambiguous role in the conflict over free mining rights. Since a number of free mining areas lay within the estates of the Crown or the Duchies of Lancaster or Cornwall, and since the Crown was keen to protect its entitlement to minerals, miners were often able to bring successful actions to certain courts, most notably that of the Duchy of Lancaster, proving both the right of free mining and the ownership of the manor in question by the Crown. Under the early Stuarts, however, outright attacks were mounted in certain areas by Crown or Duchy officials and lessees on the right of free mining. This was in part a consequence of the general movement of royal estate policy in the early seventeenth century, which was directed towards increasing revenues through raising rents, redefining customary tenures and rights, and leasing manors. As a part of this policy, in both the Forest of Dean and in Derbyshire, the Crown came into direct conflict with the free miners. In the Forest of Dean the Crown sought to enclose the Forest, suppress the right of free mining and let both land and minerals to gentry entrepreneurs. A less ambitious scheme developed by the King's Attorney-General, Sir Robert Heath, saw the removal of a large and profitable mining area called the Dovegang circuit from the King's Field of Derbyshire. These attacks on mining law went hand in hand with a broader policy of raising rents and leasing out to private individuals what had hitherto been considered common rights to stone, furze, coal, and waste land.[54] The miners did not, however, forget their lost rights. The disruptions of the civil wars and Commonwealth period allowed both miners and their opponents new opportunities to settle old scores. In the Mendips and in Derbyshire mounted and armed gentlemen confronted and attacked miners digging on land the rights of which were subject to dispute. It was reported from the Mendips that the miners had been 'driven from the hills', while both in Derbyshire and the Forest of Dean the temporary collapse of elite authority led miners to reoccupy those fields from which they had previously been ejected.[55]

Instances of mining disputes resulting in physical violence were relatively rare. More typically, opponents of the miners' rights attempted to abolish or subtly erode the miners' right through the agency of the law rather than through direct confrontation. This was very much easier in those areas where the right of free mining was difficult to prove with reference to written documentation. Lead miners in Teesdale insisted that they enjoyed the right of free mining 'without the memory of every man now lyvinge', but their lord redefined their right as a privilege, and leased the lead deposits of the manor to a gentleman entrepreneur. Similarly, in Swaledale the free miners were ejected by their lord after the discovery of rich lead deposits, and the area was thereafter subject to intensive exploitation by waged labourers.[56] The Crown and manorial authorities tried the same trick in Derbyshire and the Forest of Dean. The Exchequer court decreed in 1613 that the Dean miners' claim to free mining existed 'of charity and grace' of the Crown, 'not of right', and was therefore open to redefinition; in Derbyshire, lords of manors insisted that the miners dug in their fields by privilege and not by right.[57] But the opponents of free mining had reckoned without the tenacity of the miners and the strength of their right. The Forest of Dean miners responded with a long campaign of both litigation and physical violence and litigation in defence of their laws, while the Derbyshire miners of Wirksworth Wapentake were more fortunate in being able to refer to a statute of 1554 which gave them free mining rights across the whole hundred.

In the process of the conflict over free mining rights, just as with other issues of custom and common right in the period, history itself became a terrain of conflict between ruler and ruled. Since customary law was founded upon the principles of precedent and common usage, contending memories of communities, industries and localities became an important part of the struggle over extractive rights and mineral resources. Aged male deponents typically referred to their fathers' or grandfathers' times, often with a high degree of accuracy, to support the claims of miners or those of their opponents. Such memories were frequently highly specific, as with the case of those miners who were able to list by name the various mineworkings occupied by their forefathers. Other deponents made reference to the 'old workemen' who 'crediblie report[ed]' the 'ancient custom' of manors in the Mendips; in the same area 'severall auntiente people' were able to confirm that the mining officers were elected from amongst the tenantry and that tolls claimed as compulsory by their lord were in fact a 'gift' of the miners. Memory of past struggles continued to condition miners' resistance in the present. Thus one 70-year-old tinner referred to his father's successful defence of the discretionary nature of tolls upon the miners' production. Old Derbyshire miners in 1616 recalled their involvement in tithe strikes in the 1570s to justify their sons' rejection of the tithe proprietors' claims upon them. The longevity of the Mine Law court of the Forest of Dean was attested to by old miners in the 1620s when that institution came under threat. Equally fundamentally, deposing miners insisted upon the ancient nature of their mining rights: 'the free miners have used always . . . time out of mind as this deponent hath heard from his ancestors and other ancient men to get mine of coal, iron and oker'. The very nature of mining law itself forced the memorialisation of the history and traditions of an industry and area. By 'Common p[rescri]bed Stannary Right', Cornish tinners were allowed to dig for ore on waste land and any 'enclosed land that hath been anciently' enclosed, but which had once been available for free mining. Where the miners' opponents came to attack their claimed rights and customs, therefore, they were forced to attack popular memories and histories. Remembered and invented traditions became objects of fierce contention, and the triumph of one interpretation of local history over another could bring with it access to material resources and institutional power.[58]

An understanding of the past became central to the miners' identity as a group, and to the defence of those rights from which that identity sprang. In some respects this is unsurprising; miners in ancient mining areas periodically chanced upon deserted underground works left by 'T'Owd man', as both Cornish and Derbyshire miners described their predecessors. The eery remains they encountered included 'shovells Spades Mattocks made all of oak and holme'. Other discoveries could be more frightening. One old miner recalled in 1686 how, as a youth, he had 'found three mens skulls one whereof was of an extraordinary bignesse & some of the bones were very great ones'. Twenty-three years earlier, other miners had broken through into a cave 'as large as a great church' in which they found a giant skeleton.[59] For many miners, the forces of the past moved about them as they worked. In order to placate the spirits of past miners, Derbyshire men left candles burning underground on Christmas Eve. This respect for the past was drawn not only from the miners' working experiences, but also from their sense of rights. Mendip miners were enjoined to respect and maintain the 'Ancient Customs of the Occupation', while many Derbyshire miners saw it to be a point of honour to 'Defend [their] Antient Mineral Customs and Privilidges acquired and settled many Ages ago, by the Care and Pains of [their] Worthy Ancestors that their Posterity might enjoy the benefit thereof'.[60] In the process of this defence, the past could come to the aid of the present. 'T'Owd Man' had not just left behind some grisly and frightening remains; he had also left physical signs of his workings which deponents to equity courts felt able to refer to in order to prove the longevity of the right of free mining in a given manor.[61]

But over the course of the early modern period it was becoming increasingly apparent that oral memory and a sense of collective history could not stand alone as proof of the miners' rights. Knowledge of 'T'Owd Man's' activities was no longer enough; documentary proof was required. Between the middle years of the sixteenth century and the middle years of the eighteenth century, it is possible to detect a gradual shift within the processes of Westminster equity courts away from oral memory and testimony as a form of evidence and towards written documentation. This process was in some respects almost imperceptible, and oral testimony remained an important source of evidence throughout the period. But the significance of the transition remains.[62] Equity courts seem to have become increasingly unsympathetic to oral memory as the sole basis for the preservation of customary rights and to have favoured opponents of such rights where they were able to present written documentation which undermined the basis of custom. Moreover, in cases involving gentlemen litigating against those lower down the social scale, the former increasingly tended to select deponents from amongst their own social class to give evidence to the court in question.[63] Such gentlemen deponents were more likely to refer to written documentation in their possession than the more humble deponents typically called upon by miners or tenants. In consequence their evidence appears to have been treated with greater respect.

As a reaction to this tendency, free miners and their courts became increasingly anxious to secure a written basis to their rights. As early as 1554 the Minery Court, observing that it possessed 'no ancient writing or prescription of Antiquity', ordered that its 'Ordinances Shall remain in Writings indented'; some decades later, and finding its jurisdiction under threat, the Mine Law court of the Forest of Dean made a similar decision. Thereafter, both courts were careful to maintain written records of their new by-laws. Where Westminster courts found in favour of the continuance of free mining rights, mining courts made instructions that the legal decision should be entered in their court books; some miners carefully collected those written documents which, they hoped, guaranteed their rights, and some sympathetic local gentlemen became expert in pleading cases on the basis of such evidence. One such document was passed on to 'a miner then held most ancient and of most credit amongst them for the benefit of the miners'; in some cases written documents asserting the right of free mining could acquire an almost totemic quality for the miners. In 1623, William Booth, a Derbyshire miner, made a deposition to the Court of the Duchy of Lanmcaster, explaining that he possessed a copy of the 1554 Act which guaranteed the right of free mining within the Wapentake of Wirksworth; he was unable to decipher it since 'he cannot read written hand', but he was able to confirm all of the thirty-one points of the Act on their being read to him. Clearly an interface existed between oral and literate forms of evidence; in the miners' minds, the one was clearly meant to supplement the other. Thus the Mendip Minery court believed that the basis of its legitimacy derived from 'ancient men's depositions' and 'divers Records pr[e]sentiments and orders' from the reigns of Henry VIII and Mary Tudor. Similarly, the remembered geographical bounds of free mining activity were ordered to be entered into the Stannary court books. Great care was taken to preserve the documents and artifacts which it was thought were the preservators of the miners' liberties. The Derbyshire miners ensured that the 'King's dish' which laid down the standard measure of lead and which was inscribed with a declaration of Henry VIII to that effect should be kept chained and on public display in the Mote Hall where the barmote was held, and should be accessible to all miners in order to prevent their being cheated by lead merchants. Similarly, the Dean miners sought to collect all such documents into their Speech House where the Mine Law court sat.[64]

From the end of the sixteenth century, handwritten copies of mining laws and charters were circulating amongst both miners and local gentlemen. The oldest transcription of the Forest of Dean laws dates from 1610, while those for separate manors in the Mendips originate from 1554, 1612 and 1633. The free mining laws of Grassington were first written down in 1642, while those for most manors in the Derbyshire lead field seem to have been produced in the late sixteenth and early seventeenth centuries. The Derbyshire miner William Booth was not alone in being unable to read written hand, and a market evidently existed for printed versions of mining laws. A complicated account of the mining laws of Wirksworth Wapentake in Derbyshire was first printed by a local gentleman in 1644, who stated in his commentary on the code that the 'Miners . . . have learned the Laws by Tradition and practice from one Generation to another, and have not learned the same out of any Books', though he also observed that 'of later times' there have been 'some Articles' produced 'which every Miner hath Ready almost at his finger ends'. These 'Articles' were presumably copies of the Quo Warranto of 1288 and the Act of 1554 which formed the original documentary basis to the Derbyshire miners' claims in the seventeenth century. These documents were reprinted in 1645 in a more accessible form by a leading miner, 'beinge a Grand Juryman [of the barmote] & willing to pleasure many myners that could not write or read Written hand'. This pamphlet proved especially popular amongst the Derbyshire miners, who frequently cited its contents in justification of their rights. The production of such printed accounts of mining law was intended to strengthen the oral memorialisation of custom rather than to stand in contrast to it; for this reason, the Derbyshire gentleman Edward Manlove wrote his account of mining law in rhyme in order to aid its recitation. Similarly, the printed versions of the Mendip and Forest of Dean laws which first appeared in 1687 were intended to be publicly read out. Miners making depositions concerning mining custom were able to justify their account of their laws with reference to having read, or having heard read, such pamphlets.[65] None the less, the increasing importance of literacy and print had some impact upon the free miners' culture and understanding of their laws. Although oral memory and testimony remained important both within the terms of their own understanding of their laws and identity and in the defence of their rights, the impact of printed or written accounts of customs and rules to that understanding was marked. From the second decade of the seventeenth century onwards, miners' depositions to courts in cases concerning their rights became increasingly complex. From the fifth decade of that century, references to their possession or knowledge of printed accounts of their laws became more frequent. By the early eighteenth century, oral memory was occupying a distinctly subordinate role in the miners' legal defence of their rights to the production of ancient documents and recent printed or written accounts of their laws.

These developments should not be schematically interpreted as a simple clash of 'popular' oral and 'elite' literate culture. The shift within the processes of the law away from the acceptance of oral testimony and memory alone forced the miners to respond creatively. They were not the passive victims of economic and legal change. They were prepared to defend their rights at law and on occasion through physical force. If that meant taking on some of the attributes of an increasingly literate legal process and culture, then they were prepared to do so. In this process the miners' understanding of their laws and rights, and thereby their political culture, was subject to subtle but noticeable change.

Moreover, in the process of writing down their laws and customs, the miners on certain occasions granted a spurious specificity and certainty to what had hitherto in most circumstances been a series of loose and informal rules designed for the maintenance of order amongst communities of small producers. A process of the reinvention of mining law and tradition was under way. This process benefited the miners in some places, and their opponents elsewhere. In Cornwall, for instance, the gentry jurors of the Stannaries were able to redefine Stannary law in their interests and almost wholly to rewrite certain laws on the basis that the old laws were 'almost wholly forgotten'. In the Mendips, where the miners' interest was stronger, the jurors of 1554 recognised that 'contention Strife and debate' had arisen from the indeterminate nature of mining law. In the process of writing down their claimed customs, they therefore announced that these new customs should be granted a spurious antiquity and 'shall from henceforth be deemed taken holden judged and Stand for ancient Customes'. It was not long before such relatively recent innovations to the mining code came to be taken as 'Old & Ancient Custome'. In some respects, this process had been going on for centuries. As early as the 1480s, the authorities had complained against the precursor of the Dean Mine Law court for 'daily mak[ing] new laws at their wills and call[ing] them from thenceforth customs'. The acceptance of custom as a part of the established legal system rested upon the ancient origins and continued use of a claimed custom; this itself led to innovations or redefinitions being dressed up as originating 'before the memory of man'. By the eighteenth century, changes to mining codes in Derbyshire, Grassington, the Mendips and the Forest of Dean were all being described as 'ancient' and existing 'Time out of Mind', as if they had been a part of the original charters granted in medieval times which formed the basis of the miners' claims.[66] The printed version of the Dean miners' laws, which by the eighteenth century had become known as the 'Book of Dennis', came to occupy a central role in the miners' legal defence of their customs up to the 1840s, and was accepted by the miners as the central statement of their claims.

But despite these early modern innovations in mining law, and the creation of texts which were later to be accepted as 'ancient', the continuities in mining law were of far greater significance than the changes. The fact that the miners of Wirksworth Wapentake in Derbyshire were able to prove that they had enjoyed continuous usage of the right of free mining from as early as the thirteenth century was of considerable importance to their successful defence of their customs. Similarly, in the Mendips and the Forest of Dean, free miners were able to stave off attacks on their rights through accessing both written documents and the living memory of aged inhabitants. Historical interest in such matters should be more than merely antiquarian. These continuities in ideas and beliefs are of greater relevance than merely another instance of the curious oral cultures of the plebeian masses of the 'world we have lost'. The continuing capacity of documents such as the 'Book of Dennis' to influence the political culture of Dean miners into the middle of the nineteenth century is indicative of the enduring strength and influence of a sense of rights and history, and of the power of memory in plebeian political culture. The implications of the loss of such memories for the capacity of the miners to maintain their assertive culture and their economic and legal independence can be starkly demonstrated with reference to the case of the mining industry of Alston Moor in Cumberland.

In the Middle Ages, the lead miners of Alston moor had enjoyed some of the most extensive liberties allowed to free miners. Their rights, which were confirmed by a number of monarchs, allowed them to take wood and ore wherever they wanted within the manor, and to elect their own mining officers. In most respects, their 'semi-autonomous' status conformed to the ideal type of the free miner. At some point in the fifteenth or early sixteenth century, however, the local lead mining industry died out. With the industry went the miners' institutions which allowed for the active maintenance both of their traditions and customs, and of the memory of their rights. When the industry was reborn in the middle of the seventeenth century, it did so under the complete control of its manorial lord. Free mining was only allowed by the permission of the lord, who granted 'tacknotes' to the miners, and no mining courts were allowed. For the most part, the lead deposits seem to have been extracted by waged labourers employed by the lord.[67] The restriction of free mining rights did not follow on only from such extreme circumstances as the extinction of a mining industry. In 1775, the crucial documents which allowed for the maintenance of the rights of the Dean miners were lost or destroyed in suspicious circumstances by a mining officer hostile to the miners' interests. In the early nineteenth century the miners' rights were restricted and redefined by Act of Parliament following the report of a Commission whose members claimed that they had been unable to find positive proof of the legal basis of the such rights, having chosen to reject the 'Book of Dennis' as without basis in law.[68]

V

It was not the case that early modern English free miners were 'lawless', that their customs were 'levelling', or that their communities were especially dangerous 'frontier societies'. Instead, in the long struggle over mining rights in such areas, one sense of the law and of good order – that of the free miners – was challenged by another – that accepted by the national elite, in which the common law upheld an ideal social relationship between ruler and ruled characterised by paternalism and deference, and in which the protection of individual and absolute property rights came to be increasingly enshrined in the edicts of equity law.

Many of the miners' rulers had their own ideas as to what should serve as the best 'Law of the mines'. These were distinct from the egalitarian logic of the barmote, the Minery court and the Mine Law court, in which a rough industrial democracy of skilled male artisanal workers held sway. The function of this 'Law of the mines' can best be seen in the instructions given by the owner of Gallantry Bank copper mine in Cheshire to his overseer in 1697. The overseer was instructed to 'make rules for the workmens, after which they must work and behave themselves in all things to it'. The labourers in this mine were required to 'doe a short prayer that God may give his blessing to their work'; after prayers, the worker was to 'goe to his post . . . in doing the contrary he shall be duly punished'. Anyone who quarrelled with his fellow worker or the Steward 'must duly be punished'. 'No body shall be permitted without leave of the Steward' to take ore, and those who did so were to be 'punish[ed] as the Steward shall think sufficient'. 'Every man must be in a Christian like behaviour', and those who were not 'shall every time be punished'. Those who 'murmur against' the Steward were to receive 'punishment'; 'All the workmen must diligently doe what the Steward ordered them to doe'; no worker should 'make more holy days in the year besides the Sunday', or they 'shall be punished'. Moreover, 'He that turned the hour glass the wrong way shall loose one shilling'. In contrast to the Dean and Derbyshire miner's collectively raised and distributed common purses, the workers of Gallantry Bank mine were required to deposit a part of their wages in a sickness fund under the administration of the 'Lord', so that the Lord should not be 'troubled to assist them' save only to 'order and dispose of the sayd money'. As for the Steward, 'he must be a man who next the honour of God search nothing then the profitt of his Masters', who was prepared to '[punish] the neglectful and viciouses . . . nor neither [show] pitty'.[69]

Some labourers in gentry-owned and controlled mines looked with envy on the independence of free miners. When the Duchy of Lancaster decided in the late 1620s to exploit the extensive lead deposits on its Lancashire estates at Thieveley, its officials were sent to enquire into how best to organise the proposed mineworkings. Derbyshire free miners were asked by one Commissioner for their comments, and they were unanimous that it was best 'to use it accordinge to the Derbyshire manner'. The Chancellor of the Duchy, however, was unimpressed. He was hostile to the idea of free mining, and opposed its introduction into Thieveley, fearing that 'the workmen being once entered into this course (which is soe much to their advantage) will hardly be reduced backe againe into better order'. Miners, he thought, required a 'diligent and watch-full overlooking of them' such as was provided by 'private and particular owners of Lead Mynes' in those parts of the Derbyshire lead field where free mining had been prevented or abolished. A form of waged labour having been introduced into the Thieveley works, the labourers refused to cooperate, 'being so inured to Derbyshire Orders[70] that they can relish no other'. In particular,

Godfray Mercer and Geo. Casson . . . two beggary fellowes, Mynors, have runne upp and downe the cuntry and disgraced the
workes and discouraged other Mynors to medle in yt so much as
possibly they could, giveinge out that there can bee no profit to
any Myner unless [the mines] bee reduced to the Derbishire
Orders.[71]

Free mining laws, then, brought real advantage to the miners. They
fostered a sense of collectivity, provided the legal basis for a real
autonomy from the discipline of employers and lords, and at times
provided a real focus for popular resistance to the wishes of their
betters.

Given this context, it is surprising to find that some historians
have interpreted the free miners' political culture as 'conservative',
'backward-looking', 'reactionary' and 'nostalgic'.[72] This interpretation is in part founded upon the miners' continuing regard for, and
defence of, their laws in the nineteenth century. Instead of reaching out to the 'sensible' ideas of general unionism and socialism,
free miners are thought to have been trapped in an early modern
time warp, remaining obsessed with the defence of their petty and
antiquated customs while the 'real' struggles were waged elsewhere.
Yet as these historians themselves point out, the miners' defence of
custom and their continuing interest in and partial experience of
relative economic and political independence contributed to the
support of such workers for ideas of industrial democracy and early
socialism.[73] An unresolved contradiction is apparent here. One
answer to this problem lies in the neo-Leninist interpretation which
ascribes 'stages' of 'consciousness' to workers' ideas; thus the free
miners could be considered a worthy but essentially anachronistic
group, striving for control over their working lives at first through
the defence of their outdated laws until the light of reason dawns
upon them, at which point they reach out towards the rational
forces of organised labour. Another interpretation, that offered
here, is to deal with the miners' defence of their customs and rights
'in terms of their own experience'.[74]

Out of the heat of the conflict with their social superiors, the
miners came to a sharper definition of their rights and customs.
These became more sophisticated and articulated over the course
of the early modern period, for all that they were being gradually
whittled away. In the course of this conflict, some miners came to a

more acute understanding of the nature of power and class relations in early modern society. The Derbyshire miners felt that their
opponents amongst the gentry and aristocracy of the seventeenth
century were their 'Rich and powerful . . . oppressors', whose
'power' derived from their greater access to the 'terrifying' forces
of the law, their ability to manipulate the instruments of government against the miners, and their 'great hand' in the local community. Both they and their compatriots elsewhere responded to
the 'combination' of 'powerful men' which had been ranged
against them with their own proceedings in law, with long campaigns of refusal of manorial dues and tithes, with night-time attacks, and with open riot. In most riots, the miners sought to direct
their attentions against the works of those entrepreneurs and lords
who were digging in fields which the miners had claimed as free
mining territory. But in the most long-running and bitter disputes
between the miners and their opponents, such crowd actions could
often turn to violence against the person. The attempts of the
Winter family in the Forest of Dean and the Manners Earls of
Rutland in Derbyshire to abolish free mining law on the lands they
claimed as their estates brought large crowds of miners out on
numerous occasions to do battle with armed gentlemen, their
retainers and their employees. Such disturbances created lasting
memories and resentments. Forty years on, the Forest of Dean
rioters were still remarking on the success of their ejection of the
Crown lessees who claimed their works, while the Winters' lands in
Dean and the Rutland estates in Derbyshire were subject to periodic
invasion by miners for some decades in the first half of the seventeenth century. Certain individuals and families amongst the miners appear to have made almost a habit out of their regular
appearance as rioters, litigants, petitioners and deponents in
defence of their rights. In this unequal contest the miners were not
always defeated; for all the injunctions made against them and their
laws, the Dean miners always tenaciously returned to their works. By
the 1690s the authorities had no answer to such defiance. In Derbyshire, while the powerful Manners family of Haddon was ultimately to be successful in its attacks on mining law, and the free
miners on their estates were to be replaced with waged labourers by
the 1660s, in many others manors in the lead field the right of free
mining was successfully defended and maintained into the twentieth century.[75]

The miners' sense of their own history may seem 'backward-looking' to modern historians, but to the miners themselves it was a crucial determinant of their own identity and culture, and not only because of the force of memory within the legal process. For some, to be a free miner meant more than merely a way of making a living; it was also a way of *being*. Knowledge of past struggles was of significance to the present and the future. In his 1747 account of mining law and custom, the Derbyshire miner William Hooson paid frequent tribute to past generations of miners who had protected the free mining laws of the area for 'posterity'; such men as had 'stood up to vindicate their good old Cause . . . delivered to them by the care and Industry of their forefathers' deserved respect, and were favourably compared to those 'base and degenerate Miners' who were merely 'submissive . . . Vasals' to 'great Men'. Hooson was writing here of his 'forefathers' of Derbyshire, but in his remarks he reflected a pugnacity, assertiveness and sense of history which was common to free miners elsewhere. Knowledge of past struggles constituted a thread of continuity which ran through the political culture of early modern free miners, forming an ideological re-source which justified resistance in the present. Tristram Tresteed, a 90-year-old Forest of Dean miner announced to the Exchequer court in 1683 that

> he is concerned in defence of the rights of the miners and hath contributed to the defence of former suits brought against the miners 40 years ago and since . . . and he will be still ready and will always contribute his share in defending any suits that shall be brought against them.

One hundred and forty-eight years later, another generation of Dean miners were engaged in the last-ditch defence of those same rights. Just as Tresteed had done, they levied a common purse and organised invasions of territories which they claimed for free min-ing, but from which they had been 'so long deprived'. In justifica-tion of their actions, they cited the Book of Dennis, first printed in Tresteed's time, and by the 1830s known as 'that little book which [the miners] consider their Magna Charta'. If the ideas and organ-isations of the 'Fellowship of Free Miners' of the early nineteenth century looked recognisably similar to that of their seventeenth century ancestors, so was their sense of independence and assert-iveness. The 'Robin Hoods' of Dean Forest of 1612 found their parallel in the actions of Warren James, the miners' leader of the 1830s who was transported for life for his defence of the 'Rights and Privileges of the Miners'. Captured by Dragoons after leading riots in the Forest, he remained defiant to the last. 'Almost as black as the coal he worked', he was told to change his clothing before appearing before the magistracy. 'No I shan't,' he retorted; 'my dress is good enough for the company I am going in'.[76]

It is clear, then, that many English free miners were reluctant to take on the deferential values expected of the early modern lower orders by both conventional social theory and many modern historians. Perhaps nobody had told the miners that they lived in a time period in which 'attitudes of obligation and deference perdured even to the point of prevailing', or that as part of the 'inexperienced and illiterate' lower orders, they were meant to have been 'politically socialized' into accepting 'without question' the wishes of their social superiors.[77] Equally, many free miners' understanding of the law does not seem to have benefited from an appreciation of its supposedly hegemonic qualities. Instead, the miners' legalistic political culture creates real difficulties for a historical understanding of the operation of the law which focuses upon the law's function as a 'means of transmitting the wishes and aspirations of authority into the popular consciousness'.[78] The law was not a fixed and predetermined force which operated upon popular culture from outside; instead, understandings of the law, property and order were open to contest between ruler and ruled.[79] There can be no doubt that in his account of the operation of the law on popular culture, Jim Sharpe is correct to identify a real desire on the part of the ruling elite of early modern England to deploy the law as a hegemonic force. What remains more problematic is the question of how ordinary people responded to that intent. In some cases, elite understandings of the law may well have acquired ideological domination; but in other instances, such as those presented here, they clearly did not. A long-running battle of ideas between the miners and their betters was waged over the law, both as a concept and in its practical operation. It was not so much that the miners rejected the law; rather that one understanding of legality came into direct collision with another. This struggle was in part about contested meanings; but those meanings derived from a conflict over material resources. Understandings of legality mattered to both the miners and their rulers because it was in the contested meanings given to property, order and the law that this material struggle assumed its political form.

It was in this conflict over their laws that the miners developed their assertive and political culture. For the free miners of early modern England, as much as for their descendants, their law was no agent for instilling respect for the authority of gentlemen, employers and nobles. Instead, it was in their laws, customs and institutions that lay the miners' means of advancing, maintaining and defending their interests, and of articulating their collective identity.

NOTES AND REFERENCES

*I am grateful to the editors, and to Garthine Walker and Keith Wrightson for their comments on this chapter.

1. D. Hay, 'Property, Authority and the Criminal Law', in D. Hay *et al.*, *Albion's Fatal Tree: Crime and Society in Eighteenth-Century England* (London, 1975), pp. 17–63.

2. J. H. Langbein, 'Albion's Fatal Flaws', *Past and Present*, vol. 98 (1983), pp. 96–120.

3. C. B. Herrup, *The Common Peace: Participation and the Criminal Law in Seventeenth-Century England* (Cambridge, 1987).

4. J. A. Sharpe, 'The People and the Law', in B. Reay (ed.), *Popular Culture in Seventeenth-Century England* (London, 1985), pp. 244–70.

5. 'The law in seventeenth-century England was one of the most important ways, perhaps the most important way, in which the people at large, the custodians of the "little tradition", participated in the "great tradition" of their social superiors': Sharpe, 'The People and the Law', p. 248.

6. 'The law as a whole represented an important means of transmitting the wishes and aspirations of authority into the popular consciousness': Sharpe, 'The People and the Law', p. 264.

7. 'Popular use of the courts was slackening; the law, perhaps, was being removed from popular culture': Sharpe, 'The People and the Law', p. 264. See also pp. 246, 247, 248, 260, 264.

8. In this emphasis, Sharpe is far from alone. See also Langbein, 'Albion's Fatal Flaws'; Hay, 'Property, Authority and the Criminal Law'; A. Macfarlane, *The Justice and the Mare's Ale: Law and Disorder in Seventeenth-Century England* (Cambridge, 1981); Herrup, *Common Peace*. While an extensive and sophisticated literature has been developed by early modern social historians concerning issues of criminality, litigation and the criminal law, the fissures, contradictions and conflicts within understandings of legality in the period have largely been evaded, and 'the law' treated as a given. For an exception, see K. Wrightson, 'Two Concepts of Order: Justices, Constables and Jurymen in Seventeenth-Century England', in J. Brewer and

280   *The Experience of Authority in Early Modern England*

J. Styles (eds), *An Ungovernable People: The English and Their Law in the Seventeenth and Eighteenth Centuries* (London, 1980), pp. 21–46.

9. See Sharpe, 'The People and the Law', pp. 250–2, in which the rise in litigation in equity and local courts is discussed, together with a brief description of the varied social background of litigants. The nature of the cases brought to such courts, and the interaction or conflict between jurisdictions and understandings of the law which such cases frequently reveal, are not touched upon in Sharpe's account.

10. Sharpe, 'The People and the Law', p. 252.

11. The customary component of early modern English law has remained an important area of debate amongst both legal historians and students of elite political philosophy. However, the 'new' social history of early modern England developed in the 1970s has failed to address the significance of disputes over local customary law in conditioning plebeian culture. This may be due to the failure of the subsequent generation of socialist historians to develop the early twentieth-century insights into custom and common rights of R. H. Tawney and the Hammonds. Thus, for instance, Hobsbawm and Rudé have dismissed issues of custom and common right as merely 'the common luggage of the pre- political poor', of little consequence to to the grander themes of the emergence of the forces of organised labour and 'political' socialism: see E. J. Hobsbawm and G. Rudé, *Captain Swing* (London, 1969), p. 43. This interpretation of the 'apolitical' nature of popular responses to the undermining of their rights has proved strangely pervasive. See also R. B. Manning, *Village Revolts: Social Protest and Popular Disturbances in England, 1509–1640* (Oxford, 1988), pp. 2–3. Moreover, the assault mounted by Kerridge on Tawney's account of custom as an issue of major conflict in the sixteenth century may have frightened many recent social historians off the subject. Interest in the significance of disputes over customary law has resurfaced in the past decade, however, in particular in the works of K. Snell, *Annals of the Labouring Poor: Social Change and Agrarian England, 1660–1900* (Cambridge, 1985); J. M. Neeson, *Commoners: Common Right, Enclosure and Social Change in England, 1700–1820* (Cambridge, 1993); R. W. Bushaway, *By Rite: Custom, Ceremony and Community in England, 1700–1880* (London, 1982); and most importantly E. P. Thompson, *Customs in Common* (London, 1991), ch. 3. The most coherent brief interpretation of the place of customary law in the early modern legal system is to be found in T. Stretton, 'Women, Custom and Equity in the Court of Requests', in J. Kermode and G. Walker (eds), *Women, Crime and the Courts in Early Modern England* (London, 1994), pp. 170–89. The publication of Stretton's monograph on women and customary disputes in the Court of Requests is eagerly awaited. I hope to write about the place of custom in early modern English plebeian political culture elsewhere. See also the contribution of Adam Fox to this volume (Chapter 3 above).

12. D. Levine, *Reproducing Families: The Political Economy of English Population History* (Cambridge, 1987), p. 12.

13. R. H. Tawney, *The Agrarian Problem in the Sixteenth Century* (London, 1912); E. Kerridge, *Agrarian Problems in the Sixteenth Century and After*

(London, 1969); T. H. Aston and C. H. E. Philpin (eds), *The Brenner Debate: Agrarian Class Structure and Economic Development in Pre-Industrial Europe* (Cambridge, 1976).

14. C. Fisher, *Custom, Work and Market Capitalism: The Forest of Dean Colliers, 1788–1888* (London, 1981), p. 174; Neeson, *Commoners*, p. 19; Hay, 'Property, Authority and the Criminal Law', p. 21; Thompson, *Customs in Common*, pp. 106, 134.

15. It is unfortunate for this reason that so little has been written on this subject. Most accounts of legal or physical disputes over customary law and common right deal with agrarian issues. Even the most important survey pays scant attention to industrial customary law in general, and extractive rights in particular: Thompson, *Customs in Common*, pp. 4, 7, 160. The only recent published work on disputes over mining rights in the period up to 1800 is to be found in D. Levine and K. Wrightson, *The Making of an Industrial Society: Whickham, 1560–1765* (Oxford, 1991), pp. 106–34; Fisher, *Custom, Work and Market Capitalism*; and A. Wood, 'Social Conflict and Change in the Mining Communities of North-West Derbyshire, c.1600–1700', *International Review of Social History*, vol. 38 (1993), pp. 31–58.

16. The lead miners of the Mendips were thought to be 'lewd vagrant and wandering persons [who] waste their goods in most lewd and viscious manner': I. S. W. Blanchard, 'Labour Productivity and Work Psychology in the English Mining Industry, 1400–1600', *Economic History Review*, 2nd series, vol. 31 (1978), p. 5. The colliers of Kingswood were equally considered to be 'filthy ruffians' and 'barbarous people': R. Malcolmson, ' "A Set of Ungovernable People": The Kingswood Colliers in the Eighteenth Century', in Brewer and Styles (eds), *An Ungovernable People*, p. 93.

17. Levine and Wrightson, *Industrial Society*, p. 276.

18. Malcolmson, ' "A Set of Ungovernable People" ', p. 124.

19. The Earl of Crawford, 'Haigh Channel', *Transactions of the Manchester Statistical Society* (Manchester, 1933), p. 10 (I am grateful to Mick Brightman for this reference); C. E. Hart, *The Free Miners of the Forest of Dean and the Hundred of St Briavels* (Gloucester, 1953), p. 209.

20. Hart, *Free Miners*, pp. 204, 234.

21. Malcolmson, ' "A Set of Ungovernable People" ', p. 90.

22. Malcolmson, ' "A Set of Ungovernable People" ', pp. 91, 95.

23. For an account of elite descriptions of Derbyshire miners in the early modern period, see A. Wood, 'Industrial Development, Social Change and Popular Politics in the Mining Area of North-West Derbyshire, c.1600–1700' (unpublished University of Cambridge Ph.D. thesis, 1994), pp. 110–16.

24. Hart, *Free Miners*, p. 165.

25. D. Underdown, *Somerset in the Civil War and Interregnum* (Newton Abbot, 1973), p. 14; J. W. Gough, *The Mines of Mendip* (Newton Abbot, 1967), p. 99; Malcolmson, ' "A Set of Ungovernable People", p. 87; A. Fletcher and J. Stevenson, 'Introduction', in A. Fletcher and J. Stevenson (eds), *Order and Disorder in Early Moden England* (Cambridge, 1985), p. 39. Such interpretations of mining comunities as 'raw, isolated frontier societies' have been criticised by A. Campbell and F. Reid, 'The Independent

Collier in Scotland', in R. Harrison (ed.), *Independent Collier: The Coal Miner as Archetypal Proletarian Reconsidered* (Hassocks, 1978), and in Levine and Wrightson, *Industrial Society*, pp. 274–8.

26. Wood, 'Industrial Development', pp. 113, 256–7; Defoe's frequently cited comments on the Derbyshire miners are to be found in D. Defoe, *A Tour Through the Whole Island of Great Britain* ([1724–6], ed. P. Rogers, London, 1971), pp. 460–68; Thompson, *Customs in Common*, p. 45.

27. Old habits die hard. Thus, for instance, David Starkey finds it possible to speak of the 'brutalising' effects of mining upon its present-day workforce: BBC 'Question Time' 25 March 1993.

28. On the periodic alliances of interest forged between local lesser gentry and free miners in the lead mining villages of Derbyshire, see Wood, 'Industrial Development', pp. 191–224.

29. Hart, *Free Miners*, pp. 192, 223.

30. Middle Temple Library, Treby's MS Reports, 22–4 Car II, p. 744 (I am grateful to Alan Cromartie for this reference).

31. See, e.g., [P]ublic [R]ecord [O]ffice STAC 8/292/1; PRO STAC 8/224/19; PRO STAC 8/24/21; PRO STAC 8/228/13; PRO E134/13 Chas I/East 14; PRO E134/5 Jas I/Mich 5.

32. G. R. Lewis, *The Stannaries: A Study of the English Tin Miner* (Cambridge, Mass., 1924), pp. 93, 95.

33. Lewis, *Stannaries*, pp. 79–83, 159, 163; Hart, *Free Miners*, pp. 5, 11, 65–6; Gough, *Mines of Mendip*, pp. 69–84; J. H. Rieuwerts, 'The Inquisition or Quo Warrant of 1288', *[B]ulletin of the [P]eak [D]istrict [M]ines [H]istorical [S]ociety*, vol. VII, no. 1 (1978); M. Daniel, 'The Origin of the Barmote Court System: A New Theory', *BPDMHS*, vol. VIII, no. 3 (1982).

34. J. W. Gough (ed.), *Mendip Mining Laws and Forest Bounds*, Somerset Record Society, vol. 45 (Taunton, 1931), passim; J. W. Gough (ed.), *Mendip Mining Orders, 1683–1749*, Somerset Record Society Supplement (Taunton, 1973), passim; Hart, *Free Miners*, p. 71; [B]ritish [L]ibrary Add. MS 6713, fols 94r–102r; G. Steer, *Compleat Mineral Laws of Derbyshire* (London, 1734).

35. On the Forest of Dean courts' business, see Hart, *Free Miners*, pp. 77–137; on those for Derbyshire see, e.g., Sheffield Archives, Bagshawe Collection 702 (1) [proceedings in various small barmote courts, 1668–75].

36. Hart, *Free Miners*, pp. 85, 97; PRO STAC 8/97/24; BL Add MS 6714, fol. 91r.

37. Wood, 'Industrial Development', pp. 173–4, 156–67, 178–88.

38. Lewis, *Stannaries*, pp. 87, 98; BL Add MS 6713, fols. 90r, 94r–102r; R. R. Penington, *Stannary Law: A History of the Mining Law of Devon and Cornwall* (Newton Abbot, 1973), pp. 21, 23, 27.

39. Gough, *Mines of Mendip*, pp. 89, 99, 107.

40. Wood, 'Industrial Development', pp. 178–9; Gough, *Mines of Mendip*, pp. 99–100; PRO E134/27 Chas II/Mich 9.

41. See, e.g., the case of the lead miners of Stanhope (Co. Durham): PRO E134/19 Chas II/East 33.

42. PRO E134/13 Chas I/Mich 42; PRO E134/27 Chas II/Mich 9; PRO E134/13 Jas I/Mich 3.

43. PRO E134/9 Jas I/Mich 15; Hart, *Free Miners*, p. 65.

44. This situation was similar in form to that over communal and official notions of order described in Wrightson, 'Two Concepts of Order'.

45. Gough (ed.), *Mendip Mining Laws*, p. 19.

46. Ibid., pp. 30, 42, 53, 64, 72–3, 78, 101.

47. Hart, *Free Miners*, p. 66; Wood, 'Industrial Development', pp. 176–7.

48. PRO E134/9 Jas I/Mich 15; PRO E134/4 Jas I/Hil 15; Wood, 'Industrial Development', p. 122; Hart, *Free Miners*, pp. 1–2, 81.

49. For aged miners' memories of their progress as youths in the Derbyshire lead mining industry, see PRO E134/3 Jas II/East 15; PRO E134/2 Jas II/Mich 21, esp. deposition of Anthony Wood.

50. Hart, *Free Miners*, pp. 104, 181, 223; Fisher, *Custom, Work and Market Capitalism*, p. 1; Gough, *Mines of Mendip*, p. 106. The connection between skill, independence and masculinity was an enduring one, in mining as in other trades. Scottish miners of the nineteenth century, for instance, spoke of being 'brothered' into their trade, and compared their 'manly independence' of Iowa and Wisconsin to the subjection of Scottish 'wage slaves': Campbell and Reid, 'Independent Collier', pp. 63, 67. On this theme for other artisanal trades, see J. Rule, 'The Property of Skill in the Period of Manufacture', in P. Joyce (ed.), *The Historical Meanings of Work* (Cambridge, 1987), pp. 99–118.

51. Hart, *Free Miners*, pp. 9, 82, 86–7, 103, 104, 105, 108, 112, 114, 120. Derbyshire Record Office 200B/M1, fol. 28. In this respect, as in others, the institutional and cultural traditions of English free miners were rather different from those of the free miners of Germany and elsewhere. Developed guild structures, and a closer proximity to urban centres, resulted in significantly differing patterns of collective organisation in Germany. See S. C. Karant-Nunn, 'Between Two Worlds: The Social Position of the Silver Miners of the Erzebirge, *c.*1460–1575', *Social History*, vol. 14, no.1 (1989), pp. 313–16.

52. PRO STAC 8/303/7; Hart, *Free Miners*, pp. 98, 188, 208, 228.

53. PRO DL4/55/46; PRO DL4/110/1666/13; PRO DL4/109/8; J. Farey, *General View of the Agriculture and Minerals of Derbyshire*, 3 vols (London, 1815), vol. I, pp. 381–2. BL Add MS 6713, fol. 83v.

54. B. Sharp, *In Contempt of All Authority: Rural Artisans and Riot in the West of England, 1586–1660* (Berkeley, 1980), chs 7, 8 covers the Crown's policies in the Forest of Dean and popular responses to it; on the Dovegang dispute, see Wood, 'Industrial Development', pp. 196–201; and J. R. Dias, 'Lead, Society and Politics in Derbyshire Before the Civil War', *Midland History*, vol. 6 (1981), pp. 48–51.

55. Gough, *Mines of Mendip*, pp. 90, 124; Wood, 'Industrial Development', pp. 239–55; PRO E134/27 Chas II/Mich 28.

56. PRO E134/17 Chas II/East 24; PRO E134/9 Wm III/Trin 18; A. Riastrick and B. Jennings, *A History of Lead Mining in the Penines* (London, 1965), p. 189.

57. Hart, *Free Miners*, p. 16; PRO DL4/72/31; PRO DL4/34/22.

58. PRO E134/32 Chas II/Mich 18; PRO E134/19 Chas II/East 33; PRO E134/9 Jas I/Mich 15; PRO E134/27 Chas II/Mich 9; PRO E134/4 Jas

I/Hil 15; Wood, 'Social Conflict and Change', p. 41; PRO E134/22 Jas I/ East 8; Hart, *Free Miners*, p. 225; BL Add MS 6713, fols 103–4v.

59. BL Add MS 6713, fol. 1v; BL Add MS 43409, fol. 28r; PRO DL4/124/1686/7; J. Pendleton, *A History of Derbyshire* (London, 1886), p. 50.

60. Gough (ed.), *Mendip Mining Laws*, p. 19. W. Hooson, *The Miners' Dictionary* ([1747] repr. Ilkley, 1979), pp. 198–9.

61. PRO E134/32 and 33 Eliz/Mich 28; PRO E134/11 Wm III/Mich 26.

62. Further research is needed on this important subject. I am here presenting a controversial argument, based on my observations from a close study of the decisions reached by the Court of the Duchy of Lancaster concerning Derbyshire lead mining cases brought before it between 1550 and 1700, and from a more general and impressionistic study of Exchequer court material concerned with mining cases from Derbyshire and elsewhere. The Derbyshire evidence is more fully elaborated in Wood, 'Industrial Development', pp. 168–9. These findings remain both preliminary and suggestive.

63. The same phenomenon has been observed by Stretton, 'Women, Custom and Equity', pp. 174–5.

64. Gough (ed.), *Mendip Mining Laws*, pp. 20, 41, 42, 137; Hart, *Free Miners*, p. 70; BL Add MS 6713, fols 103r, 109v; PRO E134/13 Chas I/Mich 42; PRO DL4/72/31; PRO DL4/105/1661/22.

65. Gough, *Mines of Mendip*, p. 82; Hart, *Free Miners*, pp. 34, 36, 46; G. Hopkinson, *The Laws and Customs of the Mines within the Wapentake of Wirksworth* ([1644] repr. Nottingham, 1948), p. 3; BL Add MS 6682, fols 65–75; PRO DL4/117/8; E. Manlove, 'The Liberties and Customs of the Mines within the Wapentake of Wirksworth' [1653], reprinted in W. W. Skeat (ed.), *Reprinted Glossaries* (London, 1873); Gough (ed.), *Mendip Mining Laws*, p. 1.

66. BL Add MS 6713, fol. 95r; Gough (ed.), *Mendip Mining Laws*, pp. 20, 115; Hart, *Free Miners*, p. 72; Raistrick and Jennings, *History of Lead Mining*, p. 114.

67. J. F. Monkhouse, 'Pre-Elizabethan Mining Law, with Special Reference to Alston Moor', *Transactions of the Cumberland and Westmoreland Antiquarian and Archeological Society*, new series, vol. 42 (1942), pp. 44, 50, 52, 54; PRO E134/11 Wm III/Mich 26.

68. Fisher, *Custom, Work and Market Capitalism*, pp. 7, 27, 29; Hart, *Free Miners*, p. 137.

69. C. J. Carlton, 'The Gallantry Bank Copper Mine, Bickerton, Cheshire', *British Mining*, vol. 16 (1981), pp. 41–3, 45.

70. That is, the rules of the barmote.

71. R. Sharpe France (ed.), 'The Thieveley Lead Mines, 1629–35', *Lancashire and Cheshire Record Society*, vol. 102 (1947), p. 7, 74–5, 160.

72. Fisher, *Custom, Work and Market Capitalism*, p. 177; Campbell and Reid, 'Independent Collier', p. 70.

73. Fisher, *Custom, Work and Market Capitalism*, pp. 43, 178; Campbell and Reid, 'Independent Collier', p. 70.

74. E. P. Thompson, *The Making of the English Working Class* ([1963] Harmondsworth, 1968), p. 13.

75. Wood, 'Social Conflict and Change', pp. 44–5, 46–9; Gough (ed.), *Mines of Mendip*, pp. 124, 127; Hart, *Free Miners*, pp. 188, 230; PRO E134/27 Chas II/Mich 28; Sharp, *In Contempt of All Authority*, p. 214.

76. Hooson, *Miners' Dictionary*, pp. 63, 174, 198–9; Hart, *Free Miners*, pp. 165, 228; Fisher, *Custom, Work and Market Capitalism*, pp. 37, 41–2.

77. J. C. Davis, 'Radicalism in a Traditional Society: The Evolution of Radical Thought in the English Commonwealth, 1649–60', *History of Political Thought*, vol. 3 (1982), p. 199; G. Schochet, 'Patriarchalism, Politics and Mass Attitudes in Stuart England', *Historical Journal*, vol. 12 (1969), pp. 413, 439.

78. Sharpe, 'The People and The Law', p. 264.

79. This chapter has focused mostly upon the operation of local customary law and its interface with central Westminster courts. The point also applies to the criminal law. See G. Walker, 'Crime, Gender and Social Order in Early Modern Cheshire' (unpublished University of Liverpool Ph.D. thesis, 1994), passim, esp. ch. 5.

9 Employment and Authority: Masters and Men in Eighteenth-Century Manufacturing

JOHN RULE

I

It is true that no individual of the poor is obliged to work for any one individual of the rich; but for one or other of them he is obliged to work, under the penalty of their withholding from him the things without which he cannot live. He is not obliged to work for A, B, C, or D, etc; but for some one or other of them he is under the necessity of working, and that kind of work, too, they please to require of him. And this power of the rich is as strong and effective as that of the most absolute monarch . . . To condemn so many to the mines; to confine such numbers to such, nauseous, irksome, unwholesome, destructive employments; is more than equal to any kingly power on earth . . . the power of wealth pervades the whole country, and subjects every poor man to its dominion . . . The manufacturer therefore forces his workmen to work for him, and to give him a share of what the work produces . . . for the poor are under a necessity of working for him on the terms held out or go without the things on which they subsist. They have no alternative but to work for him, or for another from whom they can have no other terms. There is no voluntary compact equally advantageous on both sides, but an absoolute compulsion on the part of the masters, and an absolute necessity on the part of the workman to accept of it.[1]

Writing in 1805, Charles Hall equated the authority of employer over employee with that of rich over poor: of capital over labour, 'wealth gives power over, and commands the labour of man'.[2] He saw through the 'myth' of the labour contract, as modern labour lawyers have described it. Otto Kahn-Freund, for example, pointed out that in individual terms what takes place between employer and employee is an act of submission at inception and a condition of subordination in operation, 'however much that subordination may be concealed by that indispensable figment of the legal mind known as "the contract of employment" '.

The contract of employment is in fact 'a command under the guise of an agreement'.[3] In 1776 Adam Smith described working for wages as the usual condition of labour:

> In Europe twenty workmen work under a master for one that is independent, and the wages of labour are everywhere understood to be what they usually are, when the labourer is one person, and the owner of the stock which employs him another. What are the common wages of labour, depends everywhere upon the contract usually made between these two parties.

He recognised, however, that the contract made between masters and workmen was between 'two parties whose interests are by no means the same' and, by implication, that it was not made between equals: 'In the long run the workman may be as necessary to his master as his master is to him; but the necessity is not so immediate.'[4]

At one level the real authority of employers over their workmen has rested in modern history on the inequality actually inherent in the contract of employment, despite the common law assumption that the buying and selling of labour power was a matter of agreement between free individuals. The historical situation is in fact more complex. On the one hand, this simple advantage has not been viewed by employers as securing for them a sufficient power of command over their workers. Accordingly, they sought and gained legislative reinforcement of their control over labour, despite their public rhetoric of 'free' labour and of the labour market. On the other hand, at times some sections of the manufacturing labour force were able to constrain the authority of their employers, even to the extent of extending their own control into some areas of the hiring and labour processes. Most importantly they did this, largely illegally for the period of our concern, through *collective* actions. As nineteenth-century legislators eventually came to

accept, collective bargaining with employers was the most significant way of reducing the fundamental imbalance of power in the
contract of employment.

II

As England's economy modernised during the eighteenth century,
its need for an enlarged free, mobile labour force grew, especially
in manufacturing and in mining. It may be true that wage-dependency had been increasing significantly over the two previous centuries, but it was then often a partial rather than a full dependency.
Further the employment sectors of manufacturing and mining, in
which forms of wage labour were overwhelmingly predominant,
expanded rapidly after 1700. Even within long-established employments, changes were tending towards the proletarianisation of
labour. In artisan trades the rise of a permanent journeyman class
was an evident feature, while even in agriculture older forms of
agreement in some regions were giving way to weekly or daily waged
hire. The point is not that waged work was not a feature of the
seventeenth century, but rather that in the eighteenth century it
became so general in extent and so much clearer in form that it not
only brought ideas of a labour market to the forefront in the
discourse of economics, but also introduced particular concerns
over authority and subordination into the discussion of social order.[5]

An expanding economy undergoing structural change away from
its traditional sectors needed a larger, freer and more mobile labour force. Meeting this need brought attendant social problems as
more and more labour was hired outside the servitude and social
control structures of the traditional preindustrial economy. Henry
Fielding, writing in 1751, put things in a long historical perspective
when he described the emergence of the modern economy from
the 'bonds' of feudalism:

> the commonality by degrees, shook off their vassalage, and be-
> came more and more independent of their superiors. Even ser-
> vants in process of time, acquired a state of freedom and
> independency unknown to this rank in any other nation; and
> which as the law now stands is inconsistent with a servile condi-
> tion. But nothing has wrought such an alteration in this order of

people as the introduction of trade. This hath given a new face to
the whole nation, hath in a great measure subverted the former
state of affairs, and hath almost totally changed the manners,
customs and habits of the people, more especially of the lower
sort. The narrowness of their fortune is changed into wealth, the
simplicity of their manners into craft, their frugality into luxury,
their humility into pride, and their subjection into equity.[6]

Daniel Defoe had offered less historical analysis, but even more
pointed comment in 1724 in his *The Great Law of Subordination
Considered.* The common people had gone through a 'kind of
general revolution, or change in their disposition, temper and
manners . . . such as I believe no nation has undergone but themselves'.[7] Many lesser writers than Fielding or Defoe echoed this
polemical lamentation. To the influential economist and spokes-
man for the 'manufacturing interest', Josiah Tucker in 1787, the
imminent prospect of France overtaking Britain's lead was because
'The subordination of the common people is an unspeakable
advantage to them in respect to trade'.[8] This discourse derived from
a tension between economic development and social change which
intensified over the eighteenth century. As Edward Thompson
put it:

> The eighteenth century witnessed a qualitative change in labour
> relations whose nature is obscured if we see it only in terms of an
> increase in the scale and volume of manufacture and trade. This
> occurred of course, but in such a way that a substantial propor-
> tion of the labour force actually became more free from disci-
> pline in their daily work, more free to choose between employers
> and between work and leisure, less situated in a position of
> dependence in their whole way of life, than they had been before
> or than they were to be in the first decades of the discipline of the
> factory and of the clock.[9]

Thompson described the eighteenth century as the one which saw
the 'erosion of half-free forms of labour, the decline of living-in,
the final extinction of labour services, and the advance of free
mobile wage labour'.[10] While the pace of change in this direction
accelerated, masters still wished to have the best of both worlds.
While passing responsibility for employment and wages to the

labour market, they also tried to retain the notion of the worker as an unfree person, a *servant*, whom they had the right to command. They expected their authority to be reinforced by government at national and local levels. Throughout the century Parliament responded to employers' petitioning by passing statutes dealing with a variety of labour matters, including the controlling of industrial disputes. At the local level employers usually opposed the traditional role of the justice of the peace in wage assessment, except when, like the woolstaplers of Exeter in 1787, they felt thenselves to be disadvantaged in the labour market. They further expected that magistrates would dispense summary justice to recalcitrant workers.[11] For its part government usually responded favourably to employer requests.

In a recent discussion of the politics of the early industrial revolution, Professor O'Brien, while pointing out that although there is no way of measuring accurately the extent or severity of the impact, collective protests did limit to some degree the power of eighteenth-century capitalists. Industrial protests were 'ostensibly real social constraints on managerial authority' which meant that the industrialists of Hanoverian Britain did not manage their enterprises 'in the climate of security, approval and autonomy enjoyed by their counterparts during the heyday of Victorian capitalism'.[12] This degree of constraint operated despite the fact that the Hanoverian state developed an almost unbroken tendency to enhance the power of employers by giving them the statutes they wanted and ignoring or removing laws which they found bothersome. As O'Brien has concluded, employers were being given a political and judicial authority over their workers, 'which left the labour market in a state of suspension between feudal servitude and the free contractual system of nineteenth-century political economy'. Parliament in fact 'did everything required to keep the legal and political framework for labour relations in a condition that preserved hierarchy, authority and the extraction of optimal work'.[13]

That the character of employment was in transition, does not however mean that the complex body of legislation and related case law known as Master and Servant law should be simply regarded as anomalistic, attempting to deal with changed realities in an archaic language and with outmoded assumptions. The Acts passed in 1747, 1766 and 1777 with their provision for the summary punishment of 'servants' for leaving or neglecting their work, should be associated, as Daphne Simon argued, with the specific labour needs of eighteenth-century manufacturing capitalism.[14] The nineteenth-century role of Master and Servant laws in colonial Australia in the transition from unfree (convict in this case) to free labour supports this notion of utility.[15]

In theory this body of law balanced claims by servants and apprentices for non-payment of wages, ill-treatment or wrongful dismissal against penal sanctions and other remedies demanded by masters for a range of offences including: absenteeism, wage payment, duration and terms of contract, responsibilities of masters and servants, and disciplining of misbehaviour by workers, including refusal to work, desertion, disobedience, and damage to tools or work. It existed alongside related contractual forms, especially those involving apprenticeship and indenture. The laws were administered by the justices and while individual complaints from servants were sometimes upheld, the balance was very unequal. The inherent inequality in this body of law is evident in the fact that offences by employers were punished by fines, those by employees with imprisonment. Labour's continuing perception of its extreme disadvantage is revealed in that repeal in 1875 followed an organised trade union campaign. The Employers and Workmen Act of that year was in its title a belated modernisation. But the symbolism of titles was not the only factor driving trade union concern, for master and servant sanctions were much used by employers to break strikes as well as to discipline individual workers.

Legislation was also enacted covering the loss or damage of employers' property in the form of materials in the worker's care. This was an important dimension of labour discipline in the context of an expanding putting-out system, which placed raw materials and goods in the process of manufacture in the homes of outworkers. Parliament passed several Acts specific to particular trades: for example, there were a number of Acts in respect of the taking of wood ('chips') from naval dockyards; others in 1722 relating to shoemaking, in 1739 to iron, wool and leather workers, in 1749 to the hat manufacture and in 1754 to watchmaking.[16] In some cases, these enactments translated the appropriation of left-over materials traditionally regarded as perquisites into criminal embezzlement. Summary powers of punishment were usually accompanied by powers of search and detention which were in themselves considered an oppression of the labour force. The worst example was the Worsted Act of 1777. This set up an inspectorate to work under a prosecuting committee of employers. Conviction was allowed on the oath of an employer, and there were open-ended powers of search and arrest on 'reasonable suspicion' that yarn had been concealed. As the Hammonds pointed out, this offended against the underlying principle of English law, the presumption of innocence.[17] In such cases where 'new' law clashed with customary expectations, plebeian understandings of the law differed from that of elite authority, just as Dr Wood has suggested they did in the case of seventeenth-century mining laws.[18]

These further examples of the criminalisation of some acts of employees reinforce the view that historically labour law has always been concerned with much more than the labour contract. It was embedded in notions of superordination and subordination, and assumed its role was to reinforce them. As it was put in one case in 1817: 'the question really is whether the master or servant is to have the superior authority'.[19]

III

Even in employments like mining which had longer histories, the beginning of the eighteenth century saw significant changes in patterns of hiring and in the organisation of labour. Dr Wood has written of lead mining: 'Many aspects of the mining industry of the early eighteenth century would have been unrecognisable to a free miner of one hundred years earlier. A revolution had occurred in the ownership, control and organisation of extraction.' The most significant was the dependence on a group of directly hired skilled miners known as 'copers', although these men still managed to retain considerable autonomy and control over the labour process. Similarly, the emergence of specialist groups of skilled workers, the 'tributers' and 'tutworkers' in Cornish mining from the early eighteenth century, owed much more to the changing labour needs of an expanding and heavily capitalising industry, than to the persistence of earlier traditions of 'free-mining'.[20] In the coalfields of the north-east, from the early eighteenth century, coal-owners were beginning to take a more direct control over mining operations and this led to the adoption of the 'bond', a change in the form of hiring which has been described as a 'crucial institutional innovation'.[21] As Levine and Wrightson have pointed out, despite the long history of the industry, the era of the labour contract only really begins with this change: 'it extended to the pitmen . . . a contractual agreement of a kind that had previously existed only between the owners of the colleries and their contracting overmen or undertakers'. Indeed it was this latter group who in the seventeenth century and earlier had been known as 'servants'. In this, and in some other employment contexts, the word seems to have described superior employees, themselves the supervisors or even the direct hirers of lower categories of labour. In the north-east, 'servant' usually implied an overman, while the term 'workman' was applied to the pitmen who laboured under his supervision.[22] It was a usage which could be found elsewhere and which sometimes continued into the eighteenth century. In suggesting in 1787 that some Cornish miners conspired with the mine captains to claim larger wages than were due, William Pryce wrote: 'There will never be occasions wanting for bad men to decoy servants, and alienate them from their bounden duty to their masters.'[23]

Outside mining, seventeenth-century historians have yet to provide much in the way of detailed analysis of changes in the way labour was hired. The evidence from mining suggests that the eighteenth century *did* see significant change: a reminder at a time when historians have been inclined to stress continuities, that historians of the nineteenth century can recognise much in the eighteenth that they do not see in the seventeenth.[24] As the non-agricultural labour force expanded, concentrations of cloth workers, iron workers, miners, cutlers and others formed what became known as the 'populous districts', and along with the growing numbers of permanent journeymen in the urban manufacturing trades were were increasingly seen as extending the problems of labour discipline beyond the concern of individual employers.[25] Such concentrated populations of wage-earners were commonly viewed as having an inherent proclivity to be 'idle and disorderly' by a ruling class sensing the weakening of the old patterns of social control and subordination. From this perspective, the discipline problems of the master aggregated into a national political concern over, for example, the way in which the labouring people spent their non-work time. The preamble to an Act of 1752 for stricter licensing of places of public entertainment illustrates the wider concern well enough:

Whereas the multitude of places of entertainment for the lower sort of people is another great cause of thefts and robberies, as they are thereby tempted to spend their small substance in riotous pleasures and in consequence are put to unlawful methods of supplying their wants and renewing their pleasures.

The Act was accordingly intended to 'prevent the said temptation to thefts and robberies and to correct as far as may be the habit of idleness which is become too general over the whole kingdom, and is productive of much mischief and inconvenience'.[26]

The important point is not to deny that some seventeenth-century employers faced problems of labour insubordination, but that when eighteenth-century employers much more generally did so, it was by then in the context of a public discourse which had already declared a lack of discipline among the lower orders to be a matter of national concern.

IV

From the beginning of the eighteenth century the ultimately determining role of the labour market was being asserted. As a newspaper from the west country clothing districts put it in 1739: 'The value of labour has its ups and downs according to the demand there is for it, the same as any other commodity', while a in a national periodical in 1733, the political significance of this had been emphasised: 'Labour as to its price, is like everything else, it rises or falls according to the proportion that there is between the demand and the quantity then in the market, all restraints are unjust let them be upon what side they will.' Both deny any special exemption for labour from the laws of the market: 'like everything else', 'the same as any other commodity'.[27] Edmund Burke put it bluntly enough in 1795: 'labour is a commodity, and as such an article of trade . . . when any commodity is carried to the market, it is not the necessity of the vender but the necessity of the purchaser that raises the price'.[28] Or, he might have added, which ensures that any purchase is made at all. For as well as asserting that wage levels were determined through it, employers could also use the market to explain levels of employment and deny any responsibility for employing the labouring poor, other than at times when they were needed.

Thus there was a tendency for employers to opt out of the reciprocities implied in the traditional rhetoric of the master–servant relationship under which employers were presumed to have a degree of responsibility towards their employees in return for their obedience. Yet the imperatives of the labour market alone did not give employers sufficient authority over their workers. They could not even ensure that labour *was* supplied when needed, or disciplined when hired. As Defoe said of the labouring poor in 1724:

> In a glut of trade they grow saucy, lazy, idle and debauch'd; when they may have work, and may get money enough to live well, and lay up for a time of less Business . . . [instead] . . . they will work but two or three days in the week, or till they get money enough to keep them the rest of the week, and all the other part of their time they lie in the alehouse to spend it.[29]

Such lamentations were frequent and widespread. From Cornwall in 1793 came the complaint:

> The common tinners continue to be very refractory and insolent: many of them refuse to work, and have not gone underground for three weeks past – They have no just cause for it; for their wages have been rather too high lately than otherwise; the consequence has been too much brandy drinking and other bad practices.[30]

When William Temple wrote in 1739 that the only way to make the poor 'sober, industrious and obedient' was to remove the means of 'idleness and intemperance, such as high wages',[31] he was in fact admitting that the eighteenth-century labour market was segmented and did not at all times operate to the advantage of the employer in his need to secure an adequate supply of disciplined labour with the relevant skills.[32] This situation is, of course, familiar to historians. It has been described in terms of 'leisure preference' and as an example of a 'backward sloping supply curve for labour'.[33] Although Levine and Wrightson have argued that there is little evidence for such a labour attitude among the northern coal hewers, that may well have been because the interruptions to their work already gave them more 'holidays' than they would have wished, and there can be little doubt that generally the 'Saint Monday' tendency was widespread.[34] It was the subject of a celebrated article by E. P. Thompson contrasting it with the time-discipline needs of industrial capitalism.[35] It does not need detailed recapitulation here, except to emphasise the point made by Karl Marx that the failure of capital in the eighteenth century to 'become master of the whole available labour time of the manufacturing workers' is the most manifest indication of its continuing need to 'wrestle with the insubordination of the workers'.[36]

V

It has been suggested that the self-interest of the employer was mirrored by increasing self-interest on the part of the worker.[37] Throughout the eighteenth century manufacturing workers increasingly came to see their interest as separate from that of their employers. Although it has been shown by Dr Walker that historians have underestimated the importance of the restored guilds in several incorporated towns after 1660, he concedes that even so manufacturing guilds 'collapsed sharply' in the 1720s and 1730s.[38] Like the Webbs he sees the rise of journeyman trade unionism in the eighteenth century as directly related to this 'important shift in relationships' between masters and journeymen.[39] The perception of a seprate labour interest opposed to that of capital was at the root of eighteenth-century trade unionism. Trade unionism emerged among the skilled workers as the gap between journeymen and masters increased and as the former saw scant prospects of themselves ever becoming independent employers, and when they ceased to expect that their interests would be safeguarded by the unprompted regulatory activities of the guild or of the paternalist state. This changed attitude was held by increasing numbers as wage-dependency both spread across and deepened within the manufacturing crafts. In dozens of trades, including large ones like tailoring, shoemaking and printing, a class of *permanent* journeymen had come into being whose standards and status had come to depend on their collective ability to defend their interests as journeymen. In other manufactures, the process of proletarianisation had taken different forms. The extension of the putting-out system, whereby merchant capitalists put-out materials to be made up at piece rates in the homes of weavers and others and then collected the completed product, had resulted in a population of workers who neither owned the materials on which they worked nor

marketed the product of their labour. They had become in effect
an outworking proletariat. Protoindustrialisation, as it has been
termed, did not necessarily result in the emergence of a labour
consciousness, especially where a continued access to land meant
the rural outworker's wage-dependency was not total.[40] However, in
most of the English areas of rural manufacturing, the contribution
of farming to livelihoods had dwindled and a village-based, labour-
selling proletariat had come into being, which had begun over time
to create its own traditions and customs and for whom forms of
industrial action became appropriate. Hence early forms of trade
unionism can be traced to rural weavers, framework-knitters and
metal workers as well as to urban journeymen.

Hostility towards employers was an increasingly recognised facet
of the consciousness of the manufacturing workers, especially of
those who had any pretension to skill. Adam Smith had perceived
that wage agreements were made between 'parties whose interests
are by no means the same' and had recognised that both masters
and men were 'disposed to combine' to protect or advance their
interest.[41] Dean Tucker, in 1758, posed the question, 'What is the
difference, in regard to morals, cheapness and goodness of work,
extent of trade, rioting, mobbing and the like', between manufactures where small independent masters worked with few journeymen and those where few masters employed many journeymen?
He supplied the answer by contrasting the industrial peace which
prevailed in the West Riding woollen trade, dominated by small
working clothiers, with the recurrent strife in the west country
where large merchant–capitalist clothiers sometimes put out work
to hundreds of weavers:

> This is the clothier, whom all the rest are to look upon as their
> Paymaster? But will they not also sometimes look upon him as
> their Tyrant? And as great numbers of them work together in the
> same shop, will they have it the more in their power to vitiate and
> corrupt each other, to cabal and associate against their masters?
> and to break out into mobs and riots upon every little occasion?
> . . . The master . . . however well-disposed in himself, is naturally
> tempted by his situation to be proud and over-bearing, to con-
> sider his people as the scum of the earth, whom he has a right to
> squeeze whenever he can; because they ought to be kept low, and
> not rise up in competition with their superiors. The journeymen

on the contrary, are equally tempted by their situation, to envy the high station and superior fortunes of their masters; and to envy them the more, in proportion as they find themselves deprived of the hopes of advancing themselves to the same degree by any stretch of industry or superior skill. Hence their self-love takes a wrong turn, destructive to themselves, and others. They think it no crime to get as much wages, and to do as little for it as they possibly can, to lie and cheat, and to do any other bad thing; provided it is only against their master, whom they look upon as their common enemy, with whom no faith is to be kept. The motives to industry, frugality and sobriety are all subverted by this one consideration, viz that they shall always be chained to the same oar, and never be but journeymen.[42]

Writing in 1758, Tucker had in mind the widespread strike of 1756 in the west country, the most serious disturbance there since that of 1726–8.[43] In between there are recorded labour disputes involving weavers or other woollen workers in Gloucestershire, Wiltshire or Somerset in 1741, 1750 and 1752, with later instances in 1776, 1787, 1791, 1792, 1793, 1799–1802 and 1821.[44] Issues ranged from strike action over wages to partly successful resistance to employers' attempts to introduce machinery. Tucker was on firm ground in insisting that collective labour action in this manufacturing district was capable at times of setting real limits to the power of employers.[45] Given this record of labour protest, it is surprising that a recent analysis of the weavers' strike of 1825 in Gloucestershire presents it not as deriving from the labour consciousness of a workforce with a hundred-year-old tradition of protest, but as the 'preindustrial' protest of weavers who were in fact small employers imbued with a petty bourgeois psychology. This extraordinary reading of the events of 1825 seems, as Randall has pointed out, to derive from a serious misunderstanding of the meaning of 'master' as applied to the handloom weavers of that area, where it did not refer to the independent working clothier found in the West Riding, but to a skilled worker who had mastered his trade, had served his time in the customary manner, could be a 'master' to others serving their time and owned his own loom, but who still took in work put out by the capitalist clothier, and who hardly ever employed waged help, using, if he had a second loom, labour from his family.[46]

Large employers, who increasingly articulated an ideology which passed responsibility for low wages to the market, and who took the position that they had no duty simply to employ the poor, but only to take up labour as they needed it, could expect no ingrained deference from the manufacturing workers they employed. Defoe used the woollen manufacture to illustrate this change. He presents a dialogue between a justice of the peace and a cloth worker who has been summoned upon a complaint that his work was being neglected:

Justice Come in Edmund, I have talked with your Master.

Edmund Not *my Master*, and't please your Worship. I hope I am *my own Master.*

Justice Well, your Employer, Mr E—, the Clothier: will the word Employer do?

Edmund Yes, yes, and't please your Worship, any thing but *Master.*

Here, as Edward Thompson has remarked, there is a change in terms of relations as subordination becomes negotiation, howbeit between very unequal parties.[47]

VI

The language generated in hostile exchanges between employers and men during industrial disputes provides one of the most revealing sources from which to examine assumptions about the expectations and boundaries of employer authority. In it employers through the eighteenth century, for all their rhetoric of contracts made in a labour market, continued to complain more of insubordination than they did of breaches of agreement. Sometimes they presented arguments derived from both sources side by side. The Gloucestershire clothiers did this in 1756 when they came together to seek the repeal of a statute the weavers had unexpectedly secured, which reasserted the role of wage assessment by justices of the peace. In one clause of their petition, the clothiers expressed the view that it was 'absolutely absurd and repugnant to the liberties of a free people, and to the interest of trade that any law should supersede a private contract honourably made between a master and his workmen'. In another they returned to the old language of

master and servant, arguing that if weavers were allowed to appeal
to justices over the heads of their employers to have their wages
increased, then there was a threat to social order:

> Because the execution of this law tends to invert the Laws of
> Society, and to destroy that due subordination which ought to be
> religiously preserved in all communities. The weavers by this act
> will be rendered more our masters than we are now theirs. A
> levelling and turbulent spirit . . . ought never to be counten-
> anced amongst the common people and labouring manufactures
> of this Kingdom.[48]

Faced by trouble from his engineering craftsmen in 1786, James
Watt wrote of the 'rebellion of the journeymen'.[49] A Lancashire
magistrate in 1759, when the cotton weavers organised in the
course of a dispute with their employers, felt bound to support
the latter, because 'such confederacies would have occasioned the
greatest confusion between the lowest class of people and their
superiors in all trades and occupations in every manufactory and in
every employ'.[50] In these and a considerable number of other trades
at various times in the eighteenth century, combinations of skilled
workers presented a significant challenge to employer authority,
because they went beyond simple disobedience, non-cooperation
or sullen resistance, to threaten and even to operate an alternative
authority.

Ironically, the source of skilled labour's power to offer collective
resistance to employers' authority lay in an institution, which in
itself was historically the closest form of bound obedience to a
master still surviving in the eighteenth century. That institution was
apprenticeship. There is no agreement among historians as to the
rate of decline of traditional apprenticeship. What is clear is that its
nature was changing by the early eighteenth century. The most
recent survey, by Dr Brooks, points out that against its general
decline, and its ceasing to be a significant avenue of upward social
ability, apprenticeship maintained or even increased its key role as
the means of entering and exercising the craft trades. Apprenticeship, often less 'regular' than before, increasingly resting on custom rather than formal binding and in many trades already passing
into an 'outdoor' relationship where apprentices no longer lived in
the homes of their masters, through the eighteenth century and
into the early nineteenth century defined the skilled working class,

differentiating it from the common labourer below and, to some extent, from a labour-employing petty-capitalist middle class above. Dr Walker too has agreed with E. P. Thompson that in this important role apprenticeship's significant crisis came over the several years preceding the repeal of statutory apprenticeship in 1814 (see below).[51]

Adam Smith had condemned apprenticeship in 1776 as something which hindred the employers 'from employing whom they think proper'. However, in the only passage of the *Wealth of Nations* where he concedes any degree of effectiveness to workers' combinations, he recognised the importance of control over apprenticeship for skilled journeymen, when he wrote of the wool combers: 'By combining not to take apprentices they can not only engross the employment, but reduce the whole of the manufacture into a sort of slavery to themselves, and raise the price of their labour much above what is due to the nature of their work.'[52] This element of control over entry to their trade was critical for the prospects of early trade unions of craft workers. A frontier of skill had to be defended against dilution of the labour force by the unskilled. In this defence, fundamental to all other aspirations such as maintaining or improving wages or conditions of labour, artisans were able to claim legitimacy not only from the 'customs of the trade', but also from statute law. A clause of the Act of 1563, popularly known as '5 Elizabeth', required that an apprenticeship be served before any trade then in being could be practised. This was not repealed until 1814. Although narrowed in scope in case law decisions and denied extension to any new trade, apprenticeship remained important as a legitimating symbol of skilled labour's rights.[53] As a verse in memory of Queen Elizabeth – appearing in 1811 in the course of an industrial dispute involving saddlers – expressed it:

> Her memory still is dear to journeymen,
> For sheltered by her laws, now they resist
> Infringements which would else persist:
> Tyrannic masters, innovating fools
> Are checked, and bounded by her glorious rules.
> Of workmen's rights she is still a guarantee[54]

Importantly, during the eighteenth century a large proportion of the population of apprentices was indentured, or attached in less formal customary manner, to skilled workmen, not to capitalist employers. This was especially the case in the manufacturing trades with large numbers of workers like tailoring or cloth production. In the former trade, a journeyman was defined in 1745 as 'one, who has by apprenticeship or other contract, served such a portion of his time to that particular business which he professes to occupy, as renders him capable to execute every branch or part of the trade, whereby he is at full liberty, if his ability and condition of life will permit, to set up in the world as a master of his profession'.[55] Typically in eighteenth-century manufacturing apprentices learned not just the skills of a particular trade, but the customs and attitudes of its skilled practitioners. Though evasion of legal requirements was widespread, large numbers of eighteenth-century skilled workers were still able to exercise through apprenticeship a degree of control over entry to their trades; to operate a restriction on numbers and to effect a 'closed shop', which in a number of trades enabled them to impose significant limitations on the everyday authority of their employers.

In their successful campaign to secure the removal of the statutory apprenticeship clauses of the Statute of Artificers, leading employers made no secret of the fact that they were contending with a fundamental trade union challenge to their authority. The 'greatest mischief' which derived from statutory apprenticeship arose

from the pretensions it countenances, and the colour it gives to the combination of workmen for the raising of wages, and the prevention of improvement. Under the privileges given by this act, many masters are not permitted to hire their own workmen. No the 'Shop Committee' must be applied to. They must be assured that all is right – that every workman has, as they pretend, been 'legally apprenticed'; that is in fact that he belongs to 'the Club'. For they make no distinction if he leagues with them. They choose too what articles shall be made, and impose large fines on whoever disobeys *their* laws. They fine men also, that work for masters who conduct their business in a manner *not approved* by them. Aye, and they compel payment too, by outlawry and proscription! Neither will they make a new article, till 'their Committee' has decreed the price; and no member of the Club *dare* execute it for less. If the master resists the decree, however extravagant . . . and obtains assistance from any well disposed journeymen, the rest instantly *quit* his shop; and until they are able to obtain admission to another, are supported from 'the fund'. In the mean time a mark is set upon the men. None will hereafter work in the same shop with them; until their peace is made by 'a fine'. But if any of them should not have been apprenticed, then is the whole artillery of the law brought out.[56]

'Are', the employers asked, 'the masters to be the slaves of the journeymen . . . they often compel their masters to submit to whatever they direct.'[57] This is, of course, an employer polemic coming at the last moment in the life of statutory apprenticeship. It is not trade specific, but its like can be found from moments of industrial conflict throughout the eighteenth century. The complaint is always the same, that the collective power of organised skilled labour was threatening or actually imposing a fundamental constraint on the prerogatives of employers and subverting their proper authority. Disputes in the serge industry of the south-west were endemic in the early decades of the century. They reached their peak in 1725–6, ending when the employers successfully petitioned Parliament for an act banning combinations of woollen workers. This act referred to weavers and others who had 'formed themselves into unlawful clubs and societies and have presumed contrary to law, to enter into combinations, and to make by-laws or orders, by which they pretend to regulate the trade and the prices of their goods and to advance their wages unreasonably'.[58] But already in 1718 the actions of the weavers and wool-combers had led to a Royal Proclamation which gave more detail of the extent to which the combined workers were constraining the powers of their employers:

[They] lately formed themselves into lawless Clubs and Societies which had illegally presumed to use a Common Seal, and to act as Bodies Corporate, by making and unlawfully conspiring to execute certain Bylaws or Orders, whereby they pretend to determine who had a right to the Trade, what and how many apprentices and journeymen each man should keep at once, together with the prices of all their manufactures, and the manner and materials of which they should be wrought.[59]

This document carries some notions of subversion which go beyond assuming powers properly belonging to employers. In presuming to use a seal and in acting as if a 'Body Corporate', the weavers and combers had taken for themselves something which only government could grant. But there is no doubt they were both attempting a comprehensive 'regulation' of their trade and seeking an advance in wages and that they were able to make such an attempt only so long as they could effectively control entry through apprenticeship. The events in the serge districts around Exeter are unusually well documented, but there is evidence from other centres that during times when their trades were generally prosperous, organised workers were capable of imposing their interests on employers. For example, the weavers of Banbury were said in 1793 to have 'associated, formed laws of their own, and set those of their country at defiance'.[60] Shortly after the passing of the Combination Acts of 1799 and 1800, Earl Fitzwilliam, referring to a strike of wool-croppers at the Leeds factory of Benjamin Gott, when that large employer had taken on men who were not members of the union, remarked that Gott was suffering from 'an infringement of a law made by parties incompetent to make any law; a law (if I may call it so) subversive of the general rights of all his Majesty's subjects'. Concluding that the 'Journeymen are now masters', he added, 'though masters cannot be vested with an unfitting authority over their servants, they may, and ought to be protected in the full exercise of their own just rights'.[61] Wool-combers were said in 1794 to have become organised across the country:

> the woolcombers are a self-constituted corporation, bound by laws of their own making, in breach and defiance of those of the Legislature, and in consequence of this Combination, they counteract all the interests and pursuits of their employers: that if a body of woolcombers disagree with their employers, no other set of woolcombers dare to succeed them.[62]

Similar complaints come from other manufactures. Disputes between journeymen hatters and their employers came to the attention of Parliament in 1777. The journeymen had a powerful union which they called the 'Congress'. Its power rested on a closed shop derived from control over apprenticeship and it seems to have been able not only to discipline its own members, but even to impose fines on masters who employed 'illegal' workmen.[63] Journeyman papermakers forced an employer to discharge an unpopular foreman. Master printers complained of the 'unlawful and dictatorial combinations' of compositors who were attempting a limitation on apprentice numbers which, 'if not frustrated', would give them 'the means within their power of enhancing the price of labour'.[64]

More detailed evidence exists for cotton printing. This Lancashire-based industry largely depended in the eighteenth century on the skill of journeymen calico printers, as they were usually known. In the first part of the century, calico printing had been a small trade based in London, but in 1783 a number of journeymen were brought up to Lancashire to establish the industry there.[65] They brought with them not just skill but the confident attitudes of city journeymen. Their new employers described them as 'gentlemen journeymen' and were from the beginning forced to pay them higher wages than was normal in country districts: 'so ill-disposed were these journeymen to the country masters, that they executed their work in a very imperfect manner, and would often tell the overlooker, when he complained of bad work, that it was good enough for the country'.[66] So long as the industry depended upon their skilled input, the calico printers operated a very effective union:

> By their combination they prevent the master employing any journeymen they do not approve of, who as *they* say is not a fair man; and all journeymen must ask the constable of the shop, for the time being, (an officer appointed by the combination) for work, before they ask the master. They can discharge a journeyman from service without his master's consent, they can advance their wages and in many instances, prevent their masters taking more apprentices than they approve of.

When masters 'did not show a readiness to comply with their commands', they ordered journeymen and apprentices out on strike.[67] When new technologies became available by the beginning of the nineteenth century, the employers' method of breaking the power of the union was to take on themselves a large number of apprentices to perform the bulk of the printing operations. In 1806, one shop employed sixty apprentices and only two journeymen.[68] The defensive response of the journeymen was to petition Parliament to set a statutory control over the ratio of apprentices to skilled men. Parliament declined to pass such an Act. Had it granted this regulation, the employers' lobby claimed, the effect would have been to 'completely subvert the relation of master and servant, in placing the former under the slavish control of the latter'.[69]

Employers had, of course, means of opposing union power. They had remedy in the law, for as Adam Smith put it: 'We have no acts of parliament against combining to lower the price of work; but many against combining to raise it.'[70] As well as use of Master and Servant law against individuals, there was the common law of conspiracy and there was the opportunity to seek an Act specific to the trade which would provide for rapid summary justice: a provision which at the end of the century the Combination Act made generally available.[71] Without such Acts, however, legal proceedings could be lengthy and bothersome, and at times of brisk trade, employers were as likely to give in to demands rather than lose output. Masters could combine to break the power of a union by sharing the burden of prosecution or implementing a lock-out, as the papermakers did in the 1796 or by using a certificate system as the calico printers did in 1790: 'that no master should employ another's servant, who had not with him such a discharge, purporting that he had finished his work, and left his master honourably'.[72] Although some unions – those of the journeymen calico printers, papermakers, wool-sorters and compositors among them – had already devised the sophisticated tactic of the 'rolling strike', that is, striking against one employer at a time as a counterploy.[73] Union power was conditional and often temporary, but closer research into eighteenth-century industrial conflict, which has been conducted in recent years, has demonstrated that in a range of trades – including some like tailoring with large labour forces – despite the presumptions of the common law, despite the tendency of statute law and despite the rapid rise to hegemony of the ideology of economic individualism, many employers of skilled workers met with a degree of effective resistance, and had from time to time to enter into agreements which can be properly placed in a context of *collective* bargaining.[74]

VII

Craft unions had most power in times of brisk trade and those who had long traditions of organisation, like the tailors or compositors, could operate at some level of effectiveness during normal times. In times of depression, or when particular trades were in decline, their actions became defensive. In this mode they were usually much less effective. When the balance of power in the labour market moved towards employers, they were not slow to take advantage. At such times, masters most justified not only Adam Smith's assumption that they were 'always and everywhere in a sort of tacit, but constant and uniform combination, not to raise the wages of labour', but also his further assertion that masters 'sometimes enter into particular combinations to sink the wages of labour'. He remarked that workmen often responded with 'contrary defensive combination', but was largely correct in his view that they did so with little prospect of success.[75] As a pamphlet produced during a dispute in the Wiltshire cloth manufacture in 1727 expressed it, there was little prospect of redress when 'such barbarous wretches as these, the Ægyptian Task-masters have resolutely united to fall their wages, load them with intolerable weight and starve them by stoppages'.[76]

The confident actions and assertive behaviour in times of better balance in the labour market gave way to a different emphasis. Journeymen unable to rely on their own collective strength appealed to authority which they considered higher than that of any individual master. On occasion this was to Parliament itself in the hope of securing a 'regulation' of their trade. Such appeals usually produced some sympathy but not the hoped for action, although the Spitalfields Act of 1773 regulating the London silk industry stands out as a clear exception.[77] More generally, workmen legitimated resistance to the impositions of employers in the name of the 'Trade'. The Trade implied a moral as well as an occupational community in which the actions of masters and men were considered bounded. When west country clothiers sought to lower their wages in 1718 by increasing the size of the piece of cloth required for the old rate, the weavers described their action as 'contrary to law, usage and custom from time immemorial'.[78] The London printworkers held a meeting in 1805 to decide how to deal with a situation in which their employers were 'disputing or denying custom' and 'refusing to acknowledge precedents which have been hitherto the only reference'.[79] Direct action such as machine breaking was sometimes legitimated by reference to 'the trade'. During a dispute over the introduction of calico printing machinery in 1786, a Manchester employer was advised in an anonymous letter that the journeymen were determined to 'destroy all

Sorts of Masheens for Printing in the Kingdom for there is more hands then is work ... [for] the ingerd Gurnemen'. He was warned, 'it will be madness for you to contend with the Trade as we are combined by oath'.[80] Moving forward to the classic Luddism of 1811, the best known Nottingham song of that era again invokes the name of 'the Trade':

> The guilty may fear but no vengeance he aims
> At the honest man's life or estate:
> His wrath is entirely confined to wide frames
> And to those that old prices abate.
> Those engines of mischief were sentenced to die
> By unanimous vote of the trade,
> And Ludd who can all opposition defy
> Was the grand executioner made.

The struggle against some hosiers' use of unskilled labour on wide frames to produce a product inferior to the traditional stocking would continue:

> Till full-fashioned work at the old-fashioned price
> Is established by custom and law.
> Then the trade when this arduous contest is o'er
> Shall raise in full splendour its head
> And colting and cutting and squaring no more
> Shall deprive honest workmen of bread.[81]

In fact, as the work of Maxine Berg and Adrian Randall has shown, popular hostility towards new machinery in some eighteenth-century textile districts did have an influence on the pace and ways in which clothiers could introduce new technologies and processes.[82] Invoking the community of the Trade identified some employers as innovators, oppressors and imposers on their workers, despite the defence of the former that, 'Both masters and servants must always be subject to changes and inconveniences.'[83] A longer justification for wage cutting was offered by the clothiers in 1756:

It is our misfortune rather than our fault if thro' the present dullness of our Trade some occasions of complaint of the lowness of wages paid to them have arisen, or that some few members of our body, whom we would by no means countenance have taken that advantage of the times, which it would not have been in their power to do in a more flourishing trade ... Why should the weavers be exempted from feeling the effects of bad times any more than their masters ... if the head and body suffer ought not every member to bear a part?[84]

Reference might be made to an old style of master who had operated within the expectations of the moral community and treated his workforce properly, in contrast to the present generation, interestingly described as 'unmasterlike masters', who were 'more and more falling their wages increasing their oppressions, and adding fresh miseries to their misfortunes'.[85]

Journeymen's perceptions of the Trade as an authority transcending that of the individual master, indicate as Edward Thompson suggested, contra the Webbs, that workers' organisations did attempt to carry on regulatory functions and responsibilities in the vacuum left by the early decline of the guild system in England, a view endorsed by Dr Walker.[86] They also to some extent allow the placing of *some* eighteenth-century disputes in the context of an 'industrial moral economy'.[87] If so, then like the moral economy of the food rioters it was a popular consciousness increasingly at odds with the views of the ruling classes. Adam Smith recognised the weakness of what he distinguished as 'defensive' combinations:

In order to bring the point to a speedy decision, they have always recourse to the loudest clamour, and sometimes to the most shocking violence and outrage. They are desperate, and act with the folly and extravagance of desperate men, who must either starve or frighten their masters into an immediate compliance with their demands. The masters upon these occasions are just as clamorous upon the other side, and never cease to call aloud for the assistance of the civil magistrate, and the rigorous execution of those laws which have been enacted with such severity against the combinations of servants, labourers and journeymen. The workmen accordingly very seldom derive any advantage from the violence of those tumultuous combinations, which, partly from the interposition of the civil magistrate, partly from the steadiness of the masters, partly from the necessity which the greater part of the workmen are under of submitting for the sake of present subsistence, generally end in nothing but the punishment or ruin of the ringleaders.[88]

In situations such as these, masters were clearly able to advance their interests and to assert or reassert their authority over their workmen. However, Smith undoubtedly underestimated the effectiveness of what he called 'offensive' combinations. Historians have only recently reassessed this. Organised journeymen, as we have seen, were in favourable trade circumstances able not only to offer effective resistance to the authority of their employers, but also able to impose unwanted restraints on them. In line with the new historiography of early trade unionism, a historian of a distinctly conservative tendency has written of eighteenth-century combinations:

> They helped to achieve what was felt to be some sort of tolerable balance of interests between different sections of the community. Although workmen's organisations in the eighteenth century often encountered failure, nevertheless they also secured a sufficient degree of success to have these effects.[89]

The Combination Acts of 1799 and 1800 undoubtedly owed the ease with which they entered the statute book to the fears of popular political disaffection engendered by the French Revolution, but there seems little doubt that the government had become convinced that there was, as William Wilberforce described it, a 'general disease' becoming endemic in the manufacturing districts. The belief had grown that trade unionism was no longer a matter to be dealt with in the context of particular disputes between masters and journeymen. It had become a 'system' threatening not only the authority of employers but the commerce and prosperity of the nation. The government was not unmindful of the potential industrial organisations might offer radical political subversion, but when it came down so clearly on the side of the employers, it was with the industrial subordination of the manufacturing labour force that it was most directly concerned.[90]

NOTES AND REFERENCES

1. C. Hall, *The Effects of Civilisation on the People in European States* ([1805] repr. New York, 1965), pp. 49–73.

2. Ibid., p. 48.

3. Cited in K. W. Wedderburn, *The Worker and the Law*, 3rd edn (Harmondsworth, 1986), p. 5.

4. A. Smith, *Wealth of Nations* ([1776], ed. E. Cannan, London, 1962), pp. 74–5.

5. For the discourse over wage-labour in the sixteenth and seventeenth centuries, see C. Hill, 'Pottage for Freeborn Englishmen: Attitudes to Wage Labour', in Hill, *Change and Continuity in Seventeenth-Century England* (London, 1974), pp. 218–38.

6. H. Fielding, *An Inquiry into the Causes of the Late Increase of Robbers* [1751], in T. Roscoe (ed.), *The Works of Henry Fielding* (London, 1849), p. 761.

7. D. Defoe, *The Great Law of Subordination Considered* [1724], 'Letter IV', reprinted in S. Copley (ed.), *Literature and the Social order in Eighteenth-Century England* (London, 1984), p. 50.

8. J. Tucker, *A Brief Essay on the Advantages and Disadvantages which Respectively Attend France and Great Britain With Regard to Trade* (London, 1787), p. 17.

9. E. P. Thompson, *Customs in Common* (London, 1991), p. 38.

10. Ibid., p. 36.

11. The Exeter woolstaplers' journeymen, the woolsorters, struck successfully for higher wages several times in the eighteenth century before 1787. When, however, they did so in that year, their employers moved promptly to get some of them gaoled by the magistrates and then petitioned for a wage assessment. The strike and its outcome are described in a bundle of documents surviving in the Devon Record Office Miscellaneous Legal Papers Box 64.

12. P. K. O'Brien, 'Political Preconditions for the Industrial Revolution', in P. K. O'Brien and R. Quinault (eds), *The Industrial Revolution and British Society* (Cambridge, 1993), pp. 129–30.

13. Ibid., pp. 130–1.

14. D. Simon, 'Master and Servant', in J. Saville (ed.), *Democracy and the Labour Movement* (London, 1954), p. 198.

15. On the Australian context, see H. Phelps-Brown, *The Origins of Trade Union Power* (Oxford, 1986), pp. 275–6; and A. Merritt, 'The Historical Role of Law in the Regulation of Employment: Abstentionist or Interventionist', *Australian Journal of Law and Society*, vol. 1 (1982), pp. 56–85. We still await a full study of the use of Master and Servant law in England and elsewhere. Since a feature of it was its enforcement by local justices, there is a serious problem with surviving evidence. For an outline of a current research project on the subject, see D. Hay and P. Craven, 'Master and Servant in England and the Empire: A Comparative Study', *Labour/Le Travail*, vol. 31 (1993), pp. 175–84.

16. 9 George I c. 27, 13 George II c. 8, 22 George II c. 27, 27 George II c. 7. For detailed discussion, see J. Rule *The Experience of Labour in Eighteenth-Century Industry* (London, 1981), pp. 130–1; J. Styles, 'Embezzlement, Industry and Law', in M. Berg *et al.* (eds), *Manufacture in Town and Country* (Cambridge, 1983), pp. 183–204; and P. Linebaugh, *The London Hanged: Crime and Civil, Society in the Eighteenth Century* (London, 1992).

17. 17 George III c. 11 and c. 56; J. L. Hammond and Barbara Hammond, *The Skilled Labourer* ([1919] repr. London, 1979), pp. 190–1.

18. See the contribution of Andy Wood to this volume, Chapter 8 above.

19. Hay and Craven, 'Master and Servant', p. 179.

20. A. Wood, 'Social Conflict and Change in the Mining Communities of North-West Derbyshire, *c.* 1600–1700', *International Review of Social History*, vol. 38 (1993), p. 49; Lord de Dunstanville, *Carew's Survey of Cornwall . . . To Which are Added Notes by the Late Thomas Tonkin, Esq.* (London, 1811), p. 35n; W. Pryce, *Mineralogia Cornubiensis* (London, 1778), pp. 175, 180, 189; L. L. Price, 'West Barbary, or Notes on the System of Work and Wages in the Cornish Mines', *Journal of the Statistical Society*, vol. 50 (1888), p. 554.

21. D. Levine and K. Wrightson, *The Making of an Industrial Society: Whickham, 1560–1765* (Oxford, 1991), pp. 360–5; J. Hatcher, *The History of the British Coal Industry, Vol. I: Before 1700* (Oxford, 1993), pp. 309–10.

22. Levine and Wrightson, *Industrial Society*, pp. 182–3.

23. Pryce, *Mineralogia Cornubiensis*, p. 175.

24. In a recent very full bibliographical essay the small amount of work that has been done on artisans and craftsmen before the eighteenth century is specifically lamented. See J. Barry and C. Brooks (eds), *The Middling Sort of People: Culture, Society and Politics in England, 1550–1800* (London, 1994), pp. 212–3. The classic history of the important west country woollen manufacture does indicate that changes in the labour pattern were happening by the *late* seventeenth century, arguing that for the century generally, there was 'no real distinction between small clothiers and other workers in industry'. In 1693, however, petitioning for a relaxation of Elizabethan apprenticeship restrictions, the large clothiers argued that although in the sixteenth century and 'many years since' weaving had been considered a good trade, that it was 'now one of the poorest'. See J. de le Mann, *The Cloth Industry in the West of England from 1640–1880* ([1971] repr. Gloucester, 1987), pp. 97–106. B. Sharp, *In Contempt of all Authority: Rural Artisans and Riot in the West of England, 1586–1660* (Berkeley, 1980), as its title implies, presents the skilled manufacturing workers as ready to defy authority in defence of their interests. But these defended interests related to the use these rural artisans made of common land and their proclivity to food rioting after harvest failure, and although Sharp describes the west country clothworkers as 'a large rural industrial proletariat' (p. 3) in a context where 'relatively large-scale capitalists had taken control of production and distribution (p. 7), he indicates hardly any level of *industrial conflict*, in the sense that Adam Smith was considering general by 1776. In a recent outstanding book, A. J. Randall, *Before the Luddites; Custom, Community and Machinery in the English Woollen Industry, 1776–1809* (Cambridge, 1991), reveals a contrasting picture for the eighteenth century. Dr Walker's reassessment of the persistence of guilds in several incorporated towns suggests that in such a relatively sheltered environment traditional forms of hiring and paying labour persisted until the 1720s, but then the 'stability of urban wage-labour conditions' began to 'change dramatically'. See M. J. Walker, 'The Extent of Guild Control in England, *c.*1660–1820' (unpublished University of Cambridge Ph.D. thesis, 1985), p. 337. For the metalworkers of the Sheffield region, cutlers and nailmakers, there also seem to have been significant

changes in methods of work and remuneration from the late seventeenth and beginning of the eighteenth century. Between 1716 and 1719, metal-workers accounted for 50 per cent of recorded occupations in the Shef-field parish registers compared with 40 per cent between 1655 and 1659, and the dual occupational structure combining metalworking with farm-ing was giving way to a total dependence on work put out by iron factors and merchant cutlers. D. Hey, *The Rural Metalworkers of the Sheffield Region: A Study of Rural Industry Before the Industrial Revolution* (Leicester, 1972), pp. 49–60.

25. Professor E. A. Wrigley has estimated that while the agricultural labour force increased by 12.3 per cent over the eighteenth century, the rural no-agricultural sector more than doubled and the urban sector almost tripled. There is controversy over the size of the respective sectors around 1700 because the considerable mixing of occupations makes firm measurement impossible. The suggestion of Deane and Cole (1962) that agriculture still employed around two-thirds of the population *c.*1750 is generally considered seriously to overstate the level of agricultural depend-ence, but even the most optimistic estimate of the size of the manufactur-ing workforce at the beginning of the eighteenth century cannot deny its considerable further enlargement by 1800. N. C. R. Crafts (1985) estimates its annual rate of growth as 0.51 per cent (1688–1759) and 1.36 per cent (1759–1801). The rates for agricultural labour are 0.05 and 0.06 per cent for these respective periods. For a discussion of these and other estimates, see J. Rule, *The Vital Century: England's Developing Economy* (London, 1992), pp. 93–101.

26. Cited in H. Cunningham, *Leisure in the Industrial Revolution* (Lon-don, 1980), p. 21.

27. Cited in R. Malcolmson, 'Workers' Combinations in Eighteenth-Century England', in M. and J. Jacobs (eds), *The Origins of Anglo-American Radicalism* (London, 1984), p. 150.

28. Cited in A. Fox, *History and Heritage: The Social Origins of the British Industrial Relations System* (London, 1986), p. 49.

29. Defoe, *Great Law of Subordination*, pp. 143–9.

30. Royal Institution of Cornwall, MSS Letterbooks of William Jenkin, Jenkin to G. Hunt, 30 August 1793.

31. W. Temple, *The Case As It Now Stands etc* [1739], reprinted in K. Carpenter (ed.), *Labour Problems Before the Industrial Revolution* (New York, 1972), pp. 20, 40.

32. For the important notion that eighteenth-century labour markets were not 'free', but segmented by particular skills as well as by age and gender, see W. M. Reddy, *The Rise of Market Culture: The Textile Trade and French Society, 1750–1900* (Cambridge, 1984), pp. xiff; and J. Rule, 'Indus-trial Disputes, Wage-Bargaining and the Moral Economy', in A. J. Randall (ed.), *The Moral Economy: Crowds, Conflict and Authority* (forthcoming).

33. For discussion of leisure preference as description or as opinion, see P. Mathias, 'Leisure and Wages in Theory and Practice', in Mathias, *The Transformation of England* (London, 1979), pp. 148–67. Professor Mathias points out that whatever employers said, they did not in fact seek to reduce

wages when they wanted an increase in labour, but nevertheless there were many occasions when employers came to agreements not to drive wages up by competing for labour. The matter is more fully discussed in Rule, *Experience of Labour*, pp. 49–61.

34. Levine and Wrightson, *Industrial Society*, pp. 253–9. On the other hand, it has been suggested from a study of Bristol that St Monday was so general that the labour force was in fact working a regular week from Tuesday to Saturday. See M. Harrison, *Crowds and History: Mass Phenomena in English Towns, 1790–1835* (Cambridge, 1988), pp. 103–11.

35. E. P. Thompson, 'Time, Work-Discipline and Industrial Capitalism', *Past and Present*, vol. 38 (1968), pp. 56–97.

36. Karl Marx, *Capital* ([1867] repr. London, 1930), vol. I, p. 389.

37. See the useful discussion in Fox, *History and Heritage*, pp. 11–15.

38. Walker, 'Extent of Guild Control', ch. 7.

39. Ibid., p. 391. Dr Walker suggests that workers' expectations from urban guilds in this respect were lowering from the 1730s. However, in some trades the final crisis of belief in government 'regulation' did not happen until the last years of the century and the early ones of the next. The Luddite disturbances of 1811 have been described as taking place at the 'crisis point in the abrogation of paternalist legislation'. E. P. Thompson, *The Making of the English Working Class* ([1963] Harmondsworth, 1968), p. 594.

40. For a guide to the numerous writings on protoindustrialisation, see L. A. Clarkson, *Proto-Industrialisation: The First Phase of Industrialisation?* (Macmillan, 1985).

41. Smith, *Wealth of Nations*, vol. I, pp. 74–5.

42. J. Tucker, *Instructions for Travellers* [1758], reprinted in Copley (ed.), *Literature and the Social Order*, pp. 86–7.

43. See A. J. Randall, 'The Industrial Moral Economy of the Gloucestershire Weavers in the Eighteenth Century', in J. Rule (ed.), *British Trade Unionism, 1750–1850: The Formative Years* (Longman, 1988), pp. 29–51.

44. This count is for the broad woollen cloth manufacture in Wiltshire, Gloucestershire and some parts of Somerset. It does not include the separate serge cloth district based in Devonshire and adjacent parts of Somerset, which also had a long tradition of labour protest.

45. It has been argued that worker protests against textile machinery in the west country, for instance, over shearing-frames in Wiltshire, in 1799–1802, deterred their introduction for twenty years. See A. J. Randall, 'The Shearmen and the Wiltshire Outrages of 1802: Trade Unionism and Industrial Violence', *Social History*, vol. 7 (1982), pp. 283–304.

46. A. M. Urdank, *Religion and Society in a Cotswold Vale: Nailsworth, Gloucestershire 1780–1865* (Berkeley, 1990), pp. 208–43. The book's dustjacket boasts that the author spent two years in England researching it. Dr Randall, who has spent ten times as long gaining knowledge and insight into the west country woollen manufacture, has strongly challenged Urdank's interpretation. See A. J. Randall, 'Industrial Conflict and Economic Change: The Regional Context of the Industrial Revolution', *Southern History*, vol. 14 (1992), pp. 74–92.

47. This passage is discussed in Thompson, *Customs in Common*, pp. 37–8. Thompson, also notes (p. 43) that the deference shown to the magistrate reveals no challenge to the 'larger outlines of power', and that the worker's wish is to be free of 'the immediate humiliations of dependency'.

48. The petitions of both the clothiers and the weavers in this dispute are reprinted in full in W. E. Minchinton, 'The Petitions of the Weavers and Clothiers of Gloucestershire in 1756', *Transactions of the Bristol and Gloucestershire Archaeological Society*, vol. 73 (1954), pp. 216–27.

49. James Watt to John Rennie, 2 July 1786, reprinted in J. T. Ward and W. Hamish Frazer (eds), *Workers and Employers: Documents on Trade Unions and Industrial Relations in Britain Since the Eighteenth Century* (London, 1980), p. 9.

50. Cited in P. Corfield, 'Class by Name and Number in Eighteenth-Century Britain', in P. Corfield (ed.), *Language, History and Class* (Oxford, 1991), pp. 125–6.

51. C. Brooks, 'Apprenticeship, Social Mobility and the Middling Sort, 1550–1800', in Barry and Brooks (eds.), *The Middling Sort of People*, pp. 55–69, 82–3; Walker, 'Extent of Guild Control', pp. 317–18.

52. Smith, *Wealth of Nations*, vol. I, pp. 136–8.

53. For fuller treatment of apprenticeship in this respect, see Rule, *Experience of Labour*, ch. 4; and J. Rule, 'The Property of Skill in the Period of Manufacture', in P. Joyce (ed.), *The Historical Meanings of Work* (Cambridge, 1987), pp. 99–118.

54. Cited in Thompson, *Customs in Common*, pp. 62–3.

55. F. W. Galton (ed.), *Select Documents Illustrating the History of Trade Unionism: The Tailoring Trade* (London, 1896), p. 30.

56. *The Origin, Object and Operation of the Apprentice Laws, With Their Application to Times Past, Present and to Come*, by The Committee of Manufacturers of London and its Vicinity, reprinted in *The Pamphleteer*, vol. III (1814), pp. 237–8.

57. Ibid., 241.

58. 'An Act to Prevent Unlawful Combinations of Workmen Employed in the Woollen Manufactures and For Better Payment of Their Wages' (12 George I C. 34), reprinted in part in G. D. H. Cole and A. W. Filson (eds), *British Working Class Movements: Selected Documents, 1789–1875* (London, 1957), pp. 87–8.

59. Ibid., pp. 86–8. For a full account of these and other labour disputes in Exeter, see J. Rule, 'Labour Consciousness and Industrial Conflict in Eighteenth-Century Exeter', in B. Stapleton (ed.), *Conflict and Community in Southern England* (Stroud, 1992), pp. 92–109.

60. A. Aspinall, *The Early English Trade Unions: Documents from the Home Office Papers in the Public Record Office* (Blatchworth, 1949), p. 19.

61. Ibid., pp. 61–4.

62. *Journals of the House of Commons*, vol. 49 (1794), p. 395.

63. Ibid., vol. 36 (1776–8), pp. 192–3.

64. Ibid., vol. 51 (1976), p. 595; E. Howe (ed.), *The London Compositor: Documents Relating to Wages, Working Conditions and Customs of the London Printing Trade, 1785–1900* (Oxford, 1947), pp. 126–7.

65. *Facts and Observations to prove the Impolicy and Dangerous Tendency of the Bill Now Before parliament for Limiting the Number of Apprentices in The Calico Printing Business, Together with a Concise History of the Combination of the Journeymen* [1807], reprinted in K. Carpenter (ed.), *Trade Unions Under the Combination Acts, 1799–1823* (New York, 1972), p. 13.

66. Ibid., p. 14.

67. Ibid., pp. 6–7, 14–20.

68. *Commons Journals,* 17 July 1806, reprinted in Ward and Hamish Fraser, *Employers and Workers,* p. 12.

69. *Facts and Observations etc,* p. 10.

70. Smith, *Wealth of Nations,* vol. I, p. 74.

71. For recent reassessments of the Combination Acts of 1799 and 1800 and their relationship to other anti-combination laws, see J. Moher, 'From Suppression to Containment: Roots of Trade Union Law to 1823', in Rule (ed.), *British Trade Unionism,* pp. 74–97; and J. Rule, 'Trade Unions, the Government and the French Revolution, 1789–1802', in J. Rule and R. Malcolmson (eds), *Protest and Survival: The Historical Experience. Essays for E. P. Thompson* (London, 1993), pp. 112–38.

72. *Journals of the House of Commons,* vol. 51 (1796), p. 595; *Facts and Observations etc,* pp. 17–18.

73. For the development of union strategies, see Rule, *Experience of Labour,* pp. 182–3.

74. For recent work on early trade unionism, see the collection of essays in Rule (ed.), *British Trade Unionism,* especially the editor's introduction.

75. Smith, *Wealth of Nations,* vol. I, p. 75.

76. *The Devil Drove Out of the Warping Bar, or the Snap Reel Snap'd: Shewing the Maddness of the Weavers and the barbarity of the Clothiers in the West etc* [1727], reprinted in Carpenter (ed.), *Labour Problems,* p. 7.

77. See L. D. Schwarz, *London in the Age of Industrialisation: Entrepreneurs, Labour Force and Living Conditions, 1700–1850* (Cambridge, 1992), pp. 204–5.

78. Public Record Office, State Papers Domestic 35/14, Petition of the Weavers of the South West, 1718.

79. Howe, *London Compositor,* pp. 84–5.

80. Appendix of Documents to E. P. Thompson, 'The Crime of Anonymity', in D. Hay *et al., Albion's Fatal Tree: Crime and Society in Eighteenth Century England* (Harmondsworth, 1977), p. 318.

81. The full text of the song can be found in R. Palmer, *A Touch on the Times: Songs of Social Change, 1770–1914* (Harmondsworth, 1974), pp. 286–8.

82. See Randall, *Before the Luddites*; and M. Berg, 'Workers and Machinery in Eighteenth-Century England', in Rule (ed.), *British Trade Unionism,* pp. 52–73.

83. *Facts and Observations etc,* p. 8.

84. Minchinton (ed.), 'Petitions', p. 224.

85. Gentlemen of Wiltshire, *Miseries of the Miserable: Or, An Essay Towards Laying Open the Decay of the Fine Woollen Trade and the Unhappy Condition of the Poor Wiltshire Manufacturers* [1739], reprinted in Carpenter (ed.), *Labour Problems,* p. 6.

86. Thompson, *Customs in Common*, pp. 58–60; Walker, 'Extent of Guild Control', ch. 7.

87. See A. J. Randall, 'The Industrial Moral Economy of the Gloucestershire Weavers in the Eighteenth Century', in Rule (ed.), *British Trade Unionism*, pp. 29–51.

88. Smith, *Wealth of Nations*, vol. I, pp. 75–6.

89. I. R. Christie, *Stress and Stability in Late Eighteenth-Century Britain* (Oxford, 1984), pp. 124–5.

90. For a fuller development of this argument, see Rule, 'Trade Unions, the Government and the French Revolution'.

Notes on Contributors

Bernard Capp is Professor of History at the University of Warwick, where he has taught since 1968. He is the author of *The Fifth Monarchy Men* (1972), *Astrology and the Popular Press* (1979), *Cromwell's Navy: The Fleet and the English Revolution* (1989), *The World of John Taylor the Water-Poet* (1994), and essays on popular literature and religious radicalism. He is currently working on a book on female networks and social space in early modern England with the provisional title *When Gossips Meet.*

Adam Fox was an undergraduate and graduate student at Jesus College, Cambridge. He was a Knox Fellow at Harvard, 1987–8, a Research Fellow of Gonville and Caius College, Cambridge, 1991–4, and is now Lecturer in the Department of Economic and Social History at the University of Edinburgh. He is the author of a recent contribution to *Past and Present* and is currently working on a book, to be published by Oxford University Press, which examines the relationship between oral and literate forms of culture in early modern England.

Paul Griffiths was a Research Fellow of Clare College, Cambridge, 1991–4, and is now Lecturer in the Department of Economic and Social History at the University of Leicester. He is the author of *Youth and Authority: Formative Experiences in England, 1560–1640* (Oxford, 1996). He is now working on a study of the social and cultural history of London in the later sixteenth and early seventeenth centuries.

Steve Hindle was educated at Fitzwilliam College, Cambridge and the University of Minnesota. He was a Research Fellow of Girton College, Cambridge, 1991–3 and Lecturer in History at Anglia Polytechnic University, 1993–5. He is now Research Fellow at the University of Warwick. He has published articles on gossip and popular protest in early modern England.

Martin Ingram is a Fellow, Tutor and University Lecturer in Modern

History at Brasenose College, Oxford. His publications include *Church Courts, Sex and Marriage in England, 1570–1640* (Cambridge, 1987) and a number of articles on crime and the law, sex and marriage, and popular customs. He has also published on the history of climate.

John Rule is Professor of History at the University of Southampton. He has published widely in the area of labour history of the eighteenth and early nineteenth centuries. In 1992 he published a two-volume social and economic history of Hanoverian England: *Albion's People: English Society, 1714–1815* and *The Vital Century: England's Developing Economy, 1714–1815*.

Jim Sharpe is a Senior Lecturer in History at the University of York. He has published two books and numerous articles on crime and related subjects in the early modern period, and is also the author of *Early Modern England: A Social History 1550–1760* (London, 1987). He is currently preparing a major work on witchcraft in England between the sixteenth and eighteenth centuries.

Andy Wood is a British Academy Research Fellow at University College London, and was previously a Lecturer in Economic and Social History at the University of Liverpool and a Research Fellow at the Institute of Historical Research, London. He is currently preparing a book entitled *The Miners of the Derbyshire Peak Country, 1540–1770*.

Keith Wrightson is Reader in English Social History at the University of Cambridge and a Fellow and Director of Studies in History at Jesus College, Cambridge. He is the author of *English Society, 1580–1680* (1982) and co-author with David Levine of *Poverty and Piety in an English Village: Terling 1525–1700* (1979 and 1995) and *The Making of an Industrial Society: Whickham 1560–1765* (1991).

Index